Everything
Jesus Taught

ALSO BY THE AUTHOR

The All Series (14 volumes)
The Holy Spirit of God
The Keeping Power of God
The Power of Prayer
Revelation: Drama of the Ages
Seasons of the Lord (4 volumes)

Everything
Jesus Taught

Herbert Lockyer

1817

HARPER & ROW, PUBLISHERS, SAN FRANCISCO
Cambridge, Hagerstown, New York, Philadelphia
London, Mexico City, São Paulo, Sydney

Originally published in five volumes.

LC 83-48431
ISBN 0-06-065259-4

84 85 86 87 88 10 9 8 7 6 5 4 3 2 1

CONTENTS

Introduction

Never since God endowed the first human with the power of speech has any human uttered more wonderful words than those leaving the holy lips of Jesus in the days of his flesh. His were not only "Thoughts that breathe, and words that burn", but mighty words that were to shape the destinies of men and nations. Down the ages multitudes have "wondered at the gracious words which proceeded out of his mouth" (Luke 4:22). The world at large agrees with the commendation of those Roman officers that "Never man spake like this man" (John 7:46). Wordsworth could liken those who had practiced the art of stately speech as having "Choice words, and measured phrases, above the reach of ordinary people."

The immediate spontaneous reaction to his oral preaching and teaching was widespread, crowds coming from every quarter to hear him (Mark 1:45). People flocked to him because his language was easy and straightforward. He stuck to plain words the common people could easily understand. He never spoke of God in nebulous terms as the "Great First

Cause," or any vague abstract, but as "your heavenly Father." His was no scholastic vocabulary forcing him to speak over the heads of his listeners. "I seek divine simplicity in him who handles things divine." His words came straight from his inmost being, natural and inevitable, proof of deity and humanity, and they reacted with the life that brought them forth, consequently transfiguring the lives of many who heard him teach.

It was as a teacher that Jesus first began to gather disciples around him, and at the outset he established himself as the world's master preacher and teacher. Luke gives us a very lifelike portrait of Jesus when he stood up on a Sabbath morn in the synagogue at Nazareth to proclaim his first sermon. After reading from Isaiah's prophecy concerning his messianic mission (Isa. 61:1–2), Jesus commenced his teaching ministry by an exposition of the ancient prediction (Luke 4:16–30), and all eyes were fastened on him. That what he taught that morning blistered the consciences of some of his hearers is evident from the fact that they were filled with wrath and tried to silence the lips echoing forth such gracious words by killing the peerless teacher himself.

The Gospels present the ministry of Jesus under the three aspects of preaching, teaching, and healing. "Jesus went about all Galilee, *teaching* in their synagogues, and *preaching* the gospel of the kingdom, and *healing* all manner of sickness and all manner of disease among the people" (Matt. 4:23). The oral ministry is described by the terms *teaching* and *preaching,* there being twenty-four references to the former task, and fourteen to the latter, in the Gospels. Friend and foe alike gave Jesus the title of teacher, or rabbi, while the true insight of the four evangelists did not overlook the elements that made him a preacher who "was not without honor, save in his own country." That a distinction can be drawn between *teaching* and *preaching* is suggested by Dr. A. R. Bond in his *Study of the Homiletics of Jesus:*

> *Teaching* has for its purpose the instruction in principles and customs, whose acceptance may be reserved by the individual for his own convenience and deliberation.
> *Preaching* has to do with the public announcement of truth, with the intention to secure immediate response from the hearer. Both terms are used in the Gospels to record the same event, and distinctions in method and ideals are not being constantly observed, Luke 20:1. The Gospel of Mark is most faithful to the shades of meaning here. The preaching of Jesus in methods and purpose is described by two Greek words which mean—
>
> The proclamation of a herald and
> The publication of good tidings.
>
> While teaching and preaching would naturally contain common traits, *preaching* is a more comprehensive term, while the teachings of Jesus upon great themes belong to the departments of Theology and Pedagogy.

Although the preaching and teaching days of Jesus were few, through his manner and method and personal mastery of audiences, he not only created the Christian pulpit but influenced the homiletical presentation of truth down the ages. The history of oratory discovers the literary contribution to the preaching of Jesus. The pulpit is the distinctive produce of Christianity, and is ever effective when it combines a preaching and teaching ministry.

Before coming to an exposition of the varied themes or topics Jesus taught, attention must be drawn to the twofold way in which he appears as a teacher.

First, *he is prominent as an evangelical teacher*. Early in the teaching of Jesus was the invitation to repent and believe his gospel, seeing that the promises of the kingdom he came to proclaim were for those saved by his grace and power. Thus he labored to bring those who had ears to hear, a new way of life. In his encounter with Zacchaeus, Jesus declared that his mission in the world was to seek and save the lost (Luke 19:10), a mission of salvation Paul elaborated on when he declared that "Christ Jesus came into the world to save sinners; of whom I am chief" (1 Tim. 1:15). Such a redemptive task underlies many of the parables and sayings of Jesus, as, for instance, what he taught about the lost sheep, the lost silverpiece, and the lost son in Luke 15. Often he spoke of eternal life for those who repented of their sins and accepted him into their hearts (John 3:16). He distinctly says that he came to "call sinners to repentance" and that at Calvary he would give his life as a ransom for a lost world. Before his birth, he received the name *Jesus,* meaning "Jehovah is Savior," since he was coming into the world as the Savior (Matt.

1:21). Thus we have John's affirmation: "In this was manifested the love of God toward us, because that God sent his only begotten Son into the world, that we might live through him" (1 John 4:9).

Many of the truths Jesus uttered were designed to emancipate the sin-bound from their shackles, as in the case of Zacchaeus. Think of the way in which multitudes of those who were weary and heavy laden found rest through his invitation to come to him (Matt. 11:28–30)! In this far-off day there are also myriads who can sing out of their redeemed hearts,

> I came to Jesus as I was,
> Weary and worn and sad.
> I found in Him a resting place,
> And He has made me glad.

Second, *Jesus is presented as an ethical teacher.* As an *evangelical teacher* Jesus taught those who were dead in sin where and how they could find eternal life, but as the *ethical teacher* he instructed those alive, in and through him, *how to live.* The saved must be sanctified and led to serve their Savior; the forgiven must learn how to be faithful. This brings us to the claims of Jesus in the very large realm of Christian and social ethics. While he did not develop any comprehensive system of social ethics, nor indeed of any kind of ethics, he did give specific precepts on many aspects of our life among men. In order to understand the full import of this ethical side of his teaching, it is necessary to understand what the world was like when Jesus came into it.

The character of his age was hard, lustful, cruel idolatrous, and evil, making the virtues of men most difficult to maintain. Some idea of the corrupt conditions prevailing at that time can be gathered from Paul's revelation in Romans 1–3. Against such a background must we place the teachings of Jesus concerning righteousness, holiness, and social justice. The term *ethical* relates to moral action, motive, or character and also treats of morals, morality, or ethics. Many of our Lord's parables and proverbs are related to the way humans should live and act in the varied relationships of life. Being concerned with human character and conduct, ethics, then, is not so much a subject of knowledge, but a source of action. They are associated with life or personality in its inward dispositions, outward manifestations and social relations.

Chief among the teachings of Jesus on morality is the Sermon on the Mount, deemed by some writers to be impracticable in our kind of world. But as Dr. W. P. Patterson reminds us, "Though the Christian ideal towers high above the general practice of our generation, it may be that that practice will one day be looked back on as belonging to the half-savage practice of the world's youth. And in the present it has often been made sublimely practicable for those whom the Holy Spirit touched, and whose hearts were set aflame with a Christ-like love of man."

With our Lord's pronouncements of his ethics, there was the promise of fulfillment. What he commands, he supplies. "Faithful is he that calleth you, who also *will do it*" (1 Thess. 5:23, 24). His preaching of the kingdom may appear to be revolutionary, and because it meant to inaugurate a new society, it was so. It was so thorough in its whole conception that, for those who were satisfied with existing societies, it seemed to turn human relationships upside down and to be quite impracticable. But Jesus came into the world for no other purpose than to bring into existence a society consisting of those who by courage and faith should find his ethics practicable and make them real. Bishop Gore remarks that this "ethical teaching of Jesus was not expounded as a philosopher or legislator might expound a system. It was given by way of proverbs or aphorisms, sometimes highly paradoxical aphorisms—and parables." The purpose of the following pages is to prove this contention.

Approaching a classification of the teachings of Jesus, it is somewhat surprising how many topics he actually dealt with, and likewise their variety. Further, no matter what theme he dealt with, he spoke "the truth, the whole truth, and nothing but the truth." Even his foes had to confess, "Master, we know that thou sayest and teachest rightly, neither acceptest thou the person of any, but teachest the way of God truly" (Luke 20:21). The answer Jesus gave to the question about taxes required by Caesar had great effect, for the questioners marveled at his answer and thereafter held their peace (Luke 20:26). The range of his teaching was remarkable and of such absorbing interest that it was no wonder that the people crowded in upon him and hung upon his words (Luke 19:3, 48).

The exact number of themes, topics, and subjects Jesus dealt with is not easy to decide since many of them are interwoven. Dr. W. Graham Scroggie in his *Guide to the Gospels* details forty of them. He observes that "we do not know the Gospels well enough until we have to some extent understood what Christ taught about these subjects, the study of which makes for our intellectual and spiritual enrichment." While it is popularly thought the teaching of Jesus implies what he said and taught as recorded in the four Gospels—and we are keeping, more or less, to what they reveal —elements of his teaching can be found in Acts and in the Epistles, and particularly in the Book of Revelation. Jesus gave the revelation of himself to John. That book contains seven letters of his which he sent to seven churches and which contain many precious gems of truth.

My controlling desire in the preparation of these volumes is to present the teaching of Jesus in a way to attract you to the master teacher himself, who will ever remain without peer or rival in the history of oratory, profane or sacred. The Christless, sordid age in which we live requires a reemphasis of the saving and ethical truths the master taught, and it is my fervent prayer and hope that this presentation will assist many in witnessing about Christ and telling of his great teachings.

Part 1

— 1 —

The Teacher

In his description of the incarnation of Jesus as the Word becoming flesh and dwelling among men, John used the pregnant phrase, "The *life* was the *light*" (John 1:4). What made Jesus' teachings most illuminative was the holy life behind them and pulsating through them. What Jesus was in himself gave weight to what he taught. Truth and personality were one. His life was not detached from his teachings, as in the case with some teachers who tell us to do what they say, but not what they do. As the supreme teacher, Jesus not only enunciated remarkable ethics, his daily life illustrated them. He not only proclaimed truth, he was *the truth* (John 14:6). The Word became *flesh*. His life was the embodiment of all his utterances. Umphrey Lee in his *Life of Christ* reminds us that

> The most important factor in the work of every successful teacher is his own personality. What he says and does gets most of its force and significance from what he is. This at once suggests one of the secrets of the unique influence of Jesus as a teacher. His words and deeds were the spontaneous expression of a character that was

complete in its symmetry and infinitely rich in its resources, and this gave to them an inexhaustible wealth
of means.

No one who listened to Jesus' public discources
could ever say, "What you are speaks so loud, I cannot hear what you say." C. Loring Brace in his monumental work *Gesta Christi* expresses it:

> The morals and truths in these teachings of a remark-
> able Being were not absolutely new—as indeed the prin-
> ciples of morality rest on the principles of human na-
> ture, and must be known, more or less clearly, to all men
> —but they were presented with such unequalled simplicity,
> and *illustrated by a life and character of such unexampled
> elevation, and purity,* and accompanied with spiritual
> truths so profound and universal, as well as with super-
> natural claims, that the whole formed a new power in
> the world for the moral renovation of man—in other
> words, a RELIGION; but one claiming to be absolute
> and universal, for all ages and races and circumstances.

The New Testament presents Jesus himself as being holy, righteous, faithful, true, just, guileless, sinless, spotless, innocent, harmless, obedient, meek,
lowly in heart, merciful, patient, long-suffering, loving, compassionate, and forgiving. Such a perfect
life shining through his teachings became the light
of men. Pharisaical teachers tried to honor God by
the saying of their lips, but what they taught fell
dead on men's hearts because their own hearts were
far from God. Being full of dead men's bones, there
was no harmony between their proclamations and
their personalities. A stanza from one of the elegies
written on the death of Sir Philip Sidney, English
poet, statesman, and soldier of the fifteenth century,

can be taken as a faraway likeness of a greater and more wonderful figure.

> A sweet, attractive kind of grace;
> The full assurance given by looks;
> Perpetual comfort in a face:
> The lineaments of Gospel books.

THE QUALITIES HE POSSESSED

A study of the Gospels reveals certain characteristic features of the oral ministry of Jesus, both public and private. He was ever conscious of the necessary functions of a teacher. Although we have no authentic history of the early life of Jesus, apart from the solitary reference to his visit to the Temple at age twelve, we have the record that he "grew, and waxed strong . . . , filled with wisdom: and the grace of God was upon him. . . . increased in wisdom and stature, and in favour with God and man" (Luke 2:40–52).

Jesus had the spiritual and moral training of a godly home and attended the village synagogue school until he was around fifteen years of age when, according to Hebrew custom, he took up the trade represented by the family, in this case, carpentry. It seems that he never went to rabbinical schools for advanced education, nor sat at the feet of a renowned philosopher, as Paul came to do with the students of Gamaliel. This lack is what the Jewish leaders had in mind when, marveling at the truths Jesus taught in the Temple, they asked, "How knoweth this man letters, having never learned?" (John 7:15).

His was a quiet development of mind and body, of outward uneventfulness, of silent garnering of experience in the midst of humble surroundings in Nazareth. He knew how to read and write (Luke 4:17; John 8:6–8) and saturated his mind with Old Testament Scriptures, and as he pondered them, instinctively knew that he was the One in whom the predictions of the prophets were destined to be fulfilled (Luke 24:25–27, 44, 45).

Jesus had no specific training in pedagogy, or studies in the art of public speech; yet when he came to his public ministry, multitudes hung upon his matchless teachings and marveled at his striking words (Matt. 22:22). It was not only the substance of Christ's teachings that excited the attention of those rabbinically trained rulers, but the fact that he had never been technically trained as a teacher, or rabbi, in the literature of their schools. To them, he was a layman and unlearned; he was not a man of letters and was unknown in the circles of professional expounders. Other men who left their mark upon the world, such as John Bunyan, William Booth, and Dwight L. Moody, had this in common, namely, the absence of a formal education. Yet how proficient they were in wisdom from above.

The marked ability of Jesus as an untrained teacher created jealousy in the hearts of the rabbis, who thus treated him as a demagogue out to deceive the people. How chafed they were as they heard him teaching with art, wisdom, and learning, exciting their wonder as he unlocked mysteries to which they thought they only possessed the key—a confessed prerogative he had to rebuke them for! Wherein, then, lay the secret of his success as a teacher without equal in world history?

HE WAS A TEACHER SENT FROM GOD

Nicodemus had an insight as to the source of the master's knowledge and power as an expositor of truth when he affirmed, "Rabbi, we know that thou art a teacher come from God" (John 3:2). Jesus confirmed this when he said to the Jewish rulers, "My doctrine is not mine, but his that sent me" (John 7:16,17). He constantly affirmed that his own ministry of preaching, teaching, and healing was but the accomplishment of the Father's will. Repeatedly he referred to being the Father's *Sent One*, his messenger carrying his message to the hearts of men. Jesus came as the Word by whom the mind of God was revealed (John 5:19–38). Proof of the divine source of his teachings came with obedience to the divine will and word (John 7:17).

Jesus was not only a teacher come from God, but a teacher who *was* God and as such, *before* all things, an evidence of his superior dignity (Col. 1:17). John emphasizes the preexistence of Jesus in the opening words of his Gospel—"In the beginning was the Word"—a beginning beyond the beginning of creation in Genesis 1:1. It is his deity, then, that gives quality to all Jesus taught. No man could speak like him, for he was the *God-man*—man's perfect God, and God's perfect man.

Then there is the obverse side of his untiring activity as a teacher the Gospels present, namely, his unbroken and unhindered closeness to God, expressed in his life of prayer. Both his words and works reveal constant communion with his Father, whose mind and will he had known from a past eternity and which he constantly obeyed. Taught of the Father, as an obedient son, he fearlessly declared the truths received from above (John 8:28). Underlying all the superb sayings of Jesus was the intuitive knowledge of God that was his as the Son. Because of this unique, eternal relationship, Jesus alone had the messages his Father wanted the world to hear. The attitude of Jesus, even toward the most sacred tradition of his people, rested upon a divine insight into the will of God not granted to everyone (Luke 6:5).

Nicodemus confessed, "Thou art a teacher come from God." The first lesson the master in Israel had to learn from the divinely sent teacher is the first and best lesson for us to learn in all this world's lessons, namely, to be born anew by the Spirit of God. Upon the ruler's acknowledgment of Jesus as a teacher from God, there came the sudden sword thrust, "Except a man be born again, he cannot see the kingdom of God" (John 3:2, 3). Revelation of divine truth is dependent upon regeneration. In order to *see*, we must be *saved*.

Until we have mastered this initial lesson of the newborn, we are not spiritually able to receive any further tuition from the teacher, whose priorities are always right. The *natural* man, or the man unrenewed through the new birth—the truth of which Jesus taught Nicodemus—cannot receive Jesus' further teachings. They can only be "spiritually discerned," or discerned by the Spirit who brings about the new birth and then abides in the renewed one as a further divine teacher (1 Cor. 2:13, 14; 1 John 2:20). It was for the benefit of the Pharisees, who were spiritually blind, that Jesus uttered his parable on the good shepherd. "But they understood not what things they were which he spake unto them" (John 10:6). Why did they not understand his gracious words? Because their hearts were closed against him. They did not believe in him and love him, and no one can appreciate the truths he taught unless he or she loves him.

— 2 —

Himself

Usually, expositors of the teachings of Jesus commence the catalog with what he taught about *God*. I feel, however, that Jesus himself should have the first place in such a study, for it is only as we know all that he was in himself as he sought to instruct men in spiritual and moral truths that we can judge his fitness to be an interpreter of the mind and will of God and of all relating to man. Thus an understanding of the things concerning himself is of vital importance. Any consideration of the Christian faith must begin with an examination of the person of Christ. A right understanding of what we believe demands an appreciation of who he really is, and true Christian experience is essentially a relationship with him. Such a relationship is crucial. If we are honest in our belief that Jesus is God's revelation of himself to man, then we shall submit ourselves to his instructions and fashion our lives according to his teaching or, in other words, become his faithful disciples.

There can be no dispute about the fact that Jesus is the one character in human history of whom more has been written and spoken than any other person. If all the books and booklets and tracts printed through the last fifteen hundred years dealing with the preexistence, incarnation, life, character, virtues, teachings, miracles, death, resurrection, ascension, and the present and future ministry of Jesus were to be gathered in one place, where is the library that could contain them all? Then, what about the countless millions of sermons that have been preached on his uniqueness, grace, and power? And what of the unnumbered host of pastors and Christian workers who, when every Sunday comes round, magnify and extol him as Savior and Lord wherever they witness on the face of the earth?

Friends and foes alike have uttered widely differing opinions about Jesus, who never ceases to be the center of universal attraction. When he lived among men, there was a division because of him. Some held that he was a deceiver, impostor, winebibber, mad, possessed with a devil; others declared him to be a great prophet of righteousness, a good man, the wisest of teachers, a beautiful character, and God manifest in flesh. But although it is interesting and profitable to gather together all that men have said about Jesus, the opinion of him that matters most is the one he held concerning himself. We can have no higher authority of who he is than what he taught regarding his many-sided self. What personal estimation of himself, then, did he declare?

Jesus had no doubt whatever as to who he was, from where he came, why he entered our world, and what the future held for him. Authoritatively and unequivocally, he affirmed his claims even though they aroused the fierce antagonism of men and re-

sulted, from the human standpoint, in his crucifixion. At Calvary, *the Truth* was on a scaffold but did
not perish. What were these unashamed affirmations
and claims of one who could not lie?

HIS PREEXISTENCE

Although it may sound somewhat paradoxical, the
statement is perfectly true: *Jesus lived before he was
born!* His beginning as the *Word* was long before his
beginning as *man* (John 1:1; Luke 2:11). In the prologue to his Gospel, John, in three crisp sentences,
announces the way in which Jesus antedated the beginning of all things: (1) His Eternal Subsistence, "In
the beginning was the Word"; (2) His Eternal Inter-
communion with God, "The Word was with God";
(3) His Eternal Identity with God, "The Word was
God."

Jesus came as "the Father of eternity" and as "the
lofty one that inhabiteth eternity" (Isa. 9:6; 57:15,
RV). His advent on earth out of a past eternity is
implied in his claim, "Before Abraham was, I am"
(John 8:58). Quite openly, Jesus spoke of the glory
he had with God the Father before the creation of
the world and also of his coming forth from the
Father (John 16:28). In his conversation with Nicodemus, Jesus asserted that he came down from heaven
(John 3:13). He came, then, as the eternal Son.

John had no hesitation in declaring that Jesus not
only antedated all things but was creator of them:
"All things were made by him, and apart from him
was not made one thing that hath been made" (John
1:3). Thus, Jesus was taken out of the category of

creatures altogether. Accordingly, what is said of him is not that he was the first of existences to come into being—that "in the beginning he already had come into being"—but that "in the beginning, when things began to come into being, he already was." Here, express eternity of being is asserted. By his pregnant language, John would have us realize that what Jesus as the Word was in eternity was not merely God's co-eternal Fellow, but the Eternal God's self. This was the Word that became flesh, as God manifest in flesh.

HIS MESSIAHSHIP

The Old Testament presents us with "the heaven-drawn picture" of the Messiah who was to come, and in the Gospels, he steps down out of the frame in the person of Christ, a name meaning "the anointed one" or Messiah (Dan. 9:25, 26). When Andrew, after his surrender to Jesus, went out to find his own brother, Simon Peter, to tell him the good news, he exclaimed, "We have found the Messiah, which is, being interpreted, the Christ" (John 1:41). More explicit is the expression of the Samaritan woman who, during a spiritual conversation with the stranger she met at the well, confessed her faith in the long-promised Messiah: "I know that Messiah cometh, who is called Christ: when he is come, he will tell us all things."

Without hesitation, Jesus immediately replied, "I that speak unto thee am *he* [the Messiah]" (John 4:26). Leaving her waterpot, the woman at the well hurried back and confessed to her fellow Samari-

tans, "Come, see a man, which *told me all things that
ever I did;* [the woman's own description of the authoritative Messiah] is not this *the* Christ?" When Jesus
urged his disciples to search the Old Testament
books, saying, "They . . . testify of me" (John 5:39),
he actually identified himself with Daniel's prophecy
of "Messiah the prince" who would come and vindi-
cate his claim as God's anointed one. Further, when
Jesus spoke of himself as "the Son of David" and as
"the Son of man," he used prophetic messianic titles.
In his sayings Jesus constantly related himself to the
past and identified himself as the promised Messiah
of Israel. The prewritten life of Jesus is an astounding miracle as we compare it with the perfect fulfillment in the Jesus of history. As Dr. A. T. Pierson
says in *Knowing the Scriptures:*

> The inspiration of that portrait came from the Heavenly
> Gallery, and not from the studio of an artist . . . Nothing
> but Divine prescience could have foreseen it, and noth-
> ing but Divine power could accomplish it.

In Jesus' simple, poor home at Nazareth, a religious atmosphere prevailed, and a treasure of a
book was daily read, namely, the Old Testament, any
roll of which was deemed precious. At an early age,
Jesus listened to Joseph and Mary as they read from
rolls of the Psalms or the Prophets or parts of the
Law. The more he listened, the deeper the conviction grew that he was the promised *Christ,* which is
the Greek equivalent for Messiah and in English is
correctly rendered by the word *anointed.* Striking, is
it not, that when he entered his public ministry, one
day he rebuked the *demons* who knew that he was the
promised Messiah, and confessed, "Thou art Christ"
(Luke 4:41)?

HIS HUMANITY

Since we are confining ourselves to what Jesus himself actually said about the themes we are considering, it is not the purpose in this present topic to elaborate upon the evidences of his humanity which the New Testament states. The Gospels present his human birth, human relationships, human emotions, and human desires. All alike proclaim that Jesus was "made in the likeness of men" and "touched with our infirmities." He became truly man, possessing all that makes a man *a man*, and his assumed manhood lived out a human life on earth. What we are out to stress is his own assumption of real humanity which emerges in some of the titles he used of himself. Two of the titles frequently used are *the Son of man* and *the Son of God*, the main distinction between the two being his relationship to man on earth and his relationship to his Father in heaven. As *Son of man*, he dwelt here below for over thirty-three years and will return to have dominion over the earth. This latter title, then, is associated with Jesus as the one who entered upon a mode of existence in which the experiences that belong to human beings would also be his. Further, as "the Son of man" he became the personification of humanity in its most perfect form. The Gospels portray Jesus as the Ideal Man. Canon Liddon expressed this characteristic feature of Christ's nature implied in the designation *Son of man* in this fitting way:

> It does not merely assert his real incorporation with our kind: it exalts him indefinitely above us all as the true representative, the ideal, the pattern Man. His is a Human Life which does justice to the idea of Humanity. He is the Archetypal Man.

The name by which Jesus most frequently designated himself was *the Son of man,* which occurs some eighty-four times in the Gospels and was a title never used of the Lord by anyone but himself. It is only used four times outside the Gospels (Acts 7:56; Heb. 2:6; Rev. 1:13; 14:14). This was not a title Jesus invented, seeing it occurs in the Old Testament (Ps. 8:4; 80:17). In Ezekiel it is used no fewer than ninety times. Daniel also employs the title (Dan. 7:13; 8:17). Jesus never defined the title nor mentioned where he found it or how he came to designate himself in such a way. As it was his favorite self-designation, he must have seen in it a most appropriate expression for the human side of his person.

Jesus named himself thus because, through his incarnation when he became flesh, he belongs to mankind—as one who in human nature has accomplished such great things for human nature—who is man, in the supreme sense, the sense corresponding to the idea—who makes real the ideal humanity. He took upon himself all the attributes belonging to human nature and shared in all that is human, sin excepted.

Allied to the title *Son of man* is another expressing his humanity, namely, *Jesus,* recurring about 240 times in the Gospels and which, as Paul reminds us, became a highly exalted name (Phil. 2:9, 10). This personal birthname of his is the Greek form of a Hebrew name found in Joshua, the successor to Moses, as in *Jeshua,* the high priest. Its full form is *Jehoshua,* meaning, "Jehovah our Salvation" (Num. 13:16), and used by and for Jesus is associated with his saving work he was to accomplish as the *man* Christ Jesus. The most striking use of such a precious name was when Jesus appeared to Saul of Tarsus on his way to persecute his followers (Acts 9:5).

How sweet the name of Jesus sounds in a believer's ear!
It soothes his sorrows, heals his wounds,
And drives away his fear.

Evident proofs of his humanity are not difficult to trace in the Gospel narratives:
He identified himself with men (Matt. 4:4; Luke 4:4).
He received the imputation of humanity (Matt. 11:19; Luke 7:34).
He made frequent references to his body and its parts (Matt. 26:12, 26; Mark 14:8, 22; Luke 7:44, 46; 22:19, 20; 24:39; Mark 14:24).
He spoke of his soul (Matt. 26:38; Mark 14:34).
He referred to human dread as he confronted death (Luke 12:50).
He gave expression to his sense of desolation on the cross (Matt. 27:46; Mark 15:34).
He deemed that nothing that is human was alien to him except sin (Matt. 7:11; 9:12; 12:34, 39; Luke 11:13, 29).

O Saviour Christ, Thou too art Man;
Thou hast been troubled, tempted, tried;
Thy kind but searching glance can scan
The very wounds that shame would hide.

IIIS DEITY

Dr. Benjamin B. Warfield, in his monumental work *The Lord of Glory*, states emphatically that "Those who will not have a Divine Christ must seek their human Jesus outside the entire evangelical literature," which is tantamount to affirming that "the Son of man" and "the Son of God" were one and the same person. Jesus was "God manifest in flesh" and, coming as the one who in a past eternity was *equal with God,* manifested Godlike attributes while among men. In the man of Galilee deity and humanity were happily wedded, the love knot between his two natures being made by the Holy Spirit in the womb of Mary. Thus Jesus came as Mary's firstborn son and as God's beloved Son.

It is perfectly clear from our Lord's own teachings that he claimed to have a unique relationship with God, had unity and equality with God, coupling his own name with that of the Father in a most natural way. Categorically, Jesus declared himself to be "the Son of God," thereby "making himself equal with God" (John 5:18, 25). God himself, Gabriel, the disciples, and evil spirits all alike spoke of Jesus as "the Son of God." While we value such outside testimony about his deity, the expressions he repeatedly used of himself as the promised "Mighty God" (Isa. 9:6) are most impressive. The title *Son of God* is found also thirty times in the Gospels, and elsewhere in the New Testament some twenty times.

He unhesitatingly allowed himself to be called *God* (John 1:1; 10:33; 20:28).

His various *I am's* can be predicated only of deity (John 14:6).

His assertion of being the sole mediator between God and man likewise affirms his deity (John 10:9); further proofs of his Godhead (John 10:30; 14:9).

He manifested, as well as confessed, the possession of divine attributes. *Omnipotence,* for instance, is asserted in his commission to his disciples: "*All* power on earth and in heaven has been given unto me" (Matt. 28:18), and his many miracles prove his sovereignty in every realm (see Mark 2:1-12). Jesus likewise claimed the further divine attribute of *omniscience*. Knowing what was in man, he surprised Nathanael when he told him, "When thou was under the fig tree, I saw thee" (John 1:47, 48; 2:24, 25). The Gospels give us other instances of his perfect knowledge. He also indicated the attribute of *omnipresence*, the ability to be everywhere at the same time. He assured his disciples that wherever they gathered in his name, he would be there in the midst of them and that he would never leave nor forsake them (Matt. 28:20; Heb. 13:5).

When Jesus made use on his own initiative of the abbreviated form *the Son*, it was evidently with the same force as the self-designation of "the Son of God." It is true that this term is applied to angels, to men, to the Jewish nation as a whole, to Jewish kings, and to all saints, but as Dr. Stalker observes in *Ethic of Jesus*, "The principal ideas which the term embodies are, that those bearing the name are derived from God as their Author, that they are the objects of His love and choice, and that they are like him in character and conduct." With Jesus as "*the* Son of God," these ideas reach perfection. When he used the expression for his own relation to God, it indicated a relationship that was not only unique, but "one that reached up beyond the competency of men or angels, till He named himself in the same breath with the Father and the Holy Spirit as an object of worship."

The Jews knew that the miracles of Jesus were not

merely signs of his supernatural power but proofs of his divine commission. They understood them, along with his words, as the substantiation of his claim, which he certainly made, to be equal with God (John 5:1–19; 10:30–33; 14:8–11). The purpose of John both in his Gospel and in his three Epistles is to show that Jesus was "the true God" who was "made flesh" (John 1:14; 20:31; 1 John 1:1–4). John's designations of him as "God" and as "the Son of God" declare a relationship entirely unique and one which is eternal. It is this unique relationship he himself declared that constitutes the only ground of his appeal to men to come to him to learn of God (Matt. 11:27, RV; 28:19–20). As Dr. Warfield puts it:

> Speaking in the most solemn manner, he not only presents himself as the Son, as the sole source of knowledge of God, and of blessedness for men, but places himself in a position, not of equality merely, but of absolute reciprocity and interpenetration of knowledge of the Father, as if the being of the Son were so immense that only God could know it thoroughly, and the knowledge of the Son so unlimited that he could know God to perfection.

The evidence of the deity of Jesus, then, is the warp and woof of the Gospels. A threefold cord that cannot be broken proves his position in the Godhead:

His assertions of equality with God the Father (John 5:17, 18, 21–23; 10:30, 33).

His prerogative to forgive sins (Matt. 9:6; Mark 2:7, 10).

His authority to give eternal life to all who believe (John 10:27, 28).

This marvelous truth of God in Christ solves all

our problems and makes all things possible. In "The
Death in the Desert," Browning imagines the death
and last words of the apostle:

> I say, the acknowledgement of God in Christ
> Accepted by thy reason, solves for thee
> All questions in the earth and out of it.

How blest we are if out of a redeemed, adoring
heart we can exclaim with Thomas as we gaze at the
crucified, risen Savior—*My Lord and my God!*

HIS PERFECTION

Jesus is the only perfect man the world has ever
known. Apart from him, *"All* have sinned" (Rom.
3:23). For any person to rise and say, "I have never
sinned," would not only be false, but presumptuous.
Yet the man of Galilee could stand before men and
ask, "Which of you convinceth me of sin?" In every
other individual, original sin can be found, and the
old Adamic nature gives Satan a foothold. But Jesus
could say, "The prince of this world cometh, and
hath nothing *in* me" (John 14:30). There was nothing
within him which Satan could appeal to or use.
The sinlessness and deity of Jesus are implied in
the announcement of Gabriel to Mary, "That *holy
thing* which shall be born of thee shall be called the
Son of God" (Luke 1:35). Then his apostles affirmed
him to be "without sin," or the lamb without blemish,
and therefore the perfect offering. Had Jesus
sinned, even once, he would have forfeited his right
to die as a ransom for sin. But "he knew no sin" and
therefore was worthy to be "made sin"—not a sinner

—"for us." Further, it is his perfection that gives efficacy to his death for sinners.

> He only could unlock the gate of Heaven,
> And let us in.

When the scribes and Pharisees brought a woman, taken in the very act of adultery, to Jesus, they tried to trap him by saying, "Moses in the law commanded us, that such should be stoned: but what sayest thou?" Jesus, as though he heard them not, stooped down and wrote something with his finger in the dust—the only time he is referred to as writing. Then looking up he said to his foes, "He that is without sin among you [could he have meant the particular sin which men had made the woman guilty of?], let him cast a stone at her." Then he continued writing, and when the woman's accusers heard the answer of Jesus, conscience-stricken they left him "one by one, beginning at the *eldest*." The only man present who was without sin was Jesus, but he never cast a stone. Graciously he said, "Neither do I condemn: go, and sin no more" (John 8:3–11). Because he was the sinless one, he was able and willing to forgive, for "Who can forgive sins but God only?"

The psalmist urges us to "mark the perfect man, and behold the upright: for the end of that man is peace" (Ps. 37:37). But only in the man Christ Jesus can there be found this combination of perfection and peace. Not only was he undefiled, but also undefilable. His untainted holiness was such that although tempted of Satan he never yielded. No temptation could fasten itself upon him. Although in close contact with sin, as the friend of sinners, he

remained pure and holy, just as the sunbeam is un-
contaminated although it constantly shines on a heap
of rubbish. Jesus will ever remain God's perfect man,
and man's perfect God. Even hell acknowledges him
to be "the Holy One of God" (Mark 1:24; Luke
4:34). As for Satan himself, he has no doubt as to the
deity and authority of Jesus!

HIS UNIQUENESS

Any reader of the four Gospels is profoundly impressed with the way Jesus asserted for himself a
peculiar dignity, and for his work, a peculiar efficacy. He comes before us as one having a unique
relationship and in the world to accomplish a unique
task and likewise having authority to make unique
demands or claims upon others. He calls himself not
a Son but *the* Son (Matt. 11:27) and because of this
unique relation to the Father has the right to make
upon the other children of God a demand for faith
and obedience. If we seek the reasons for claims
without parallel in any other person, we can find
them in three particulars:

Jesus is in the Father's confidence, and from him
the other children obtain their knowledge of the
Father (Luke 10:22).

Jesus fully possessed the privileges and fulfilled
the obligations which are involved in sonship (John
8:29).

Jesus, by his death, procured the means of procuring for his own the highest blessings (Mark 14:24).

The absolutely filial Son, then, perfectly fulfilling
the Father's will, earned the right to exercise all au-

thority. In virtue of his death and resurrection, he could declare, "All power is given unto me" (Matt. 28:16–20). As for his unique claims, men tried to deny them, but they remained in their realization as evidences of his deity.

He claimed absolute authority and infallibility as a teacher and declared that he alone knew the mind of God the Father and that he alone could reveal him (Matt. 7:24, 26; Luke 10:16; John 5:24).

He affirmed that heaven and earth would pass away, but that his authoritative words would never pass away (Matt. 24:35) and that his teachings were based upon the Old Testament (Matt. 9:13; 12:7 with Hos. 6:6; John 5:39; Luke 24:27, 44).

He declared that he came not only to teach the truth, but was the personification of the Truth (John 14:6).

He proclaimed the august power of judging men and allotting them to their eternal destiny, asserting that the Father had committed all judgment to him (John 5:22; Matt. 25:31–46).

He united himself with the Father and the Spirit as together constituting the Godhead (Matt. 28:19).

He not only predicted the fact and manner of his death, but also that his was the power to lay down his life and take it up again (Matt. 9:15; 16:21; Luke 9:22; 18:31–33).

He also claimed that his death was not inevitable, but that it had a universal significance (John 12:32–33), that it had a bearing upon the unseen world (John 12:31), that it was the purpose of his incarnation (John 12:27), that it was to be a vicarious death (Matt. 26:28; Mark 10:45), and that it would eternally glorify the Father (John 12:28; 13:31; 17:1).

HIS DEATH AND RESURRECTION

As soon as a child is born, it commences the journey to the grave, for all come into the world under the sentence of death. Death is an appointment which every person must keep. "It is appointed unto men once to die." But at the birth of a baby we never think of it as being born to die, but born *to live*. But with Jesus who came to give his life as a ransom for sinners, it was different. He is the only one who came into the world for the purpose of dying. Virtually, he died in a past eternity, for he came as the lamb slain from *before* the foundation of the world. Thus, Jesus was born crucified. Among·his many utterances none is so positive or strikes a grander and more universal note than the one his disciples heard: "The Bread that I will give is my flesh, which I will give for the life of the world" (John 6:51).

This is why Jesus had so much to say about his death and resurrection, and upon the example and authority of Jesus, Paul, in his Epistles, gives the first place to this cardinal truth of the Christian faith. Peter, in his sermon to the Sanhedrin, accused the rulers, elders, and scribes of the death of Christ "whom ye crucified" (Acts 4:10), but Jesus himself declared that his life was not *taken* by others, but *given*. Think of these great utterances: "I lay down my life for the sheep"; "I lay down my life, that I might take it again"; "I lay it down of myself. I have power to lay it down, and I have power to take it again" (John 10:15, 17, 18). His death, then, was voluntary; "No man taketh my life from me." Such wonderful declarations point back to the sacrificial work of Jesus as conceived and accomplished in the eternal counsel of God, where his sacrifice of himself was not *exacted,* but was his own spontaneous offering in harmony with his Father's will. At Jesus' trial before Pilate, the ruler was perplexed at the silence of the majestic prisoner before him and said, "Speakest thou not unto me? knowest thou not that I have power to crucify thee, and have power to release thee?" Jesus, breaking his silence, replied, "Thou couldest have no power at all against me, except it were given thee from above" (John 19:9–11; see Matt. 26:52, 53). Here is proof that his death was voluntary. "He gave himself for our sins."

That such a death was also vicarious and substitutionary comes out in some of Jesus' sayings. "This is my body, broken for *you.* . . . My blood . . . shed for many for the remission of sins" (Matt. 26:27, 28). "The Son of man came . . . to give his life a ransom for many" (Matt. 20:28). To these we could add all the references of the apostles who witnessed his death and resurrection. George Bernard Shaw spoke scornfully of those "who actually make their religion centre in the infamy of loading the guilt and punishment of all their sins on an innocent victim." Yet this was what the innocent victim himself said he would do, namely, die in our room and stead. This was why, under the inspiration of the Holy Spirit, the prophets were able to describe the sufferings of Jesus *before* he was born. As Peter puts it, they were able to "testify beforehand of the sufferings of Christ." Chief among those prophets was Isaiah who, in vivid word pictures, poured a flood of light upon the atoning sacrifice Jesus was born to accomplish. Underscore in your Bible at Isaiah 53 these phrases:

A tender plant, a root, no form, no beauty, despised, esteemed not, bore our griefs, carried our sorrows, stricken, smitten, af-

flicted, wounded, buried, chastisement, stripes, on him iniquity,
oppressed, led as a lamb to the slaughter, dumb, prison, cut off,
grave with the wicked, bruised, an offering, unto death, with
transgressors, bore our sin.

Is it any wonder then that the four Gospels give such space to his death? One-third of the material in the Gospels has to do with the events in the last week of Jesus, who, when he spoke of his death, linked onto it his resurrection. It is pointed out that two of the Gospels do not relate the birth of Jesus—Mark and John; two do not relate his Sermon on the Mount in full—Mark and John; but all four narratives record with fullness of detail the fact of his death and resurrection. One-third of Matthew, one-third of Mark, one-fourth of Luke, and one-half of John are devoted to the last hours of Jesus. Thus about one-third of the material making up the four Gospels relates to the last week of Jesus.

The prominence given to the death and resurrection of Jesus in the biographies of the Gospels is in strange contrast to the biographies of the notable men in history. For instance, in a recent biography of Daniel Webster, the American statesman, just 5 of the 803 pages which deal with his career tell of his death at Marshfield in 1852. Several years ago a life of the poet Shelley appeared in which just 3 pages out of a total of 1,389 pages described the sad story of his death by drowning near Leghorn in 1822. But in the three years of his public ministry, Jesus constantly predicted, not only his death, but also the manner and purpose of it. Further, the way he intensely felt about the end for which he was born can be seen in the way in which from the beginning of his ministry, he steadfastly set his face toward Jerusalem where he was to be crucified.

It would take several pages to tabulate all his sayings about his decease at Jerusalem. Here are a few:

"Destroy this temple, and in three days *I* will raise it up . . . He spake of the temple of his body" (John 2:18–22).

"The sign . . . the Son of man shall be three days and three nights in the heart of the earth" (Matt. 12:39–40).

"The Son of man must be lifted up" (John 3:14).

"The Son of man shall be betrayed into the hands of men: and they shall kill him, and the third day he shall be raised again" (Matt. 17:22, 23; 20:18, 19).

In the parable of the vineyard, Jesus portrayed himself as the heir, the husbandmen would slay (Matt. 21:33–39). A striking feature of our Lord's frequent references to his death is the way he spoke of it as the great hour of his life and work. Twice over it is recorded that his enemies were unable to arrest him for *"his hour* was not yet come." He believed that he was "immortal until his work was done." He knew when the hour of his departure would come (John 13:1; 17:1), and when it did, he died, not as a victim, but as a victor, crying with a loud voice, *It is finished!* Jesus was not referring to the termination of the terrible anguish he knew could be his, but to the accomplishment of the task he came from heaven to fulfill. It was thus in anticipation he could pray, "Father, I have finished the work which thou gavest me to do" (John 17:4). This is why many of the old divines referred to the death and resurrection as "the finished work of Christ." At dark Calvary he laid hold of the principalities and powers of

hell and robbed them forever of their authority. Describing the manner of his death, he said, "I, if I be
lifted up . . . will draw all men unto me," and the
wondrous cross on which he died as the prince of
glory has never lost its magnetism—and never will—
for in heaven the unending song will be, "Worthy is
the lamb that was slain" (Rev. 5:12).

> In the Cross of Christ I glory,
> Towering o'er the wrecks of time;
> All the light of sacred story
> Gathers round its head sublime.

Thus, as James Denny expresses it in *The Death of
Christ*, "The forfeiting of His free life has freed our
forfeited lives."

With all the foregoing unique claims of Jesus before
us, as well as all of his other sayings, how apt is the
observation of Canon Liddon that "Jesus distinctly,
repeatedly, energetically preaches himself." In any
other person the constant *I* would be obnoxious and
evidence of arrogant presumption. Jesus, however,
was all he claimed to be. There are only two possible
reactions to all of his claims and demands, namely,
acceptance or rejection. We must believe him to be
the unique Son of God as he affirmed himself to be,
or regard him as a deceiver and a blasphemer. To all
who love and trust him, he is fairer and greater than
all the world beside.

How one wishes he possessed the qualifications enabling him to understand and expound fully the
character, the experience, the excellency, and the
greatness of Jesus who had the stamp of perfection
imprinted indelibly on all that he did and said! He
always did the right thing and uttered the right

word. Never once was it necessary for him to retrace a step or recall a saying. Words were rightly spoken and like "apples of gold in pictures of silver"; and his deeds were rightly performed. As we watch him moving among men, he was the complete master of every situation, able to weigh each circumstance and each event in its value and able to act therein in complete accord with truth and righteousness. The world has never seen his like since! Dr. Alexander Stewart, one-time professor of systematic theology in St. Andrew's University, Scotland, wrote in his *Life of Christ,* way back in 1906, "He who would worthily write the life of Jesus Christ must have a pen dipped in the imaginative sympathy of a poet, in the prophet's fire, in the artist's charm and grace, and in the reverence and purity of a saint."

BIBLE STUDY QUESTIONS

Take time to turn to each Scripture reference and mark the verse or a portion in your Bible.

1. Explain the statement, "Jesus lived before he was born."
2. Trace in the Gospels the proof of Christ's divinity.
3. What is the meaning of the name *Son of God?*
4. Did Jesus claim he was infallible?
5. What did Jesus say was the purpose of his death?

— 3 —

God

Theologians have taken all the Bible says about the being, attributes, and actions of God and formulated that information into what they call *systematic theology.* As with the Old Testament, Jesus makes no studied definition of God but rather assumes all that God is in himself. Richard Glover says in *The History of Jesus,* "It would be right to say that Jesus puts before us no system of God, but rather suggests a great exploration, and intimacy with the slow and sure knowledge that imtimacy gives. He has no definition of God, but he assumes God, lives on the basis of God, interprets God; and God is discovered in his acts and his relations."

Further, having lived with God in a past eternity, and cognizant that he had been sent by God into the world to manifest his sacrificial love for sinners, Jesus never spent time seeking to prove the existence of God. To him, the Father had ever been a living, bright reality, and so, simply yet confidently, he taught that God *is* and that, consequently, men should accept his revelation of his being and obey him. When we examine all that Jesus said and taught about God, however, we do not find an orderly presentation of God's nature and functions in what he revealed of his Father. But by gathering all he did teach about God, it is not difficult to trace clear lines of delineation. One day Philip asked Jesus, "Lord, show us the Father, and it sufficeth us." His reply was most revealing and emphasized his equality with God as he declared in the saying, "I and my Father are one." "Jesus saith unto him, Have *I* been so long time with you, yet hast thou not known *me*, Philip? he that hath seen *me* hath seen the *Father;* how sayest thou then, Shew us the Father?" (John 14:8, 9).

Jesus came as the culmination of the revelation of God, and if we would know what God is like, all we have to do is to study the ways, works, and words of his beloved Son, for it was his face that reflected "the light of the knowledge of the glory of God" (2 Cor. 4:6). From his own teachings we have the assertion that he *alone* is the medium of the revelation of God (John 5:20; 17:25, 26). "All things are delivered to me of my Father; and no man knoweth who the Son is, but the Father; and who the Father is, but the Son, and he to whom the Son will reveal him" (Luke 10:22).

Coeternal and coequal with God, Jesus has a most intimate knowledge of the character and characteristics of God (John 1:18). Personifying Christ as the wisdom of God, Solomon says, "Then was I by him, as one brought up with him: and I was daily his delight, rejoicing always before him; Rejoicing in the habitable part of his earth: and my delights were with the sons of men" (Prov. 8:30, 31). One cannot have such a close relation with a person as this without knowing all there is to know about him, which brings us to our meditation of what Jesus taught about God because of the perfect relationship between them as Father and Son. "Show us the Father and it sufficeth us," said Philip, and as we are to find, a true knowledge such as Jesus taught is sufficient for all our needs. In what ways, then, did the Son reveal the Father in his teachings?

THE NATURE OF GOD

Is it not somewhat amazing that truth about God, which Jesus probably never unfolded to his disciples, he revealed to a woman of doubtful character? His teaching on the essence of God and of the spirituality of worship was reserved for the woman of Samaria at the well where Jesus rested. Although a Samaritan, this female water-carrier yet looked for the Messiah to come and had the priceless privilege of seeing him in the flesh. Then, as a worshiper, she was more concerned about the *place* of worship than the *spirit* of worship, and thus informed Jesus, "Our fathers worshipped in this mountain; and ye say, that in Jerusalem is the place where men ought to worship" (John 4:20).

Jesus replied by saying that the *sphere* of worship mattered little, but that the *spirit* of worship was all important. "True worshippers shall worship the Father in spirit and in truth" (John 4:23, 24). He then links the true, spiritual nature of worship to the spirituality of God, "God is Spirit"—a truth previously taught by Solomon in his dedicatory prayer at the opening of the Temple (1 Kings 8:27). The two defining terms, *in spirit* and *in truth*, express the con-

crete character of the new form of worship in which
Jesus instructed the Samaritan woman. Paul instructs
us to "worship God in spirit" (Phil. 3:3), and the *spirit*
is the highest organ of the human soul, by means of
which it has communion with the divine, unseen
world. The link between human nature and the divine is in the human spirit, which in the believer is
the shrine of the Holy Spirit (1 Cor. 6:19). All true
approach to God must therefore be *in spirit* (Eph.
6:18). This first feature marks the *intensity* of this
worship; while the second, *in truth*, the corollary of
the first, is expressive of the inward character of
worship coming from a spirit in harmony with the
nature of the one worshiped.

Since God's very nature and essence is *Spirit*, all
true worship must be spiritual, as well as all that is
associated with the place and mode of worship. To
worship God *in truth* is not merely to worship in
sincerity, but with a worship corresponding to the
nature of the object. *God is Spirit*, not *a* Spirit. *Spirit*
is the emphatic word; *Spirit* is God. The phrase thus
describes the *nature*, not the *personality* of God, as in
other expressions, such as, *God is light* and *God is love*
(1 John 4:16). The *first person* of the Trinity, then, is
before us in his eternal essence, *God is Spirit*, in contrast to that which is material and of the flesh. The
third person of the Trinity is named the *Holy Spirit*,
being of the same nature and essence as God. But
what about the *second person* who became the man
Christ Jesus and no longer an invisible Spirit?

Before his incarnation, Jesus was of the same nature and essence as God and the Holy Spirit, but
when he took upon himself the likeness of our flesh,
the composition of the Trinity was altered. The first

and third persons remained eternally the same—
Spirit—but when Jesus the second person of the
Trinity went back to heaven, he took with him the
human body he had lived in for over thirty-three
years, withal glorified! Thus, the center of attraction
in the heavenly abode, where "the spirits of just men
are made perfect," is some of humanity's dust, glorified and seated at the right hand of him of whom
Jesus spoke as "God is Spirit." Something of this
sublime truth emerges in that memorable conversation on the Emmaus Road between our Lord and the
two disciples returning, as they thought, from the
grave containing the dead body of him they loved.
When, ultimately, Cleopas and his companion met
the eleven and recounted their experience of having
met and talked with the risen Lord, who had also
appeared to Simon Peter, he appeared to them all.
But although he spoke in the tone they should have
known, saying, "Peace unto you," the disciples were
"terrified and affrighted, and supposed that they
had seen a spirit."

Then calming their fears, Jesus went on to utter
the remarkable words, "Behold my hands and my
feet, that it is I myself: handle me and see; for a
spirit hath not flesh and bones, as you see me have"
(Luke 24:38–40). Further, to prove that he was no
apparition or specter from the world of the dead, he
asked for something to eat (Luke 24:41; John 21:5).
No shadow or ghost would have asked for food. Ellicott has an apt statement on this crucial test of the
reality of the resurrection body in his *Commentary on
the Whole Bible:*

> The question whether there was not only the power to
> receive food, but a life in any sense dependent upon the

laws which govern the bodily life of men, leads us into a region of problems which we cannot solve, and on which it is profitless to dwell. What seems suggested is a spiritual existence capable, by an act of volition, of assuming, in greater or less measure, the conditions of corporeal.

One wonders how many *true worshipers* who fully understand Christ's teaching on spiritual worship are among those who congregate in places of worship on the Lord's Day?

THE LOVE OF GOD

It would take a book itself to contain a full exposition of all Jesus manifested and taught of the love of God. Scratched upon the wall of a prison cell were found these expressive lines:

> Could we with ink the ocean fill,
> Or were the skies of parchment made,
> Were every stalk on earth a quill,
> And every man a scribe by trade?
> To write the love of God above,
> 'Twould drain the ocean dry;
> Nor would the scroll contain the whole,
> Though stretched from sky to sky!

But one came as the personification of such boundless love and wrote out its message in his own heart's blood for all the world to read. Jesus taught that love was not only one of God's transcendent attributes but his very being or essence. God *is* love! Further, what he preached, he personified, for Jesus taught the love of God by the life he lived. The apostle of love learned this as he lay on Jesus' breast and listened to his heartbeat and thus repeated twice over one of the most precious phrases in the Bible, *God is love!* (1 John 4:8–16). As Jesus was one with the Father, the earthly life he lived, of necessity, reflected the love and goodness of God. By his gracious deeds, acts of pity and compassion, he revealed the love of God to men and demonstrated to them that

> The love of God is broader,
> Than the measures of man's mind:
> And the heart of the Eternal
> Is most wonderfully kind.

Heathen religions set forth a God who is an angry being and in contrast in need of appeasement. Christianity, however, is the only religion that manifests the supreme being as *love,* from whom all true love is derived. God's whole nature is love, and thus Jesus spoke in terms of endearment when he came to the theme of God's interest in his creatures and of his affection in acts of loving care and sacrifice in behalf of the objects of his love. God is symbolized in a fourfold way:

God is Spirit (John 4:24);
God is light (1 John 1:5);
God is truth (John 14:6);
God is love (1 John 4:8, 10).

Spirit, light, and *truth* are expressions of his essential nature; *love* is the expression of his personality corresponding to his nature. God not only loves, but *is* love; it is his very nature, and Jesus taught that this nature must be the sphere in which all who abide in God must abide (see 1 John 4:16). With the four Gospels open before us, may the Spirit of love lead us into the truth Jesus taught concerning the eternal love of God.

A filial love. As the Son of God, Jesus could pray, as he did in his High Priestly Intercessory Prayer, three times over that he had ever been the object and recipient of the love of the Father. "Father, thou hast loved them, as thou hast loved me" (John 17:23). "Thou lovest me before the foundation of the world" (John 17:24). "I have declared . . . that the love wherewith thou hast loved me, may be in them, and I in them" (John 17:26).

As for God himself, he presents Jesus as his *well-beloved* Son (Matt. 3:17; 17:5; Luke 20:13). The first and foremost object of God's love is his own Son, who shared the love of his Father in a unique sense. Between Father and Son there existed an eternal affection, the Son being the original and eternal object of the Father's love—a love warming the heart of the Son before the world began. Since God's love is *eternal,* it must have an eternal object, and it did in the eternal Son. As already pointed out, Jesus often spoke of his preexistence. When he became man, his life radiated the love of his Father, just as his lips taught such a sublime truth.

A universal love. This was the startling yet wonderful aspect of God's love to Nicodemus which he learned during a midnight conversation with Jesus on the subject of regeneration. The narrow exclusivism of this ruler of the Jews (he conceived of God as loving only the Jewish nation) was shattered as, listening to the teacher sent from God, he heard him say, "For God so loved the world" (John 3:16).

The word Jesus used for *world* did not mean the universe he created in six days and pronounced as being "very good." It was not "The earth, with its store / Of wonders untold," not the world men lived

in, but all the men living in the world, as the hymn
reminds us:

> God loved the world
> Of sinners lost
> And ruined by the Fall.

The world Jesus said that God loved was not the
sum total of the material universe considered as an
orderly system, but the sum total of humanity on the
earth, the human race, the sum total of human life
in the ordered world, considered apart from, alienated from, and hostile to God, and apart from the
earthly things which seduce men from God, so
clearly evident from other sayings of Jesus (John
7:1; 15:18; 17:9, 14). What a Gospel this is to
preach, to proclaim to those who are dead in trespasses and sins that God loves them and waits to love
them out of their sin into fellowship with himself!

The emphasis in the opening phrase of this
greatest text in the Bible is the little word *so;* no one
can plumb its depth. A mother asked her small
daughter how much she loved her, and throwing her
chubby arms around her neck said, "So much,
mother!" At Calvary, God threw his arms around a
lost world and cried, *So much!* The very origin, then,
of salvation for the lost lies in the love and mercy of
God, and, seeing that such divine love is active and
identifies itself with its object, it is more than mercy
or compassion.

An individual love. It may seem somewhat general
to many when they hear the blessed news, "God so
loved the world," and thus Jesus made the truth *individual* when he went on to say, "whosoever believeth." It may be hard for one to separate himself

from the millions who have lived, are living, and will yet live and say to his heart, "God loves me"; yet this was the aspect of divine love that captivated the heart and transformed the life of Paul: "Who loved *me*, and gave himself for *me*" (Gal. 2:20). Says Richard Glover:

> It is easy to talk in a vague way about the love of God. But the love of God implies surely the individual; love has little content indeed if its object is merely a collective noun, an abstract, a concept. But that God loves individual men is very difficult for us to belive in earnest. The real crux comes when the question rises in a man's own heart, "Does God love *me?*" Jesus says that he does, but it is very hard to believe, except in the company of Jesus under his influence. Jesus throughout asserts and reasserts the value of the individual to God.

The matchless parables of Jesus on the lost sheep and the lost son were designed to assure lost sinners that "there is joy in heaven in the presence of the angels of God over *one* sinner that repenteth"; that the joy God had when he created the world, he likewise experiences when sinners in his world repent and surrender to his claims.

A sacrificial love. What marvelous truths are condensed in the twenty-five words forming John 3:16! Truly, it presents the maximum of truth in the minimum of words, one of which is the simple word *gave*, representing as it does the full limit of sacrifice—the test of love's reality. Man once offered to God his only son, and the surrender must have broken Abraham's heart; could God, then, in a matter of love for a lost world, remain behind his creature? What a difference, however, between the two fatherly sacrifices—Abraham's son, Isaac, was spared; God's Son was crucified. The word used here for *gave* implies not only the sending but surrender, even to the last limits of sacrifice. The sinner's redemption was not extorted from the divine love; it was at the center of such love. The supreme manifestation of the love of God is expressed in the gift of his only begotten Son to die for the sins of the world.

> Inscribed upon the Cross we see,
> In shining letters, God is Love.

Further, it took the cross, with all it represented in pain, shame, ignominy, and death, to reveal the yearning of God's heart to redeem the lost. What was the shape of the cross? Well, it *went down*. A deep socket was made in the ground, and the end of the cross sunk into the socket in order to steady its grim load. And God's love, seen at Calvary, goes down—down beneath all human sin. A sinner may be so far down, with his feet on the lowest rung of the ladder, but there is something still lower. Underneath are the everlasting arms waiting to embrace the repentant sinner. Then the cross *went out* on either side to which the victim was nailed. And, at Calvary, we see "two gaunt arms stretched out to save." Jesus was crucified with outstretched hands symbolic of his eagerness to embrace those who are lost in sin. "Come unto me!" The cross also *pointed heavenward*, suggesting the truth that the sacrificial love of the Father and the Son elevates and raises all who believe from their dead self to a higher life.

> Let me love Thee, come revealing
> All Thy love has done for me;
> Help my heart, so believing,
> By the sight of Calvary;

> Let me see Thy love despising
>   All the shame my sins had brought;
> By Thy torments realizing
>   What a price my pardon bought.

There is a further thought crowded into this one verse which has been used by the Holy Spirit more than any other to bring the lost back to God, namely, the seeming contradiction between *God so loved* and *perish.* How could a God, loving as he does, permit any sinner to perish or to suffer eternal condemnation? Godet, in his most valuable commentary, has this answer:

> This spontaneous love of the Father for the sinful world is not compatible with the wrath and threatenings of judgment; for here is not the love of communion, which unites the pardoned sinner to God; but a love of compassion, like that which we feel towards the unfortunate or enemies. The intensity of this love results from the very greatness of the unhappiness which awaits him who is the object. Thus are united in this very expression the two apparently incompatible ideas which are contained in the words: *so loved* and *may not perish.*

A reciprocal love. While Jesus taught God's love for all men, whether sinners or saints, he likewise affirmed that God had a deeper love for those united by faith and love to him. Listen to him as he prays, "Thou lovest them, even as thou lovest me" (John 17:23). His very own redeemed children are not on the outskirts of God's love but in the very center of it. "The Father himself loveth you, because ye have loved me" (John 16:27). This is love in a more intense form than that spoken of for the world in John 3:16. It indicates the fatherly affection of God for the believer in the sacrifice of Jesus, his well-beloved Son.

But our Lord went on to teach that if God so loves us we ought to love him in return and that we ought also to love the Savior who died that we might be forgiven. In answer to a question once propounded to him, "Which is the great commandment in the law?" Jesus replied: "Thou shalt love the Lord thy God with all thy heart, and with all thy soul, and with all thy mind. This is the first and great commandment. And the second is like unto it, Thou shalt love thy neighbour as thyself" (Matt. 22:37; Mark 12:29–34; see Deut. 10:19; Lev. 19:18).

Do not these demands intend to claim for God the affection of redeemed hearts in all its extent and in all its intensity? James Stalker in his *Ethic of Jesus* says:

Love to God is a capability of the heart the influence of which when it comes to fruition, cannot but be deep and transforming; whereas a member of the human family who does not love God is lacking in one of the functions of a complete humanity.

Further, Christ, being God, also taught that he must have first place in the affections of those redeemed by his blood (Matt. 10:35–38; Luke 14:26). Did not the Master instruct Peter that love to him is the only acceptable motive in service for him? Three times he asked Peter, "Lovest thou me?" and three times he replied, "Thou knowest all things: thou knowest that I love thee" (John 21:15–17). Then loved by him and loving him involves loving all others who love him. Love for the brotherhood is a natural consequence of love of the Fatherhood. The degree to which we are to love others is *as thyself*, said Jesus (Matt. 22:39), which means according to the strict observance of the Law. But according to his teaching, our love for others is to supersede this standard: "A new commandment I give unto you, that ye love one another; *as I have loved you,* that ye also love one another" (John 13:34).

The exhibition of love of this Christlike character toward fellow believers is the badge of true discipleship. "By this shall all men know that ye are my disciples, that ye love one another" (John 13:35; 15:17). The manifestation of such love must also be shown toward those who do not share our faith in Christ and our love for him. Did he not instruct his disciples to love their enemies, those who spoke evil of them and despitefully used them (Matt. 5:43–48)? God loved us when we were yet his enemies, and as those professing to be his it is incumbent upon us to emulate his love for the unloving and unlovable and not render evil for evil. Is this not the grand love Jesus teaches in his moving parable of the good Samaritan?

> Love Divine all loves excelling,
>   Joy of Heaven, to earth come down!
> Fix in us Thy humble dwelling,
>   All Thy faithful mercies crown.

THE HOLINESS OF GOD

Another facet of the divine character, so arresting in the teaching of Jesus, is that of God's august *holiness.* In the most remarkable prayer ever prayed Jesus addressed God in this twofold manner: "Holy Father" (John 17:11) and "Righteous Father" (John 17:25). The original word for *holiness* is associated with the term "without blemish" and also with "righteous" (Mark 6:20, RV). John the Baptist is described as a "righteous man and an holy." The virtues of holiness and righteousness or justice are sometimes combined as a divine name, "Just and holy is his name," "O Lord holy and true" (Rev. 6:10), "Just and right is he" (Deut. 32:4). Jesus spoke of his Father as "holy" and "righteous," and he was righteous because he was holy. "Holy is his name" (Luke 1:49; Isa. 57:15). Throughout the Old Testament the holiness of God is characterized by stainless purity and awful majesty—a conception resident in what Jesus meant of God as "holy" and "righteous." Such holiness implies absolute separation from moral evil, and perfect moral purity—a condition man can never attain in this life. In the Psalm of divine holiness, God is declared to be "high above all peoples" (Ps. 99:2).

Yet God commands his children to reflect upon the marked features of holiness—"Ye shall be holy, for I the Lord your God am holy" (Lev. 19:2; 1 Pet. 1:16). In the section of his Intercessory Prayer where Jesus addressed God as "Holy Father," the emphasis is upon the sanctification of his own, "Sanctify them" (John 17.9–19). The titles holy and righteous in effect imply that Jesus was saying, "O Father, thou art holy and righteous. Make these my own followers like thyself!" Hastings' Dictionary of the Bible, in the article on "The Holiness of God," observes:

> The holiness which Jehovah requires, and which is evidently to be thought of as to some extent of the same nature as His own, includes—
> Honesty, Lev. 19:11, 36.
> Truthfulness, Lev. 19:11.
> Respect for Parents, Lev. 19:3; 20:9.

Fair dealing with Servants, Lev. 19:13.
Kindness to Strangers, Lev. 19:34.
The weak and helpless, Lev. 19:14, 32.
The poor, Lev. 19:9.
Social purity, Lev. 20:11, 18.
Love of neighbours, Lev. 19:18.
Abstinence from blood as food, Lev. 17:10.
From unlawful mixtures, Lev. 19:19.
From fruit of newly planted trees for the first 3 years, Lev. 19:23.
Priestly compliance with special rules about mourning and marriage, Lev. 21:1–15.

Such required holiness was partly ceremonial, partly moral, without any apparent difference between the two, and this double aspect of holiness is stressed throughout the Bible and is present in the teaching about Jesus' Father, who was not only *holy* but *righteous* in all his ways. Ancient Israel thought of all connected with God as holy. For instance, he dwelt in a holy heaven, sat on a holy throne surrounded by holy attendants, and had an arm and a way called holy (Ps. 20:6; 47:8; 89:7; 98:1, Isa. 35:8, etc.). In his Sermon on the Mount, where Jesus enjoined upon his own the practical, ethical side of holiness, he enforced his exhortations with the call, "Be ye therefore perfect, even as your Father which is in heaven is perfect" (Matt. 5:48).

There is a tendency today, even among some theologians, to dwell on the love and goodness of God as revealed in the life and teachings of Jesus, and to ignore what he also taught about the holiness and justice of God. A distinction drawn is that the stern and unloving despot of the Old Testament is not the God of love and of mercy Jesus portrayed when here

among men. But this is a libel both upon the Old
Testament and upon the Lord Jesus. It is contrary to
fact to say that the Old Testament reveals only the
holiness and justice of God but does not tell of his
love and mercy, just as it is equally false to say that
in the Gospels Jesus speaks only of the love and
mercy of God and says nothing of his holiness and
his righteous judgments.

If anything, Jesus gave us a higher conception of
God's holiness and justice because he gave men a
new and higher conception of sin. Not only did he
magnify the love and mercy of God in many of his
sayings and parables but in others emphasized that
men must be judged and punished, that if they despised his goodness, they must face his severity.

Jesus told of the vineyard owner who destroyed
"those wicked husbandmen" who ill-treated the servant and son (Matt. 21:33-41).

Jesus told of the man who scorned the wedding
garment provided for guests and was cast into outer
darkness (Matt. 22:1-14).

Jesus told of the five foolish virgins who came too
late and knocked too late, and of whom the bridegroom said, "I know you not" (Matt. 25:1-13).

Jesus told of the steward who was cast into outer
darkness because he hid his talent in the earth (Matt.
25:14-30).

Jesus is the judge in the final assize dismissing into
everlasting punishment those who failed to show
compassion on the poor and needy (Matt. 25:31-46).

Jesus made his bitter cross

> The trysting place where Heaven's love
> And Heaven's justice meet.

God, because of his holiness, hated sin; and because of his justice, he demanded death for sin. At Calvary, his justice was satisfied, for Christ died for the sin of the world; and his love was manifested in that he gave his only begotten Son to die as the sinless substitute for sinners.

> Jehovah bade His sword awake,
>   O Christ, it woke 'gainst Thee!
> Thy blood the flaming blade must slake;
>   Thy heart its sheath must be—
> All for my sake, my peace to make;
>   Now slays that sword for me.

THE SOVEREIGNTY OF GOD

One of Charles Wesley's great hymns is founded upon the saying of Jesus, "Father, all things are possible to thee" (Mark 14:36). The last verse of the hymn reads:

> All things are possible to God;
> To Christ, the power of God in me;
> Now shed Thy mighty Self abroad,
> Let me no longer live, but Thee;
> Give me this hour in Thee to prove
> The sweet omnipotence of love.

The teachings of Jesus reveal how he constantly experienced "the sweet omnipotence of love." Often we find him exalting the omnipotence, all-mightiness, and sovereignty of God, and in his miracles, revealing the same supremacy in every realm. The very first miracle he performed "manifested forth his glory" as the prophesied "mighty God" (John

2:10; Isa. 9:6). Both the incarnation and the resurrection of Jesus proclaim that the highest form of "power belongeth unto God" (Ps. 62:11; Luke 1:35; 1 Thess. 1:10). His tribute to his Father's omnipotence emerges in such utterances as:

"With men it is impossible, but not with God: for with God all things are possible" (Mark 10:27; Luke 18:27).

"Father, all things are possible to thee" (Mark 14:36).

"The work I do in my Father's name" (John 10:25).

"The Father that dwelleth in me, he doeth the works" (John 14:10).

"The throne of God, and him that sitteth thereon" (Matt. 23:22).

To this saying of Jesus we can add another of similar import: "Thine is the kingdom." Here he teaches us that over all is God's throne and that because of his sovereignty he can exercise his omnipotent power on our behalf; therefore, seeing he is supreme, we should have faith in him.

"My Father worketh hitherto, and I work" (John 5:17, 27).

"I must work the works of him that sent me" (John 9:4).

"The Father that dwelleth in me, he doeth the works" (John 14:10).

The foregoing work-sayings are related to the manifestation of the miracle power of Jesus, and in both references there is the oneness between the Father and the Son in the exercise of their omnipotence. Jesus justified his work in the healing of the impotent man on the Sabbath by his *perfect subordina-*

tion which existed between his activity and that of his Father (John 5:10–30). Often the utterances of Jesus are like a flash of light breaking forth from the inmost depths of the consciousness of Jesus, from the point of mysterious union where he inwardly received the Father's impulse. These sudden and immeasurable profound outbreakings of thought distinguish the language of Jesus from all other language (see Luke 2:49; John 2:19).

The sayings of Jesus can be given this sense: "My Father works *continually* (that is without allowing himself to stop on the Sabbath) and, for myself, I work in the same way, without being bound by the legal statute." The display of "the sweet omnipotence of love" admits of no interruption, particularly in the salvation of the lost. Because of the miracle Jesus performed on the Sabbath, justifying his claim thereby that he was equal with God in his omnipotence, the Jews sought to kill him (John 5:18).

Referring to his miracles, displaying his omnipotence as they did, Jesus went on to utter a somewhat staggering statement: "Greater works than these shall he do; [that is, the one believing in him] because I go to my Father" (John 14:12). By *greater* works, Jesus did not mean that the apostles would accomplish more marvelous and spectacular miracles than Jesus himself performed, although throughout the apostolic age they were empowered to perform miracles. *Greater* means, not more stupendous, but more excellent and abiding. It was wonderful to raise those who died and were buried, but they all died again later on. It is a greater work to be the means of raising those who are dead in trespasses and sins to walk in newness of life and to become alive forevermore. It is a greater work to lead those who are spiritually blind to the Savior that theirs might be eternal sight, than to give sight to one who is physically blind. The miracles of Jesus were of a material, physical, and temporary nature, but the works he gives us to do are *greater* in that they are spiritual and eternal in nature.

THE CARE OF GOD

Peter, who knew what it was to become the object of divine concern and the recipient of divine care, was the apostle who exhorted the saints to cast all their care upon God, seeing that he cared for them. How precious is the phrase, "He careth for you" (1 Peter 5:7). The lament of David, when hiding in a cave from murderous Saul, was, "No man cared for my soul" (Ps. 142:4). Yet he went on to declare that God cared for him, fugitive though he was. Prominent in the teaching of David's greater Son is God's care, interest, and provision for his children. In various sayings, Jesus calls us to remember that God loves, God knows, God cares, and God can do great things for us. There is no common concern, no matter of food or clothing, no mere detail of the ordinary round of common duty and common life—father and mother, son and daughter, husband and wife—that God is not interested in and is not at hand to undertake.

In the Old Testament, although God is presented

as one caring for his redeemed people, he is more prominent as the author of nature, the archbishop of the universe. "The sea is his, and he made it; and his hands formed the dry land" (Ps. 95:5). "He taketh up the isles as a very little thing" (Isa. 40:15).

These and similar passages magnify God as the creator and sustainer of the world. But when we reach the Gospels, it is most noticeable that in his teachings about God, Jesus chiefly emphasizes his interest in the individual. He emphasizes God's heart rather than his power to make a sea or dry land, his knowledge of the cares and needs of his children and his ability to undertake for them. Jesus has taught us that God thinks out man's life in all its relations and provides all that is necessary for it. The cure for all anxiety, says Jesus, is trust in the Father's care. "Take no thought for your life, what ye shall eat . . . what ye shall put on . . . your heavenly Father knoweth that ye have need of all things" (Matt. 6:25–34). "One sparrow shall not fall on the ground without your Father . . . Ye are of more value than many sparrows" (Matt. 10:29, 31).

It is beyond our comprehension to understand God's power as described by the psalmist: "He telleth the number of the stars; he calleth them by name" (Ps. 147:4). But it is comforting to know that "The very hairs of your head are all numbered" (Matt. 10:30) and that "There shall not an hair of your head perish" (Luke 21:18). How precious and consoling are the words, "Your Father knoweth"! He knows all that there is to know about every child of his—their needs, their struggles, their worries, and their worth.

> In every hour in perfect peace,
> I'll sing He knows! He knows!

If a father cannot refuse his child bread, can God withhold from any child of his that which is good? (Matt. 7:11).

If God is interested in flowers, thinks about their colors, takes care of them so that even "Solomon in all his glory" is not equal to them, will he not be more concerned in his own who are as trees planted by him? (Matt. 6:30; Ps. 104:16).

If he who created the birds knows that in one of their nests there is one fewer sparrow today than there was yesterday, will he not feel it more deeply when the humblest of his children suffer? (Matt. 10:31).

If God makes his sun rise on the good and on the bad and sends his rain on the just and the unjust, should we not bless him for his generosity of heart for acting as a friend in either case? (Matt. 5:45).

If he could command twelve legions of angels (seventy-two thousand) to protect his Son, why should we charge our souls with care when in a tight spot (Matt. 26:53)?

With such a provider and protector constantly with us to meet our needs and to preserve us from any harm, should we not learn to rest with joy in all that God is in himself as the friend that sticketh closer than a brother? Has he not promised to bear both you and your burdens? Jesus assures us that the Father "seeth in secret" the needs we try to hide from others and blesses us openly with all we require (Matt. 6:4).

> Enough; this covers all my wants;
>   And so I rest;
> For what I cannot, He can see,
> And in His care I saved shall be,
>   For ever blest.

THE FATHERHOOD OF GOD

Jesus taught the love and goodness of God by teaching men the fatherhood of God. *Father* was his favorite way of addressing God and speaking about him. Sometimes it was *our* Father, at other times *your* Father, or *my* Father, or just plain *Father*. The most prominent truth Jesus taught about God is that he is *Father*—a term applied to him 189 times in the Gospels, 124 of which are found in John. Discussing whether or not fatherhood is the culminating expression in revelation for the love of God, Dr. Stalker goes on to say in *The Ethic of Jesus:*

> The name of heavenly Father irradiates the teaching of Jesus, and has supplied to human imagination a plastic and fecund image, from which thoughts of the Deity, just and attractive, have been evolved. Jesus gave to his own conception of what human fatherhood may be peerless expression in the figure of the father in the Parable of the Prodigal Son; for this is no ordinary father, but one clothed with resources, dignity and wisdom, and, above all, invested with the magnanimity of forgiveness. It suggests the sublime thought of Paul, that it is not human fatherhood which enables us to comprehend Divine Fatherhood, but rather the Fatherhood of God that begets and shapes the fatherhood of man. "The Father from whom every fatherhood in heaven and on earth is named," Ephes. 3:15, R.V. *margin.* And this may suggest the further reflection that, not only do all pure forms of earthly love point upwards to features of the Divine love, but that in the Divine Being there is something great and incomprehensible from which all these earthly fires have been kindled, and which is expressed in the final testimony of revelation that *God is Love.*

The first recorded words of Jesus are those he uttered in the Temple when he was but twelve years of age. Answering the rebuke of his earthly parents for his ardent attachment to the House of God and for his thirst for instruction from the custodians of the oracles of God therein, Jesus said, "Wist ye not that I must be about my Father's business?" (Luke 2:49). In this primary confession lies the germ of all that was most original in Jesus' subsequent doctrine of divine fatherhood. Dr. H. R. Mackintosh says in *The Doctrine of the Person of Christ,* that "the recurrence of the sweet and deep name, *Father,* unveils the secret of his being. His heart is at rest in God." This rest in the paternal aspect of God is not only the very note of the being of Jesus but also of all his teaching. He taught us that our prayers are to begin with "Our Father, who art in heaven." In his own prayer life, there was the constant use of this precious, filial title. For instance, in his High Priestly Prayer found in John 17, Jesus uses the name in three different ways, corresponding to the three parts of this marvelous prayer.

The first part of the prayer is *personal* (John 17:1–8). In this section, Father and Son are in close communion, with the Son expressing the wish for the Father to glorify him in his final work of the cross and then restore him to his preexistent glory with the Father. As the Son is here telling the Father all that he had accomplished (see the four *I haves,* John 17:4, 6, 8), there is no need of any addition to the simple, filial term *Father,* used twice in this portion of the prayer (John 17:1–5).

The second part of the prayer is *special* (John 17:9–19). Christ no longer prays about himself as indicated by the opening phrase, "I pray for them." Then note the exclusion, "I pray not for the world." His intercession, therefore, in this part of the prayer is *particular*—he prays for his own, and the burden of his request is that they might be kept from evil, sanctified. Hence, the significance of the title used, *Holy Father* (John 17:11), the only time God is addressed this way in Scripture. It was as if Christ were praying, "Father, because thou art holy, transform these whom thou hast given me into thy likeness!"

The third part of the prayer is *universal* (John 17:20–26). The change of emphasis is most noticeable in the outset of this last section, "Neither pray I for *these* alone." Thus, the intercession of Jesus moves in three widening circles—he prays for *himself,* he prays for his *church,* he prays for the *world.* Looking down the vista of the ages he could see the great multitude who would come to crown him as Redeemer through the witness of the church, and he interceded, "for them also which shall believe on me through their word." The term used here is *righteous Father* (John 17:25), which is most fitting. Had divine righteousness not been personified in the life of Jesus and vindicated by his death as the substitute for sinners, there would never have been the gospel of redemption to proclaim to a lost world.

In these apostate days when there is a good deal of loose thinking and loose talking about the universal fatherhood of God and the brotherhood of Man, it is most imperative to decide what, exactly, Jesus taught about divine fatherhood. Is God the Father of all men whether they are saints or sinners, virtuous or vile, religious or renegade? Are all men brothers, irrespective of any religious relationship? Is the teaching of Jesus as "the truth of the fatherhood of God a figure of speech of extremely uncertain application, sometimes describing the relation of all men to God and at other times the peculiar relation of believers," as one writer suggests?

Wherever, in the Gospel, Jesus is represented as calling God *Father,* this is not an assertion of ancient Greek and of the modern liberal teaching that God is the universal Father of the human race, but a declaration concerning Jesus' own relation to God and the relation of those who are born anew by the Holy Spirit and who, having received him as the "Spirit of Adoption," are entitled to cry *Abba, Father!* The absolute use of the title *The Father* is characteristic of John who never uses the singular *Father* without the article, except in address.

On the distinction between *"The* Father" and "My Father," Canon Westcott observes in *The Gospels:*

Generally it may be said that the former title expresses the original relation of God to being, and specially to humanity, in virtue of man's creation to the divine image; and the latter more particularly the relation of the Father to the Son incarnate, and so indirectly to man in virtue of the Incarnation. The former suggests those thoughts which spring from the consideration of the absolute moral connection of man with God; the latter those which spring from what is made known to us, through revelation, of the Incarnate Son with God and with man.

Although the outstanding truth Jesus taught about God was that he is *Father,* in no passage does he explicitly speak of God as the Father of all men. As Dr. Griffith Thomas in *Principles of Theology* asks, "If the universal Fatherhood of God and the universal sonship are assumed, how is it that there is not a single clear instance of either truth in the New Testament?" Jesus took it for granted that many of his hearers were familiar with Old Testament teaching as to the fatherly nature of God as a God who was all-wise, all-powerful, all-holy. Those who listened to the priceless teaching of Jesus about his Father's love and care would recall David's revelation, "Like as a father pitieth his children, so the Lord pitieth them that fear him" (Ps. 103:13; see Exod. 4:22, 23).

Jesus, however, enriched this splendid spiritual inheritance of the doctrine of God as set forth by prophet and psalmist and revealed that God as Father was not only the protecting God of Israel as a nation, but the Father of individuals upon whom he lavished the utmost resources of a Father's wise and tender care. The God Jesus proclaimed and manifested, was the forgiving Father in the parable of the prodigal son (Luke 15:11). But that he is not a Father condoning sin is taught in the parable of the wrathful king in his judgment upon the unmerciful servants (Matt. 18:23). Jesus never stressed the care of the Father for his children at the expense of his chastisement of them.

Professor W. P. Patterson suggests in *Christ and the Gospels* that there are at least *seven aspects* of the relationship of an earthly father to his children that can be used to illustrate the higher relationship between God as Father and his offspring.

1. To the father, children owe their existence.
2. From the father they borrow his nature and likeness.
3. The father provides for their wants.
4. The father educates and disciplines them.
5. The father holds intimate intercourse with his children.
6. The father is graciously disposed to forgive their offenses.
7. The father makes his children his heirs.

It is not difficult to trace the analogy in the teaching of Jesus concerning the fatherhood of God in these particulars. In his parables, discourses, and sayings Jesus loved to reveal how the human was a shadow of the Divine.

Created by the Father. Ever in the background of our Lord's teaching about fatherhood and sonship is the fact that "he made us and not we ourselves." *All* things—including man—were made by him (John 1:3). Jesus himself, coeternal with the Father, was without a beginning, but man owes his existence to God, the Father of all mankind, in respect to creation (Acts 17:28). That man was God's creative masterpiece is an article of Old Testament doctrine which Jesus fully recognized and had no need to emphasize. The prophets freely acknowledged God to be their maker and used the favorite figure of his ability to fashion man, namely, that of the potter. "O Lord, thou art our father; we are the clay, and thou our potter: and we are all the work of thy hand" (Isa. 64:8, see also Isa. 29:16; Jer. 18:1–10).

In the natural realm, the husband becomes a father when his seed matures in the womb of his wife, and parenthood becomes a living, loving, and abiding reality. Thus, as we trace our organic, earthly origin back to our parents, in like manner, we trace man's original existence to God who created him (Gen. 1:26, 27; 2:7). There is an element in the fatherhood of God, therefore, involving our relationship to him through creation. Yet he is not only the God of creation; he is also the God of redemption—a far greater and more sacrificial work than creation.

> 'Twas great to call a World from naught;
> 'Twas greater to redeem.

Through original sin we were alienated from God and became spiritually dead; we can only experience a restored relationship with God through all his beloved Son accomplished on our behalf and by the regeneration of the Holy Spirit through which we become the sons of God (John 1:11–13; Gal. 4:4–7) and receive the privilege to cry *Abba, Father!* The fatherhood and sonship Jesus constantly refers to in his teaching is not that of *natural* man's relationship to God as the Creator, but rather, *redeemed* and *regenerated* man's relationship to him as the Redeemer. It is the fatherhood of *re-creation* rather than that of *creation* which Jesus emphasized. And because it is the fatherhood of grace, other men only become my brothers as they share my experience of God's saving grace and mercy. Thus, all men do not sustain the same basic eternal relationship with our loving, heavenly Father. Those who do, Jesus named as *saved;* and those who do not are *lost.* The much discussed question raised by several writers can be dealt with at this point, namely, Did Jesus conceive of God as the Father of all men, or only as the Father of those who are within the family-kingdom? Professor Patterson's answer is convincing:

> It may be that Jesus applies the name of the Father to God only in relation to the children of the Kingdom, but the palpable meaning of his teaching is that God is the Father of all men, while yet it is not possible for him to be the Father, in the full sense of the word, of those who are living in impenitence and in alienation from him. He is the Father of all to the extent that they are created by him, are made in his image, have their wants supplied by him, and are disciplined by him; but just as it is impossible for an earthly father to forgive a contuma-

cious son, to hold intercourse with an absent son, and to make him an heir who has already squandered his portion, so it is impossible for God to be in the full sense a Father to those who shun his face and spurn his gifts.

That the Pharisees, in spite of their religious pretensions, had no relationship with God as the heavenly Father whom Jesus revealed is evident from his stern declaration that God was not their Father but that they were the offspring of their father, the Devil, and that their life and works were proof of their satanic parentage (John 8:38–44).

Sharing the Father's nature and likeness. We often say of a boy that he has the habits, temperament, and features of his father. God created us in his own image and likeness (Gen. 1:26, 27). We were made and meant to be Godlike in all the virtues of the Godhead. Christ came as "the image of God" (2 Cor. 4:4; Col. 1:15; Heb. 1:3). If, therefore, we want to know what God is like all we have to do is to gather from the Gospels how Jesus revealed him by his life, teaching, and works. It is the Spirit's ministry, in turn, to produce in us Christlikeness of character and to make visible the image of the heavenly.

Sin has terribly defaced the divine image in man who, more than ever, is becoming devillike in character and conduct. It is hard to see any Godlike virtue in the vicious gangsters and terrorists who set no value on human life. Yet no matter how illegible the original Godlikeness may be in the most degraded heart, grace can restore the image as Christ proved in the lives of those disfigured, deranged, and destitute through demon-possession. He immediately transformed them into new creatures.

Objects of the Father's provision. Among the poor,

sometimes parents bring children into the world they are not financially able to provide for—a tragedy so common in undeveloped countries. But God our Father is found saying, "I have made, and I will bear" (Isa. 46:4). Running all through the teaching of Jesus on the fatherhood of God is the assurance that all his children by faith will never lack any good thing, that he bears full responsibility for all who trust him as their Father in heaven. Jesus taught that we are to have no concern about what to eat, drink, or wear, for the Father has anticipated all our needs and made provision accordingly (Matt. 6:25–34). He who feeds the sparrows and clothes the lilies will not suffer any child of his to be in need (Ps. 23:1). Jesus used the human relationship as a reflection of the heavenly when he encouraged his disciples to pray for what they required: "If ye then, being evil, know how to give good gifts unto your children, how much more shall your Father which is in heaven give good things to them that ask him" (Matt. 7:11). That divine provision includes spiritual blessings as well as material gifts is explicit in Luke's account of our Lord's parable on divine fatherhood (Luke 11:11–13).

Fatherly discipline and education. Jesus himself was never in need of any disciplinary action either by his earthly parents or by his heavenly Father. Of the latter he could say, "I do *always* the things that please my Father!" Of the former we read that Jesus was "subject unto them" and consequently increased "in favour with God and man" (John 8:29; Luke 2:52). Because of divine grace, Jesus, in tasting death for every man, became perfect as the captain of salvation through his sufferings, but he never questioned or murmured against the permissive will of his Father. The guiding principle of his whole life was, "Not my will but thine be done." There was that solitary moment in his experience when he seemed to query his Father's responsibility of him as an obedient Son, "My God! My God! why hast thou forsaken me?" But this was quickly followed by his final act of surrender, "Father, into thy hands I commend my spirit."

As the Father's erring sons and daughters we are in constant need of his disciplinary and educative actions. Loving us, he chastises us, for "he dealeth with you as with sons; for what son is he whom the father chasteneth not?" And whatever he provides and permits in the way of correction is for our profit that "we might be partakers of his holiness" (Heb. 12:3–11). Implied in what Jesus taught about the divine education of souls are these two aspects gathered from a child's earthly training:

1. A child's education, though arduous, painful, and not always fully appreciated, is designed for the child's profit. Thus in his Sermon on the Mount, Jesus indicates the great reward here and hereafter of God's children who are subjected to poverty, sorrow, persecution, and calumny (Matt. 5:1–12).

2. Because of his inferior knowledge, a young child does not always appreciate the wisdom, kindness, and necessity of fatherly discipline, even when asked to take same on trust and believe that a father knows what is best for his child. Similarly, Jesus taught that where we cannot trace the significance of God's purposes, we must trust him, seeing that, because of his perfection, he is incapable of making a mistake or taking a wrong turn in the ordering of

our lives. We must rest in our heavenly Father's love
when and where we cannot comprehend his purpose. Is this not the attitude Jesus had in mind when
he prayed, "Yea, Father, for so it was well-pleasing
in thy sight" (Matt. 11:25, 26).

> Ill that He blesses,
> Is our good;
> And unblest good is ill.
> All is most right that seems most wrong,
> If it be His sweet will.

Living on intimate terms. The lamentable drift of
children from their parents in our modern society is
put down to lack of communication between them.
There is a lack of mutual confidence, trust, and understanding, and consequently parents and children
seldom thrash out together many of the problems
and important issues of life. Between father and son,
mother and daughter, there must be close fellowship
if the family tie is to remain unbroken. As children
of our heavenly Father we are privileged to communicate with him about all that concerns us at any
time. Did not Jesus teach that if we ask the Father
about anything, in his name, that he will hear and
answer us?

As we shall see more clearly when we come to the
Master's teaching about prayer, God offers to communicate with his children, to hold intimate intercourse with them, even in secret. It is an alien idea
for an earthly parent to hold aloof from his children,
keep them at a distance, and seldom converse with
them. Jesus taught that we have immediate access
into the presence of our heavenly Father through his
mediation (John 14:6), which on our side means
prayer, and on his side, *response.* Does not the Master

assure us that "whatsoever ye shall ask in prayer, believing, ye shall receive" (Matt. 21:22)? He also encourages us to seek both spiritual and material blessings, and the parables of the importunate widow and of the friend at midnight teach us to be persistent in solicitation of what we need (Luke 11:5; 18:1). How the Father-heart of God is pleased when he hears a child of his pray.

> Nothing between, Lord, nothing between;
> Shine with unclouded ray,
> Chasing each mist away,
> O'er my whole heart bear sway—
> Nothing between.

The virtue of fatherly forgiveness. Jesus not only preached divine forgiveness but practiced it. When he came to his cruel death, his prayer for his murderers was, "Father, forgive them; for they know not what they do!" In his parental prayer, Jesus taught us to ask the Father to forgive our trespasses, knowing as he did that his Father was graciously disposed to forgive his children's offenses on the basis of sincere repentance. Professor Patterson would have us bear in mind that

> God's way with sinners is not the way of a man with his enemy, to whom he refuses on any terms to be reconciled, or of a creditor with his debtor, who insists on full payment, but that of a father, who meets a penitent son in a spirit of magnanimity, rejoices over his return, and receives him back to his home. The point of our Lord's three great Parables in Luke 15 is that, while the respectable world was sceptical about the restoration of the erring, and frowned on those who attempted it, there is in Heaven a charity that believeth all things, and joy unspeakable over one sinner that repenteth.

As sinning children we have the assurance of a Father's pity and pardon through all his unsinning Son accomplished when he died for the sin of the world.

Heirship. There are many parents who have found it hard to make ends meet in the building up of a home and who, consequently, have nothing tangible to bequeath their children. Yet they are rich indeed if theirs is the heritage of a saintly and sacrificial parentage. On the other hand, there are children who become heirs of valuable possessions, of money and estates. That our heavenly Father destines us as his children to an inheritance is a distinct and large topic in the teaching of Jesus. Paul reminds us that if we are sons of God, then "if a son, an heir of God through Christ." Also in his Epistles, the apostle has much to say about the riches of our inheritance in Christ. What a great saying that was Jesus uttered for the encouragement of his own! "Fear not, little flock; for it is your Father's good pleasure to give you the kingdom" (Luke 12:32).

The privileges and riches we are heirs to because of the divine fatherhood would take long to enumerate. Among the many, however, we possess as children, in fact or in promise, there are the following blessings our all-powerful Father is able and willing to bestow:

The immediate forgiveness of our sins.

Unhindered access to him in prayer.

All necessary provision for the supply of bodily and spiritual needs.

Unerring guidance when perplexity arises.

Safe protection amid persecution and danger.

All supernatural power to aid us.

The prospects of rewards for faithful service.

The assurance that our names are written in heaven.

These privileges which are ours as heirs are summarily described by Jesus as *life* and as *salvation* (Matt. 7:14; Mark 9:45; Luke 19:9). As to their exceeding value, they are emphasized in particular maxims, such as Matthew 16:26, and in the parables of the hidden treasure and the pearl of great price (Matt. 13:44–48; see the author's work, *All the Parables of the Bible*). As we await the final benefits of our heirship, hardships and perils may be ours, but our habitual mood as children of an almighty Father must be one of peace, repose, and even of joy (Matt. 11:28–30; Luke 6:23; John 16:33).

Nor does it seem that any bitter experiences can be such as to justify disbelief in the Divine Fatherhood, because the witnesses to the truth include those who have tasted the extremity of human sorrow. The paradox of it is that the belief in the Fatherhood of God comes to us attested by many who were beyond other sons and daughters of affliction, and owes its place in the world's heart above all to him who, dying in unspeakable agony, said, "Father, into thy hands I commend my spirit."

With the sacred record and the inner assurance that the Father of our Lord Jesus Christ, whom he eternally loved and implicitly obeyed, is likewise our heavenly Father (John 20:17), what love, trust, and peace should be ours. We must learn how to rest in the joy of all that he is in himself. "The recurrence of the sweet and deep name, *Father*, unveils the secret of the being of Jesus," says Dr. H. R. Mackintosh. "His heart is at rest in God." This same rest, the very note of all the being and all the teaching of Jesus, must possess our hearts.

The central object in our Lord's oral ministry was to induce men to base all life on God and to have constant faith in him as the Father who knows all about our needs before we express them in words. Why waste breath telling him what he knows already? If, as redeemed children, we continually bask in the sunshine of God's fatherhood, every concern of ours will be his first concern. The way to faith in God and to love for man is as of old to come nearer to the living Jesus who said, "Have faith in God" (Mark 11:22).

BIBLE STUDY QUESTIONS

Take time to turn to each Scripture reference and mark the verse or a portion in your Bible.

1. What does it mean to worship God in Spirit?
2. Describe the meaning of the term *God is Love.*
3. Can a Christian do greater works than Christ?
4. List six aspects of God's fatherhood.
5. Does faith in God bring any reward?

— 4 —

The Holy Spirit

Referring to his complete identification with his Father in nature and works, Jesus could say, "I and the Father are one." He could have likewise affirmed, "I and the Holy Spirit are one," for the Gospels reveal a holy intimacy existing between Jesus and the divine Spirit. Jesus' use of the phrase, "I, by the Spirit of God" (Matt. 12:28), must not be limited to the casting out of demons recorded in the narrative, for it applies to our Lord's every action. He lived and walked in the Spirit, and all Jesus taught about the Spirit's actuality and activities was the natural outcome of the most blessed and harmonious fellowship between these two members of the Godhead. A word or two is therefore necessary as to the ministry of the Holy Spirit in the life of Jesus. The fine flour, unleavened (Jesus), was mingled with oil (the Spirit).

First, in his incarnation, our Lord emptied himself or "stripped himself of the insignia of majesty" and became subject to the Father's will and lived his life in the realm of that will. He likewise became dependent upon the life-giving Spirit who was the one responsible for Jesus' becoming man (Luke 1:35) and who imparted to him his full empowerment in all his preaching and teaching.

Second, in the days of his flesh, the Spirit seemed to have labored exclusively with Jesus, concentrating all his energies upon him as he went about doing good and healing all who were oppressed of the Devil (Acts 10:38). After Jesus' wondrous birth by the Spirit, there is no reference to the Spirit's association with any other individual until after his resurrection when Jesus said, "Receive ye the Holy Spirit." John could say, "The Holy Spirit was not yet given unto men" (John 7:39). There had to be a man both able and willing to receive the Spirit in his fullness before he could come in his plenitude to men, as he did at Pentecost. For the first time in Jesus, the man was able to receive the Holy Spirit in his entirety.

The authority of immediate knowledge of all aspects of truth, then, wedded to the power of the Holy Spirit, gave the teachings of Jesus an original element. Thus, prominent among his doctrines was the personal leadership of the Spirit in the individual and corporate life of Christianity (John 14:26). Jesus recognized that his purposes of salvation would be accomplished through the power of the Holy Spirit as he brought home to the consciences of individuals the import of the preached words of Jesus. It was the Spirit who enlightened the minds of our Lord's auditors and brought to fruition a full harvest from his seeds of truth. In fact, when he commenced his public ministry that Sabbath in the synagogue of Nazareth, it was with the recognition of the power and work of the Holy Spirit in his life, works, and teachings (Luke 4:18, 19).

In us Abba, Father! cry;
Earnest of our bliss on high;
Seal of Immortality,
Comforter Divine.

The fact of the leadership of the Spirit in the life of Jesus is stressed in the accounts of his temptation after his baptism in terms like "led by the Spirit," "The Spirit driveth him," "He was full of the Spirit," and that God gave his Son the Spirit "not by measure" (Matt. 4:1; Mark 1:12; Luke 4:14; John 3:34).

Jesus could speak of himself as "him whom the Father hath sealed," and as it is by the Spirit of God we are sealed (Eph. 4:30; John 6:27), we are taken back to the forecast of John the Baptist, that Jesus would come as the baptizer in the Holy Spirit. The Spirit's ascent upon Jesus attested or sealed the Father's approval of his Son and gave great value to his teaching, not only about the Spirit, but about every other topic. Because of his own baptism with the Spirit by the Father, Jesus had the authority and ability to baptize in the Spirit (Matt. 3:11; John 1:33). It must be observed that the Gospels never speak about "the baptism *of* the Holy Spirit," but always *in* or *with* the Spirit, the element in whom we are baptized.

Dr. W. Graham Scroggie suggests that the chief source of Christ's teaching on the Holy Spirit is his Upper Room discourse and the continuance of it on the way to Gethsemane (John 14–16) and then gives an outline of what Christ taught in his conversation with his own. But as there are valuable references to the Spirit's ministry in the other three Gospels which John does not mention, these too must be brought into the Master's overall teaching on such an important theme. The following features are unmistakably plain.

HE TAUGHT THE SPIRIT WAS A PERSON

To Jesus, the Spirit was no mere influence or force or emanation from God but was a real person as he himself was, only without a visible body as Jesus had. All the elements of personality were his. For instance, *terms* of personality of the Spirit were continuously employed by Jesus. Pronouns like *he, him,* and *himself* are frequent throughout the Gospels (Mark 12:36). Count up the personal pronouns Jesus used of the Spirit in John 14:16–17, 26; 15:26; 16;7, 8, 13, 14, and you will be forced to conclude that our fellowship is not with a *something* but with *someone;* not with an exertion of divine energy but with a person of the Trinity; not with an *it* but with *him.* The Revised Version gives *him* for *it* in Romans 8:16, 26. True spiritual worship is dependent upon belief in the Spirit's personality. May we experience the same intimate fellowship with the Holy Spirit, the living and conscious exerciser of true personal will and love, even as Jesus continually enjoyed!

Further, the *qualities* and *operations* of personality were attributed to the Holy Spirit by Jesus in his revelation of him. The Spirit can teach, reveal, and communicate truth (John 14:26; 16:13). The Spirit can lead, receive, glorify, speak, announce, and assist (John 14:16, 26; 15:26; 16:13, 14, 15; Mark 13:11).

The Spirit can impart joy and gladness. That Jesus himself was anointed with the oil of gladness (Ps.

45:7; Heb. 1:9) is evident from Luke's account of the feelings of Jesus when the seventy returned from their mission and reported what mighty things had been accomplished. "In that hour Jesus rejoiced in the Spirit" (Luke 10:21). Weymouth translates the phrase, "At that hour Jesus was filled by the Holy Spirit with a rapturous joy." Paul reminds us that "the fruit of the Spirit is . . . joy," and the Spirit was the source of our Lord's joy and is likewise the one who inspires us to be glad in the Lord. Twice over Jesus declared his joy was fulfilled in his disciples. Because of his inner fount of joy in the Spirit, Jesus carried no forbidding countenance but had a somewhat gracious and attractive person, drawing all classes, even children, to him. Do we know what it is to joy in God by the Spirit who indwells us (John 14:16, 17)?

Further, Jesus believed, not only in the *personality* of the Holy Spirit, but also in his *deity*. Had he not been the third person of the blessed Trinity, the Spirit could never have accomplished the works ascribed to him by Jesus. Only a divine person can convict men of sin, regenerate the sinner's heart, cast out demons, and judge Satan. Jesus plainly states that *associations* of deity were the Spirit's (Matt. 28:18, 19; John 14:16, 26; 16:14, 15); attributes of deity were his (John 14:17, 26; 16:7, 12, 13; Luke 2:26, 27); actions of deity were, and are, his (John 3:5; 16:8–14; see Luke 4:1; 12:12).

As to the *character* of the Spirit, the same is indicated in the various titles Jesus used of him, each of which carries its own significance.

The Spirit of Truth (John 14:17; 15:16; 16:13). He is so called because he inspired holy men to understand the truth, then sent it forth. But the Spirit is not only the revealer of truth, he is a constant *witness* to it (John 15:26, 27; 16:12, 13, RV). The receptive and teachable minds of the apostles found their impression of the truths Jesus taught quickened by the Holy Spirit. He had promised the enlightening of the Spirit to lead his followers into a larger appreciation of his gospel (John 14:26). Promises of the future light and leadership of the Spirit had to be coupled, however, with obedience to qualify them for increased gifts of revelation. Jesus believed that his disciples would remember the truth he taught them and that this truth committed to the lives and memories of the disciples would greatly extend the influence of his teaching through the enlightenment, illustrative presence, and leadership of the Spirit of Truth who would specially empower the immature church after Pentecost. Thus, all the Books of the New Testament became possible under the direct guidance of this selfsame Spirit (1 Pet. 1:11, 12; 2 Pet. 1:21). What delight we experience when the Spirit of Truth brings to our remembrance so many of the beautiful truths Jesus taught.

The Holy Spirit (John 14:26; Luke 11:13). The Spirit is thus named some one hundred times in Scripture under this title. *Ghost,* by the way, never used in the Revised Version, is an old English word for "Spirit." The qualifying term *Holy* reminds us, not only of his own inherent holiness, but also that he is the source of our holiness. "Be ye holy, even as I am holy"—such a command can only be realized as the Holy Spirit imparts divine holiness.

The Spirit of Power (Luke 4:14, 18; 24:49; Acts 1:8;

Rom. 15:19). Power is the predominant feature of the Spirit's ministry, and such power is not *something* but *someone*, even the Spirit himself. Power is the manifestation of his presence. This is evident in the life and work of Jesus. We read of his returning in the power of the Spirit and his fame spreading abroad. All the miracles of Jesus were performed through the Spirit, especially the cure of demoniacs which was a conspicuous feature of the Master's miraculous ministry. "I, by the Spirit of God." The disciples were promised that power would be theirs as the Holy Spirit came upon them. Jesus knew that their preparation to continue his ministry on earth would come by the empowerment of the Spirit, and apostolic history reveals what he accomplished through the apostolate.

The Spirit's unceasing power is seen in the conviction of sin (John 16:8, RV; see Acts 2:37); the regeneration of the sinner (John 3:3, 5); and in the sanctification of the saved sinner (John 17:17; 1 Cor. 6:11; 1 Pet. 1:2).

The Finger of God (Luke 11:20 with Matt. 12:28). It is Luke, the beloved physician, who knew all about the human anatomy, who tells us that Jesus used the illustration of a *finger* to describe the Holy Spirit as a medium of power. Head, arm, and fingers are united in any action. The head plans and directs; then the strength of the arm through the fingers carries out the plan. How marvelously the fingers operate to carry out the dictates of the mind! The analogy resident in our Lord's symbol of the Spirit as the "Finger of God" is apparent. God is the *head;* Jesus is spoken of as the *arm* of salvation; and the

Spirit is the *finger*, fulfilling the divine task both in the world (John 16:8–11) and in the church (John 14:26; 15:26; 16:12–15).

The Comforter (John 14:16; 15:26). After announcing his coming departure from his own, Jesus exhorted them not to be troubled in heart or mourn because of the coming separation. He would pray the Father, and the Father would give them one like himself to take his place. Jesus was careful to identify the coming *Comforter* as "the Spirit of Truth" and as "the Holy Spirit." Such a title means an advocate, a pleader, a defender, and is transliterated as *Paraclete*, a term John applied to Jesus (1 John 2:1; see Rom. 8:26). Since Jesus had taught much about the Holy Spirit, it must have been assuring for the disciples to hear him speak of the promised Comforter as *the Spirit of your Father* (Matt. 10:20), the only time in Scripture he is thus named. Does such a title not imply that like Jesus the Spirit shares the care, concern, and compassion of the Father—the God of all comfort—for his children?

Further, in the original, the English word *another* has a twofold meaning, namely, *another of the same kind* and *another of a different kind*. Which word do you think Jesus used when he promised, "I will send you *another* Comforter"? It was *another of the same kind*. Thus, the Comforter was to be like Jesus, represent him in every way, and act as Jesus' other self. The statement, "It is expedient for you that I go away," must have perplexed the disciples. How could it be suitable for Jesus to leave them in a world of evil?

Actually our Lord's statement teaches the omnipresence of the Holy Spirit. In the days of his flesh, because of the limitations of his humanity, Jesus could not be in more than one place at a time. If comforting the saints in Bethany, he could not be in Galilee consoling his followers there. Now, by his Spirit, from whose presence none can flee (Ps. 139:7), he is everywhere at the same time. Wherever there is a child of God in need, anywhere in the wide world, the Comforter is there to console, strengthen, and intercede. Truly, great is this mystery of our godliness! Thus, the mission of Jesus, commissioned by the Father, and empowered by the Spirit, continued after the ascension and will only cease when the church is raptured at Christ's return.

Jesus recognized the unique ministry of the Holy Spirit, as well as his authority, just as the Book of Acts reveals how the early church lived under the impact of the Spirit's presence and presidency, when he warned against ill-treating or despising the Spirit, who has been called "the Vicar of Christ." The reception hall of the Temple, so suitable for preaching and teaching, with all sorts of people having access to Jesus without the formalities of invitation, was the place where he uttered some of his most famous sayings and discourses. For instance, it was there that he refuted the calumny of the Jewish rulers and declared their blasphemy against the Holy Spirit (Matt. 12:31, 32; Mark 3:29, 30).

The Pharisees had condemned Christ himself with blasphemy (John 10:33, 36), and there was his forgiveness for that, but for blasphemy against the Holy Spirit there was no forgiveness, either now or hereafter. Those scribes and Pharisees knew in their hearts that Jesus was virtuous and a true representative of God; yet they declared that he achieved his works by the power of Beelzebub, Jesus himself identified with Satan (Luke 11:18). Thus, calling good evil, and speaking of evil as being good, they were in grave danger of a deadening conscience or of killing their conscience. Prejudice and pride can blind men to that which is of God and lead them to attribute the working of the Spirit of God to evil energies and motives.

The unspeakably solemn topic of blasphemy against the Holy Spirit reminds us that if such a sin cannot be forgiven, neither in this world nor in the world to come, how great is our need of forgiveness before we reach this irretrievable state. This particular sin is a state of heart and mind rather than an isolated act. We have the divine assurance that the blood of Jesus Christ is able to cleanse us from *all* sin, but what is finally unpardonable is the willful, conscious, and final rejection of the pardon God offers man in Christ. There are those who live in fear that they have committed this unpardonable sin, but the very fear they manifest is evidence that they have not committed it, for those who have are insensitive to any fear. Only those who are hardened in heart can attribute a work of mercy and kindness and goodness on the part of Christ to the power of Satan. Fear of committal of this sin against the Spirit is one of the Devil's devices to keep despairing hearts from him who prayed for his murderers, "Father, forgive them; for they know not what they do!" The solemn task of the teacher is to warn sinners of the peril of procrastination with emphasis upon the old-time call, "Today, if ye will hear his voice, harden not your heart" (Heb. 4:7).

Jesus summed up his teaching concerning the ministry of the Holy Spirit, saying that his death would prepare the way for the coming of the Spirit to his church and that without his death on the cross the gracious work of the Spirit in the church would not be possible (John 16:7). Through all Jesus accomplished by his death, resurrection, and ascension, the gifts and graces are now possible for believers to appropriate (Gal. 5:22–23; 1 Cor. 12:1–11; Eph. 4:4–13). The power of the Spirit in our lives today is limited only by the degree of our willingness and capacity to experience his fullness (Eph. 5:18).

Because the teachings of Jesus have a purifying effect and also form a basis of fruitful praying (John 15:3, 7), how important it is to give heed to his prominent instruction concerning the Spirit. In his reference to the quickening power of the Spirit, "It is the Spirit that gives life" (John 6:63), Jesus went on to affirm that the truths he taught "are Spirit and life." Godet says that the meaning of the declaration of Jesus is:

> My words are the incarnation and communication of the Spirit; it is the Spirit who dwells in them and acts through them; and for this reason they communicate life.

This is why the Spirit uses, not only all the sayings of Jesus, but the Scripture as a whole as his sword to conquer the souls of men (Eph. 6:17; Heb. 4:12). The Holy Spirit is the inspirer of Holy Writ, and he always rides triumphantly in his own chariot.

BIBLE STUDY QUESTIONS

Take time to turn to each Scripture reference and mark the verse or a portion in your Bible.

1. In which ways was Jésus led by the Holy Spirit?
2. Does the Holy Spirit have personality?
3. Who is the finger of God?
4. What is the meaning of the word *paraclete?*
5. What is blasphemy against the Holy Spirit?

— 5 —

The Scriptures

The only part of the Bible Jesus had was the Old Testament. He came from heaven, took upon himself frail flesh, and died that the New Testament could be written and thus complete the Word of God, which is the sword of the Spirit. Liberal-minded theologians and preachers, believing that man evolved from a monkey and was not a direct creation of God as Genesis declares, disparage the reading and use of the Old Testament because of the inaccuracies and inerrancies they say it contains. These same critics claim that a warlike atmosphere pervades the Old Testament and that God is presented as a cruel and revengeful tribal deity. They fail to appreciate Christ's constant debt to the part of the Bible for which they have no time.

Foreign to the portrait Jesus gives us in his teachings of God as our loving, heavenly Father is the austere, unjust God of the Old Testament. But what did Jesus himself have to say about the origin of his beautiful and influential teachings the modernist tells us we should concentrate upon? The critics who marvel at the range and force of all the Master taught and who are loud in their assertions that the Gospels are preferable in every way to the Old Testament description of the vindictiveness of God it presents, forget that all that Jesus did teach was not conceived in his own mind but *received* directly from his Father—the God of the Old Testament whom modernistic preachers tell us to shun. "All things I have heard of my Father I have made known unto you" (John 15:15). "I have given unto them the words thou gavest me" (John 17:8, 14). The gracious words proceeding out of the mouth of Jesus, causing his listeners to wonder, were words he repeated out of the Book of Isaiah (Luke 4:16–22 with Isa. 61:1). Peter had in mind all the authors of Old Testament books when he affirmed that as "holy men of God they spake as they were moved by the Holy Spirit" (2 Pet. 1:21; 1 Pet. 1:11). Thus the seal of divine inspiration and authenticity is stamped upon the Living Oracles, as Stephen called the Old Testament (Acts 7:38; see Rom. 3:2; Heb. 5:12; 1 Pet. 4:11).

A very remarkable feature the Gospels present of Jesus is the way he spent the whole of his public ministry in expounding the Old Testament Scriptures. Never once—even by the slightest hint—did he warn his disciples about the supposed errors and contradictions which present-day critics say they contain. As Sidney Collett in the *Scripture of Truth* so aptly expresses it:

> Is this not unlike our Lord, when we remember in what scathing language he showed up and denounced the errors of his day, Matt. 23, and how quick he was to detect and to correct errors or faults even in his own people, Luke 9:55, that he should have known—as he must have known—of these errors, and yet that he

should have remained silent about them? Had any such errors really existed, would he not as "the faithful and true witness," Rev. 3:14, have sounded a warning note, making it clear that certain passages had somehow got into the Old Testament Scriptures which were not inspired by his Spirit, and were therefore not trustworthy; knowing—as none else could know—how many myriads of souls would be staking their eternal well-being upon some of the very words of Scripture?

But instead of this, what do we find? Why, we find his unfailing testimony to be exactly the opposite. Whenever our Lord referred to the Scriptures, he invariably did so in terms calculated to inspire the most absolute confidence in every word. And the whole record of his life fails to furnish one single exception to this rule.

A careful study of what the Master taught reveals how the Old Testament Scriptures were continually upon his lips because they were always hidden in his heart. As coinspirer of them, he knew their contents from Genesis to Malachi, hence his abundant quotations. Jesus mentioned twenty Old Testament characters and quoted from nineteen different books. Take away from his teachings references to events, experiences, and exhortations related in the Old Testament, and there is little left. Think of this coverage of his from the only part of the Bible he had. He refers to:

the creation of man
the institution of marriage
the history of Noah, Abraham, and Lot
the destruction of Sodom and Gomorrah
the appearing of God to Moses in the bush
the manna the Israelites lived on
the Ten Commandments

the tribute money under Mosaic law
the ceremonial law for lepers
the great moral law of the Decalogue
the brazen serpent Moses reared in the wilderness
the Law regarding rows
David's flight to the high priest at Nob
the glory of Solomon and the queen of Sheba
Elijah's sojourn with the widow of Sarepta
the healing of Naaman
the killing of Zechariah (see the charts in the appendix).

These direct references, as well as other indirect ones, reveal the Master's intimate knowledge of the Old Testament and how his inner life felt the formative force of the past and explain why his words were rich in phraseology. In fact, he associated himself as the living Word with the written feeling that both were one. In Jesus, the Word became flesh.

Both are light.

Old Testament: "The commandment is a lamp; and the Law is light" (Prov. 6:23).

Jesus: "I am the light of the world" (John 8:12).

Both are truth.

Old Testament: "Truth shall spring out of the earth" (Ps. 85:11).

Jesus: "I am . . . the truth" (John 14:6).

Both are spiritual food.

Old Testament: "Man doth not live by bread only, but by every word that proceedeth out of the mouth of the Lord doth man live" (Deut. 8:3).

Jesus: "I am the bread of life" (John
                    6:35).
Both are life.
Old Testament: "I have set before thee this day
                    life" (Deut. 30:15).
Jesus: "I am . . . the life" (John 14:6;
                    1 John 5:11, 12).

It is most profitable to go over the claims Jesus
made for Old Testament writers and to investigate
the exact quotations he used from their writings to
prove that they were the heaven-drawn picture of
himself. Of the whole of the books of the Old Testament Scripture, Jesus could affirm, "Search the
Scripture . . . they are they which testify of me"
(John 5:39). When questioned concerning the resurrection, Jesus answered, "Ye do err, not knowing the
Scriptures" (Matt. 22:29). The ground of his constant appeal can be found in phrases like, "Have ye
not read?" "It is written"; "The Scripture cannot be
broken" (John 10:35).

For many years, modernists or higher critics who
reject the worth, authority, and inspiration of the
Old Testament have maintained that the art of writing was not known until long after the time of Moses
and that, consequently, he could not possibly have
written the Pentateuch, or the first five books of the
Bible. Yet Jesus persisted in saying that Moses did
write these initial books. "Moses wrote you" (Mark
10:5). "Moses wrote of me" (John 5:46). The Jews
could assert, "Moses wrote unto us" (Mark 12:19).
The derogatory answer to this divine seal upon Mosaic authorship of the Pentateuch is that Jesus
shared the ignorances and prejudices of his day.
This modernist position is tantamount to saying that
Jesus was not the Truth.

The important statement of Jesus after his resurrection is a remarkable testimony to the divine inspiration of the Old Testament: "All things must be fulfilled, which were written in the law of Moses, and in the prophets, and in the psalms, concerning me" (Luke 24:44).

The trio used here, *the law, the prophets, the psalms,* was the expression used by ancient Jews to represent the whole of the Old Testament. How, therefore, could Jesus make such a statement if any parts of those Scriptures were uninspired and incorrect? Not once did he utter one word which could possibly lead his hearers to expect any flaw in the Old Testament. On the contrary, he solemnly charged his disciples with folly and slowness of heart because—like liberal-minded preachers of today—they did not believe *all* that the prophets had written of him. "O, foolish ones and slow of heart to believe *all* that the prophets have written" (Luke 24:25; see 24:26, 46). What a wonderful expositor Jesus proved himself to be when "Beginning at Moses and *all* the prophets, he expounded unto them in *all* the Scriptures the things concerning himself" (Luke 24:27).

Thus, whenever Jesus referred to Old Testament Scriptures, he invariably did so in terms calculated to inspire the most absolute confidence in all they contained. The Gospels fail to furnish one single exception to such a witness. "Verily I say unto you, until heaven and earth pass, one jot or one tittle shall in no wise pass from the law, until all be fulfilled" (Matt. 5:18; Luke 21:22). Dr. A. R. Bond says that in all but five examples of direct quotations from the Old Testament, Jesus used some sign of quotation:

"It is written," ten times
"It is said," eleven times
"Have read," five times
"Reads," once
"Fulfilled," once

"Jesus' method of quoting was fragmentary and composite. He made sword thrusts with pointed verses. He often combined original passages into one statement. His homiletical purposes did not require citation of the complete thought of the writer. He chose his passages for wisdom in application rather than for literary ends." If Jesus had any favorite Old Testament Book, it must have been Isaiah, with its clearest appreciation of the coming Messiah, his humiliation, sufferings, and glory. This evangelical prophet was a kindred spirit to Jesus. Because all the prophets gave witness to Jesus (Acts 10:43), Sidney Collett reckons that "there are altogether about 1,000 Prophecies in the Bible—about 800 in the Old Testament and about 200 in the New. Of these, in the Old, no less than 333 center in the Person of Christ." Remarkable! This means that no matter where the Old Testament is opened you can see Jesus, for this portion of the Bible is a portrait album of him. What is said of the Temple is equally true of the Old Testament Jesus loved and revered, "Every whit of it uttereth his glory" (Ps. 29:9, margin).

Let us look more particularly at the way Jesus applied much of the Old Testament to himself and also to the future. As already indicated, when he commenced his public ministry at the age of thirty, the eyes of all in the synagogue at Nazareth were riveted upon him as he took the ancient scroll of Isaiah and reading the two opening verses concluded by saying, "This day is this Scripture [Isa. 61:1, 2] fulfilled in your ears" (Luke 4:17–21). He saw himself as the fulfiller of Isaiah's prediction.

At the outset of his ministry there came his temptation in the wilderness (Matt. 4:1–11). Three times over Jesus was assailed by Satan, and each time the tempter was defeated, not by any manifestation of the divine glory and power, nor even by his own challenging answers to satanic suggestions. Jesus achieved victory by falling back upon written words from which saints of successive ages have gathered courage and strength. Three thrusts from the Book of Deuteronomy (8:3, 6:13, 14, 16), and Satan was foiled—as he always is by the Sword of the Spirit.

The length to which the modernists—false teachers of our time—are prepared to go in their destruction of the authenticity of Scripture is proven by their arrogant assertions that the Book of Deuteronomy was not written by Moses but was a pious forgery of the time of Josiah to give greater weight in bringing about the much needed reforms of his day. Satan himself, although "the father of lies," knew perfectly well that the book was not a forgery or full of untruths and that Jesus would never use such a book in his defense. Had Moses not been divinely inspired to write this fifth book of the Pentateuch, it would never have had power to defeat Satan in his threefold effort to induce Jesus to sin.

Further, in common with David, Paul, and John, Jesus had much to say about the "time of the end" (Dan. 11, 12; 2 Thess. 2; Rev. 19). His teachings are laden with references to the mighty scenes and events of the last days. Daniel and the apostles with united voice declare that the great adversary will be destroyed by the coming of Jesus himself, and Jesus' own declaration is identical with theirs (Matt. 24:14, 15; 25:31, 32; 26:63, 64; Mark 13; Luke 21:24). In fact, he quoted the words of Daniel about the daily sacrifice being taken away and the abomination that maketh desolate being set up. A remarkable feature is that Jesus spoke expressly of the prophet Daniel by name, adding the words which, in effect, constitute his commendation of the study of the Book of Daniel, "whoso readeth, let him understand."

Although the book claims Daniel as its author (Dan. 8:1, 2, etc., see also Ezek. 14:14, 20; 28:3), the modernists deny such authorship. Because of its exact predictions we can understand why it has been assailed. E. B. Pusey, in *The Prophets,* says in his preface:

> The Book of Daniel is especially fitted to be a battlefield between faith and unbelief. It admits of no half measures. It is either Divine or an imposture.

Pusey goes on to show that to write any book under the name of another and give it out as his is in any case a forgery. If the writer was not Daniel, as Jesus said he was, then the book is one continued lie in the name of God, seeing the book ascribes everything to God. In the last book of the Bible, Jesus gives us a full revelation of himself, which must be studied alongside its Old Testament counterpart from which the Master loved and taught—the Book of Daniel.

As Jesus neared the end of his ministry and the cross threw its shadow across his pathway, his testimony to the veracity and value of the Old Testament carries a still more sacred and personal import. Listen as he tries to impress upon his disciples the truth they found hard to believe: "Behold, we go up to Jerusalem, and all things that are written by the prophets concerning the Son of man shall be accomplished" (Luke 18:31; see Isa. 53). "For I say unto you, that this which is written must be fulfilled in me, And he was reckoned with transgressors: for that which concerneth me hath fulfillment" (Luke 22:37, RV; Isa. 53:12).

On the very night of his betrayal by Judas, beneath the shade of Olivet, three times over Jesus pointed to the fulfillment of Old Testament Scriptures in himself (Matt. 26:31, 53, 54; Mark 14:48, 49). Three of his seven sayings upon the cross were words of Scripture, and he died with the language of David on his lips: "Into thine hand I commit my spirit" (Ps. 31:5; Luke 23:46).

Jesus often referred to resurrection in general and to his own resurrection in particular during his public utterances. He clearly proved from the Old Testament the fact of resurrection, declaring that "God is not the God of the dead, but of the living" (Exod. 2:6–15; Matt. 22:20–33). To higher critics the Book of Jonah is a mythical story, but Jesus believed in the existence of Jonah as a prophet and in the book bearing his name as an authetic record of Jonah's experiences. Jesus saw a remarkable analogy between Jonah's entombment in the whale and his deliverance from a watery grave and his own death, burial, and resurrection (Jon. 1:17 with Matt. 12:40). It would seem, however, as if the strongest testimony Jesus bore to the Old Testament was after his resurrection. As already indicated, on the very day he rose a mighty victor over the grave, he met two forlorn disciples on the way to Emmaus who were so disconsolate because they thought that the body of Jesus was still reposing in Joseph's new tomb. Then Luke informs us, Jesus rebuked his sad followers: "Ought not Christ to have suffered these things, and to enter into his glory? And beginning at Moses and all the prophets, he expounded unto them in all the Scriptures the things concerning *himself*" (Luke 24:25–27, 44–46).

Luke, physician and historian, also tells us that he wrote the Book of Acts to record "all that Jesus began both to do and teach" and that until the day he ascended on high he continued to teach the apostles truths pertaining to the kingdom of God (Acts 1:1–3). Sufficient, then, has been said to prove that Old Testament Scriptures are full of Christ, even as he was full of them. How privileged we are to have the whole Bible, all of which centers around him who came as the Word of God. As Martin Luther expressed it, "There is one Book—The Bible. There is one Person—The Lord Jesus Christ." We believe his witness to the ages: "In the volume of the book, it is written of me." May we be found emulating his love for the Scriptures and also his fearlessness in declaring their message to a world in dire need of such! May we ever believe of Scripture that

It is the golden casket
  Where gems of truth are stored:
It is the heaven-drawn picture
  Of Christ, the Living Word.

BIBLE STUDY QUESTIONS

Take time to turn to each Scripture reference and mark the verse or portion in your Bible.

1. Show that Jesus had an intimate knowledge of the Old Testament.
2. Why did Jesus quote so often from the Book of Daniel?
3. What Scriptures did Jesus use in his conflict with Satan?
4. What Scriptures did Jesus quote as he died on the cross?

Part II

— 6 —

His Authority

In this designation of Jesus the term *authority* implies an independent commission from God that carried with it the power of its execution. It was somewhat fitting that Matthew should conclude his full report of our Lord's teaching, as enshrined in the Sermon on the Mount, with the observation, "He taught them as one having authority, and not as the scribes" (Matt. 7:29). This prolonged teaching period had a profound effect upon the auditors, for we read that when Jesus had ended his remarkable discourse "the people were astonished at his doctrine" (Matt. 7:28). The word for astonished implies *amazement* and suggests how overwhelmed the people were, not only by his teaching, but still more by himself, as he revealed the truth.

Two features impressed the rapt listeners, namely, the difference between Jesus and all other teachers ("not as the scribes"), and the authority he manifested ("he taught them as one having authority"). He spoke as if he were accustomed to receiving obedience from all. "Where the word of a king is, there is power" (Eccles. 8:4). Jesus never troubled himself about quoting authorities as the scribes were in the habit of doing. His was a God-given authority, born of infallible insight into the mind of God. Jesus never taught on personal authority as did the scribes in their dogmatic utterances. "My doctrine is not mine." His was the authority of God-inspired truth, not of personality.

The second observation of the people was that Jesus taught *not as the scribes*. We can only appreciate this remark if we know how and what the scribes taught. Alexander Whyte, in his rare work, *The Walk, Conversation, and Character of Jesus Christ Our Lord,* refers to the depths of imbecility found in the teaching of the scribes.

> Their own books, preserved to this day, prove to us that the New Testament, plain-spoken as it is, has not told us the half of the scandal of the life and teaching of the scribes and the Pharisees. You would simply not believe the frivolities, and the superstitions, and the downright immoralities of the teaching and preaching of the Scribes and the Pharisees, as all these things stand written in their own records. And it was the grace and the truth, it was the wisdom and the beauty of our Lord's teaching and preaching, all taken together with the heavenly holiness of life that led Matthew to give us such a full report of the Sermon on the Mount, and then to add to it this conclusion that our Lord did not teach as the Scribes.

The scribes were mere retailers of what others said. They loved to cite some great name to prove that their teachings were not original but approved by those with a renowned reputation for learning. Even today, writers and teachers are careful about quoting authorities and give authority for a statement for the advanced interpretation of Christianity, all of which has its value and makes for accuracy. But with Jesus it was totally different, as the people noticed. While he was always quoting Scripture, and taught how he was fulfilling it, he is never found quoting the rabbis of his time. This method was new to the scribes, who knew nothing of teaching what they had come to know from a heart-experience of intimacy with God, the source of truth.

These Jewish leaders were simply parrots, constantly repeating the learned traditions of their fathers—a method for which Jesus rebuked them. They knew nothing of the utterance of fresh, vibrant messages for the needy hearts they professed to teach. As for Jesus, his teachings were striking, apt, forceful, and of far-reaching influence. They also testified to his divine authority and of his sinless separateness from other teachers with whom he is often grouped and compared. Comparative teachers there may be, but the teacher sent from God is not one of them. Shakespeare reminds me that "Comparisons are odorous," and the matching of Jesus with ancient philosophers is one of these odorous comparisons, simply because none can be compared with him who is incomparable, separate, and supreme in the realm of pedagogy. "Who teacheth like him" (Job 36:22)?

There is no other explanation why the ethics he orally communicated in the small provinces of Galilee and Nazareth became the ethics of the world to live by. The teachings of Jesus have shaped the thinking of the world and are still shaping it. The man of Galilee was no dreamer, no mere visionary. The Gospels present him as an ardent revolutionary willing to suffer for what he taught. As T. R. Glover in his *Jesus of History* asks,

> When we make our picture of him, does it suggest the Man who has stirred mankind to its depths, set the world on fire, Luke 12:49, and played an infinitely larger part in all the affairs of men than any man we know of in history?

All who listened to Jesus in his itineraries, as well as multitudes all down the centuries who have studied his spoken word, testify that his speech was without parallel. There is never any real danger of overestimating his greatness. The risk is that of underestimating this most wonderful teacher the world has ever known, who transcends our categories and classification. We never exhaust him; and one element of Christian happiness is that there is always more in him than we supposed.

THE METHODS HE EMPLOYED

We now come to examine how Jesus put his authoritative message across. We know that he never had the countless volumes on homiletics that

preachers and teachers have access to today to
help him shape his public discourses. Because of
his omniscience and omnipotence, he had no
need to sit down and write and rewrite his messages, then tape them in order to mark their effect, and memorize them. In every opportunity
that arose for public or private tuition, he knew
exactly what to say and how to declare the truth
required. Discussing the habits of Christ's mind,
the way it moved and the characteristics of his
thinking, Richard Glover wrote in *History of Jesus:*

> We note a certain swiftness, a quick realization of a
> situation, a character, or the meaning of a word. Men
> try to trap him with a question, and he instantly "rec-
> ognizes their treachery," Luke 20:23. When they ask
> for a sign, he is quick to see what they have in mind,
> Mark 8:11-13. He catches the word whispered to
> Jairus—half hears, half divines it, in an instant, Mark
> 5:36. He is surprised at the slowness of mind in other
> men, Matt 15:16; Mark 8:21. And in other things he
> is as quick—he sees "the kingdoms of the world in a
> moment of time," Luke 4:5; he beholds "Satan fallen
> like lightning from heaven," Luke 10:18—two very
> striking passages, which illuminate his mind for us in
> a very important phase of it. We ought to have been
> able to guess without them that he saw things in-
> stantly and in a flash—that they stood out for him in
> outline and colour and movement there and then.

Further, one cannot examine the teachings of
Jesus without being impressed with his close observation of nature and of human life and relationship and with his economy of words in using these
observations as illustrations of truth. He was

never verbose. His language was always well chosen, simple, direct, and natural. It was likewise free from quotations, except scriptural ones. Then what a gift he had of arresting attention: "Whosoever will save his life shall lose it" (Matt. 16:25), which came with a spontaneous flash and lives in the memory. A notable feature of the sayings of Jesus is that they are hard to forget.

It is also evident that, along with other teachers of his time, Jesus did not teach, as we do in this highly developed age, by orderly, logically matured propositions. Ancient teaching was informal. There were no three-deckers—"firstlies," "secondlies," "thirdlies"—so common in Alexander Maclaren's *Expositions of Scripture*. However, Alexander Whyte tells us that Jesus always practiced an ancient rule of Greek and Roman oratory, though he had never learned the rules of any oratorical school:

> Out of the native wisdom of his own mind, and out of pure love of his heart, our Lord always "captivated the ears of his audiences" at the opening of all his discourses. What could be more conciliating, and indeed captivating, than the opening words of his very first sermon? What could take hold of a congregation better than the beautiful beatitudes with which he began his great Sermon on the Mount?

Some early centers of learning were known as *Peripatetic* schools because in them master and students walked about as they talked—which Jesus was fond of doing. Then before his time there was the famed *Socratic* method of informal question and answer, a method so common of our Lord's teaching. Even at the early age of twelve, Jesus had the gift of putting and answering questions (Luke 2:42–47). In fact, the questions he asked and others asked of him, and the answers he gave, as recorded in the Gospels, afford a profitable aspect of study.

Although Jesus sometimes taught formally, as in the synagogue or on the mountain side, much of his teaching was what we might call *table talk*, as scenes of teaching prove. Often his environment suggested answers to questions or subjects to be dealt with. Passing through wheatfields, walking along the roadside, or sitting by a wayside well prompted truths he wanted people to hear. Because of his omniscience he knew the questions men would ask of him before they were uttered, and so he was ready with a perfect answer, thereby causing those who heard him to be "astonished at his understanding" (Luke 2:47). In ancient times, "the city was the education, and the market-place the school where most of the most-abiding lessons were learnt."

Said the old Greek poet Simonides, "The city teaches the man," and it does, more than we realize. As we know, Jesus grew up in an Oriental town, in the middle of its life—a town with poor houses, bad smells and worse stories, tragedies of widow and prodigal son, of unjust judge and grasping publican—yes, and comedies too—all of which colored his public utterances. Human relationships likewise added their quota to his unique teachings. The education of Jesus was not bookish even though he may have had access to the works of prominent teachers and philosophers. Some writers claim to have found traces of other books in his teachings.

While Jesus was thoroughly immersed in the Old Testament, primarily, he found his education in home and shop, in the desert, on the wayside, and in the marketplace. As a boy, he watched those around him and weighed their words more closely than they guessed; their words provided "grist" for his mill. We sometimes say of preachers that their sermons "smell of the lamp," which means they are very bookish. But the illustrations and parables Jesus used in his teachings were full of humaneness and thus easily understood by his hearers.

Jesus had the art of taking experiences common to himself and to his audiences alike and using them to enforce his truths. His love of home, of bird and beast, and of the wild, open countryside as a country-bred peasant boy came through when he entered his public ministry. The lines of Wordsworth are so true if applied to Jesus:

> The earth
> And common face of Nature speaks to Us
> Remarkable things.

Much of the teaching of Jesus reveals the environment of his years of preparation. He was intimately associated with Galilee which was the center of many industries of the home and where there were factories of pottery and fine linen and dye-works. The caravans of the world's commerce

passed through along the great trade routes. Dr.
George Adam Smith reminds us that "Judea was
on the road to nowhere; Galilee is covered with
roads to everywhere." Thus, the life and scenes
the boy Jesus looked out on were full of action,
with Roman legions and the litters and equipages
of wealthy noblemen passing to and fro. Then
among the birds, animals, and flowers of the country, the child Jesus found much to interest his
developing mind.

When, at about the age of fifteen, he left the
village school to follow the trade of the home,
Jesus became a carpenter and builder. The Ara-
maic word for "carpenter" means more than a
worker in wood; it is also used to indicate a
worker in stone (Matt. 13:55; Mark 6:3). Does not
this practical experience at the bench and of outside construction lie behind Jesus' sayings connected with his trade? For instance, we have his
references to the making of plows and yokes
(Matt. 11:29, 30), lampstands (Matt. 5:15, 16),
building of houses (Matt. 7:24–27), and barns
(Luke 12:16 81). It is possible, then, to recon-
struct from the range of Christ's teachings a picture of the kind of house and environment in
which he lived before beginning his brief ministry
at the age of thirty. Consider the following summary of his illustrations:

1. *Indoors*
     Women grinding corn (Luke 17:35)
     Heating the oven (Matt. 6:30)
     Making the bread (Matt. 13:33)
     Sweeping the floors (Luke 15:8)

Mending the clothes (Mark 2:21)
The value of money (Luke 15:8, 9)
Children at meals (Matt. 7:9–10)
Children in bed (Luke 11:7)
2. *Outdoors*
Flowers (Matt. 6:28)
Chickens (Luke 13:34)
Sheep (Luke 15:4)
Ox in a pit (Luke 14:5)
Foxes (Luke 9:58)
Eagles (Luke 17:37)
Small seeds, big trees (Mark 4:31, 32)
Sowing and reaping, wheat and corn (Matt. 13:24; Mark 4:3)
The marketplace, buying sparrows (Matt. 10:29; Luke 12:6)
bargaining (Matt. 5:33–37)
measuring (Luke 6:38)
children at play (Luke 7:32)
The sea, the dragnet (Matt. 13:47, RV)
the fishermen (Mark 1:17)

Further, his teachings suggest a wider outlook. They were not only parochial but universal, as the following aspects prove:

A nobleman who would seek a kingdom from Rome, which Archelaus, a son of Herod the Great, did (Matt. 2:22; Luke 19:12)
An ancient king with his slaves and dependents, great and small (Matt. 18:23)
Stewards, bad and good (Luke 12:42)
An unjust judge (Luke 18:2)
A banker (Luke 19:23)
A householder hiring laborers (Matt. 20:1)
Trading, in pearls (Matt. 13:45)

in oil (Matt. 25:9)
in weapons (Luke 22:36)
in cattle (Luke 14:19)
in slaves (Matt. 18:25)
in land (Matt. 13:44; Luke 14:18)
Robbery, on the road (Luke 10:30)
in the house (Matt. 6:19)
Marriage, groomsmen and maidens in attendance
  (Matt. 22:2; 25:1; Mark 2:19)
The burden of debt (Matt. 18:28)
The result of youthful dissipation (Luke 15:12)
The misuse of wealth (Luke 12:16-21)
The art of hospitality (Luke 14:7)
Prudent and eager resourcefulness (Luke 16:3)
The scribes and Pharisees (Matt. 23:2), the
  Sadducees (Mark 12:18-27), the publicans
  (Luke 18:9), the Samaritans (Luke 9:52),
  Gentile foes (Matt. 10:28)

Does not such a coverage of the lessons Jesus
garnered from these varied aspects of life greatly
help a living knowledge of him in his boyhood,
youth, and manhood, which is in every way to be
desired, since it is one of the chief objects of Christian education?

The life of women, as portrayed in some of
Jesus' parables and sayings, is what he saw in his
own mother's home, for example, the woman who
lost part of her precious house-money (Luke 15:8
-10), two women grinding at the mill (Luke 17:35),
the housewife washing her crockery, outside and
in (Luke 11:39), the woman hiding leaven in the
meal (Matt. 13:33), a mother mending torn
clothes (Matt. 9:16), the mother's task to satisfy
healthy appetites of children who did not confine

themselves to bread, but wanted fish and eggs as well (Matt. 7:10; Luke 11:11–12).

As the creator and lover of nature, Jesus drew many of his similes and metaphors from the birds of the air, the fish of the sea, and the fruits and flowers around. His teachings ever live because of their illustrations taken from sheep, oxen, hens, sparrows, foxes, eagles, and camels, sowing and reaping. Because Jesus knew nature, being on closer terms of intimacy than any other, the four facts he noted in nature are its mystery, its regularity, its impartiality, and its peacefulness.

As Jesus attended the village school and played with his school-fellows, he learned how they could be sulky at times (Luke 7:32). Some of the games of the children come out in his illustrations:

> At weddings and at funerals,
> As if His life's vocation
> Were endless imitation.

As to personal traits associated with his teaching, Jesus made much use of his eyes; so we have several references to his *looking* (Mark 3:5; 8:33; 10:23). Love, grief, and anger are emotions given of his looks. Jesus had feelings and expressed them, even in indignant utterances (Matt. 23:14; Mark 11:17). Characteristics of his mind as a teacher were a certain swiftness, a quick realization of a situation, a character, or the meaning of a word. Sometimes the scribes and Pharisees would try to trap him with a saying or a question, and he would instantly recognize their trickery and amaze them by his foreknowledge and swift reply (Matt. 9:11–13; Luke 20:23). We read that the Pharisees provoked "him to speak of many things . . . seeking to catch something out of his mouth, that they might accuse him" (Luke 11:53, 54). The more he preached to the Pharisees, the more bitter their opposition grew, until at last, determined to silence him, the cry arose, "Away with him, crucify him!" But those precious lips of his never uttered a single word which they could catch to bring an accusation against him.

PARABLES AND PROVERBS

It must be clear, even to the most casual reader of the Gospels, that Jesus had a unique way of using the popular medium of parables and proverbs. Further, he did not create the parabolic form of teaching, seeing there are many parables in the Old Testament. He at least developed it with high originality, and gave it a deeper spiritual import. Parables have the quality of making truth clearer to those who see the point. To others, without spiritual insight, they are only stories (Mark 4:11–12, Luke 8:18). Says Bishop Gore, "The parables of Jesus, as they appear in the world's literature are masterpieces, and are easily rememberable—we may almost say unforgettable." (See the author's volume, *All the Parables of the Bible*.)

As for the incomparable proverbs of Jesus, with their method of *parallelisms*, what pregnant maxims they are. For instance, when Jesus said, "He that is not with me is against me," the proposition is intelligible, and we can appreciate the truth expressed. All of his proverbs, it will be found, are principles stated in extremes, without modification, often requiring to be balanced by their seeming contraries. Studying the form of our Lord's teaching, we have to get at the *principle* behind the proverb, at the same time not forgetting that the short-pointed paradoxical form of instruction is meant to stimulate us, and to warn us that the conduct required of us in such and such cases will be extreme and difficult conduct, as in the somewhat hard proverb, "If any man . . . take away thy coat, let him take thy cloak also" (Matt. 5:40).

Bishop Gore reminds us of another Jewish habit of speech Jesus emulated, the building up of sentences on the framework of *not-but,* two hundred examples of which have been counted in the Gospels alone. "Labour *not* for the meat which perisheth, *but* for that meat which endureth unto everlasting life" (John 6:27). Some of the sayings of Jesus containing *not* and *but* mean exactly what is said, namely, that the first alternative is literally excluded. But more often it is intended only to depreciate the first by comparison with the second, as in the above Proverb, where Jesus certainly did not mean to condemn what he approves—honest work for an honest living—but only intended to fix our attention on a more important kind of labor.

All aspects of the teachings of Jesus, notably his precepts of admonition and instruction and chains of discourses, should be closely studied by those who are called to preach and teach the Word. The best-known example of the *chain* method is the Sermon on the Mount (Matt. 5–7), which, according to some writers, when compared with the Sermon on the Plain (Luke 6:20–49), creates the impression that the Evangelists strung various sayings together into a single discourse, or that they found them strung together that way in tradition. But the preface to the Sermon on the Mount suggests that it was a complete sermon delivered without any break. "When he was set . . . he opened his mouth, and taught [his disciples]" (Matt. 5:2).

THE RESULTS HE ACHIEVED

In H. Twell's heart-moving hymn, "At Even Ere the Sun Was Set," there is the line, "No word from Him can fruitless fall." The prophecy of Isaiah can certainly be applied to the matchless and eternal words leaving the holy lips of Jesus when among men. "So shall my word be that goeth forth out of my mouth; it shall not return unto me void, but it shall accomplish that which I please, and it shall prosper in the thing whereto I sent it" (Isa. 55:11).

Because of the divine source and substance of the teachings of Jesus, they cannot fail in their mission. "The word which ye hear is not mine," he could say, "but the Father's which sent me" (John 14:24). This, then, is the secret of the abiding influence of his utterances, and eternity alone will reveal the marvelous results of all Jesus taught while here below (1 John 2:14). We have, of course, the immediate effect of his teachings and the continuing influence of "the grace poured into his lips" (Ps. 45:2).

— 7 —

Man

Jesus had every right to discourse about *man* because by his condescension he became the only perfect man the world has ever known. *Behold the man!* (John 19:5). And well might we behold him, for there was never before his like as a man, and there never will be again. As co-sharer in the creation of man, Jesus knew that he had been fashioned in the divine likeness, for was he not included in the plural, "Let *us* make man in *our* image, after *our* likeness" (Gen. 1:26)? Jesus, then, without whom "was not any thing made that was made" (John 1:3), knew everything about the constitution and purpose of man whom he assisted in creating.

From the dateless past, the Son of God, by his incarnation, became the Son of man, a title denoting an essentially human being and which he used of himself some eighty times in the Gospels. It is the title by which he most frequently designated himself. In passing, however, let it be said that although he became the Son of man, he was not the Son of *a* man. He is the only Son the world has known who did not have a human father. He was conceived of the Holy Spirit (Matt. 1:20). The terms, *Son of man* and *Son of God,* then, form a pair and aptly describe the two sides of our Lord's person, namely, his deity and his humanity.

Coming in the fashion of a man (Phil. 2:8), never man spake like this man, and all through the Gospels the humanity of Jesus is most evident. By becoming "the man Christ Jesus," he entered into a personal experience of human emotions, human desires, and human frailties, and his temptations, travail, trials, and tears have forever endeared him to mankind. Man is irresistibly drawn to him as he remembers that he is the one touched with his infirmities. He became like man, sin excluded. Although rich in his prerogatives in past glory, he became poor when he took upon himself frail flesh to die as man's deliverer.

Being man, Jesus knew what was in man and was able to penetrate his thoughts and read his intentions. He could teach more clearly than the philosophers of his time about the vital problems of man's destiny because he had known it from the beginning of mankind. When Jesus entered his public ministry of preaching and teaching, man was asking:

> But what am I?
> An infant crying in the night;
> An infant crying for the light;
> And with no language but a cry!

Jesus understood such yearnings and answered this infant cry with himself. As Dr. A. R. Bond movingly puts it in his most remarkable volume, *The Master Preacher:*

Upon his heart fell the shadows that saddened others; the minor chords of human woe made his own heart-strings quiver with the sympathetic melody; the threnody of misfortune and the dirge of death found a response in his tenderness and help. He entered into fellowship of a common life with his fellow-men, alive to their disappointments, touched by the feeling of their infirmities, tempted with their struggles, and able to succour every tempted soul. He knew the trials, aspirations, and needs of men, for his insight into life was piercing, comprehensive, clear, and interpreted by his own experience.

His words were authoritative with the strength of a fulness of his entrance into the entire life of the world. His mind and heart garnered the full harvest of human experience, excluding the thorns and thistles, which they could not house. His preaching caught the authority of the double relationship. Out of his complete Divine Sonship he could bring the message which could be applied according to his knowledge of men that he brought from his complete human Sonship.

These, then, are the thoughts to have in mind as we consider what Jesus had to say concerning man. By reason of his birth when, as God, he became flesh, he had a complete experience of human nature and complete knowledge of man (John 2:24–25; 4:29).

Touched with a sympathy within, He knows our feeble frame:
He knows what sorest trials mean for He has felt the
same:
But patient, undefiled, and pure the great Redeemer
stood,
While Satan's fiery darts He bore, and did resist to
blood.

Since no man knows the things of a man like the
man of Galilee, let us now try to piece together
what he taught about man whom Lord Byron described in "Manfred" as "Half dust, half deity,
alike unfit/To sink or soar." I prefer St. Augustine's appraisal: "Man wonders o'er the restless
earth, the flowing waters, the sight of stars, and
forgets that of all wonders, man himself is the
most wonderful."

MAN IS A DUAL BEING

Jesus taught that man has a spiritual side to his
make-up as well as a physical, that he is soul and
spirit as well as body. Is this not borne out in his
reply to Satan during the temptation in the wilderness? Throughout this severe testing period lasting forty days and forty nights, Jesus fasted and at
the end of the satanic onslaught was very hungry.
"He had not felt the need of food while absorbed
with the contemplation of the work on which he
had now entered," says Richard Glover in *History
of Jesus*. "But when the strain is over, he found

himself helpless and feeble through want of bodily sustenance" (Matt. 4:1-3; see Mark 3:20, 21; John 4:31, 32).

Tempting Jesus to assuage his hunger by displaying his omnipotence, tauntingly Satan said, "If thou be the Son of God, command that these stones be made bread." Then came the crushing reply of Jesus based upon Deuteronomy 8:3: "Man shall not live by bread *alone*, but by every word that proceedeth out of the mouth of God" (Matt. 4:3, 4). Jesus needed bread, for he was hungry; and man must have the bread he is able to bake for his physical needs which Jesus himself recognized when he taught men to pray, "Give us this day our daily bread." But the question arises, If, in the first miracle he performed, Jesus turned the water into wine to meet a need at the marriage feast in Cana, why did he not respond to the seemingly harmless suggestion to provide the bread he certainly required being "an hungered"? One imperative lesson we must learn in life is that every act is wrong which is done from wrong motives, however innocent in itself it may seem to be. Had Jesus displayed his power and made the bread he required, he would have yielded to the doubt Satan insinuates in his question.

Jesus went on to give us one of those arrestive *buts* of his: "But by every word that proceedeth out of the mouth of God." Material bread is necessary to sustain life in the body; Jesus, the Word of God, is the bread of heaven to nourish the spiritual side of man (John 6:26-35). The folly of man today is to live for bread alone. He obeys the tempter's voice, *Make bread!* Thus he lives only for the gratification of the physical side of his being, forgetting that he is also a "living soul" (Gen. 2:7), for whom food has been provided both in the written and in the living Word.

All around us are multitudes very much alive physically but dead spiritually. Speaking of widows, Timothy writes, "She that liveth in pleasure is dead while she liveth" (1 Tim. 5:6). There were church members in Sardis of whom John wrote, "Thou hast a name that thou livest, and art dead" (Rev. 3:1). Such may appear to be paradoxical, but far too many are alive yet dead. They make every provision for their material and natural needs but are not mindful of the deeper need of the soul for the true bread from heaven. Would that we could hear those who live only for bread for the body cry, "Lord, evermore give us this heavenly bread of life the soul must have!"

MAN HAS AN INHERITED EVIL NATURE

Jesus did not believe that in every man is the divine spark, nor did he teach that "God is slumbering in the heart of every man, and only needs to be awakened." Running through all his references to the heart of man is the Old Testament truth that man was born in sin or born with an evil nature with propensities toward iniquity. He knew, as no other, that in unregenerated man there was no good thing, that his throat was an open sepulchre, with the poison of asps under his lips (Rom. 3:9–20). Think of our Lord's scathing exposure of the professedly religious Pharisees: "O generation of vipers, how can ye, being evil, speak good things? . . . An evil man out of the evil treasure bringeth forth evil things" (Matt. 12:34, 35). "If ye then, being evil [not only *doing* but *being* evil]" (Luke 11:13). "Out of the *heart* of man proceed evil thoughts . . . All these evil things come from within, and defile the man" (Mark 7:20–23).

He who was without sin knew perfectly well the evil of which the human heart is capable (Matt. 15:19) and all about falsity, even in professed religionists (Matt. 15:8). When Paul spoke of "the natural man," he meant man as he is *naturally* sinful and used this figure of speech for that evil nature common to all men and which is equivalent to our Lord's phrase about men "being evil." Descriptions like "sinful inclination," "evil disposition," "apostate will," "original sin," and "native depravity," which theologians use, all imply the same truth Jesus taught, namely, that man is born with a bias toward evil and needs to be reborn by the Holy Spirit and made a new creature in Christ Jesus, or "the spiritual man." Proud, obstinate man may reject what Jesus taught about his heart corruption and lost estate, but in his vain effort to reform himself he knows only too well that there is an evil force in his nature beyond his control which can only be dislodged by a greater power than himself.

MAN IS CAPABLE OF GREAT WICKEDNESS

Because of the poisoned well within man, in no uncertain terms Jesus described the putrid waters capable of flowing from a tainted source. "Out of the abundance [the overflow] of the heart the mouth speaketh" (Matt. 12:34). This is true of purity as well as impurity. Everything depends on what a man *wills*. Says Richard Glover in *Jesus and Man:*

> It is the inner energy that makes a man; what he says and does is an overflow from what is within—an overflow, it is true, with a reaction. It is what a man *chooses*, and what he *wills*, that Jesus always emphasizes:
> *God knoweth your hearts* (Luke 16:15).

Jesus used the illustration about the impossibility of a good tree bearing corrupt fruit or a corrupt tree producing good fruit (Matt. 7:15–20). Then, in his teaching regarding the defiling streams coming out of a man, Jesus listed the manifestations of wickedness to expect:
"Evil thoughts, adulteries, fornications, murders, thefts, covetousness, wickedness, deceit, lasciviousness, an evil eye, blasphemy, pride, foolishness" (Mark 7:21, 22).
Knowing all there is to know about man, is it not amazing that in spite of all the sin he is capable of, Jesus was mindful of him and gave his precious blood to make even the vilest clean?

MAN IS A LOST SINNER

In his teaching concerning man, Jesus often used the word *lost,* and no other descriptive term is as fitting as this, for man is a lost being. Through the Fall, he lost the original powers with which his creator endued him. Robert South, in a famous sermon, said that "Aristotle was but a wreck of an Adam, and Athens but the rubbish of an Eden." How completely sin has defaced the divine image in man! That man has lost his righteousness and happiness is clearly evident as we look at the state of the world today!

But masses of lost souls mattered to Jesus who summed up his work in the world as he met one of them in the squalid little figure of a man, Zacchaeus, whom people around despised. "The Son of man is come to seek and save that which was lost" (Luke 19:10). Zacchaeus was one of these, but Jesus came into his life, and the man held in contempt became a transformed person and a pioneer of Christian generosity (Luke 19:1–10). Then the taunt flung at Jesus really described what he was and wished to be: "The friend of publicans and sinners" (Luke 7:34; Mark 2:16).

The constant foes of Jesus, the scribes and the Pharisees, tried to fill the cravings of the lost for God with the Law; and when the Law failed to satisfy such a yearning, they had nothing further to suggest, except their fixed ideas. "God heareth not sinners" (John 9:31). But Jesus taught that his Father did care for and hear sinners. The reli-

gious leaders left the masses alone, having no feelings whatever about them being as sheep without
a shepherd. Jesus taught that God loved them so
much as to give him, his only-begotten Son, that
they might be saved (John 3:16). Is not this truth
illustrated in the threefold parable of the lost
Sheep, the lost coin, and the lost son (Luke 15)?

> I was lost, but Jesus found me,
> Found the sheep that went astray.

The term *lost*, however, has a twofold implication,
namely, something lost with every possibility of
recovery or something lost with no possibility of
recovery. Our railways have what they call the
Lost Property Office. Goods, lost or left behind by
passengers, are held so that they can be applied
for and reclaimed. But when there is an air disas-
ter and the report is printed of all who died, the
usual phrase employed is, "All lives on the plane
were lost." Alas! for them there was no recovery,
save as charred corpses.

This twofold significance is attached to the
word *lost* as Jesus used it. He came across many
who were lost in sin, like the woman taken in adultery, but he found her, as the shepherd found the
lost sheep. No matter how lost a soul may be, while
the door of mercy stands ajar, he or she can be
recovered by the seeking Shepherd. According to
Paul's testimony, in him the Savior recovered the
chief of sinners.

Jesus also taught the further implication of the
word *lost*, namely, something lost with *no* possibility of recovery. If the lost determine to remain

lost, despising the salvation offered them, then, dying in their sins, they die lost forevermore. "If ye believe not that I am he, ye shall die in your sins" (John 8:21, 24). When Jesus spoke of a man "losing his own soul," he implied an *eternal* loss as well as a present one. Then when he taught that if men finally reject him as their only Redeemer, they must certainly *perish,* such a term does not mean annihilation or cessation of being, since man is immortal, but everlasting banishment from the presence of a thrice holy God (John 3:16; Rev. 20:15; 21:27).

MAN'S SOUL IS OF INESTIMABLE VALUE

Shakespeare's Hamlet exalts God's masterpiece in creation in this fashion:

> What a piece of work is a man! how noble in reason! how infinite in faculties! in form and moving how express and admirable! in action how like an angel! in apprehension how like a god!

While sin has debased man's nobility and changed him from being angellike into a diabolical creature, in his purest form he is still a reflection of his creator. The incomparable value of man's soul makes understandable the mission of Christ as a Redeemer. Synesius, who lived about A.D. 410, wrote that "A thing of price is man because for him Christ died." In his estimation of man's worth, Jesus said that he is more valuable than the entire universe. "What is a man profited, if he shall gain the whole world, and lose his own soul? or what shall a man give in exchange for his soul" (Matt. 16:26)?

Because the vital loss of soul is irreparable, its redemption is most precious (Ps. 49:8), and nothing less than the precious blood of the sinless man can avail to restore him to what his Maker intended him to be. Through grace, man receives still higher value as a member of the body of Christ who assured his own that the very hairs of their head were numbered and that they were of more value than many sparrows. What a tragedy, then, for God's supreme handiwork to languish in hell!

> To lose one's wealth is much,
> To lose one's health is more,
> To lose the soul, is such a loss
> That nothing can restore.

MAN MUST REPENT AND BE REGENERATED

A sinner by birth, then a sinner by practice, man must repent of his sin and be born anew by the Spirit of God in order to become a "new man." The pathway from his sinnership to his saintship consists of three steps: (1) "Repent ye" (Mark 1:15; Luke 15:10); (2) "Come unto me" (Matt. 11:28); and (3) "Follow me" (Matt. 4:19).

Jesus came calling sinners to repentance, for if they remain ignorant of their condition, they will never realize the necessity of regeneration. To Nicodemus, a man deeply religious and highly educated, Jesus said, "Ye must be born anew" or "born from above." It is sadly possible for a man to be sincerely religious and yet not be a Christian after the standard of Christ. "Except a man [religious or irreligious] be born again, he *cannot* see the kingdom of God" (John 3:3–7). Man may think that his own righteousness is a sufficient passport into the kingdom, but all his righteousnesses are as filthy rags in God's sight. So whether he is good or bad, a man must come to see that he is a beggar on God's grace and mercy and that unless he comes to him in his way, and on his terms, he is a lost sinner in danger of eternal condemnation.

Jesus alone claims to be the Savior of man, the satisfier of his deepest needs and the giver of rest to his burdened soul (Matt. 11:28; John 7:37–38). He asks nothing of sinners but genuine sorrow for sin and unreserved surrender to his claims. But once a person becomes a Christian, Jesus demands all that he is and has, and that thereafter nobody and nothing must interpose between himself and the soul of his follower.

BIBLE STUDY QUESTIONS

Take time to turn to each Scripture reference and mark the verse or a portion in your Bible.

1. In what ways was Jesus uniquely different, yet one with all mankind?

2. How did Jesus show us that spiritual and physical gratification are both necessary?

3. Describe the condition and character of the lost sinner.

4. Explain what is required of man in each step from sinner to "new" man.

— 8 —

Sin

Much of what we have said about the nature of man is also relevant under this section. Having seen something of the *fruit* of sin in him, we now consider the *root* of sin, or what Jesus taught about this intrusion into God's universe. The tragic fact of sin is involved in Christ's doctrine of man. It is taken for granted that we cannot formulate a complete doctrine about sin from the few scattered references to it by Jesus in the four Gospels. For this, we need the coverage of the Bible as a whole. Confining ourselves, therefore, to what the Master taught about this topic, we observe the following features (see my book, *All the Doctrines of the Bible*).

First, Jesus could not have ignored the problem of sin even if he had wished to ignore it, for he came into the world to die for its sin. Before his birth, he was called *Jesus*, a name implying that he would save people from their sin (Matt. 1:21; John 1:29). Sin was the keynote of the preaching of John the Baptist, who was likewise the herald of the sinless Lamb who would bear away such sin. Dr. Alexander Whyte points out:

> If we would enter truly into any of our Lord's texts, and would really and truly take home to ourselves any of our Lord's sermons, we must continually keep in mind what, exactly and exclusively, his errand was in the World. *SIN* was his errand in the World, and it was his only errand. He would never have been in this world at all, either preaching sermons, or doing anything else, but for *SIN*.
>
> He could have done everything else for us without coming down into this world at all; everything else but take away our sin. And thus it is that our sin is the key wherewith to open up all he ever did, and all he ever said, while he was with us in this world. And thus it is also that unless your sin is ever before you, neither Jesus Christ himself, nor his coming, nor any of his texts, nor any of his sermons, will ever be understood by you.
>
> You will not understand or comprehend one single clause of his first text, Luke 4:16–19, nor one single sentence of my present sermon upon his first text, unless you attend all the time as a sinner, and as nothing else but a sinner. You must be poor, as only a sinner is poor.

T. R. Glover's chapter, "Jesus' Teaching about Sin," in his *Jesus of History*, shows how our Lord's view of sin is very different from those current in that day.

> Man set sin down as an external thing that drifted on to one like a floating burr—or like paint, perhaps, —it could be picked off or burnt off. It was the eating of pork or hare—something technical or accidental;

or it was (many thought) the work of a demon without, who could be driven out to whence he came. Love and drunkenness illustrated the thing for them —a change of personality induced by an exterior force or object, as if the human spirit were a glass or a cup from which it could be emptied and the vessel itself remain unaffected.

Jesus has a deeper view of sin, a stronger psychology, than these, nor does he, like some quick thinkers of today, put sin down to a man's environment as if certain surroundings inevitably meant sin. Jesus is quite definite that sin is nothing accidental— it is involved in a man's own nature, in his choice it comes from the heart, and it speaks of·a heart that is wrong.

JESUS SPOKE MUCH ABOUT SIN

"He that is without sin among you, let him first cast a stone" (John 8:7). Jesus was the only one who ever lived without sin; yet he never cast a stone against a sinful woman taken in adultery.

"Whosoever committeth sin is the servant of sin" (John 8:34; 9:24).

"If I had not come and spoken unto them, they had not had sin: but now they have no cloak for their sin" (John 15:22).

"He will reprove the world of sin" (John 16:8, 9).

"He that delivered me unto thee hath the greater sin" (John 19:11).

"Behold the Lamb of God, which taketh away the sin of the world" (John 1:29; 18:14).

JESUS CALLED MEN SINNERS, OR MEN LIVING IN SIN

"I am come to call ... sinners to repentance" (Matt. 9:13).

"The Son of man is betrayed into the hands of sinners" (Matt. 26:45).

"Sinners also love those that love them" (Luke 6:32, 33).

"Sinners also lend to sinners to receive as much again" (Luke 6:34).

"God be merciful to me a sinner" (Luke 18:13; 19:7; John 9:24).

"A friend of ... sinners" (Matt. 11:19).

"Suppose ye that these ... were sinners above all men" (Luke 13:2, 4).

Chief among those Jesus named sinners were the publicans, Pharisees, and Sadducees. As Professor Stalker points out, they represented three notorious forms of *sin,* each of which lay like a burden on Jesus' spirit till he relieved himself in their exposure and condemnation.

The sin of the publican. Jesus linked "publicans and sinners" and "publicans and harlots", together, for these were the "lost sheep," those who had broken through the fences of religious and social observance by which Jewish life was regulated and distinguished from the world at large, thus allowing themselves to become a reproach and a menace to all by whom these barriers were respected. The Pharisees and scribes, observing how the publicans and sinners were eager to hear Jesus preach and teach, murmured among themselves, "This man receiveth sinners, and eateth with them" (Luke 15:2).

But who and what were these publicans, the most despised sinners among sinners? In Britain, *publicans* are those who run "public houses," or drinking saloons, in which intoxicating liquors are sold and drunk. But in our Lord's day publicans were tax gatherers or farmers. The Herods auctioned to the highest bidder the right to exact and collect taxes in specific areas. The buyer would subdivide the area and auction portions of it to smaller men. Agents employed in the actual collecting of the taxes were called *publicans*. Naturally these public tax gatherers wanted to retrieve as soon as possible the money they had "staked," with the result that in the main they were *extortioners* (Luke 3:12, 13; 19:8). The fact that degenerate Jews would serve the Romans and the Herods in this way made them hated and despised (Matt. 9:10–13), and they were looked upon as having forfeited their nationality and gone over to the pagans. Thus, the very worst that could be said of any man was that he was "an heathen man and a publican" (Matt. 18:17).

Yet the attitude of Jesus to this lowest type of sinner was one of the most singular and characteristic features of his ministry. Little of his indignation was directed against those guilty of carnal and public sins. His scathing denunciations were reserved for sinners of a wholly different cast. Toward the publicans Jesus manifested a surprising leniency, not to say partiality. His enemies were not lying, then, when they condemned him as "a

gluttonous man, a friend of publicans and sinners." Jesus attended a feast that Matthew, originally Levi the publican, gave at his house. When
Jesus went home with Zacchaeus, chief among the
publicans, the Pharisees chided that he had gone
to be a guest with a man who was a sinner (Luke
19:7; see Matt. 11:19; Luke 7:34).

But those publicans and sinners with whom
Jesus was so friendly never received the impression
that he was condoning their manner of life or that
he was making himself one of them. They were
perfectly aware that Jesus had come to save them
from the evil way of life—which he did! He was
not blind to their faults, but he never forgot that
they were human beings worth restoring, hence,
his astounding statement that "the publicans and
harlots" would enter his kingdom before the carping priests and elders (Matt. 21:23, 31). Matthew
became a disciple and was chosen as one of the
twelve (Matt. 9:9; 10:3). Fitting, is it not, and
somewhat dramatic, that unjust taxation—that historic root of bitterness through past ages—should
end in contemplation of Jesus who said to an outcast and guilty tax collector, the words summarizing his mission on earth: "The Son of man
is come to seek and to save that which was lost"
(Luke 19:10).

The sin of the Pharisee. Originally, the Pharisees
were a commendable party. Their group probably
arose as a protest against the encroaching Greek
influence, before the time of the Maccabees,
which led them to adhere even more strictly than
was necessary to the old Mosaic ways. During

Jesus' day there were a few Pharisees who remembered these worthy foundations. Saul of Tarsus who became Paul the apostle was not ashamed of having been one of this minority (Acts 23:6; 26:5–7). Gamaliel, also, was a good example of the better sort of Pharisee (Acts 5:34).

As a party, however, the Pharisees degenerated into an assembly of talkers rather than actors. Religious hypocrisy became their most glaring sin which called forth some of the most scathing denunciations to leave the tender lips of Jesus (Matt. 5:20; 16:6, 11, 12; 23:1–39). If it seemed as if he displayed extraordinary tolerance to the sins of the publicans and harlots, he made up for it by his blunt exposure of the Pharisees. What contempt he poured upon them in his Sermon on the Mount when he turned into ridicule their habits of prayer, fasting, and almsgiving! To him, they were sinners far worse than the publicans, whom the Pharisees hated, because their sins were of a religious nature. How Jesus scorned their holy-looking dress, long prayers, and lip-sermons! Of these professed religious teachers Jesus said, "They say and do not." He had no hesitation in calling them "children of the devil."

The most direct collision with these religious hypocrites is preserved for us in the sermon of Jesus to the multitudes and to his disciples, recorded for us in Matthew 23. In tones ranging from the most biting sarcasm to holy indignation Jesus exposed the Pharisees, his avowed enemies. He named them "children of hell" and compared them to "whited sepulchres, which indeed appear beautiful outward, but are within full of dead men's bones, and of all uncleanness." Then came his Seven Woes in which he revealed how the Pharisees had carried iniquity to the point of perfection. Their glaring sin was a foreshadowing of "the mystery of iniquity," and its wickedness was not realized by the populace because it masqueraded in the garb of sanctity. The poor publicans knew they had plenty to repent of, but the Pharisees were not aware of anything for which repentance was necessary. In fact, they seemed incapable of repentance.

Shakespeare, in "Love's Labour Lost," says, "Now step I forth to whip hypocrisy," which Jesus did most mercilessly, and how those Pharisees cringed under the whip! Laurence Stern, of the seventeenth century, wrote that "Of all the cants which are canted in this canting world, the cant of hypocrites may be the worst." Jesus thought it was and thus sought to destroy such a false, religious mask. In Matthew 23, Jesus denounces hypocrisy as so great a sin. In expository fashion Richard Glover elaborates on this helpful outline in *History of Jesus*:

Hypocrisy is a hard taskmaster (23:4).
Hypocrisy lives only for the praise of men (23:5–7).
Hypocrisy is most mischievous (23:13–22).
Hypocrisy concerns itself with the small things of religion (23:23, 24).
Hypocrisy deals chiefly with externals (23:25–28).
Hypocrisy reveres only what is dead (23:29–32).
Hypocrisy finds a fearful judgment (23:32–36).
Hypocrisy receives an unexpected lament (23:37–39).

While the vice of hypocrisy today may differ from the way the Pharisees condoned it, combining as they did "the maximum of formalism with the minimum of reality," and although we may have no intention of falsity, we may maintain habits and ways after the feelings which originated them have died away, leaving us as hypocrites. The sure and only cure for any tendency to such a sin is to live beneath the eye of God, with all its infinite comfort and constraint. Deceit is an abhorrent sin in his sight. As this is a vice specially besetting all who inherit a religious life and creed, which they are unwilling to let go, but have no devotion enough to keep up—a sin, therefore, easily besetting those who have Christian homes and Christian upbringing,—we should give heed to the Savior's lessons on it. Perhaps the most moving words Jesus ever uttered were those where he was found lamenting over those who would not let him show that, although he severely upbraided such sinners, he loved them in the midst of their wickedness and hypocrisy. "I would . . . ye would not."

The sin of the Sadducees. The Sadducees, further enemies of Jesus, were named after Zadok, or Sadduc (2 Sam. 8:2), the high priest, the most important founder of a branch of the priesthood, and a descendant of Aaron (1 Chron. 24:3). Between the Pharisees and Sadducees there were marked differences. The former were traditionalists, while the latter, a Jewish politico-religious party, took their guidance from Scripture alone and not from the ruling of the elders. The Sadducees denied the Pharasaic doctrine of the resurrection of the body and of existence in hell; they also rejected the reality of angels (Mark 12:18; Acts 23:8) and the rewards and punishments of a future life.

The Sadducees not only denied the immortality of the soul and the resurrection of the body, they also rejected the traditions of the Pharisees who believed that Moses delivered the doctrine of a future life to the elders (Acts 23:8). Josephus asserts that this party believed that the soul dies with the body and that there is no divine providence. In their encounter with Jesus in regard to the resurrection, there is an element of contempt implied in the illustration which they used as an indication they did not take him seriously (Matt. 22:25; Mark 12:20; Luke 20:29).

Nevertheless, the Sadducees were afraid of the effects of Jesus' teaching and united with the Pharisees to interfere with his mission and to destroy the church he came to build (Matt. 16:1–4; 22:23–33; Acts 4:1–22; 23:6–10). Although the doctrines and practices of the Sadducees were conspicuously alien to the teachings of Jesus and to the conduct he enjoined, he did not denounce them as he did the Pharisees. In fact, he never rebuked them save along with their opponents the Pharisees; whereas he frequently denounced the Pharisees alone. The Sadducees seemed to look upon Jesus as a harmless fanatic who, by his strong denunciations of the Pharisees, was weakening their influence much to the satisfaction of the Sadducees.

This aristocratic and somewhat priestly party

did not play anything like so important a part in
the life of Jesus as did the Pharisees. He did not
confront the Sadducees nearly as often as he did
the Pharisees. Only at the very end of his ministry
do we find the Sadducees openly identified with
the opposition to the influence and teaching of
Jesus. Only when he claimed to be the Messiah
did they become more vocal and promptly decreed his arrest and death. The arrest of Jesus,
however, was to be in secret, "lest a tumult arise
among the people" (Matt. 26:5). Later on, Paul,
although a Pharisee, was an agent of the Sadducean high priest in the persecution of the church.
It is interesting to observe that after the resurrection the Pharisees became less hostile to the followers of Jesus; but the Sadducees maintained their
attitude of suspicion and hatred (Acts 4:1).

While the Sadducees were not as numerous as
their opponents the Pharisees, theirs was a prominent sect, and priestly descent had an influence
comparable to their rivals. They were a political
party, of priestly and aristocratic tendency, as
against the more religious and democratic Phari
sees. They were a skeptical party whose religious
beliefs lacked warmth and conviction. They
gained, however, complete ascendancy in the
Sanhedrin, and later, under the leadership of
Annas, or Ananias, they put James, the brother
of Jesus, and others to death (Acts 23).

Josephus, the Jewish historian who has given us
full characteristic features of the sects in existence
at the time of our Lord's birth, says that "while
the Pharisees had amiable manners and cultivated

concord among all, the Sadducees thought they were very boorish." While such a want of manners is not usually associated with an aristocracy, it yet describes the Sadducean cruel horseplay indulged in when Jesus was tried before an irregular meeting of the Sanhedrin (Matt. 26:67, 68). It also accounts for the shout of Ananias at Paul's trial before the same tribunal to "smite Paul on the mouth," on which occasion the Sadducees were certainly rough and overbearing (Acts 23:1–10).

Professor James Stalker in *The Ethic of Jesus* suggests that the particular sin of the Sadducees was that of *worldliness* and that the weakness of their religious sentiment was due to that sin. Loose ideas of spiritual and eternal realities resulted in concerns of the present life. The rich fool, who pulled down his barns to build greater and was so absorbed in his property—the mere shell and husk of life—while his soul and his eternity were of no concern to him, illustrated precisely the spirit and sin of Sadducean worldliness. "Worldliness," says Professor Stalker, "stifles the very faculty of religion: and on a cold, cynical heart the appeals of religion fall like seed upon a rock."

Josephus informs us that the Sadducees had influence with the rich. On the other hand, the Pharisees, like Jesus, drew their adherents chiefly from the poor. Association with the wealthy classes caused the Sadducees to look upon money as the sign and symbol of all earthly possessions and proved that it is an enslaving power when valued and pursued for its own sake. By his statements in the Sermon on the Mount, Jesus taught that when men accumulate the apparatus of life instead of living, they become forgetful of the fact that a man's life does not consist in the abundance of the things which he possesses. "Blessed are the poor" was the opposite pole from Sadduceeism. There is one object on which the Sadducee in human nature casts itself by an inevitable instinct, and to which it clings with appalling tenacity—this is money. The teaching of Jesus is astonishingly severe regarding the heaping up of treasures on earth (Luke 6:24; Matt. 6:19, 20).

The sins of publicans, of Pharisees, of Sadducees, and of men in general were only "the outcropping above the surface of a solidarity of evil beneath the surface, which is the property of the race as a whole" and forced Jesus to level at his own generation a reiteration of invective without a parallel: "This is an evil generation . . . a generation of vipers . . . a wicked and adulterous generation." One wonders what he would have to say about human society today if he were here in the flesh and surveyed the mounting toll of crime, violence, vandalism, drug and drink and sex addiction, bloodshed, and war. Because of its corrupt state, the world is becoming ripe for another judgment similar to what it experienced in Noah's day. God loved the world, and his only begotten Son shed his blood for it because it was a world lost in sin. As the Lamb, Jesus bore away the sin of the world, but alas! so few in a "world of sinners lost, and ruined by the Fall" appropriate the emancipation from sin which he secured.

JESUS USED METAPHORS TO DESCRIBE THE HAVOC WROUGHT BY SIN

We sin when we say, do, or intend to do what we know to be alien to the will and Word of God. The term *sin* is used of anything felt, done, or said which is contrary, consciously or otherwise, to the mind of God. The word *sin* itself means a falling from or missing the right way. It also implies transgression of the law (Rom. 4:15; Heb. 10:26). The Westminster Catechism states "Sin is any want of conformity unto, or transgression of, the law of God." Sin springs in the individual man from a perverted and depraved mind. All forms of evil come "from within," said Jesus. The heart of man is the seat of impurity covering every kind of sin (Matt. 15:18, 19).

Sin is blindness. Carlyle wrote that "the beginning of a man's doom is that vision be withdrawn from him." Jesus said, "Thou blind Pharisee" (Matt. 23:26)! Then he told the Pharisees that they were "blind leaders of the blind" (Matt. 15:14) and likewise "blind guides" (Matt. 23:16, 17; see John 9:40, 41). This teaching of Jesus as to spiritual blindness corresponds to Paul's words about the mind being darkened (Rom. 1:21; 2 Cor. 3:14). Because Satan as the god of this world had blinded the minds of those who believe not, Jesus came as the light of the world.

The whole world was lost in the darkness of sin.
The Light of the world is Jesus.

He came that the eyes of man's darkened understanding might be enlightened, and his miracle of giving sight to those who were physically blind was a parable of what he is able to accomplish in the spiritual realm. At the commencement of his ministry, in his first sermon Jesus declared that he had come into the world for the recovering of sight to the blind, meaning, the spiritually blind, as well as those with sightless eyes (Luke 4:18). Such spiritual blindness is dark ignorance of mind, for the heart excluding the light of truth is in the blackness of midnight. John Bunyan in *Pilgrim's Progress* personifies *Ignorance* and sends him to the blackness of darkness forever. The tragedy is that men love darkness rather than light because of their evil deeds (John 1:5; 3:19; Matt. 6:23).

Sin is bondage. That a sinner is in bondage and fettered by Satan can be gathered from our Lord's teaching in his discourse on himself as the light of the world (John 8:12–50). Listening to his priceless words, the consciences of the Jews were stung as they heard him say, "Whosoever committeth sin is the slave of sin." Then came the twofold utterance: "Ye shall know *the truth*, and the truth shall make you free. . . . If *the Son* therefore shall make you free, ye shall be free indeed" (John 8:32, 36). There is no contradiction between these two statements. The one is the complement of the other, for *the Son* is *the Truth* (John 14:6), and he only, through the truth, can emancipate a sinner from the shackles of his sin and set him gloriously free (Rom. 6:14). His chains fall off, and, freed, he follows his mighty Emancipator, rejoicing in a blood-bought liberty. Charles Wesley taught the church to sing:

> Long my imprisoned spirit lay
>   Fast bound in sin and nature's night;
> Thine eye diffused in quickening ray,
>   I woke, the dungeon flamed with light;
> My chains fell off, my heart was free;
> I rose, went forth, and followed Thee.

There are other aspects of sin we could enlarge upon, such as the utter bankruptcy it reduces the sinner to until he becomes "full of hypocrisy and lawlessness" (Matt. 23:28), depraved like bad trees unproductive of any but rotten fruit (Matt. 7:16), destitute of faculties their sin abused (Matt. 25:28, 29), disorganization of the whole being, and with instincts perverted, fit only for "outer darkness" (Matt. 22:13). Yet running all through the teaching of Jesus about *sin* and his constant contact with sinners of all kinds is the witness that he himself was without sin. Although "made sin for us," he was never a sinner but always "separate from sinners" (2 Cor. 5:21; see 1 Pet. 2:22; 1 John 3:5).

Jesus appeared to put away sin by the sacrifice of himself, and his sinlessness gives efficacy to such a sacrifice. None could convict him of sin or find any fault in him; therefore, as the sinless Son of God, his blood is able to cleanse sinners of their sin, and transform them into saints (1 John 1:7).

> There was no other good enough
>   To pay the price of sin.

He only could unlock the gate of Heaven
And let us in.

BIBLE STUDY QUESTIONS

*Take time to turn to each Scripture reference and
mark the verse or a portion in your Bible.*

1. Explain Jesus' purpose in coming into the
   world.
2. Contrast publicans and sinners with the Pharisees.
3. How are the Sadducees characterized?
4. What actually is the nature of sin?

— 9 —

Repentance

Arising out of Christ's teaching about sin is what he taught about *repentance* for sin. As we have already seen, the tragedy of human sin reveals, by contrast, the height of man's original destiny and, therefore, the necessity of a deep penitence because of his fall. More than the philosophers of his time, Jesus understood the nature and consequences of sin and thus urged upon sinners repentance toward God and faith in himself as the means of their recovery to divine favor. The terms *repent* and *Repentance* occur over twenty-five times in the four Gospels, and in the majority of references were used by Jesus. Two or three times, *repentance* is given as the watchword of the forerunner of Jesus who preached "the baptism of repentance for the remission of sins." The commencement of our Lord's ministry is described by Matthew, "From that time began Jesus to preach and to say, Repent: for the kingdom of heaven is at hand" (Matt. 4:17). Here repentance is set forth as the first aspect of Jesus' ministry.

After his choice of the twelve, Jesus commis-

sioned them in their humbler way to begin where
he did. Mark tells us that the disciples "went out
and preached that men should repent." Repentance, then, in its full scriptural sense, is the sum
and substance of the gospel of Jesus Christ. In his
mind, the need for repentance was as universal as
the fact of sin and the possibility of salvation.
With utmost authority and freedom Jesus taught
the sinfulness of man, but he was equally certain
that sinners, even the worst, could be saved, no
man having gone too far in sin as to be beyond his
power to deliver. "Him that cometh to me I will in
no wise cast out." The gospel hymn reminds us
that "his blood can make the vilest clean."

Further, there can be no deep, genuine repentance—an essential condition of salvation—apart
from the convicting ministry of the Holy Spirit
revealing to the sinner the nature of his sin, not
merely against himself or others, but first of all
against God (John 16:7–11, RV). Is this not proven
by our Lord's teaching in his illustration of the
prodigal son who, out in the far country, "came to
himself"? This phrase is equivalent to repentance
in the prodigal's soul who, thus convicted, framed
the repentant petition he would present to his loving father once they met again. "I have sinned
against *heaven* [not first against his father, but
heaven] and in thy sight, and am no more worthy
to be called thy son" (Luke 15:21). When a soul is
made conscious of sin by the Spirit, it is primarily
of sin against God and of not having believed in
him. David, in contrition, confessed, "Against
thee, thee only, have I sinned" (Ps. 51:4)! Jesus
taught of the Spirit's ministry: "He will reprove

the world of sin . . . Of sin, because they believe not on me" (John 16:9)!

For a complete understanding of what the Master taught on the topic of *repentance*, it is essential to combine his several references to it in his seven letters to the churches (Rev. 2:3) with those to be found in the Gospels. Five of those churches received a direct call to repentance from Jesus who used several designations of himself in all seven letters.

Ephesus. This church had left (not lost) her first love and must repent and do her first works or lose her light-bearing power (Rev. 2:4, 5).

Pergamos. In this city the church had plunged into sensuality and priest-worship and was called to repent or be smitten (Rev. 2:16).

Thyatira. Alas! the church here had gone deeper into adultery and the abominable practices of the ancient Jezebel and must repent or suffer tribulation (Rev. 2:21, 22).

Sardis. Here was a church with a name to live but was spiritually dead and must repent or face judgment (Rev. 3:3).

Laodicea. This last of the seven churches was one so proud, self-righteous, and self-satisfied, with Jesus, not inside and the center and source of its life, but outside on the doorstep. This church must also repent and give Jesus his rightful place within it (Rev. 3:19).

WHAT IS REPENTANCE?

A gospel hymn simply puts it, "Repentance is to leave the sins we loved before," but while it results

in such a cleavage, more is involved in contrition
of soul. The word itself has several connotations.
In the New Testament two words are translated
repent. One original word means to "care afterwards," or a sorrow or remorseful regret which
may lead to turning (Matt. 21:29) or which may
not (Matt. 21:32), as in the case of Judas whose
repentance was merely regret (Matt. 27:3). This
particular word occurs six times and is twice translated in the revised version as *regret* (2 Cor. 7:8).

The second word, however, far more common
and stronger in meaning, is used in all the teaching concerning repentance and is the equivalent
of the Old Testament word *turn,* or *return,* one of
the Hebrew terms used some six hundred times.
Applied to man, then, it means turning away
from sin to God (Acts 20:21) and occurs, in the
noun and verb forms, some fifty-seven times.
Thus, as used by Jesus, to repent implied to *turn,
rightabout-face,* or go the opposite way and do the
opposite thing, a turning based upon deep sorrow
and remorse for and abhorrence of sin, produced
by a revelation of divine holiness and hatred for
sin. The three steps in this about-face are expres-
sively set forth by David: "I thought on my ways,
and I turned my feet unto thy testimonies. I made
haste, and delayed not to keep thy commandments" (Ps. 119:59, 60).

At the heart of the word *repent* is the idea of
changing one's mind for the better or to *have another
mind*—the term for "mind" covering feelings, judgment, desires, and purposes. There is implied a
complete reversal of the sinner's entire nature—
intellectual, affectional, and moral. Repentance is

a change of mind resulting in a change of life. When Martin Luther discovered, while reading his Greek Testament, that the Greek word for repentance means literally a change of mind, he experienced a great new light that revolutionized his life and service. When he discovered that biblical repentance means a change of heart, he was launched into a fierce battle against the Roman church in which he had been brought up and which he had tried to serve.

Several writers have emphasized the radical significance of the term. Archbishop Trench wrote in *The Miracles of Our Lord,* "Repentance expresses that mighty change in the mind, heart, and life wrought by the Spirit of God."

Similarly, Thomas Chalmers observed in the *International Standard Bible Encyclopedia:* "Repentance describes that deep and radical change whereby a sinner turns from the idols of sin and self unto God, and devotes every movement of the inner and outer man to the captivity of His obedience."

When Jesus told men to repent, he likewise meant the voluntary change in the mind of the sinner whereby he turns from his discovered sin (Matt. 9:12, 13). Professor Stalker in *The Ethic of Jesus* concludes his chapter on Christ's teaching concerning such a drastic change: "This was repentance: it is an upheaval of the nature from its foundations; it turns the life upside down; it is a decisive breach with the past; it is a great venture for the future."

What must be stressed, however, is that repentance, in itself, is not sufficient, and it is not salva-

tion although it results in salvation. Repentance is
only a condition of salvation and not its merito-
rious ground. A sinner may be a truly repentant
soul, yet never know what it is to be blessedly
delivered from his sin made so clear to his conscience by the Spirit of God. Penitential tears avail
for nothing if they do not result in entire committal to Christ. The prodigal not only "came to himself," he also "arose and came to his father." What
is the use of repentance unless we bring forth
fruits worthy of such contrition (Luke 3:8)? Such
expression of sorrow over sin is only profitable
when it leads to remission of sins (Luke 24:47)
and functions as repentance unto life.

> It is not thy tears of repentance nor prayers,
>   But the blood that atones for the soul:
> On Him then who shed it thou mayest at once
>   The weight of iniquities roll.

Whether repentance is a gradual movement of
a convicted soul, or a sudden and complete turning away from the evil of the past life, as with Saul
on that Damascus Road, it must be allied with
faith if it is to result in salvation. While it is true
that repentance precedes faith and brings faith
and that there can be no saving faith without repentance, it is also true, in a very real sense, that
repentance and faith go together and are inseparable and mutually dependent. Could anything be
more concise and compelling as the message of
Jesus as he went forth to preach the gospel? "Repent ye, and believe the gospel" (Mark 1:15). But
such believing repentance is not a once-for-all act.

Once saved by grace through repentance and faith, the saved one must practice habitual repentance, not for the sins already blotted out by God, but for daily sins of omission and commission. John uses the continuous sense in his word of assurance, "As we keep on confessing our trespasses, the blood of Jesus keeps on cleansing us from all sin" (1 John 1:7, 9). Carlyle says, "In Repentance too is man purified. It is the grand Christian act."

When Jesus instructed his disciples in the grace of forgiveness, he said that if those who trespassed against them repented of their action, they were to be forgiven (Luke 17:3, 4). No wonder they prayed, "Lord, increase our faith"! When repentance is coupled with faith, there is always divine forgiveness for our trespasses (Matt. 6:12). True repentance, then, involves confession, contrition, and correction.

Confession (Luke 15:18). It is folly to hide anything, for God knows all the inner secrets of the heart. As the familiar features of the father looked down on the prodigal and he saw "the venerable figure, the melting eye, the gentle smile— all sunk into his heart; till, casting himself in imagination before it, he cries, 'Father, I have sinned.' "

Contrition (Luke 22:61, 62). There must be genuine grief because of sin against divine love (see Eph. 4:30). The value of repentance accompanied by confession is that it brings the sinner and the God sinned against face to face; for "the core of repentance is to recognize, not what our sinful life has been to ourselves, or even to others, but what it has been to God."

Correction (Luke 15:19). Repentance is always practical and expressed by how we act and how we live. Where necessary, amends must be made. For instance, repentance for a theft is expressed by giving back stolen property (Luke 19:7-9; see Matt. 27:3). A slanderer must retract the false statement, and an unkindness must be amended by extra kindness. Wrongdoing may be atoned for by doing better in the future. Repentance and faith are not mere sentiments, but, like hope and love, essentially practical, involving the exercise of the will to fulfill every obligation. Jeremy Taylor wrote that "true Repentance must reduce to act all its holy purposes . . . A holy life is the only perfection of Repentance."

Several of Jesus' references to repentance remind us of deep feelings of the soul that we would like to see more of in these sinful and callous days in which we live.

WHO DOES AND WHO DOES NOT REPENT?

Jesus came to call sinners to repentance (Matt. 9:13), and there is joy in heaven when the cry is heard arising from a heart smitten by conviction, "God be merciful to me a sinner" (Luke 15:7; 18:13). Sent out by the Master to preach the gospel, the disciples called upon men to repent and greatly rejoiced when they saw men sorry for their sins (Mark 6:12; Luke 10:17, 20). Two of the most incomparable illustrations of genuine repentance to be found anywhere are those given by Jesus in the parable of the prodigal and in the woman who was a sinner (Luke 15:11–32; 7:36–50).

In connection with the prodigal, Dr. Stalker in *The Christology of Jesus* says that the striking phrase, "came to himself," shows that the first element in repentance is *awakening*. He observes:

> When a man awakens out of sleep, we say he comes to himself. The Greek means literally "he entered into himself"—a remarkable phrase; for who is denoted by *he* and who by *himself*? It sounds as if in one person there are two men, the one of whom has been home but now returns. So, in common parlance, we say, a man is "out of himself," or, "beside himself," meaning that he is mad. And, indeed, sin is a brief madness; it is a drunken sleep, out of which a man has to awaken and be himself. Or "he entered himself" may suggest another line of reflection. The interior man may be conceived as a picture-gallery or corridor, hung with the scenes of one's own past, into which, in hours of leisure and reflection, one can enter and follow one's own course step by step and stage by stage.

When the prodigal was far from home, he sat down among the swine, and the past came up before him. In the cold reality of retrospect he saw everything in an entirely different light. All the glamour, excitement, and intoxication of his free life had gone; completely disillusioned, he returned home to confess, "Father, I have sinned against heaven, and in thy sight, and am no more worthy to be called thy son" (Luke 15:21). This is the kind of repentance that creates joy in heaven, and Jesus had the satisfaction of seeing many prodigals turning from their sin to him.

The other illustration the graceful pen of Luke records is that of the woman twice referred to as a sinner, the term being used in the sense of unchastity (Luke 7:37, 39). The impressive feature of the scene Luke describes is that this sinful woman never uttered a word or confessed her sin as the prodigal did. Yet from what Jesus said of this woman and of her actions, we see repentance in its purest form. To quote again from Stalker's *Ethic of Jesus:*

> Heis was a flight from a besetting sin and lost life, and in pursuit of a better life, the vision of which had risen before her eyes, that she ventured in where she dared not well be seen. There was a certain boldness in her action: but this was necessary in order to make a public break with the past. On the other hand, humility pressed her down to the earth; shame constrained her to unbind her hair and let its heavy tresses fall to hide the burning blushes; sorrow for her sins, which were many, burst in tears from her eyes. The shattering of the box of ointment may have been the final sacrifice of an instrument of her evil calling. But it would not be easy even to name all the emotions surging through her soul—timidity, admiration, gratitude, love, enthusiasm.

The eloquent silence of this sinner's repentance touched the heart of Jesus, leading him to utter some of the most beautiful sentiments, both in the parable of the creditor and the two debtors, and in his response to the woman's tears and sacrifice. Addressing Simon, he said, "Wherefore I say unto thee, her sins, which are many, are forgiven; for she loved much: but to whom little is forgiven, the same loveth little." Then came the glorious message of Jesus, thrilling the soul of this debased female and transforming her into a new creature: "He said unto her, thy sins are forgiven thee . . . Thy faith hath saved thee; go in peace" (Luke 7:48, 50).

There are many who, when deep conviction grips them and their sins come up before them, have, like the woman who was a sinner, no language but a cry. Dumb with silence, they hold their peace (Ps. 39:2). But he who is ever quick to respond to a deep recognition of guilt can read the meaning of the silence and the travail behind the tears and blesses the repentant heart with a free and full forgiveness.

There are other passages, however, in which Jesus describes the nature and the peril of those who felt there was no cause for repentance in their lives. Think of his woe pronounced on Chorazin and Bethsaida for their unconsciousness of sin. He compared them with Tyre and Sidon: "They would have repented long ago in sackcloth and ashes" (Matt. 11:20, 21; see 21:29, 32).

Cities were upbraided because they repented not, and Jesus' own generation received his judgment because it failed to repent of its sin. Nineveh repented at the preaching of Jonah, and here was a greater than the runaway prophet; yet they spurned his preaching (Matt. 12:38–42). Jesus said that there were those so hardened in sin that

they would not repent if a preacher arose from
the dead to preach to them (Luke 16:31). But the
gracious Savior left those who were blind to their
need of soul-repentance for sin. "Except ye repent, ye shall all likewise perish" (Luke 13:1–5).
Shakespeare asks:

> What then? What rests?
> Try what repentance can. What can it not?
> Yet what can it when one cannot repent?

It would seem from the teaching of Jesus that
repentance is not necessary for all men, as, for
instance, when he spoke of joy in heaven over one
sinner that repents more than over ninety-nine
just persons who need no repentance (Luke 15:7).
Then he also said, "I am not come to call the righteous, but sinners to repentance" (Matt. 9:13),
which is equivalent to the previous verse where
Jesus chides those who think themselves sinless
and in no need of repentance with the observation, "They that be whole need not a physician,
but they that are sick."

In the context of these verses Jesus is dealing
with two classes, namely, publicans and sinners,
scribes and Pharisees. Now, he did not imply that
the former certainly needed to repent; but that
the latter, signified by the "ninety-nine just persons" and those who were "whole," had no need
of repentance. *All* have sinned, and *all* must repent and believe if they are to be saved from their
sin. Jesus knew only too well that the publicans
and sinners were in dire need of repentance and
that they knew they were. He also knew that of all

sinners the scribes and Pharisees were the worst
since they were religious hypocrites; therefore, we
cannot believe he meant they had no need of repentance.

What Jesus, as the superb teacher, subtly implied was that the ninety and nine persons
deemed themselves to be just and in no need of
repentance, or so whole as requiring the aid of no
physician. Because of their Pharisaic sins these
self-righteous men required repentance far more
than the "one sinner that repented" and had
deeper need of divine healing than those who
knew they were sick. Jesus came to call *sinners* to
repentance; because the Pharisees did not deem
themselves to be in such a class, he had no message for them. It was in irony, then, that Jesus
referred to them as just persons with no need of
repentance, for his scathing denunciations of
their unjust lives as "children of the devil" reveal
them to be sinners of the worst degree. Their self-
righteousnesses were more filthy than the swine-
smelling rags in which the prodigal returned
home. Because of his repentance he exchanged
his rags for the best robe in his father's house.

To summarize then, repentance, as taught by
Jesus, is an evidence of the Spirit's ministry in the
soul, making the contrite one conscious of his
need of deliverance from besetting sins of the
past. Further, the motives for Repentance are
chiefly found in the goodness of God, in divine
love, in the pleading desire to have sinners saved,
in the inevitable consequences of sin, in the universal demands of the Gospel, and in the hope of

spiritual life and membership of the kingdom of heaven (Mark 1:15; Luke 13:1–5; John 3:16; see Acts 17:30; Rom. 2:4; 1 Tim. 2:4). Attention has been drawn to the first four Beatitudes of Jesus (Matt. 5:3–6) as forming a heavenly ladder by which penitent souls pass from the domination of Satan into the kingdom of God. We have:

A consciousness of spiritual poverty dethroning pride,

A sense of personal unworthiness producing grief,

A willingness to surrender to God in genuine humility,

A strong spiritual desire developing into hunger and thirst to enter into the experience of one who wholly abandons sin and heartily turns to him who grants repentance unto life.

BIBLE STUDY QUESTIONS

Take time to turn to each Scripture reference and mark the verse or a portion in your Bible.

1. How is repentance an essential condition of salvation?
2. What is repentance?
3. In what ways is repentance expressed?
4. Who must repent? Why?

— 10 —

Forgiveness

Since divine forgiveness is an integral part of our *salvation,* we should have included it under such a head, but as such a virtue as taught by Jesus comprises God's forgiveness of man, and man's forgiveness of man, it merits a chapter of its own. Whether used of God or man in the Gospels, the word *forgiveness* means to discharge, dismiss, acquit, let loose from, to remit a debt or sin, to pardon. It also implies giving up an inward feeling of injury or resentment, the removal of a feeling of anger and restoration for a feeling of favor and affection (see Acts 13:38, 39). The kindred terms *forgive, forgave, forgiveness* occur some forty times in the four Gospels. A peculiarity of John's Gospel is that none of these terms are found in the Authorized Version. In the Revised Version at John 20:23 *forgive* replaces "remit."

A UNIVERSAL NECESSITY

All men have need to join in the prayer, "Forgive us our debts" or trespasses, "for *all* have

sinned, and come short of the glory of God."
"There is none righteous, no, not one" (Rom.
3:10, 23). They have no righteousness of their
own, making them acceptable to God. All have
broken his laws and, therefore, require forgiveness if fellowship with him is to be restored. Jesus,
who had much to say about *forgiveness,* never
sought it from God simply because, as he himself
confessed, "I do always those things that please
[my Father]." As the sinless one, he never infringed
any divine commandment and so had no cause to
seek God's forgiveness. He, likewise, never had
any reason to ask forgiveness of any individual
because "harmless" as well as "holy" he never injured anyone while here on earth. The man after
God's own heart had to write, "I will be sorry for
my sin" (Ps. 38:18), but Jesus never had to say,
either to God or to man, "I'm sorry for what I've
done, please forgive me." All others, having
sinned against God and man, require forgiveness
from both. Further, divine forgiveness is of supreme importance for all who have trespassed
against God, for if they die in their sin, unfor-
given by God for Christ's sake, then they are forever lost. Blessed is the man whose transgression
is forgiven, however, and who knows that his sin
has been covered by the precious blood of Jesus
(Ps. 32:1; 103:3).

A DIVINE PREROGATIVE

We may be able to forgive injuries others cause
us, but only God can forgive sin. Even the carp-

ing, critical scribes realized this, for they asked, "Who can forgive sins but God only" (Mark 2:7)? They had just heard Jesus say to the palsied man whom he had healed, "Son, thy sins be forgiven thee" (Mark 2:5). What those scribes were ignorant of was that Jesus had every right and authority to forgive sins since he was God manifest in flesh. Thus, whenever Jesus forgave a sinner, he revealed his deity. More than once he made the penitent one rejoice over the gift of forgiveness.

"He said unto her, Thy sins are forgiven" (Luke 7:48).

"Thou art made whole; sin no more" (John 5:14).

"Neither do I condemn thee; go, and sin no more" (John 8:11).

Constantly, Jesus reminded his foes that as the Son of man he had power on earth to forgive sins (Matt. 9:6). To Jesus, the author of forgiveness was always God, and when he spoke of his own power to forgive sins, he always saw himself as God's representative and spokesman and medium. When they criticized him for this power, he attested his right by miracles. It was also his power to forgive sins that lent authority to his preaching and likewise declared that by his act God his Father had also forgiven the penitent. As Dr. Bond expresses it in *The Master Preacher:*

God had revealed himself in Jesus that man might have the blessing of forgiveness personalized and applied. Through this divine right Jesus caught the ear and heart of the sinner whom all other teachers had spurned and despised, but whom Jesus made the basis of his work. In two worlds his Word became supreme—the world of the penitent sinner and the world of the rejoicing saint.

At Calvary Jesus recognized the divine prerogative to forgive sinners when he prayed, "Father, forgive them; for they know not what they do" (Luke 23:34). In passing, it is striking that the *first* and *last* recorded sayings of Jesus begin with "Father" (see Luke 2:49; 23:46). No one else could have spoken these words, for they are utterly unlike anyone else. By *them* we understand both Jews and Gentiles, for both shared in his crucifixion (see Acts 4:26, 27). But what is meant by the words, "They know not what they do"? Jesus, speaking out of a divine consciousness, implied, "They do not know *who* it is that they are crucifying." Did not Paul substantiate this when he wrote, "Which none of the princes of this world knew: for had they known it, they would not have crucified the Lord of glory" (1 Cor. 2:8).

Christ's dying plea for the forgiveness of those humanly responsible for his death did not mean, "Take no notice, as though this sin of sins had not been committed." Had this been the implication of his prayer it would have been less than kind, for it would have been a plea for them to remain in sin and death. No, it was a supplication that God would open their eyes that they might discover the hideousness of their sin and, seeing it in its true light, might in a searching repentance, aided by God's grace, change in their hearts and seek forgiveness and restoration which the Savior longed should be theirs. While ignorance may mitigate the criminality of sin, it never exonerates it. F.W. Faber wrote:

> Jesus, Who to Thy Father prayed
> For those who all Thy Love repaid
> With this dread cup of woes—
> Teach me to conquer, Lord, like Thee,
> By patience and benignity,
> The thwarting of my foes.

In his teaching on *forgiveness*, Jesus made it plain that the exercise of such a divine prerogative to forgive depended upon the repentance of the penitent, even as the Old Testament taught. The transgressor had to admit his sorrow for sin and show that he meant to amend his ways (Josh. 24:19; Ps. 86:5; Jer. 5:1, 7). Once this had been done there was no hesitation on God's part to forgive (1 Kings 8:36, 56; Ps. 103:3). Thus, in his instruction in the art of forgiving, twice over Jesus said, "If he repent, forgive him" (Luke 17:3, 4). It has ever been his nature to forgive, but first those requiring his forgiving grace must repent (Luke 18:13; see Ezek. 33:11; Hos. 14:1). Without genuine repentance for sin there can be no divine forgiveness. Jesus went on to declare that within this condition no limit should be put on forgiveness even though it is required "until seventy times seven" (Matt. 18:21–35), a phrase meaning endlessly, or so often as it may be required.

Peter went beyond the current generosity of his day in respect to the limit of forgiveness. God denounced punishment on Damascus, Tyre, and Judah, in a formula always beginning, "For three transgressions of . . . and for four" (Amos 1, 2). This suggests that the nations had concluded in four transgressions the limit of forgiveness, but Peter went one better and asked if *seven times* would be the limit of forgiveness the Savior would approve. What Peter had to learn was that "forgive" means *forthgive*, that is, to *dismiss* absolutely from thought. Jesus suggests that he who really forgives does not keep count of the offenses pardoned. Some say they forgive but cannot forget. But they do not forgive if they do not forget, so far as any resentful memory is concerned. As Peter found it hard to enter into the spirit of this grace, Jesus added a parable to show our infinite obligation to forgive.

There had to be at all times the cultivation of the spirit of forgiveness, but only on the basis of repentance and confession. If we have not this spirit, then God will not hear or heed our prayers. Is this not the spirit Tennyson exhorts us to manifest:

> O Man, forgive thy mortal foe,
> Nor ever strike him blow for blow;
> For all the souls on earth that live
> To be forgiven must forgive—
> Forgive him seventy times and seven:
> For all the blessed souls in Heaven
> Are both Forgivers and Forgiven.

There is one sin, however, Jesus said a forgiving God cannot forgive. It is blasphemy against the Holy Spirit, known as the *unpardonable sin,* reference to which is found under the section, "About the Holy Spirit." Mark calls this "the eternal sin" (Matt. 12:31, 32; Mark 3: 28–30). For this particular sin, the sinner can never have forgiveness (Mark 3:29). The solemn words of Jesus regarding this tragic state were uttered after his clash with the Pharisees and in them he was referring to a condition of soul the Pharisees manifested by their words, actions, and attitude. As James N. Dow puts it in his *Gem Dictionary of the Bible:*

> In life their souls were dead; they were completely impervious to the influence of the Holy Spirit. Such a soul cannot possibly find its way back to the beginning and start again. It is, in fact, dead. God cannot forgive such a soul for such a soul is unable to receive and appreciate forgiveness. It has gone too far ever to return.

A HUMAN OBLIGATION

It will be further found that in his teaching Jesus emphasized the relationship between the two aspects of forgiveness, namely, God's forgiveness of man, and man's forgiveness of man. Passages like the following are most emphatic in this warning:

"If ye forgive men their trespasses, your heavenly Father will also forgive you: But if ye forgive not men their trespasses, neither will your Father forgive your trespasses" (Matt. 6:14–15).

"Forgive, and ye shall be forgiven" (Luke 6:37).

"Likewise shall my heavenly Father do also unto you, if ye from your hearts forgive not every one his brother their trespasses" (Matt. 18:35).

With this teaching of his Lord in mind, Paul likewise relates the two phases of forgiveness when writing to the Ephesians: "Forgiving one another, even as God for Christ's sake hath forgiven you" (Eph. 4:32). In two Parables, namely, the two debtors and the prodigal son (Matt. 18:21–35; Luke 15:11–24), Jesus sets forth the same related phases of forgiveness.

> Return my son,
> To thy Redeemer!—Died He not in love!—
> The sinless, the Divine, the Son of God—
> Breathing Forgiveness 'midst all agonies;
> And *We*,—dare we be ruthless?

At the heart of the teaching of Jesus then was the insistence that the human who would not forgive the human could never be forgiven of God. Nothing of this kind had been conceived in the world before, and Jesus enforced it in his parable about those who, having a proper estimate of the greatness of the forgiveness extended to themselves, would find it too difficut not to forgive—even their enemies. Forgive meant they would be compelled by love to forgive. Mutual forgiveness indicates the condition of the heart accepting divine forgiveness with humility. Both in the Lord's Prayer and in his instruction to Peter, Jesus seems to say, "How dare you ask God to forgive you when you refuse your forgiveness to a brother?"

God's forgiveness involves the restoration of happy relationships, but this is impossible if his children continue to harbor toward each other a spirit which is so much out of harmony with the spirit of him with whom is forgiveness that he might be feared. We must do to others as we wish God to do to us; if we refuse to forgive, our own forgiveness is denied (Matt. 18:21–35). If he was unwilling to forgive us, as we are to forgive those who offend us, we would never be saved. Forgiven himself, Stephen illustrated in his martyrdom how to emulate the divine example (Acts 7:60). Jesus made the forgiving spirit an antecedent to prayer, "When ye stand praying, forgive, if ye have ought against any" (Mark 11:25). This is what Stephen did. It would seem as if Jesus deemed an unforgiving spirit to be one of the most heinous of sins. As God sets the example of ready clemency, the child ought to imitate the Father (Matt. 5:45). Great stress is laid on forgiving injuries, of which Jesus cited three kinds: injury to the person (Matt. 5:39); loss of property (Matt. 5:40); defamation of character (Matt. 5:11).

Ever practical, Jesus gave instructions as to the steps to be taken in securing reconciliation, beginning with a private session to talk things over (Matt. 18:15–17). Every effort must be made to win the wrongdoer to repentance, and only when he has exhausted every effort may the effort be abandoned. The object of the brother seeking the restoration of his fellow believer is that of gaining him for the truth. The word *ought* Jesus constantly used is the Greek form of the verb for "owe." If forgiven by him, we are debtors to others in that we must manifest toward them the same magnanimity. "How much owest thou unto my Lord" (Luke 16:5)? We cannot measure the debt of gratitude we owe him for the forgiveness of our sins and then the debt we must discharge toward those who sin against us. Does not the sentiment of Longfellow make a fitting conclusion to the teaching and example of Jesus regarding the grace of forgiveness?

... Why shouldest thou hate then thy Brother?
Hateth he thee?—Forgive! For 'tis sweet to stammer one letter
Of the Eternal's language;—on earth it is called *Forgiveness.*
Knowest thou Him?—Who forgave, with the Crown of Thorns on His temples!
Earnestly praying for His foes, for His murderers,— say dost thou know *Him?*
Ah! thou confessest His name, so follow likewise His example!

BIBLE STUDY QUESTIONS

Take time to turn to each Scripture reference and mark the verse or a portion in your Bible.

1. What does forgiveness mean?

2. Discuss why Jesus never asked the Father for forgiveness.
3. How could Jesus forgive sins?
4. What is man's part in forgiveness?

— 11 —

Salvation

In the purpose of God, repentance should result in salvation. Made conscious of his need as a sinner, the repentant one must be brought to see the Savior, hanging on the tree for his emancipation from the thralldom of past sin and as his guarantee that sin shall not again have dominion over him. When the keeper of the prison was smitten with conviction by the manifestation of divine power in the great earthquake that shook the prison to its foundations, he came trembling before Paul and Silas, and cried, "Sirs, what must I do to be saved?" And the miracle happened, for the jailer rejoiced and believed in God with all his house (Acts 16:25–34).

That *salvation* was a topic dear to the heart of him who came to save is evident from the many references to it in his oral ministry. Jesus used the term *to save* about twenty-seven times, and *salvation* twice. The meaning of these evangelical terms is "integral in all his teaching, and is illustrated by his whole ministry." Dr. Graham Scroggie goes on to say in *A Guide to the Gospels* that "salvation is a central idea in which others meet, such as sin, repentance, faith, regeneration, justification, life, righteousness, and it stands in contrast to the ideas of lost, destruction, perish and death." The salvation Jesus came to provide for the lost he illustrated in his parables of the Pharisee and the publican, the lost sheep, the good shepherd, the good Samaritan, the great supper, and the wedding feast.

Before devoting ourselves to a study of what Jesus taught regarding the topic of *salvation,* it is necessary to take notice of three related terms he used and which in evangelical parlance are deemed to signify the same spiritual experience of a sinner when his is a heartfelt sorrow for sin, namely, *conversion, regeneration,* and *justification.* That these are not simply different words describing the initial work of grace in the soul is evident from an examination of them.

CONVERSION

Three times Jesus used the word *convert* in three different ways. First, it spoke of the character of his mission, "Lest at any time . . . they should be converted and I should heal them" (Matt. 13:15; Mark 4:12; John 12:40). In the second he employed the word in his teaching on humility, "Except ye be converted, and become as children" (Matt. 18:3). Then there is the reference to Peter's fall and recovery, "When thou art converted, strengthen thy brethren" (Luke 22:32).

In gospel crusades, numbers are given of *converts*, their "conversion" being reckoned as tantamount to their full surrender to the claims of Christ. But Peter was not one who needed a conversion of this order, for he was both a disciple and an apostle already and called *blessed* by Jesus because of his confession of his master's messiahship and deity. What, then, did Jesus mean when he said to Peter, "When thou art converted"? The word *convert* itself means to turn again. Peter, in his denial, followed Jesus afar off or turned away from him, so there came the assurance that when he had turned back to his forsaken Lord again, he would be able to forewarn others.

Conversion, then, is a human act and one that can be repeated many times. A truly regenerated person may backslide, but under the impulse of the Spirit slides back or returns to the Lord. When Jesus called those who were his chosen ones to be "converted," he was teaching them a lesson on the necessity of lowliness of heart and that, although grown men, they must turn back again to childlike innocency, trust, and guilelessness. Under conviction, a person may turn toward the Savior, "Turn thou me" (Jer. 31:18), but if the turned one is to be healed, the turning must result in faith and surrender.

Conversion is the movement of the soul toward grace; regeneration is the infusion of that grace within the soul. The sinner must be converted *unto the Lord* (Ps. 51:13). After an evangelistic campaign many of the so-called converts are seen and heard of no more or they may journey for awhile on the Christian pathway then disappear because, as Jesus put it in his parable of the sower, they do not have the *root* in themselves (Matt. 13:21). Their conversion is proven to be merely external, consisting only of a temporary profession. *Conversion* is the motion of the creature toward God, but *regeneration* is the motion of God within the creature whereby he becomes a new creature of creation, in Christ Jesus. Conversion is a human act, and one that can be repeated, but regeneration is a divine act that once accomplished can never occur again. "Whatsoever God doeth, it shall be for ever" (Eccles. 3:14).

REGENERATION

This term occurs only twice in the New Testament and in each case implies a *re-creation*. When our Lord said, "Ye which have followed me in the regeneration" (Matt. 19:28), he was referring to the re-creation of the social order and to the renewal of the earth when his kingdom comes (Isa. 11:6–9; Rom. 8:19–22). But when Paul used the same word in writing of "the washing of regeneration" (Titus 3:5), he was speaking of the new birth of a convicted, believing person born anew, "not of blood, nor the will of the flesh, nor of the will of man, but of God" (John 1:13). Through such a re-creation, the sinner becomes a son of God (John 1:12).

While Jesus did not use this evangelical term *regeneration* of a believing person, all that it represents in this connection was fully taught by him in his memorable night conversation with Nicodemus when he uttered his fiat: "Ye must be born again [or born anew]" (John 3:7). Man is born in sin and must be reborn if he is to enter the kingdom of heaven. "Except a man be born again— born from above—he cannot see the kingdom of heaven" (John 3:3). As the result of his departure from God, man became degenerated, and in order for him to be restored to fellowship with God he must be *re*generated. Comparing conversion with regeneration and other works of grace, we have these differences:

Conversion is our turning to the Lord; regeneration, his turning unto us to bring us into sonship.

Conversion is the expression of longing for life eternal; regeneration is the impartation of this life.

Further, regeneration differs from *adoption* in that the latter entitles us to heaven, while the former is a guarantee of heavenly bliss. Then there is the distinction between *justification* and *regeneration*—the former acquitting us from the charge of guilt, being effected by the obedience, death, and resurrection of Jesus; the latter being the work of the Holy Spirit. Comparison between these two acts of grace must be carefully defined.

Regeneration does not justify, nor does justification regenerate, although there cannot be the one without the other (see Titus 3:5–7). They are separate and distinct from each other in every respect, but inseparable, both occurring at the same time by the same act of faith. Justification cancels the guilt of the repentant sinner. Regeneration imparts a new nature, a spiritual resurrection into a new life. Other ways of expressing differences are as follows:

Regeneration is a change of nature; justification is pardon for sin.

Regeneration is a work done *within us;* justification is work done for us.

Regeneration is a change of *character;* justification is a change of *relationship.*

Regeneration shows God as *creator,* or *life-giver;* adoption shows him as a *loving Father.*

Justification leads us to think of him as a righteous yet merciful *Judge;* forgiveness reveals him as a sovereign or king, cancelling the past violation of his law.

At this point, a word or two may be fitting concerning God's act in declaring a person righteous and altogether free from the demands and penalty of his broken law.

JUSTIFICATION

This act or decree of God made in heaven whereby he alone declares a believing sinner righteous through the merits of a substitute was surely in the mind of Jesus in his parable of the Pharisee and the publican who went up to the Temple to pray (Luke 18:9–14). The Pharisee was at pains to justify himself, even as Jesus revealed more when he condemned the Pharisees as a whole for justifying themselves before men (Luke 16:15). Likewise the lawyer with whom Jesus dealt was "willing to justify himself" (Luke 10:29). But with the repentant, abased publican, it was different, for like other publicans he "justified God" (Luke 7:29). In contrast to the Pharisee, the publican had no righteousness of his own, no fasting, no tithing to present as a plea. The Pharisee prayed with *himself*, but the distressed publican, so smitten with contrition, would not lift up so much as his eyes to heaven. All that he could do was to cry in agony, "God, be merciful to me a sinner" (Luke 18:13).

The remarkable feature about this prayer that Jesus put into the lips of the publican is that the word *merciful* is that used of "the blood-sprinkled mercy-seat" (Lev. 16:5) and of "propitiation," Paul's great term (Rom. 3:25). So, as Dr. C. I. Scofield suggests, his prayer might be paraphrased, "Be toward me as thou art when thou lookest upon the atoning blood." This was why, as Jesus put it, "This man went down to his house justified *rather* than the other" (Luke 18:14). In this sentence Jesus declares a sinner righteous before God because of the substitutionary act of another. As the Westminster Catechism expresses it,

> Justification is an act of God's free grace wherein He pardoneth all our sins, and accepteth us as righteous in His sight, only for the righteousness of Christ imputed to us and received by faith alone.

Allied to this justification is *reconciliation* whereby enmity is exchanged for friendship (see Rom. 5:10, 11, margin). As the judge, God pardons and justifies; as the Father, he forgives and reconciles. In the evangelical realm, *justification* becomes ours by:

God (Rom. 3:26; 4:5; 8:33).
Christ (Gal. 2:16).
Grace freely (Rom. 3:24; Gal. 2:16).
Faith (Gal. 3:8).
His blood (Rom. 5:9).
His knowledge (Isa. 53:11).

All the gospel truths we have just mentioned are wrapped up in salvation, a topic so prominent in the teaching of Jesus.

SALVATION

Before Jesus became man, he knew how sin had left its serpent's trail upon men and that divine wrath rested upon a world of sinners; and it was because he heard the wail of the lost and as God the son was manifested in flesh, that all flesh might be saved. This is why that when we come to consider his ministry we find that in his teaching, *sin* and *salvation* were complementary terms, the prevalence of the former carrying with it the possibility of the latter. Jesus came into a lost woild, died, and rose again that abounding sin might give way to the more abundant salvation and grace.

Entering his brief but dynamic mission, Jesus caught up the slogan of John, his forerunner, *Repent ye!* and proclaimed it. In his thinking and teaching the need for repentance was as universal as the fact of sin and the provision of salvation.

Although he declared that "God so loved the world," he did not generalize in his teaching, which was always based on individualism. In his thought, the individual was the unit of salvation, as evidenced by his "whosoevers." We hear and read a great deal today about a social salvation and about the utopia of an ideal republic. But the individual is forgotten.

Jesus, however, came as an individual Savior to preach an individual evangel. This is why the bulk of his wonderful topics were presented to individuals and why he directed his appeal to the conscience of each person. Jesus made real the republic of God to each individual believer in whose heart and life the forces of good became operative and dominant. The simple heart of one man or woman gave him suitable audience. Fresh from his own heart, these truths came into the individual life of select men and women, creating new ideals and hopes and forming new character and destiny, as Nicodemus, the woman at the well, and others experienced.

The embodiment of salvation. In consideration of such a glorious, evangelical theme, it is important at the outset to realize that salvation is not *something* but *someone.* "Behold, God is my salvation." When godly, aged Simeon took up the child Jesus in his arms and looked at his sweet, innocent face, he said, "Lord, now lettest thou thy servant depart in peace, according to thy word: For mine eyes have seen the salvation" (Luke 2:29, 30). Having seen salvation personified in him who was born a Savior, Simeon wanted to go to heaven. Salvation, then, is not merely a spiritual gift that Jesus offers; it is *himself*

Further, his mission to save is embodied in his human name *Jesus,* which means, "Jehovah the Savior" (Matt. 1:21). Used as an acrostic, this peerless name spells our salvation:

> *J* esus
> *E* ternally
> *S* aves
> *U* s
> *S* inners

> *Call Him Jesus!* He shall save us
> From the tyranny of sin;
> From its condemnation save us,
> From iniquity within.

The doctrine of salvation. What, exactly, is the nature of this gift the giver is in himself? When Jesus said to Zacchaeus, "Today is salvation come to this house," it actually came in his person. Then he pronounced in no uncertain terms why he left the glory and took upon himself frail flesh. "The Son of man is come to seek and to save that which was lost" implied that Zacchaeus was one of the sinners in deep need of salvation (Luke 19:7, 9, 10). But what constituted such a salvation for this rich, prominent tax gatherer? It meant his recovery as a fallen man, from a state of sin and unbelief, his deliverance from condemnation and guilt, and his restoration to divine favor and holiness. No wonder Zacchaeus received Jesus joyfully!

Redemption is God's provision for man's emancipation from iniquity; *salvation* is the bringing

about or realization of such a deliverance. The
former is like making and equipping a lifeboat,
while the latter is like being rescued by means of
a lifeboat. Salvation, or being saved, in its evangelical sense signifies the work the Savior at once ac-
complishes in and for the sinner who yields to
him, and it includes forgiveness or pardon, regeneration, justification, and adoption. The list of our
salvation rights is formidable as a study of relevant passages reveals. Suffice it to say that Jesus,
by his finished work at Calvary, can save all who
believe from Satan and all his works (see Matt.
18:11). This was the truth Nicodemus learned
from the lips of Jesus, namely, that *redemption* is
the basis of regeneration and that a new creation
is only possible through the precious blood. Listening to Jesus as he spoke of the necessity of a re-
birth, the master of Israel asked, "How can these
things be?" Then Jesus said only through his being lifted up to die upon the cross as the manifestation of God's love for a lost world (John 3:9–16).

The necessity of salvation. Because all men are sinners, Jesus came not to destroy them but to save
them, not only from present sin, but from eternal
destruction which would be theirs if they died in
their sin. From his remarkable teaching given to
the woman at the well, it would seem as if those of
his own nation were only those in dire need of
salvation, for Jesus said, "Salvation is of the Jews"
(John 4:22). Godet, however, translates this
phrase as "Because salvation comes from the
Jews," meaning that through them salvation was
to come to the world. Jesus himself, who came as

the Savior of the world, was a Jew, and his apostles, who were so wonderfully used in the salvation of multitudes in the early days of the church, were Jews. "It was at Jerusalem that the living God has made himself known: and that it is by means of the Jews that he intends to give salvation to the world."

Both Jews and Gentiles are born in sin, for the whole world is guilty before God, and *all* have sinned and come short of his glory and must be saved if they are to escape eternal woe for their sin. It is thus that Jesus, in himself, is the only light to lighten the Gentiles and the only glory of his people Israel (Luke 2:32). The jailer recognized the necessity of salvation when he cried, "What *must* I do to be saved?' But Paul had an immediate answer, "Believe on the Lord Jesus Christ, and thou shalt be saved" (Acts 16:30, 31). Would that the masses of godless men and women today could be made conscious of the imperative need of God's matchless saving grace and power (Luke 3:6).

The conditions of salvation. As used here *condition* means something necessary to, yet not the cause of, a certain result. God is willing and able to save sinners, but there are things they must do before the gift of salvation becomes theirs. What is the use of his being the horn of salvation (Luke 1:69) unless we appropriate him as such and drink out of such a horn? If, as Jesus said, he is "the door," and it is only as we enter into him that we can be saved, then it is useless to stand outside the door. Entrance is the condition of salvation (John 10:9).

If he is "the Truth," then it is only as we receive his testimony that we can be saved (John 5:34).

The *first* condition of salvation is *repentance,* which, as we have already shown, involves a deep conviction of sin when the penitent one sees himself to be guilty of sin before God and deserving of punishment. Unless there is contrition for sin, and the willingness to renounce a sinful past coupled with a full confession of sin to God, the salvation he offers cannot be given. All of this is what Jesus taught in his parable of the prodigal son.

The *second* condition is *faith,* the only ground or foundation of which is the death and resurrection of Jesus. While repentance and faith are the conditions required of the sinner who would be saved (Mark 1:15), the procuring cause of salvation is the redeeming work of Christ (John 3:16). "He that believeth on the Son hath everlasting life" (John 3:36). When a sinner is urged to exercise faith in Christ for salvation, and says he cannot believe, he must be reminded that even the faith, like the salvation, is the gift of God (Eph. 2:8). God gives to all the power to believe, but the act of believing is the sinner's own, just as the power to walk is God's gift, though walking is man's own act.

Faith, which is belief or trust, may be either faith with understanding, often called "intellectual faith," or faith in action, referred to as "practical faith" or "heart faith." *Intellectual faith* is believing some*thing* with the mind; *Heart faith* is the act of trusting some*one*. A sick man exercises the former kind when he believes that his doctor is able to cure or relieve him; he manifests the latter kind when he trusts or commits himself to the doctor's advice and treatment. In his parable of the sower, Jesus spoke of the Devil taking the word out of the hearts of those who hear it, "lest they should believe [with their hearts] and be saved" (Luke 8:12). It is possible to believe with the mind all the Bible says, yet lack saving faith. The demons, James described, had intellectual faith, for they believed what the Bible taught—and trembled— but were unable to manifest saving faith (James 2:19).

The woman who was a sinner, and who by her actions displayed contrition and repentance, re- vealed *intellectual faith,* for she knew who Jesus was, and also *saving faith,* for he said to her, "Woman, thy faith hath saved thee" (Luke 7:50). Saving faith, then, is that act of personal heart- trust by which the sinner commits himself to God and accepts as his own the salvation God so freely offers. Blind Bartimaeus was another who exer- cised both kinds of faith and had the joy of hear- ing Jesus say, "Thy faith hath made thee whole" (Mark 10:52; see 9:23, 24).

It would seem as if Jesus added a *third* condition for salvation, for when he commissioned his disci- ples to go out into all the world and preach the gospel to every creature, he said, "He that believ- eth *and is baptized* shall be saved" (Mark 16:16). This does not imply that if a sinner repents of his sin and by faith accepts Christ as his personal Sav- ior, yet fails to be baptized, that he is not saved, for Paul distinctly says, "By grace are ye saved through faith" (Eph. 2:8). If baptism is essential to salvation then the dying thief who repented and believed, was not saved. Barnes in his *New Testament* commentary explains:

> Jesus did not say that a man *could not* be saved without baptism, but he has strongly implied that where this is neglected, *knowing it to be a command of the Saviour*, it endangers the salvation of the soul. *Faith* and *Baptism* are the beginnings of a Christian life; the one the beginning of piety *in the soul*, the other of its manifestation *before men*, or a profession of religion.

The sacrament of baptism provides an outward and visible sign of inward grace and represents the grafting into the body of the regenerated one. Baptism by immersion portrays identification with Christ in his death, burial, and resurrection (see 1 Cor. 12:13; Rom. 6:3–10; Col. 2:12). While not an essential condition to salvation, baptism is essential to obedience to Jesus who left us an example in his own baptism that we should follow his steps. Throughout the early church, baptism was an accompaniment of salvation. The rite of baptism practiced by John the Baptist was a baptism unto repentance, but Jesus who was baptized by John had no sin to repent of. Nevertheless, his act identified him with those he had come to save. With him, baptism was a symbol of self-dedication in purity of heart to the service of God, the symbols of the dove and the voice assuring Jesus that the Spirit of the Lord was upon him as he commenced his great task as the Savior of the world.

The tenses of salvation. Phrases like "abundant salvation," "full salvation," "save to the uttermost" (Heb. 7:25), imply developing phases, aspects, or tenses of salvation. A simple hymn expresses it:

Jesus saves me all the time,
Jesus saves me now.

Did he himself not say, "He that endureth unto the end shall be saved"? (Matt. 10:22; 24:13, 22). Jesus came to provide, not only life, but life more abundant (John 10:10). We must not limit salvation to what is accomplished when, in the hour of decision for Christ, we received him as our personal Savior. This evangelical term has a wider meaning, signifying a daily and full deliverance from sin and its consequences, until redeemed in soul *and body,* we are taken into heaven. A drowning man at sea is *saved* when pulled into a lifeboat, but in a fuller sense his salvation includes a daily recovery from exhaustion and injury, the necessity of food and clothing, and conveyance to and housing on shore. So a sinner is *saved* when forgiven and accepted by God; in another sense he is *being saved* all the time until *finally saved* in heaven. Thus a believer is one

Who has been saved—*Past:* Penalty of Sin.

Is being saved—*Present:* Power of Sin.

Has yet to be saved—*Prospective:* Presence of sin.

Paul, who was deeply immersed in all the topics the Master taught, and who is still the unrivaled expositor of them, dearly loved the doctrine of salvation Jesus proclaimed. As a servant of the most high God, Paul lived only to declare the way of salvation, which he did with marvelous results. This Christ-honoring apostle rings the changes on the three tenses of salvation in his Roman Epistle.

Past tense. In verses Romans 1:14–16, Paul gives us a trio of *I am's,* the last being, "I am not ashamed of the gospel of Christ: for it is the power of God unto salvation to every one that believeth." Salvation, then, is a gift we receive the moment we accept, by faith, the Lord Jesus as our personal Savior. This is a salvation from *the penalty of sin.* Convicted by the Holy Spirit of our sin, and of our consequent condemnation, for "the soul that sinneth it shall die," and through our reception of the crucified, risen Lord, our guilty past was blotted out. Then came the assurance that God would remember our sins against us no more forever, and so reconciled to God through the Savior, we were able to sing:

'Tis done, the great transaction's done,
I am my Lord's, and He is mine.

Thereafter, we could confess, "Praise God, I am saved!" Yes, and once saved in this way, we are saved forever, for such a salvation embracing regeneration, justification, and adoption can never be repeated. One may lose the joy of such a salvation for a little, but never the divinely wrought salvation itself, for we have been saved with "an everlasting salvation in the Lord," as Isaiah expresses it. This, therefore, is the initial feature of the salvation so freely offered to the sinner, the reception of which blots out his past sins.

For nothing can untwine
Thy life from mine.

Present tense. When God saves a person and banishes the guilt behind him, he does not take away from him any possibility of sinning. The old nature is not eradicated but remains. The believing sinner, however, is made the recipient of a new nature, hence the constant conflict Paul reminds us of in the phrase, "When *I* [saved Paul] would do good, evil [the old Saul of Tarsus] is with me." The *penalty* of sin, associated with the past, has been banished, but the *power* of sin remains, and thus salvation is necessary from the government of sin and is promised in the declaration of victory. "Sin shall not have dominion over you." So, although I can say, "I have been saved," I can also say, "I am being saved." This is the salvation we show forth day by day in victory over the world, the flesh, and the Devil.

But how is this daily salvation made possible? In the fifth chapter of Romans, we have a remarkable passage, the import of which all too few saved sinners understand. "For if, when *we were* enemies, we were reconciled to God by the death of his Son"—salvation in its past tense, a salvation effected by the sacrifice of the cross—"much more, *being* reconciled [or being saved], we *shall be saved* by his life" (Rom. 5:10). Here we have a twofold salvation—one by *his death,* the other by *his life.* This latter aspect cannot refer to Christ's earthly life. We hear a good deal about living like Jesus, but there is no salvation through mere imitation. No, the words, *his life*, refer to his present life, his risen, glorified, throne life in heaven. Because he is alive forever more and all power has been given unto him, he is able to save us moment by moment from sin's seductive snares. Appropriating his risen life, we can be more than conquerors. The question then is, Although saved, are we being saved?

> Love's resistless current sweeping
> All the regions deep within,
> Thought, and wish, and senses keeping
> *Now,* and *every instant,* clean
> Full salvation!
> From the guilt and power of sin.

Prospective tense. Blessedly saved and continuously saved, we yet live in a sinful world with its insistent temptation to sin. Saved from the *penalty* of sin and daily saved from the *power* of sin, we need to be saved from the *presence* of sin and such an aspect has been provided in him who is our salvation. Dealing with the return of Jesus for those saved by grace, Paul reminds us that if we can read the signs of the time, then we must bestir ourselves from spiritual lethargy, for "Now is our salvation *nearer* than when we believed" (Rom. 13:11). Did we not receive salvation when we first believed? Yes. Do we not receive salvation as we keep on believing? Yes. Then what salvation is this Paul says is *nearer*? The answer is that Jesus who in himself is our salvation is nearer the rapture than when we received him as our Savior.

When he does "appear the second time without

sin unto salvation," he will gather his truly saved ones around him and remove them from the entire presence of sin. Then, "the church will be saved to sin no more." Receiving us unto himself he will translate us to a sinless world in which we shall be perfectly holy and in no further need of salvation. What a great salvation God has provided us with, and because it was purchased at such tremendous cost, and confers so many blessings to cover our past, present, and future, we dare not neglect it (Heb. 2:3). For sinners who deliberately neglect it, there is no escape. Escape from what? Jesus warned sinners against the eternal condemnation if they died in their sin, rejecting his proffered salvation (John 8:24).

BIBLE STUDY QUESTIONS

Take time to turn to each Scripture reference and mark the verse or a portion in your Bible.

1. Compare and contrast conversion, regeneration, and justification.
2. What is salvation and what does it include?
3. What conditions accompany salvation?
4. Discuss briefly the three tenses of salvation.

— 12 —

Righteousness

All the truths enunciated by Jesus were, first of all, experienced by him who came as the personification of truth. "I am . . . the Truth." Thus, when he exhorted those around him to "search the Scriptures," meaning, of course, the Old Testament portion of the Bible, he was only urging others to do something he had daily joy in doing. He was able to expound unto his disciples in *all* the Scriptures the things concerning himself because his mind was saturated with every phase of truth they presented. The virtue we are now to deal with is a case in point, for *righteousness*, divine and human, pervades the Old Testament, and Jesus knew it to be one of its most prominent ideas.

In the Gospels, Jesus is before us as one with a passion for righteousness which may be called "a peculiarly Hebrew instinct." In his Sermon on the Mount, *righteousness* is seen to be one of the elements of blessedness, for after expounding his Beatitudes, Jesus returns to *righteousness* and makes it the text of his ensuing discourse. His

characteristic phrase, "Hungering and thirsting after righteousness," is but another way of saying,
"Blessed is he that doeth righteousness" (Ps.
106:3). Jesus not only "preached righteousness to
the congregation," he was the paragon of such a
virtue. Although in Bible usage *justification* is the
act of pronouncing one righteous, seeing the literal root of the word *justification* is to "make righteous," *righteousness* as used by Jesus not only implied this significance but also included rightness
according to the divine standard, or conformity
to the will and nature of God himself.

From our Lord's teaching on *righteousness* both
its religious and practical aspects are emphasized.
Not only was it a term he used for the behavior of
man to man, but also one indicating the prize of
the favorable verdict of God on a man's character
and conduct. Through grace, made righteous, the
believer must live and act righteously. The root
idea of *righteousness* is "right"—right before God
and right before men—and it is used this way by
Jesus (Matt. 20:4–7; Luke 12:57). Whoever is
right with God is, or should be, righteous in all his
ways. It has been pointed out that in the teaching
of Jesus the word *righteousness* and its cognates are
also translated *just,* five times (e.g., Matt. 5:45);
righteous, eighteen times (e.g., Luke 5:32); *justify,*
four times (e.g., Matt. 11:19); *judge,* once (e.g.,
Luke 12:14); *righteousness,* eight times (e.g., John
16:8, 10).

It is from these various terms Jesus used that
we are able to discover that righteousness em-
braces *morality,* or man's relation to men, and *religion,* or man's relation to God.

GOD IS THE ABSOLUTE RIGHTEOUSNESS

Absolute in *holiness*, God cannot be anything else but absolute in righteousness. Jesus called God, *righteous Father*, a term corresponding to the Old Testament revelation of his righteousness, "The righteous God" (Ps. 7:8, 11). "The Lord God of Israel is righteous" (Ezra 9:15). This also coincides with the Pauline phrase, "The righteousness of God" (2 Cor. 5:21; Phil. 3:8, 9). As the source and sum of righteousness, God is just and righteous in all his ways, as Jesus often confirmed.

CHRIST WAS ALWAYS RIGHT IN HIS JUDGMENT OF ALL THINGS

Had he not been the sinless one, Jesus' claim, "My judgment is just [or righteous]" (John 5:30), would have been arrogant assumption. To him, righteousness meant being *right* in all things, God ward and manward. Jesus fulfilled *all* righteousness and urged *all* to follow him in such a virtue (Matt. 3:15). God made him to be our *righteousness*, and actually the "righteousness of God" *is* Christ, not his obedience to the Father, but himself (1 Cor. 1:30). Righteousness then is not only a policy and mode of practice but a *person*, and we become the righteousness of God in him (2 Cor. 5:21). As the righteous one, Jesus alone can make a sinner right with God, as he is made righteous by faith (Rom. 4:3; Gal. 3:6). Those who are *right* have repented of their sins (Matt. 9:13). Isaiah spoke of the Lord clothing him with "the robe of righteousness" (Isa. 61:10), and when Paul speaks about "putting on the Lord Jesus Christ" (Rom. 13:14), he infers that the believer is one who is clothed with divine righteousness. Count Zinzendorf expresses this wonderful truth in his great hymn on such righteousness:

> Jesus, Thy blood and righteousness
> My beauty are, my glorious dress;
> Midst flaming worlds, in these arrayed,
> With joy shall I lift up my head.
>
> His spotless robe the same appears,
> When ruined nature sinks in fears;
> No age can change its glorious hue;
> Its glory is for ever new.

THE HOLY SPIRIT CAME TO CONVINCE THE WORLD OF WHAT WAS RIGHT

In his teaching concerning the threefold work of the Holy Spirit toward the world, Jesus said when the Spirit came, as he did at Pentecost as the gift of the Father and of the Son, that he would convict the world "of sin, of righteousness, of judgment" (John 16:8–11).

It will be noted that Jesus gave righteousness the middle position, or as the intermediate one between the two others, signifying, as Godet observes, "*righteousness* applying itself to *sin* to produce *judgment*." Ever since Pentecost the Spirit has been active, convicting sinful and unjust men of the necessity of the new birth to make them holy and righteous. To quote Godet again:

Thus by the testimony of the Spirit the world, righteous in its own eyes, will be declared sinful; the condemned malefactor will be proved righteous; and the true author of this crime will receive his irrevocable sentence. Such are the three ideas contained in this passage, whose powerful originality it is impossible not to recognize.

HUMANITY IS DIVIDED INTO TWO CLASSES

A distinctive feature of the teaching of Jesus was his way of classifying different types of men. For instance, he described those who were *wrong* (Matt. 23:28, 29, 35), and those who were *right* (Matt. 5:45; 13:17, 41, 43. Men may not like these clearly defined classes; yet they are in one or the other group. Further, Jesus spoke of *right* as a virtue implying *wrong*. All householders were not righteous, but Jesus, as the perfect hirer of laborers for his vineyard, assures them, "Whatsoever is right I will give you . . . Whatsoever is right, that shall ye receive" (Matt. 20:4, 7).

WRONG PEOPLE OFTEN IMAGINE THEY ARE RIGHT

That this was the sin of the Pharisees is evident from our Lord's constant condemnation of their self-righteousness. The ruling idea of his Sermon on the Mount was *righteousness*. The kingdom he spoke of was inwardly one of righteousness as its outstanding character. The whole of his discourse is taken up with this theme in contrast, not only with habits of living, but also with traditional maxims. As Professor Stalker states in *The Ethic of Jesus*, "Through the Sermon on the Mount, from first to last, there runs a strain of the most passionate moral earnestness. Never elsewhere in the world has there been taught so inward or difficult a morality; but it was to be the high prerogative of the Kingdom of God to realise it." Continuing his piquant contrasts, Jesus warned, "Take heed that ye do not pour righteousness before men, to be seen of them" (Matt. 6:1). True Christian righteousness is first inward. The so-called righteousness of the scribes and Pharisees was external, but that which Jesus taught was internal. The righteousness of those he exposed was made up of ostentatious words and actions; his righteousness we are to earnestly seek flows from the innermost thoughts and feelings. Those who trusted, not in God, but in themselves, had a conventional righteousness, that is, a brand intended only for the eye of society, but Christ's was a righteousness of the conscience, having regard only for God's eye.

The Pharisees were taken up with an outward show of righteousness and were the wrong people who imagined they were right, hence, the appeal of Jesus, "Except your righteousness shall exceed the righteousness of the scribes and Pharisees, ye shall in no case enter into the kingdom of heaven" (Matt. 5:20). The rest of the Sermon on the

Mount is actually an exposition of this verse, the righteousness required of Christians being contrasted first with that prescribed in the Mosaic Law and the traditional exposition of that law (Matt. 5:21–48), with contemporary Pharisaic custom (Matt. 6:1–18), and with the ordinary course of this world (Matt. 6:19 to the end of the sermon).

Repeatedly Jesus exposed the so-called *right* of the *wrong* Pharisees as having been manufactured. Their goodness was not derived from a living nature, the beauty of which is originally connected with the root from which it springs. The paraded words and deeds of the Pharisees appeared to be good, but their hearts were corrupt. They "justified themselves," were "highly esteemed among men but an abomination in the sight of God," "trusted in themselves that they were righteous, and despised others," and were not as "other men are" (Luke 10:29; 16:15; 18:9, 11, 14). The sermon of Jesus excited his avowed enemies to anger, not only because of his truly righteous life, but because he told them in no uncertain terms that righteousness must be an experience and not identified with ceremonials. If they would enter the kingdom their Pharisaism must vanish, and as sinners they must have the righteousness imputed and imparted. They must "seek his righteousness." As a teacher, Jesus demanded a height of character and attainment never even dreamed of by Moses and the prophets. He never abrogated their teachings but sharpened the edge of every precept and enlarged the scope of every principle they set forth.

THOSE WHO YEARN TO BE RIGHT CAN BE RIGHT

Jesus made it clear that the publican who could only cry, "God be merciful to me a sinner," went home *justified* rather than the Pharisee who exalted himself to such a degree as to say that he was not as low, morally, as "this publican." But yearning to be right with God, the publican found the true righteousness which the Pharisee never did because he trusted in himself that he was righteous and he despised others (Luke 18:9–14). Among the *Blesseds* of Jesus is, "Blessed are they which do hunger and thirst after righteousness; for they shall be filled [with him who is our righteousness]" (Matt. 5:6). All who yearn to be *right* before God, and are made *right*, exercise judgment of others which is right: "Judge not according to the appearance, but judge righteous judgment" (John 7:24).

Our preeminent duty, then, is to pursue that which is *right* in God's sight, even as Jesus taught, "Seek ye first the kingdom of God, and his righteousness" (Matt. 6:33). In this compelling exhortation Jesus returns to a similar one in his wonderful sermon where he instructed his own: "Lay not up for yourselves treasures on earth, where moth and rust doth corrupt, and where thieves break through and steal" (Matt. 6:19).

Those who are the Father's children must aspire to higher things—treasures in heaven—immortal pleasures of the immortal soul. They must seek, not visible wealth, but God's kingdom and

God's righteousness. What is the difference between these two eternal treasures? God's *kingdom* represents his rule, blessing, acceptance, protection, and salvation. God's *righteousness* is God's character, God's life in the soul; God the Son himself was made our righteousness, and we are to incarnate the righteousness of the kingdom.

Notice must be taken of the adjective Jesus used, *first,* meaning preceding all others. What a man endeavors to secure *first,* and chiefly, mirrors his essential character. Paul could say, "For me to live is Christ." What a man puts after "For me to live is ——," shapes his life and determines his destiny. Many perish through putting God's kingdom and his righteousness *second* in order of time. They fail to put first things *first.* Their argument is "Let us first do this or gain that, then we will seek God's kingdom." Others perish from placing the concerns of God second in order of importance. Yet if God is given the *first* place in every phase of life, then all that is necessary to life is *added,* or thrown into the bargain. If all that concerns God is our *first* concern, then all that concerns us will be his chief concern. Jesus left his own in no doubt regarding the price we must be prepared to pay if he, our righteousness, is first in all things. "Blessed are they which are persecuted for righteousness' sake: for theirs is the kingdom of heaven" (Matt. 5:10).

> Seek this first—Be pure and holy
> Like the Master, meek and lowly;
> Yielded to His service wholly:
> Seek this first.

BOTH THE RIGHT AND THE WRONG WILL BE ULTIMATELY RECOMPENSED

Jesus spoke of a coming judgment when he will sit upon the throne of his glory to reveal who are right and who are wrong. The latter, not clothed in His righteousness, and therefore not conspicuous in righteous acts, go away into *everlasting punishment,* but the righteous in heart and action pass into *life eternal* (Matt. 25:31–46). As the Master sent the twelve forth to preach, teach, and heal, among the assurances they were cheered by was, "He that receiveth a righteous man in the name of a righteous man shall receive a righteous man's reward" (Matt. 10:41; Luke 14:14). What a day that will be when our *Jehovah Tsidkenu* returns for those made righteous by God in Christ who came the first time as the personification and perfection of righteousness!

> When clothed in His brightness transported I rise,
>   To meet Him in clouds of the sky,
> His perfect salvation, His wonderful love,
>   I'll shout with the millions on high.

BIBLE STUDY QUESTIONS

Take time to turn to each Scripture reference and mark the verse or a portion in your Bible.

1. Why is righteousness in our lives important?
2. What is the relation of righteousness to each of the Godhead?

3. Contrast God's and man's views of righteousness.

4. What is the hope of the one who wants to be right?

Part III

— 13 —

Faith and Faithfulness

We group these two excellent virtues together seeing that the one results in the other. *Faithful* means "full of faith in," and "loyalty to," the one in whom our faith reposes for salvation and sustenance. When Paul wrote of "the faith of God" (Rom. 3:3) and of "the faith of Jesus Christ" (Gal. 3:22), the Greek word he used for "faith" was *pistos*, meaning, "fidelity," and thus the Revised Version gives "faithfulness" in these references. The margin of the Revised Version gives us, "the just shall live by his faithfulness" (Hab. 2:4). Whether we think of the major or minor topics Jesus taught, we cannot but be amazed at their wide range. His teaching reached all limits of our life Godward and also in respect to human conduct. It will be found that he gave the guiding principle for life in its varied responsibilities and duties, and what he taught about that principle is deathless.

FAITH

The Bible uses a trio of terms to express the same act of man, namely *faith, believe, trust.* The first occurs over twenty times in the Gospels; the second, some one hundred twenty-five times, with John giving us ninety references out of this number; the third, some nine times. Outside the four Gospels, these three terms are used hundreds of times.

Faith is the noun for "believe" and is a word with a noble heritage. From the Latin *fides,* it came to mean the sense of personal honor and mutual loyalty attaching to the pledged word. For the believer, it implies steadfast adherence to Jehovah's word, a passive fidelity becoming an *active* faith to live by.

Believe suggests trust and confidence and is the word used by John more than anyone else. John only employed the noun *faith* once (1 John 5:4).

Trust carries the idea of taking refuge in, or leaning upon. When used of Jesus it is most suggestive. "He trusted in God" (Matt. 27:43). At all times, especially in his darkest hours, Jesus found refuge in, or leaned upon, his heavenly Father. The New Testament conception of this term is that of *trust* in a person, in his word and promise, then *mutual trust,* or the expression thereof in troth or pledge.

We live by *faith* in our ordinary lives. Daily we manifest faith, belief, trust. Professor James Stalker reminds us in *The Ethic of Jesus:*

> Although faith is a theological term and is of incessant occurrence in the language of religion, it is, nevertheless, in the first place a purely human act; it is an element in ordinary life, without which the world could not go on for a single day. Every hour we are performing acts of faith towards our fellow

men, as well as acts of disbelief; and, if we analyze what faith toward man is, we shall obtain a key to the question of what faith towards God or Christ is. It is entirely in accord with the mind of Christ to look upon the life of faith toward men as a school in which to acquire a knowledge of faith on a higher level.

For an understanding of all the implications of *faith*, it is necessary to study the Bible as a whole. Our purpose in these volumes is to examine what Jesus taught on any given topic or theme. As to the subject before us, he distinguished between *faith*, as representing belief and trust in himself, and *faith* as the body of revealed truth, or Christianity, or the Christian faith. In his parable of the unjust judge, Jesus said, "When the Son of man cometh will he find *the* faith on the earth" (Luke 18:8, RV, margin). He will find plenty of faith in false cults and religious systems, but *the* faith is already a scarce commodity in a world of growing apostasy. *The* faith is that which Jude says we must "earnestly contend for . . . which was once delivered unto the saints" (Jude 3). The word *faith*, together with the corresponding verb *believe*, has in the teaching of Jesus a remarkable variety of meanings.

The chief elements of this Christian faith are the death, burial, and resurrection of Jesus; that in dying he atoned for human sin and in rising he abolished death, and that faith in "the word of the cross" is at the same time "the word of faith" (Rom. 10:8; 1 Thess. 4:14; Col. 1:5, 13). We recognize that in some verses "the faith" may, and doubtless does, refer to doctrine; yet this is not always a necessary inference since it is rather the rule that, in Greek, abstract nouns take the article, even when that article cannot be expressed in English. But even so, when doctrine is called "the faith," as by Jude for example, it is because faith in God is back of it.

The nature of faith. Many and varied are the answers to the question, What is faith? *Faith* is believing, and *believing*, we trust. Faith in God is believing all he has declared, accepting his word as true, and trusting him to fulfill all he has promised. Dr. R. A. Torrey states in *What the Bible Teaches:*

> To believe God is to rely upon or have unhesitating assurance of the truth of God's testimony, even though it is unsupported by any other evidence, and to rely upon and have unfaltering assurance of the fulfillment of his promises, even though everything seems against fulfillment.

Trust is the result of faith. It steps out upon God because it believes him. It commits to God and rests there, happy because it does not have a thought that he will fail. This is the sentiment resident in Jesus' exhortation, "Have faith in God" (Mark 11:22). Such *faith* is our side of union with him and is our means of possessing all his benefits—pardon, justification, holiness, life, peace, and glory. The Gospels make it clear that contact with Jesus gave to the words *faith* and *believe* a greatly increased use and heightened potence. Thus "believing" meant to Jesus' disciples more than before since they now had him to believe in; and *believers*, "they that had believed," became a standing name for his followers (Acts 2:44; Rom. 10:4, etc.).

Old Testament *faith* is backward looking to

Egypt and the Exodus, while the New Testament *faith* is forward looking to the kingdom. Where the Old Testament is saying, "Believe that it will happen yet," the New Testament is saying, "Believe that it has happened," which it did in the coming of Jesus as the Messiah. Peter, believing this, was called *blessed* by Jesus (Matt. 16:16–17).

The degrees of faith. When Paul wrote of God dealing to every man "the measure of faith" (Rom. 12:3), the apostle did not imply that God measured out more faith to some than others. Paul was dealing with Christian service and with the idea that members of Christ's body "have gifts differing according to the grace that is given." But the teaching of Jesus recognizes varying degrees of faith, with some around him manifesting more faith than others.

"*According* to your faith be it unto you" (Matt. 9:29). The greater the faith, the greater experience of his power.

"Lord, *increase* our faith" (Luke 17:5). With its increase there came the increase of trust in him and a daily increase of desire to serve him. Here are some of the phrases arresting our minds in his teaching about *faith:* "great faith" (Matt. 8:10; 15:28; Luke 7:9); "little faith" (Matt. 6:30; 8:26; 14:31; 16:8; Luke 12:28).

It may be as small as a grain of mustard seed, but the virtue of faith consists, not in itself, but in the fact that it gives God his opportunity. "No faith" (Mark 4:40); "faithless" (John 20:27), or less, empty of faith. "Full of faith" (Acts 6:8) is God's ideal for every child of faith. Which degree of faith is ours? The Bible gives the best definition of *faith* ever coined: "Now faith means putting our full confidence in the things we hope for, it means being certain of things we cannot see" (Heb. 11:1-3, Phillips trans).

The object of faith. Scripture has much to say about false and wrong objects of trust and confidence. Many trusted in idols of their own creation (Ps. 115:8). Others trusted in their horses and chariots or in their riches. But a strong faith in a false object cannot save, whereas even a weak faith—"Lord, I believe, help thou my unbelief"—in a right object can accomplish mighty things. As Wordsworth asks,

> Who the line
> Shall draw, the limits of the power define,
> That was imperfect Faith to man affords?

1. *God as object of faith.* Sayings like "Have faith in God" and "Ye believe in God" reveal how Jesus directed the faith of men toward his Father as the supreme object of their trust, and therefore such faith becomes the underlying grace for everything that is pleasing to God. Enoch "pleased God. But without faith it is impossible to please him" (Heb. 11:5, 6). This is the reason Satan strives to undermine the believer's faith in God by bringing in doubt, worry, anxiety, and the like, to hinder the believer's close fellowship with God. Because of all God is in himself, faith in him is never misplaced or disappointed. Coming to God, we "must believe that he *is* [all Scripture declares him to be], and that he is a rewarder of them that diligently seek him" (Heb. 11:6).

2. *Christ as object of faith.* Greatly perturbed over

the announcement of the coming departure of Jesus, the distressed disciples listened to words that have comforted myriads down the ages, "Let not your heart be troubled: ye believe in God, *believe also in me*" (John 14:1). Here Jesus places himself on the level of equality with God and deems such equality no robbery (Phil. 2:6). Therefore, equal with God, Jesus claimed equal faith and confidence, and no faith in God is valid unless there be a corresponding faith in Jesus who came as the culmination of the revelation of his father. The Son was "in the Father, and the Father in" the Son (John 14:11). Professor Adolph Von Harnack says that while Jesus preached *faith*, it was a faith toward God, not toward himself. But his statement, "Believe also in me," proves that he did direct faith toward himself, as well as toward God.

Christ, then, is also the supreme object of faith and of salvation by his grace. What a volume of evangelical truth is condensed for us by Paul in his gospel creed: "*Repentance* toward God, and *faith* toward our Lord Jesus Christ" (Acts 20:21). Says Stalker in *The Ethic of Jesus*, "Faith is, at the core, not the acceptance of beliefs or dogmas, but a relation or bearing towards Christ himself—a transaction between person and person." As we study all that Jesus said about believing in him, we cannot but conclude that *faith* was his chief and incessant demand from those who listened to his teaching, which, as it advanced, suggested that he required unparalleled faith, not so much in his miracle works, producing a "miracle-faith," but in *himself*, along with the message he taught.

As the author and finisher of faith (Heb. 12:2),

the mission of Jesus was a constant appeal for faith, with his own person as its chief ground and matter, as John emphasizes most strikingly in his *apology* for his great gospel: "These are written, that ye might *believe* that Jesus is the Christ, . . . and that believing ye might have life in his name" (John 20:31). After concentrating on *himself* the faith of men, giving to faith thereby a new heart and energy, Jesus finally fastens that faith upon his *death;* he marks this event for the future as the object of the specifically *saving* faith. Thus, to Paul, Christian faith was to "believe that Jesus died and rose again" (1 Thess. 4:14). All "who received him" (John 1:12) and who "believed on his name" in a complete sense, came to experience that faith acquired a scope undreamed of before; it signified the unique attachment to the Person of Jesus—a human trust, in its purity and intensity such as no other man had ever effected, which grew up into and identified itself with the possessor's belief in God, transforming the latter in doing so, and which drew the whole being of the believer into the will and life of his Master. This must have been the kind of faith that Long-fellow had in mind when he wrote:

> Faith is enlightened Hope; She is Light, is the eye of affection:
> Dreams of the longings interprets, and carves their visions in marble.
> Faith is the Sun of Life, and her countenance shines like the Hebrew's,
> For She has looked upon God! The heaven on its stable foundation
> Draws She with chains down to the earth.

The power of faith. Mark gives the dual aspect of the effect of faith: "Father, all things are possible to thee" (Mark 14:36). "All things are possible to him that believeth" (Mark 9:23). The former is the guarantee of the latter. What a mighty spiritual upheaval there would be in our personal lives, and collectively in the church, if only we could live under the impact of these two pertinent sayings of Jesus! The physical cures and spiritual blessings he distributed were conditioned by the one requirement, *Only believe!* How slow we are to learn that God is seeking those who will dare to believe him for great things in order that he may do great things with and through them!

> Expect great things from God,
> Attempt great things for God.

We can link on to the above passage the teaching of Jesus in which he recommended believing prayer, "All things whatsoever ye shall ask in prayer, *believing,* ye shall receive." We must also believe that he is able to perform the miraculous, "Believest ye that I am able to do this?" Out of this came his promise that faith would endow his disciples with miraculous power, "These signs shall follow them that believe." Jesus, the teacher in the art of faith, demonstrated that he was able with equal success to deal with the necessities of the body and with the maladies of the soul. That faith, as a channel of power, was a constant theme of Jesus can be gathered from the following unique utterances:
While in Nazareth, "He did not many mighty

works there because of their unbelief" (Matt. 13:58).

To the storm-tossed disciples, "Why are ye so fearful? Where is your faith?" (Mark 4:40; Luke 8:25).

To anxious Jairus, "Only believe, and she shall be made whole" (Luke 8:50, RV).

To the woman with a blood issue,. "Thy faith hath made thee whole" (Mark 5:34).

To the centurion, "I have not found so great faith, no, not in Israel" (Matt. 8:10; Luke 7:9).

To the blind man, "Believe ye that I am able to do this? According to your faith be it unto you" (Matt. 9:28, 29).

To the disciples, "If you have faith and doubt not, you shall ... do this which is done to the fig tree" (Matt. 21:21). "O faithless generation, how long shall I bear with you" (Mark 9:19, RV)?

To the Syrophoenician woman, "O woman, great is your faith! Be it done for you as you desire" (Matt. 15:28, RSV).

To Peter, sinking in the sea, "O man of little faith, why did you doubt" (Matt. 14:31, RSV)?

The disciples to Jesus, "Why could not we cast it out?" His reply, "Because of your little faith" (Matt. 17:19, 20, RSV). "If you have faith ... nothing will be impossible to you" (Matt. 17:20–21).

To Martha, at the grave of Lazarus, "If you would believe you would see the glory of God" (John 11:40, RSV)?

To the multitudes at Capernaum, "This is the work of God, that you believe in him whom he has sent" (John 6:29, RSV).

What amazing things Jesus can accomplish for

those whose faith laughs at impossibilities and
shouts, *It shall be done!* A remarkable feature of his
miraculous work is the way he blessed and honored what we might call *substitutionary* faith. An
illustration of this appears in the contact Jesus
had with the Syrophoenician woman (Mark 7:24
–30), which is one of the instances when the person
requiring healing was not present and the faith
exercised had to be by another on her behalf. The
same response of Jesus to *substitutionary* faith is
found in the centurion's experience. His servant,
for whom he had a deep affection, was grievously
ill, and the presentation of his plight to Jesus elicited the reply, "I have not found so great faith,
no, not in Israel" (Matt. 8:10). It was *great* in that
it was faith exercised on behalf of another. "As
thou hast believed [for another] so be it unto thee."

Then there is the further classic instance of
the palsied man whom four of his friends ingen-
iously succeeded in placing at the feet of Jesus.
Here is another cure apparently given without the
cooperation of the faith of the patient. Poor fellow, doubtless he was too far gone to know what
was going on! Yet as soon as he saw Jesus, personal faith was likely awakened by the antecedent
faith of his quartet of friends. "Jesus, seeing *their*
faith, said to the sick of the palsy, son, be of good
cheer, thy sins are forgiven thee." All four bearers
had faith in the power of Jesus to heal their
friend in his bodily restoration. But their combined faith on his behalf, coupled with the hal-
lowed presence into which they had brought him,
awakened faith in the paralytic himself, not only
for the bodily cure, but for the higher blessing of

forgiveness as well. Christ bestowed both. In all cases of spiritual healing, however, the cooperation of *personal* faith is absolutely essential. "What must *I* do to be saved? Believe on the Lord Jesus Christ, and *thou* shalt be saved" (Acts 16:30, 31). Brought to Jesus with his back on a bed, the paralytic went home with his bed on his back, a transformed man in body and soul. Always disappointed at the conspicuous lack of faith, Jesus was correspondingly delighted by the display of faith, whether it was personal or substitutionary (see Matt. 17:14–21).

The accompaniments of faith. While faith alone is sufficient to save a soul from sin, often it is connected with other virtues. Yet faith, in itself, cannot save. It is but the channel of salvation, for we are "saved by grace *through* faith" (Eph. 2:8). An essential associate of faith is *repentance* which precedes and brings into faith (Matt. 21:32; Mark 1:15). Without genuine repentance involving a deep consciousness of sin, and the confession of it, there cannot be saving faith. Paul emphasizes this fact when he unites repentance and faith (Acts 20:21), proving that they go together and are inseparable and mutually dependent. When both are experienced, many blessings accrue. Repentance is directed "toward God," while faith is directed "toward our Lord Jesus Christ."

Further, faith and salvation are joined together. Without faith, that is, saving faith involving the act of personal heart trust by which the sinner commits himself to God and accepts as his own the salvation he so freely offers, there can be no deliverance from the penalty of sin. Jesus said to

the woman who was a sinner, "Thy faith hath
saved thee," and in his parable of the sower, he
described a certain class of hearers subject to satanic pressure, "lest they should believe and be
saved." In his Temple discourse Jesus warned the
Jews that unless they believed that he was the sent
Messiah they would die in their sins (John 8:24).
Hearing such an ultimatum, "many believed on
him."

Then, as we have already indicated, faith and
prayer are presented as being good companions.
"Whatsoever ye shall ask in *prayer, believing*, ye
shall receive." We may say prayers, but what do
we know about *believing prayer?* It is only such
faith that can remove the mountains of which Jesus spoke. This brand of faith is not dependent
upon sight or feeling. In true Christian experience the order is threefold—*fact, faith, feeling*.

Feeling, or evidence from the senses, cannot
precede faith, and faith accepts the facts before us
in the Word. The *fact* is that, as Jesus expressed it,
we are lost in sin and that he alone is the Savior
who can save us. Then *faith*, accepting the fact,
comes to prove that what God says is true. Then
comes the *feeling*, the amount of which depends
upon the degree of faith. We have "joy and peace
in believing" (Rom. 15:13). Jesus, in the parable of
the sower, spoke of those who put feeling before
faith. They had "joy" as they heard the word but
became offended because the root was not in
them (Matt. 13:20, 21).

Yet again, we find works as an accompaniment
of faith. "Faith without works is dead" (James
2:26). There are "works of the law," works we are

to accomplish for the purpose of earning or merit-
ing salvation. But these *works* are the opposite of
faith (Rom. 3:20; Eph. 2:8–10). We do not work
in order *to be* saved but because *we are* saved. We
are saved by faith alone but not by the faith that
goes alone. Actually, there is no contradiction between the salvation by faith Jesus taught and the
doctrine of justification by faith Paul loved to
preach and the theme of justification by works of
which James wrote. They are supplementary
truths. In his *Bible Handbook* Henry H. Halley expresses the difference thus:

> Paul preached faith as the basis of justification before
> God, but insisted that it must issue in the right kind
> of life. James was writing to those who had accepted
> the doctrine of Justification by Faith, but were not
> living Right, telling them that such Faith was No
> Faith at all.

One writer suggests that the seeming contradiction between Paul and James is resolved if we use
faith as employed by James in the sense of creed
or orthodox belief. The context is taken up with
faith as the acceptance of what God had said:
"Abraham believed God." Jesus said, "This is the
work of God, that ye believe on him whom he hath
sent" (John 6:29). The creedal confession of the
orthodox Jew, taken as a passport to salvation, is
stated in James 2:19, RV: "Thou believest that *God
is one*" (see Deut. 6:4). Thus briefly, James presses
the futility of creed without life; Paul, the necessity of reliance in order to receive "life and
peace." What James sought to express is given a
poetic exposition by Coleridge:

Think not the Faith by which the Just shall live
Is a dead creed, a map correct of Heaven,
Far less a feeling, fond and fugitive,
A thoughtless gift, withdrawn as soon as given;
It is the affirmation and an act
That bids Eternal Truth be Present Fact.

Last of all, there is Paul's trio in his marvelous hymn of love in which he joins three graces in an indissoluble union. "Now abideth faith, hope, love, these three; and the greatest of these is love" (1 Cor. 13:13, RV). *Faith* makes all things possible; *hope* makes all things bright; *love* makes all things easy.

One would have liked to enumerate the heroes of faith of which Scripture is full. What a remarkable portrait gallery we have of these heroes and heroines in Hebrews 11! May we, like them, leave behind us "a good report through faith"! Faber would have us remember:

How can they live, how will they die,
    How bear the cross of grief,
Who have not got the light of faith,
    The courage of belief.

FAITHFULNESS

A good tree bringeth forth good fruit, said Jesus, who also described *faithfulness* as the commendable fruit of *faith*. Among men faithfulness represents trustworthiness, or the state or quality of being faithful in all things. A faithful friend is one upon whom we may safely lean or rely.

Raised to the divine sphere, the same virtue characterizes each person of the godhead.

God is absolutely faithful. The predominant theme of the Old Testament is the faithfulness of God. "Great is thy faithfulness," which reached even unto the skies (Lam. 3:23; Ps. 36:5; 119:90). The religious value of this moral attribute is connected with God's gracious promises of salvation, making him, thereby, the firm and secure object of religious trust. John reminds us that God's faithfulness, as well as his righteousness, is manifested in the forgiveness of sin (1 John 1:9). Further, God is often presented as faithful in an absolute sense as to contrast him with men who are faithful only in a relative sense and who appear as changeable and faithless in comparison with the faithfulness of God (see Isa. 49:15).

God the Son is manifestly faithful. Like Father, like Son! Divine attributes became visible in the life and works of Jesus who without arrogant assumption claimed such an attribute of faithfulness for himself. He told John to write to the church at Laodicea that he "the Amen" was "the faithful and true witness" (Rev. 3:14), a fact John also subscribed to concerning Jesus (Rev. 1:5; 19:11). When Jesus is spoken of as a "faithful high priest" (Heb. 2:17; 3:2, 6), the reference is to his fidelity to his obligations to God and to his saving mission among men. When he appears as the victorious warrior, it will be as the one "whose name is faithful and true." While on earth, Jesus never violated his trust of the divine commission. As God's steward he was found faithful in his adherence to the divine message, "I have given unto them the words which thou gavest me" (John 17:7, 8; see 1 Cor. 4:1, 2). This is why his words, like himself, are pronounced "faithful and true" (Rev. 21:5; 22:6). And the injunction is that we ʼare to "speak the same divine words 'faithfully'" (Jer. 23:28).

Because Jesus was the perfect personification of faithfulness and trustworthiness, his exhortations to faithfulness carry great weight. There was never any contradiction between his counsel and his character. What his lips enunciated as to loyalty to God and to his Word and cause, his life enforced. He not only preached and taught truth, he was the embodiment of it. "I am . . . the truth." As the prophecy of him puts it, "Faithfulness was the girdle of his reins" (Isa. 11:5).

God the Holy Spirit is inherently faithful. All three persons of the godhead are equal in all divine attributes. Thus, the Spirit shares the trustworthiness of the Father and the Son and is ever our faithful guide, leading us into all truth. "The fruit of the Spirit is . . . faith," or faithfulness, steadfastness (Gal. 5:22, RV).

> Truthful Spirit, dwell with me!
> I myself would truthful be,
> And with wisdom kind and clear
> Let Thy life in mine appear;
> And with actions brotherly
> Speak my Lord's sincerity.

1. *Jesus commends faithfulness in the service of God.* In the Gospels, the term *faithful* appears seven times, and four times Jesus used the opposite term *faithless*. In his teaching, he expected his own to be faithful to God and to one another. Wher-

ever *faithless* occurs (Matt. 17:17, etc.), it means, not untrustworthy, but *unbelieving*. Shakespeare, in *Merchant of Venice*, describes Shylock as a "faithless Jew" simply because he was an unbeliever in Christ.

The illustration of "the faithful and wise servant," blessed by his master for loyalty during his absence, which Jesus used in the parable of the fig tree, was meant to incite his disciples to faithfulness and steadfastness during his absence (Matt. 24:35). Then, in the following parable of the talents, he commends those who have been true to their trust and condemns those who have betrayed it. May each of us so live as to earn his praise at the end of the day, "Well done, thou good and faithful servant" (Matt. 25:14–30). Jesus also recognized the necessity of faithfulness among ourselves: "If ye have not been faithful in that which is another man's, who shall give you that which is your own" (Luke 16:12)?

2. *Jesus commands faithfulness until the end.* While he commended faithfulness to his disciples while among them on earth, after his ascension, Jesus sent letters to seven churches. To the church at Smyrna the message was, "Be thou faithful unto death" (Rev. 2:10). This was not only a plea for undying loyalty, but a command to be faithful until the end of the road—a command as binding as any other from his lips. It is not our privilege to be faithful to him but our *duty*, and duty is *debt*, and debt is something *we owe* to another. The important question is, Are we striving to pay our debt?

Faithfulness is a debt we owe to God. All of us

are in divine debt and try to smother the voice as it asks, "How much owest thou thy Lord?" Are we as faithful as we should be in honoring his cause, his day, his Word? Do we recognize his redemptive claim upon all we are and have and upon our talents, time, and treasures?

Faithfulness is a debt we owe each other as fellow believers. What a lamentable breakdown of love, trust, confidence, and loyalty there has been among ourselves! What strange representatives we are of Jesus who is the same yesterday, today, and forever in all his virtues! Did he not say, "I have called you friends" (John 15:15)? Alas! too often we act more like *fiends*—to drop the *r* —than friends. What need there is to preserve the fellowship of the saints.

Faithfulness is a debt we owe the world at large. Jesus paid the debt, even to the uttermost farthing, in agony and shame. When he graciously saved us, it was not only that we might be happy on our way to heaven, but that we might, in turn, become channels of blessing in a lost world. We are not loyal to our charge if we fail to warn the godless of their peril if they linger and die in their sin. In this day of the glad tidings of grace, we dare not hold our peace. If we do, then we are traitors to our trust.

Faithfulness is a debt we owe ourselves. It is incumbent upon us to seek after personal, spiritual culture and devotion, and cultivate loyalty in every phase of our life. If negligent regarding personal holiness and rectitude, faithfulness in other directions will not be evident. "To thine own self be true." If such a manifold debt seems to be beyond our ability to discharge, we have the encouraging promise, "Faithful is he that calleth you [to faithfulness], who also will do it" (1 Thess. 5:24).

How practical Jesus was in all his oral ministry! He was never over the heads or out of touch with his audience. For instance, in his parable of the unjust steward, he says, "He that is faithful in that which is least is faithful also in much" (Luke 16:10).

"Because thou hast been faithful in a very little" (Luke 19:17). Trifles! How guilty we are of neglecting them! Yet as Michelangelo replied to a friend who chided the famous sculptor for spending so much time over insignificant details in his carving, "Trifles make perfection, and perfection is no trifle." We strive to appear loyal in the more conspicuous realms of life, forgetting that it is only by being faithful in the small unnoticed things and duties that we gather strength to be faithful in the greater responsibilities. "A little thing is a little thing, but faithful in a little thing is a great thing." Jesus did not neglect to gather the fragments after he fed the hungry. Is this not the thought Tennyson has captured in his verse?

> He bowed Himself
> With all obedience to a King, and wrought
> All kind of service with a noble ease,
> That graced the lowliest act in doing it.

3. *Jesus certified rewards for faithfulness.* Servants who had been faithful "in a very little" were given "authority over ten cities" (Luke 19:17). Those with ten talents, or with five, who used what they had to the best of their ability were rewarded. But

the man with the one talent, who was not faithful in the use of it, lost it. We read that he wrapped it in a napkin or handkerchief; he hid his talent in the very thing he should have used to wipe the sweat from his brow as he toiled to double his talent. "Use it or lose it" is the lesson Jesus taught in his parable.

Then there is his wonderful promise to the church of martyrs in Smyrna. "Be thou faithful unto death, and I will give thee a crown of life" (Rev. 2:10). Facing extreme suffering, tribulation, and martyrdom, the faithful witness himself inspired those saints to let their lamp of loyalty blaze away until its light was extinguished by their horrible death.

When my life is past, how glad I shall be
That the lamp of my life has blazed out for Thee.
I shall not mind whatever I gave of labour or
    money one sinner to save;
I shall not mind that the way has been rough, that
    Thy dear feet led the way was enough.
When I am dying, how glad I shall be
That the lamp of my life blazed out for Thee.

Because faithfulness unto death has been the royal road of others all down the ages, may we be found planting our feet in their footprints and following them over the pathway of faithfulness to the Lord and his cause. Jesus spoke of "Antipas . . . my faithful martyr, who was slain among you, where Satan dwelleth" (Rev. 2:13). For him, and for all others dying for their Lord, there is "a crown of life." What the Savior is to reward at his judgment seat is not fame, but fidelity; not success, but sincerity; not how much we have done, but what motives have actuated us. Faithfulness is to be the basis of reward in eternity.

> Keep us faithful, keep us pure,
>   Keep us evermore Thine own!
> Help, O help us to endure,
>   Fit us for Thy promised crown.

It may never be our privilege to wear a martyr's crown. A horrible death for Christ's sake may not be our end. If it is, then he will grant dying grace even as he did to the saints in Smyrna. What we sadly need is grace to live faithfully, day by day, wherever his providence has placed us, no matter how humdrum our lot may be. Whether our talents are many or few, if loyal to God with what he has given, then his "Well done, good and faithful servant, enter into the joy of thy Lord" will be ours.

> Blessed are those who die for God
>   And earn the Martyr's crown of light;
> Yet he who lives for God may be
>   A greater Conqueror in His sight.

BIBLE STUDY QUESTIONS

Take time to turn to each Scripture reference and mark the verse or a portion in your Bible.

1. What is the nature and compass of faith?
2. What is the link between the objects of faith and the power of faith?
3. Speak of the accompaniments of faith.
4. Why is faithfulness in Christians important?

— 14 —

Humility

The commendable virtue, *humility*, is praised but seldom practiced. Men find it hard to believe that the best way up is *down*, or as Jesus puts it, "He that humbleth himself shall be exalted" (Luke 14:11; 18:14). A simple hymn reminds us:

Our highest place
Is lying low,
At our Redeemer's feet.

Although the word *humility* does not appear in the Gospels, its close relative *humble* occurs four times and means "to make low." John Bunyan in *Pilgrim's Progress* reminds us:

He that is down needs fear no fall.
He that is low no pride,
He that is humble ever shall
Have God to be his guide.

Solomon affirmed that "Better it is to be of an humble spirit with the lowly, than to divide the spoil with the proud" (Prov. 16:19). Proud man finds it hard to believe that the only true independence is in humility; for the humble man expects nothing, and cannot be mortified—expects nothing and cannot be disappointed. Humility is also a healing virtue; it will cicatrize a thousand wounds, which pride would keep forever open. But humility is not the virtue of a fool, since it is not consequent upon any comparison between ourselves and others, but between what we are and what we ought to be—which no man ever was. "No man," that is, except Jesus, meek and lowly in heart, will ever remain the perfect model of the grace of humility, as old Thomas Dekker of the sixteenth century describes:

> The best of men
> That e'er wore earth about Him, was a sufferer,
> A soft, meek, patient, humble, tranquil spirit,
> The first true Gentleman that ever breath'd.

One met those who were proud of their humility. Coleridge said:

> The Devil did grin,
> For his darling sin
> Is pride that apes humility.

Archbishop Trench warns:

> If humble, next of thy Humility beware!
> And, lest thou should'st grow proud of
>   such grace, have care!

Marcus Aurelius of ancient Roman times affirmed that "Nothing is more scandalous than a man that is proud of his humility." Uriah Heep, one of Charles Dickens' characters, says, "I am well aware that I am the 'umblest person going . . . My mother is likewise a very 'umble person.

We live in an 'umble abode . . . We are so very 'umble."

When the disciples disputed which of them should be the greatest, Jesus took a towel and washed their feet (John 13:1–17). In this symbolic act of divine condescension we are given an example of the Master's better and unique way (Phil. 2:3–8). How little did the disciples understand his assumption of the task of a slave! How slow they were to take his hint, "If I, the Lord, and master, have washed your feet, ye also ought to wash one another's." It is likewise hard for our proud hearts to realize how the mightiest stoop to the lowliest unless we have ourselves done the things he did, letting his spirit possess and move us. The glamor of a great position, appealing to our sense of self-importance and power, must give way to the real appreciation of what it means to be helpful in ways simple, unseen, and even perhaps unpleasant. Sincere humility is the pathway to an understanding of the lowly Jesus and indeed of God himself. In "Recessional," Rudyard Kipling wrote that there "Still stands Thine ancient sacrifice, /An humble and contrite heart.

Another forcible illustration of *humility* Jesus gave his disciples was on that day when he set a child in their midst. How patient he was in teaching these men the meaning of humble service. By a simple deed, taking the little one in his arms, he sought to teach by action (Matt. 18:1–10). The innocent child resting in the arms of Jesus—the picture of trust, confidence, peace, and love— preached the sermon to those around who sought for greatness. The baby preacher seemed to say to these ambitious disciples, "Shame on all your quarreling about prominence and high places. Look at me. I am much higher up in the kingdom of heaven than you. You must get clear of all your proud thoughts and fancied greatness and become lowly and simple-minded and childlike, or in the new kingdom you will have no place at all, much less a high place."

Paul said that when he became a man, he put away childish things (1 Cor. 13:11). Let it be noted that he said *childish* and not *childlike* things, such as innocency, simplicity, trust, lowliness—virtues the apostle manifested even when he became "Paul the aged," believing that "before honour is humility" (Prov. 15:33). In his further instructions, Solomon reminds us that "By humility and the fear of the Lord are riches, and honour, and life" (Prov. 22:4). Both Paul and Peter describe *humility* as an "apron" all saints should don. "Put on therefore, as the elect of God . . . humbleness of mind, meekness" (Col. 3:12). "All of you be subject one to another, and be clothed with humility" (1 Pet. 5:5). "Wear the overall of humility in serving one another" (Phillips trans.). Micah reminds us of three things the Lord requires of us, "To do justly, to love mercy, to walk humbly with thy God" (Mic. 6:8).

When we meditate upon all the Lord is in himself—his august holiness, his almightiness, his absolute sovereignty—what worms we are in his sight, and how we should humble ourselves in his sight (James 4:10). Jesus would have us like himself, "lowly in heart" and empty of all self-pride. As we have seen, he taught by action that

among the things God abominates are the proud
heart and look (Prov. 6:16, 17). "Wherefore he
saith, God resisteth the proud, but giveth grace
unto the humble" (James 4:6).

May ours be the constant experience of "the
stainless peace of blest humility"! Henry Vaughan
reminds us:

> His life while here, as well as birth,
> Was but a check to pomp and mirth;
> And all man's greatness you may see
> Condemn'd by His humility.

BIBLE STUDY QUESTIONS

*Take time to turn to each Scripture reference and
mark the verse or a portion in your Bible.*

1. What two acts of Jesus teach us humility?

— 15 —

Money

(Poverty and Riches)

No one can study the four Gospels without being deeply impressed, not only with all Jesus taught about money, poverty, and riches, but also with his own personal experience of poverty from the hour of his birth which, of course, gave tremendous weight to his oral instruction on such a topic. Here, again, Jesus *was* what he taught. Why did the Father permit his beloved and only-begotten Son to be born in a stable and laid in a manger? Did he not come as the Prince of Peace, and are not princes born in palaces?

We read that there was no room in the inn for Mary to have her child. Surely, if God made the world, he could have decreed that Jesus should be born in a more fitting place than the corner of a stable with straw as a bed? The big world into which he came had plenty of room for others, yet for the Lord of glory, the Savior of the world, all it could give was the crib holding food for the oxen (Isa. 50:3). Why was it so? No other kind of poverty could have made us rich. As he left heaven for the stable, he emptied himself, or stripped himself of the insignia of majesty, as Lightfoot expresses it, and in the borrowed stable commenced a life of poverty lasting until he died naked on a cross.

Starting poor, Jesus made himself accessible to all. Had he been born in a palace, those seeking him would have needed permissions and introductions, but no formalities are needed for access to a *stable*. The shepherds found an open door, and so, from the beginning Jesus has been easy of approach. When he came to his public ministry, he taught "that which is highly esteemed among men is abomination in the sight of God" (Luke 16:15). God illustrated his contempt of the world's values when he chose a manger for the cradle of his Son, and not one of ivory and gold, lined with costly silks and delicate witcheries of art, such as princes receive.

Further, the holy child Jesus was born among *beasts*. Does this describe the character of the world that received him not, despised and crucified him? He found a good deal of the stable in the world in which men had "changed the glory of God into an image . . . of four-footed beasts" (Rom. 1:23). He came to identify himself with the world in all its bestiality, sin, and wretchedness. He made himself poor so that he could descend to the human lot of the world at its lowest point, and there is no depth he does not know and from which he cannot save. Now he is able to "raise up the poor out of the dust, and lift up the needy out of the dunghill; that he may set him with princes" (Ps. 113:7, 8).

The home in which the infant child was to spend the first thirty years of his life was a poor one, which is proven by the offering Joseph and Mary brought to the house of the Lord for the circumcision of Jesus when he was but eight days old. "To offer a sacrifice . . . a pair of turtledoves, or two young pigeons" (Luke 2:21–24). Not able to afford a lamb as a burnt offering, the ancient law allowed the parents to substitute a cheaper gift (Lev. 12:8). The two pigeons, then, costing little, were an indication of the poverty of Joseph and his espoused wife. Coming, thus, in such a state of poverty, Jesus manifested that it is not dishonorable to be poor. No condition in life is dishonorable where *God* places us. As Barnes' *Notes* put it, "God knows what is best for us, and he often makes a state of poverty an occasion of the highest blessings. If *with* poverty he grants us, as is often the case, peace, contentment, and religion, it is worth far more than all the jewels of Golconda, or the gold of Mexico."

But although that Nazareth home was a poor one, its inhabitants did not live on the borderline of starvation, as millions are doing today. Parents and children were among the genteel poor of the village with enough to live by, with care. They were not caught in a poverty trap. Since it was a godly home, the prayer of Solomon would often rise from its very humble exterior: "Give me neither poverty [of the extreme sort] nor riches; feed me with food convenient for me: Lest I be full, and deny thee . . . Lest I be poor, and steal" (Prov. 30:8, 9).

Then, if it be true, as assumed, that Joseph, the

breadwinner, died when Jesus was a youth, the burden of providing for his widowed mother, his three brothers, and, at least, two sisters (Mark 6:3), fell upon his shoulders. As he is described as a "carpenter," Jesus took on the responsibility of the family business and for many years worked hard to meet the needs of his humble home until, at the age of thirty, he was manifested to Israel. His own hands ministered to the necessities of his home, with its frugal living. As Mary's firstborn, Jesus labored hard and long at the bench to keep the homefires burning, as his gnarled hands testified. Cruel men gave to this "carpenter" wood and nails as he died.

Found in fashion as a working man in that carpenter's small shop, Jesus revealed the toil of divinity and the divinity of toil. As he labored to keep the beast of extreme poverty from the door, Jesus provided, from his personal experience, an impressive background to all he taught concerning money, poverty, and riches. Born poor, and ever subject to a condition of indigence, he lived that way until he died without anything material to leave his relatives as mementoes—not even the clothes he wore!

As we approach his brief yet blessed ministry of about three years, it is not difficult to formulate his many references to the poor and the rich, and to the peril of possessions. Jesus taught of such, not only with authority, but with added power of example. Perhaps we can take the last aspect *first* and discover something of his material poverty as a traveling preacher and teacher. An impressive fact is that, having created all things, Jesus lived on borrowed things. Both his cradle and his grave were borrowed, just as were the drink of water from a fallen woman, the ass he rode on in triumph, and the boat in which he slept. Women ministered unto him of their substance. It is Paul who lived "as having nothing, and yet possessing all things," who reminds us that it was because of his grace that Jesus, "though he was rich, yet for your sakes became poor, that ye through his poverty might be rich" (2 Cor. 6:10; 8:9). The word for *poverty* used here, which is the same Jesus used to described the church at Smyrna (Rev. 2:9), means "beggary." Through him who lived like a beggar, we are greatly enriched.

What pathos is behind these two connected statements which John records: "Every man went unto his own house. . . . Jesus went unto the Mount of Olives" (John 7:53; 8:1). There was no one with feeling enough to offer Jesus a bed, and so out into the cool air of the evening he went and, with the darkness of the night to cover him, spent the lonely hours in communion with his Father. To the unnamed scribe who said to Jesus, "Lord, I will follow thee whithersoever thou goest," the reply was that one that must have dampened the inquirer's ardor: "Foxes have holes, and the birds of the air have nests; but the Son of man hath not where to lay his head" (Luke 9:57, 58).

Like the apostle Paul, Jesus, in his itinerary missions, had "no certain dwelling place." In his assertion of his own poverty, Jesus dashed the hopes of the avaricious scribe. The very foxes and birds have places of repose and shelter, but he was as a wanderer and an outcast from the abodes of men.

He came unto his own, but they received him not. Alexander Whyte comments in *The Walk, Conversation, and Character of Jesus Christ Our Lord:*

> He would not have lacked where to lay his head as long as you had a house to call your own. And I fully believe you; but, at the same time, you must clearly understand him, and must in nothing mistake him. You must distinctly understand that it was not his *head* that was without a pillow so much as his *heart*. I do not suppose that our Lord, at his worst, had often to sleep in the open air and on the bare ground. But for all that, he was in reality as lonely and as homeless as his plainest-spoken proverb said he was. Take his proverb home to yourself. You never wanted a table to eat at, or a bed to sleep on. But you know only too well what it is to be very lonely and neglected at a crowded table, and very desolate in a luxuriously furnished apartment. And what he really complained about in Israel, and still complains about among us, is the very few who, with any warmth, entertain his truth in their mind and himself in their heart. . . . With all your willingness to put him up in your house, how does it stand with your mind and your heart? How are you entertaining his message in your mind and your heart at this moment? "Behold . . . I stand at the door and knock!"

As a preface to what Jesus taught about *money*, it may prove helpful to list his outstanding sayings on riches and on poverty.

RICHES

"The deceitfulness of riches, choke the word" (Matt. 13:22).

"Verily I say unto you, That a rich man shall

hardly enter into the kingdom of heaven" (Matt. 19:23, 24; Mark 10:23, 24).

"A rich man of Arimathaea, named Joseph, who also himself was Jesus' disciple" (Matt. 27:57).

"The rich he hath sent empty away" (Luke 1:53).

"Woe unto you that are rich" (Luke 6:24)!

"He that layeth up treasure for himself, and is not rich toward God" (Luke 12:21).

"When he heard this, he was very sorrowful: for he was very rich" (Luke 18:23).

"Zacchaeus . . . he was rich . . . the half of my goods I give to the poor" (Luke 19:2, 8).

POOR

"Blessed are the poor in spirit" (Matt. 5:3).

"Sell all that thou hast, and give to the poor" (Matt. 19:21; Mark 10:21).

"Ye have the poor always with you" (Matt. 26:11).

"There came a certain poor woman, and cast in two mites . . . all that she had" (Mark 12:41–44; Luke 21:3).

"When thou makest a feast, call the poor" (Luke 14:13).

"The Spirit of the Lord is upon me . . . to preach the gospel to the poor" (Luke 4:18).

"The poor have the gospel preached to them" (Matt. 11:5).

MONEY

"Thou shalt find a piece of money" (Matt. 17:27).

"He hid his lord's money" (Matt. 25:18, 25).

"They gave large money unto the soldiers" (Matt. 28:12, 15; Mark 14:11).

"He beheld how the people cast money into the treasury" (Mark 12:41).

"Take ... neither money" (Luke 9:3; Mark 6:8).

"Gavest thou not my money into the bank" (Luke 19:15, 23).

"They were glad, and covenanted to give him money" (Luke 22:5).

"He poured out the changers' money" (John 2:15).

While the term *poor* means to be impoverished, the kindred term *poverty*, which has its root in *poor*, is not found in the Gospel, but used three times elsewhere in the New Testament (2 Cor. 8:2, 9; Rev. 2:9) and signifies "to be reduced to a state of beggary or pauperism." *Penury*, used of the widow and her two mites (Luke 21:4), is not found elsewhere apart from the reference in Proverbs 14:23. The two words used for *poor* set forth two degrees of poverty.

Pénes. This word does not indicate extreme poverty but simply a condition of living from hand to mouth, a bare and scant livelihood, as in the case of the widow (see also 2 Cor. 9:9).

Ptōchós. Jesus used this term when he said, "Blessed are the poor" (Luke 6:20); Paul employs the same term in 2 Corinthians 6:10. This term indicates a condition of abject poverty such as Lazarus experienced when he begged for crumbs from the rich man's table (Luke 16:20). This, also, is the word Paul used to describe the extreme form of poverty Jesus voluntarily took upon himself for our sakes (2 Cor. 8:9). He became a "mendicant," a "beggar," in order that we might be saved.

THE RIGHT VALUE OF POVERTY AND RICHES

Although born of a poor mother, Jesus was buried by a rich man, and in his superb teaching emphasizes the true significance of poverty and of wealth. What he taught about *money* includes many things associated with life in this world. Nowhere does he condemn private ownership and property in itself. He knew that was a recognized part of the world system of his time. When, in the solitary instance, Jesus required a prospective follower to abandon his property, he told the rich young ruler not to give away all his tangible assets but to *sell* them, thereby affirming property rights and the legitimacy of bargain and sale (Mark 10:17–23).

The correct value of private property and of advantages accruing from the investment of money received from such is surely taught in the parables of the talents and of the unjust steward. "Thou oughtest to have put my money to the exchangers, and then at my coming I should have received mine own with interest" (Matt. 25:27).

From the whole tenor of Scripture we learn that material riches are neither good nor bad in themselves, but only as they are properly and/or improperly used. Further, they must be looked upon as transitory, must not be trusted in, but used to provide the most precious and glorious realities of the spiritual realm (Matt. 10:23; Luke 18:24; Eph. 2:7; Col. 1:27). Jesus, then, instructed men how to use their wealth wisely and well. When he exhorted his disciples to "make . . . by means of the mammon of unrighteousness," he meant that we should use the wealth which God has committed to us as stewards in order that we may win souls with it for him and his kingdom, just as the unfaithful steward used the goods with which his master had instructed him to make friends for himself.

The opposite picture is found in the record of Dives and Lazarus. Here we have the sad portrait of a selfish rich man who grossly abused his trust, who failed to make friends with his money, and who, in hell, would have given anything for such a friend (Luke 16:19–31). Around Jesus were those of considerable means. Nicodemus, Joseph of Arimathaea, and Zacchaeus were rich men, as were probably Matthew, James, and John (Mark 1:19–20; John 19:27). Mary, Martha, and Lazarus also appear to be people of means to entertain as they did. The possession of wealth, then, was not condemned by Jesus as sinful, but, on the contrary, could be counted as a sign of the blessing of God (see Eccles. 5:19; 6:2).

Further, as God is the maker of rich and poor alike (Prov. 22:2), Jesus rightly evaluated poverty. "Blessed are the poor." The most precious gift offered to men is the gospel of redeeming love and grace. This is seen in the Master's reply to the messengers from John the Baptist. He first enumerated the works of benevolence he was performing and then added, as the crown and climax, "And to the poor the gospel is preached." If

Jesus had his rich disciples, he also had poor ones he equally loved. His foremost follower, Peter, confessed one day, "Silver and gold have I none, but such as I have give I thee" (Acts 3:6).

The church today has plenty of silver and gold but no power to say to a world crippled by sin, violence, and bloodshed, "In the name of Jesus Christ of Nazareth, rise up and walk." A. L. Waring would have us sing:

> There is a certainty of love
> That sets my heart at rest;
> A calm assurance for today
> That to be poor is best.

The poor widow who had only two farthings to her name and dropped them both into the treasury-box was, thereby, a 100 percent tither for she gave "all her living." She did not have the cares, worries, frustrations, and sorrows of the rich men who gave of their "abundance" and not of their "want." The widow left the Temple happy that her all was on the altar and that the one to whom she had surrendered all would see to it that further mites would be forthcoming.

Did not Jesus, who for our sakes became poor and yet made his grave "with the rich in his death," say to his disciples, "Ye have the poor with you always" (Matt. 26:11)? Then he added, "But me ye have not always" and was the poorest of the poor in his humiliation! The prophecy of Jesus has not failed of fulfillment, for even today there are myriads more poor people in the world than rich. The problem of poverty, whether self-produced or otherwise, is an international dilemma that can only be solved as nations and men give heed to the teachings of Jesus concerning the glamour of riches and the pressure of poverty. He taught that when the spiritual nature is awakened the whole environment of man is transformed as a matter of course. His gospel was not one of meat and drink, loaves and fishes, better clothes, finer houses, increasing wages. He knew that these would follow in their order. "All these shall be added unto you." His preeminent precept was, "Seek *first* the kingdom of God and his righteousness." This is the message poor and rich alike must heed.

Money cannot buy the greatest blessings in life. Izaak Walton, of the sixteenth century, wrote in his *Compleat Angler:*

> Look to your health; and, if you have it, praise God, and value it next to a good conscience; for health is the second blessing that we mortals are capable of; a blessing that money cannot buy.

God's richest gifts are "without money, and without price." Solomon would have us know that money answereth all things (Prov. 8:18). But no matter how much or little we may have, it cannot secure deliverance from sin, peace with God, and life forevermore.

RESPONSIBILITY TOWARD THE POOR

The poor home in which he lived, the work at the bench, and the constant struggle to make ends meet, left their indelible mark upon Jesus. He looked around him and saw how slender was the livelihood of those, stunted and undeveloped and having few pleasures, who worked the grudging soil or toiled all night at sea and found nothing. Such toilers had little time to pray or to cultivate spiritual beauty; yet he called them to seek first food for their souls before bread for their bodies. One of the purposes of his Sermon on the Mount was that as God feeds the ravens and arrays the lilies in all their glory, so he will provide all that is necessary for those who put him first in their lives. His mercy is more necessary than money, and his grace more necessary than gold.

The continual presence of the poor in our own communities, or countries, or in the underprivileged areas of the world is an unceasing reminder of our personal obligation to distribute our money to the necessity of the poor, especially to the saints among them (Rom. 12:13; 15:26). Is it not this pressing obligation Jesus emphasized in his teaching regarding the judgment of the nations (Matt. 25:31–46) where reward awaits those who minister to the poor and needy in his name? But for those failing to relieve the destitute, feed the hungry, and clothe the naked there was condemnation. Such negligence is reckoned by the Master as being against himself: "Inasmuch as ye did it not to one of the least of these, ye did it not to me."

In like manner, Dives suffered eternal loss for his failure to share his money with Lazarus, the beggar at his gate. It was also this thoughtlessness concerning the less fortunate that condemned the prosperous farmer whom Jesus called a *fool* for having left out the needy. The rich young ruler was likewise smitten with grief when told to sell

his property and give to the poor. Ordinary benevolence may relieve the poor, feed the hungry,
clothe the naked, and house the homeless, but still
deeper, spiritual needs characterize a poverty-
stricken humanity as far as the things of the soul
are concerned, and which can only be met by the
gospel Jesus came to proclaim. Professor Stalker
in *The Ethic of Jesus* observes:

> Where the light of the Gospel shines, the blessings of
> civilization abound also. Those, therefore, to whom
> the spirit of Christianity prevails to such a degree as
> to overflow upon others are the true disciples of
> Jesus and the true benefactors of humanity; and they
> hold in their keeping the secret of Jesus.

Jesus had no self-interests. He lived and died for
others and seeks through us to find "the other
sheep" he also must have within his fold.

THE ENSLAVING POWER OF MONEY

Francis Bacon, the essayist, said, "Riches are a
good handmaid, but the worst mistress." This is
but another way of saying that money is a good
servant, but a hard, cruel master. Bacon also said
that "Money is like muck, not good except it
be spread." "Rich, and increased with goods," the
Laodiceans were blind to their real condition—
"wretched, and miserable, and poor, and blind,
and naked"—and also ignorant of the true wealth
to be found only in Jesus (Rev. 3:17, 18). Paul did
not say that *money* is the root of all evil, for there
is nothing evil in money itself. What he did say

was that "the *love* of money is the root of all evil," having the power over those who covet it to their spiritual detriment to "pierce themselves through with many sorrows" (1 Tim. 6:10). Literally, "love of money" means "lover of silver" and corresponds to those Jesus describes as "covetous," which means, "lovers of silver" (Luke 16:14). Because of the Pharisees' inordinate love of silver Jesus was forced to "pour out these changers' money, and overturn the tables" (John 2:15).

The tragic influence of money over a person is likewise illustrated by Jesus in the parable of the sower in which he describes how "the deceitfulness of riches, choke the word, and he becometh unfruitful" (Matt. 13:22), meaning that covetousness destroys spiritual life and ruins godly aspirations. While it is not sinful to be rich, wealth can be very dangerous and perilous to one's salvation (Matt. 19:23). And, it is because of the danger of losing the soul through the possession of wealth that so many exhortations are found in Scripture aimed especially at those who have an abundance of this world's goods but who fail to share with those not similarly blessed (James 1:10, 11; 5:1). That it is blessedly possible for rich men to be saved is evident from Zacchaeus and Joseph of Arimathaea.

As a class, the rich were severely condemned by Jesus. "Woe to you that are rich! for ye have received your consolation. Woe unto you that are full! for ye shall hunger" (Luke 6:24–25). The only kind of idolatry Jesus warned against was the worship of *money*. Listen as he says, "Ye cannot serve God and mammon" and as he told men "to lay up treasure in heaven." To illustrate how the irresponsible and godless rich receive their consolation in this world only, Jesus related the incident of Dives and Lazarus (Luke 16:19–31). The rich man here is not portrayed as a particularly wicked man, but he was condemned for what he had left undone and endured the torments of hell. He did not go to hell because he was rich but because he allowed his riches to enslave him, making him callous to the terrible need of the beggar at his gate whose sores the dogs licked and whose belly was constantly empty. Also note that Lazarus did not go to Paradise because he was poor. He was carried by the angels into Abraham's bosom solely because, in spite of his supreme poverty, his trust was in the God of Abraham.

That money can be a dangerous and damning thing to possess is also taught by Jesus in his further illustration of a rich farmer, the only man he called a *fool*. He was a fool in the way he allowed his money and possessions to dominate his life and thinking and become the root of evil. What Bacon said in one of his essays is applicable to this wealthy farmer: "He does not possess wealth, but his wealth possesseth him." He became the slave of his silver, and on the day he planned to increase his hoard, he was smitten with sudden death by God (Luke 12:16–21).

It was fitting that Jesus should conclude this story about the rich fool with the statement, "So is he that layeth up treasure for himself, and is not rich towards God." The final phrase, "rich towards God," is a perfect description of Christ's ideal for those blessed with money, and suggests a development of the Godward side of human nature in prayer, aspiration, charity, generosity, and all the other qualities that go to the fashioning of a noble manhood. This is what Jesus desiderated for everyone; and to miss it, which was fatally possible, was, in his eyes, the greatest of calamities.

The rich, foolish farmer suffered his ever-growing wealth to injure his own self, or make serious inroads upon his moral personality, and, thereby, stain his soul. When the stroke of judgment fell, he lost his soul, eternally. How unlike the apostle Paul he was who, being poor, made many rich! The warning of the psalmist is, "If riches increase, set not your heart upon them," but upon God who gave them for beneficent purposes (Ps. 62:10). When Jesus sent his disciples forth, he instructed them to "provide neither gold, nor silver, nor brass in your purses" (Matt. 10:9). Whom he calls, he equips and provides for. John Milton in *Paradise Lost* describes Satan as the evil inspirer of man's covetousness.

> Mammon led them on,
> Mammon, the least created spirit that fell
> From heaven, for ev'n in heav'n his looks and thoughts
> Were always downward bent, admiring more
> The riches of heaven's pavement, trodden gold,
> Than aught divine or holy else enjoy'd
> In vision beatific.
> 　　　Let none admire
> That riches grow in hell; that soil may best
> Deserve the precious bane.

How adverse to the teaching of Jesus and to the whole tenor of Scripture is the assertion of George Bernard Shaw who, in the preface to *The Irrational Knot*, declared, "Money is indeed the

most important thing in the world; and all sound
and successful personal and national morality
should have this fact for its basis."

This godless writer also wrote that "All great
truths begin as blasphemies"—a blasphemous
statement in itself. "Righteousness—not money—
exalteth a nation" is a great truth of Scripture;
and did not Jesus affirm that the basis of a truly
sound personal morality is the seeking *first* of
God's righteousness and his kingdom? Love to
him with the ensuing love for a lost humanity constitutes "the most important thing in the world."

THE HIGHEST USE OF MONEY

When he drew attention to the poor widow casting all the money she had into the collection box
of the Temple, Jesus was teaching the highest use
of money, namely, the giving back to God of his
own. "The silver and the gold are mine, saith the
Lord." Thus, whether we have much or little
wealth, we have nothing we did not receive from
him who is the giver of every good and perfect
gift. Jesus praised the full surrender of the widow's two mites because she was "rich toward
God" and received, in return, "gold tried in the
fire" that she might be rich (Rev. 3:18). That sacrificial widow, like Jesus himself, had little money to
give away. There was a time when he had no
money with which to pay the tribute (Matt. 17:27).

Money is not, however, the only thing, or even
the chief thing, to be given away. Though Jesus
gave money, he gave far oftener sympathy,
health, relief from disablement and life. Wher-

ever he went, he was distributing such blessings on every hand, restoring to the diseased and deformed the power of earning money for themselves. Still, money is of high value when it is used for the chief end of glorifying God. When the widow gave her all to God, she, in effect, said by her action, "What is mine is thine"; and we can be assured that God said to her heart, "What is mine is thine" and provided for her further mites for her own living and for the divine treasury.

Jesus said of the rich that they "cast in much" and of "their abundance" (Mark 12:41–44), which means they gave of their superfluous store, or what they did not *need*. Theirs was no self-denial. The widow, however, although she only had two small coins to give—the smallest in use among the Jews—gave "more than all they which cast into the treasury." She gave more in proportion to her means and was therefore more acceptable to God. Jesus did not mean that what she gave was more in material value than all which the others had put in but that she revealed more love for God's sacred cause, more self-denial, more sincerity in her surrender (see 2 Cor. 8:12). Devoting all the property she had to God, she went back home happy in the assurance that he would hear the scraping of the barrel and would supply her needs. She knew that God was no one's debtor.

Often material riches are used to illustrate the most precious and glorious realities of the spiritual realm (Rom. 9:23; 11:33). The term *poverty* is likewise used to describe a penury in spiritual things. Among our Lord's Beatitudes, the first in the series is "Blessed are the poor in spirit" (Matt.

5:3). This means that all have an inner joy and peace, not of this world, who know they have no self-righteousness, no worth of their own to present to the Lord as a ground of their salvation, who feel their utter bankruptcy of spirit apart from the riches of divine grace. Without such spiritual wealth we are poor, naked, miserable, and wretched (Rev. 3:17).

No merit of thine own
Upon His altar place;
All is of Christ alone,
And of His perfect grace.

When Paul wrote of those who were "lovers of their own selves" (2 Tim. 3:2), he used a term for *love* in the sense of "avarice" which implies a seeking to retain and hoard all that is acquired (Luke 12:21). Even with our spiritual wealth, such hoarding is detrimental to our growth in grace. Paradoxical though it may seem, it is only as we scatter what we know of Christ that we save (Eph. 3:7, 8; Heb. 11:26; Mark 12:41).

There was a man, some thought him mad,
The more he gave, the more he had.

BIBLE STUDY QUESTIONS

Take time to turn to each Scripture reference and mark the verse or a portion in your Bible.

1. In what way was Jesus prepared to speak of poverty and riches?

2. How did Jesus teach the correct value of private property?

3. What is our obligation regarding the poor?

4. What caution did Jesus teach about money?

— 16 —

Prayer

It is very easy to write about *prayer* but very hard to practice what the Bible calls "praying in the Holy Spirit." No one should presume to discourse about the necessity and nature of communion with God unless he is experiencing the blessedness of a deep, personal prayer life. To teach about prayer he must be a Spirit-inspired *pray-er*. Such a holy exercise is conspicuous in the teaching of Jesus because he knew, from experience, its power. He not only taught men the many facets of prayer, prayer was his life, and his life was a prayer. St. Francis of Assisi is said by his biographer Thomas of Celano not so much to have prayed as to have turned into prayer. Are we not told that "in the days of his flesh, . . . he offered up prayers and supplications with strong crying, and tears"? No wonder Jesus' tear-saturated intercessions were heard (Heb. 5:7)! Perhaps it is because our prayers are too dry, formal, and mechanical that they never reach heaven.

Those long nights of intercession beneath a starlit sky, and those Gethsemane agonizing prayers, gave Jesus authority to teach others about prayer and to present such a topic with great weight and abiding influence. Men asked him to teach them how to pray because they knew he lived a life of unbroken fellowship with his father. His was an abiding "correspondence fixed with heaven." Examining what the Gospels record concerning Jesus and prayer, three features are clearly evident, namely, what he taught about such a topic, the models of prayer he gave us, and his own experiences in prayer.

HIS ENUNCIATIONS REGARDING PRAYER

It is a most profitable exercise to gather from the Gospels all Jesus had to say on this important topic. His instructions were not only direct, but extensive and profound. He did not teach his disciples how to preach but certainly guided them as to how they should pray and approach the mercy seat. What Jesus taught about prayer illuminated what he meant by God, and conversely his conception of God threw new light upon the whole problem of prayer. No one can miss the fact that Jesus believed in prayer, prayed himself, and unfolded the secrets of fruitful praying to his disciples. His summonses and encouragements to prayer coupled with his own heavenward sighings mark him as the prince of humanity, even in the realm of prayer. John the Baptist was Christ's forerunner in the art of teaching men to pray, for seeing and hearing Jesus at prayer, his disciples asked, "Lord, teach us to pray, as John taught his disciples" (Luke 11:1). What were some of the elements of intercession he imparted to his own?

In his name. First and foremost it was to be remembered that Jesus is the only mediator between God and man and that he himself taught that no man can approach God save through him (John 14:6), *"But by me."* Nothing could be more explicit than his enunciation that "Whatsoever ye shall ask in my name, that will I do, that the Father may be glorified in the Son. If ye shall ask anything in my name, I will do it" (John 14:13–14).

God is glorified in answering prayers offered to him in the name, and for the sake of, his beloved Son. Prayer is operative only when certain principles are observed, and the most important of these is the presentation of our petitions in the name of Jesus which means in reliance upon all that he is in himself and in all that he has accomplished on our behalf. Anticipating the fruits of Calvary, and his intercessory ministry in heaven as the great high priest, Jesus went on to say, "Hitherto have ye asked nothing in my name; ask, and ye shall receive, that your joy may be full" (John 16:24).

This condition, *in my name,* introduced a new element in man's contact with heaven and was a prerogative for New Testament believers and for us as born again ones in Christ. Even among men, if one approaches a friend for help which he is not able to give himself, but has a friend who can assist, he says, "Go to so-and-so, and mention my name, and he will give you what assistance you require." The character of the friend giving his name is a guarantee of the fulfillment of the request made.

To this we can add what John, who records so much about our Lord's praying and teaching, had to say: "If we ask anything according to his will, he heareth us" (1 John 5:14, 15). Often we pray but receive not because we ask amiss. Our prayers are not according to all the name of Jesus represents, nor according to God's purpose. From God's side the same principle operates, for he hears our petitions and answers them "for Christ's sake" (Eph. 4:32), which is tantamount to blessing us in his name. Whatever he deems is best we should have, he graciously bestows. With his higher, perfect wisdom he knows if what we ask for is good for us, spiritually, and responds to our petitions accordingly.

> O Will, that willest good alone,
>   Lead Thou the way, Thou guidest best:
> A little child, I follow on,
>   And trusting, lean upon Thy breast.

Continuous. Paul must have had the teaching of Jesus in mind when he exhorted the Thessalonians to "Pray without ceasing" (1 Thess. 5:17). In order to enforce such continuous prayer, Jesus told his disciples, "To this end, that men ought *always* to pray, and not to faint" (Luke 18:1–8). These verses, along with verse 9 in the same chapter, are among the few instances in which a parable is introduced by a distinct statement as to its drift and nature. Persistency in prayer is illustrated in the *continual* coming of the widow to the judge and in our Lord's own words about his elect "crying day and night unto him" (Luke 18:5, 7). The truth Jesus taught by his parable of the unjust judge and importunate widow is that if the wicked and heartless judge for whom one could only feel scorn and contempt, yielded to the repeated solicitations of the widow who only asked for justice, not vengeance, how much more will the infinitely good and merciful God give of his best to those who earnestly seek him.

Another illustration Jesus used to enforce the truth that his father ever responds to the ceaseless intercession of his own is the story of the friend at Midnight (Luke 11:5–10). The continued knocking at the door of a neighbor, by the friend desiring bread for his friend who had traveled far, was at last responded to when the neighbor arose and gave his friend what he needed. Importunity was rewarded, and for our hearts the lesson is Ask, Seek, Knock, and he who hears and answers sincere prayer will open the door of his provision and grant us bread enough and to spare.

Doubtless there are those somewhat perplexed by the exhortations to be "always praying" and "praying without ceasing," those for whom the cares and duties of home or the responsibilities of business demand the attention of the best part of their waking hours. Monks and nuns, separating themselves from the outside world to live in secluded monasteries, may be able to assume the posture of prayer for hours, but for the rest of us who have to work in order to live little time is left to give to a season of prayer and intercession. Yet while we cannot be in the posture or attitude of prayer all the day long, we can live in the spirit of prayer, and like Nehemiah of old with the heavy work of restoring the walls, we can shoot up arrow prayers to heaven. The days of Jesus were loaded with preaching, teaching, and healing, but he never lost touch with his father. Unfailing God-consciousness, ever a semblance of prayer, was his.

Private and public. Further, Jesus had much to say about these two aspects of prayer with the first feature determining the quality and effectiveness of the second. Revealing the hypocrisy of the public exhibition of prayer by the Pharisees, Jesus said to his own, "But *thou*, when thou prayest, enter into thy closet, and when thou hast shut thy door, pray to thy Father which is in secret; and thy Father which seest in secret shall reward thee openly" (Matt. 6:6). The shut door secures freedom from contact with the world, and in our "closet," or any room in which we are least likely to be disturbed, we can have uninterrupted communion with God. "Commune with your own heart upon your bed, and be still." While family prayers are most advantageous in helping to keep the family together, each within the family should have some part of the home where he or she can meet alone with God. Jesus "went up into a mountain apart to pray." Public prayer of ostentation is abhorrent to the Lord, who always chose the quiet and solitary place for his intercourse with his Father. The real prayer is to the Father in secret —his affair.

But Jesus also recognized the necessity of mutual prayer in public and so gave us the parable of the Pharisee and the publican, the two men who went up into the Temple to pray (Luke 18:10). United prayer is also operative when two or three gather in his name (Matt. 18:19, 20). The ten days of waiting for the coming of the Spirit, as commanded by Jesus, were spent in prayer meetings (Acts 1:14). It was at a riverside where prayer was wont to be made that Paul gained his first convert in Europe (Acts 16:13). A prayer meeting is a spiritual thermometer of the life of a church.

Reverent and familiar. When we pray, it must be to "our Father who is in heaven" (Matt. 6:6, 9). *Father* implies a precious, privileged relationship. Approaching him, we can only gain an audience as we come in sincerity and truth (John 4:24). We often sing, "What a privilege to carry everything to God in prayer," and this privilege side of prayer must not be forgotten. We are saved from all irreverence, formalism, and unreality when we come to pray as we remember that we are entering the presence of the most high God. Social barriers may keep us from conversing with the high and noble of the land. A pauper, however, has the same privilege of coming into the audience chamber of the King of kings as any earthly sovereign. "Prayer," said an old Jewish mystic, "is the moment when Heaven and Earth kiss each other."

If all due sincerity and earnestness and reverence are ours as we "approach the mercy seat where Jesus answers prayer," then whatsoever we ask for is granted. If we feel that we lack the faith and obedience making prayer possible, Jesus suggests that we can ask for them and have them. He gives us an illustration of the man who prayed, "Lord, I believe; help thou mine unbelief."

Further, we are not to be afraid to ask for great things. Clement of Alexandria said, "Ask the great things, and the little things will be added unto you." John Newton taught the church to sing his great hymn, "Come, my soul, thy suit pre-
, pare."

> Thou art coming to a King,
> Large petitions with thee bring;
> For His grace and power are such
> None can ever ask too much.

Definite and precise. Jesus condemned the Pharisees for their "much speaking" and "vain repetitions" as they assumed the posture of prayer in the public place where they could be seen and heard. Encouraging his disciples to pray, however, he stressed the necessity of knowing what you want to ask of God who will only give us the good things we ask him for. We are not to beat about the bush or be verbose. After all, God knows what we need *before* we ask him (Matt. 6:8). Jesus taught men to avoid *vain repetitions—vain* meaning "empty." Terence, in one of his poems, makes a husband say to his wife who had been offering thanks to God for the deliverance of their child from danger, that she must cease "stunning the gods with thanksgiving, unless thou judgest them by thyself that they cannot understand a thing unless they are told of it a hundred times."

The repetitious prayers of Mohammedanism, Judaism, Romanism, and Anglicanism, couched though they may be in solemn language, are so

cold, formal, and mechanical. Yet all repetitions
are not vain as we learn from the prayers of Jesus
in Gethsemane where he prayed the first time, the
second time, and the third time *saying the same
words* (Matt. 26:39–44). Some people would never
dream of commencing or ending a day without
repeating the Lord's Prayer. If they do so with all
due thought, warmth, and reverence of heart, saying the same words will make the ancient prayer
fresh every time.

That there are definite things to pray for is
found in the teaching of Jesus on the holy art of
praying. He taught his own to pray for the forgiveness of sins, for deliverance from evil, for the coming of his kingdom. Perhaps the only place where
he asked his disciples to pray for his great mission
is in the request, "Pray ye the Lord of the harvest
that he will send forth labourers into his harvest"
(Matt. 9:38). Says T. R. Glover in *The Jesus of History*, "Identification with God's purposes—identification with the individual needs of those we love
and those we ought to love—identification with
the world's sin and misery—these seem to be his
canons of prayer for us, as for himself."

Believing and watchful. Prayer and faith were often coupled by Jesus, "Whatsoever ye shall ask . . .
believing, ye shall receive" (Matt. 21:21, 22). When
it comes to the acceptance of the infinite possibili-
ties of prayer in the Holy Spirit, the majority of us
are unbelieving believers. Reproving his disciples
for their unbelief in connection with the lunatic
boy, Jesus gave them an illustration of believing
prayer (Matt. 17:20). He then went on to say that
by "prayer and fasting" faith is fostered in the

soul. *Prayer* helps spiritually, and so does *fasting,*
which means simplicity and spare use of food and
self-denial.

Several times Jesus recognized that men do not
really *quite* believe that their prayers will be answered; they are of "little faith." Repeating in one
form or another, that "all things are possible with
God," to "have faith in God," with the full weight
of his personality behind these exhortations, must
have given them the full value he intended. To
see him at prayer and to hear what he had to say
about it must have given faith of itself. The keynote of all prayer is the thought that our Father in
heaven listens to our petitions and answers them
as he deems best for our good and his glory.

Allied to *faith* is *obedience.* We must not cease to
pray, or cease to obey. It is not one or the other.
Dwelling upon the new promise and privilege in
prayer, Jesus links together two if's: "If ye
shall ask anything in my name, I will do it. If ye
love me keep my commandments" (John 14:14,
15.) Asking, even in his name, is not sufficient
unless we acquiesce in all he demands of us. As
believers we must walk on two feet—*trust* and
obey. Answered prayer is assured when, with
Tersteegen, we too can pray:

> Thy wonderful grand will, my God,
>   With triumph now I make it mine;
> And faith shall cry a joyous *Yes*
>   To every dear command of Thine.

Not only must we draw near to God with a true
heart in full assurance of *faith* (Heb. 10:22), a willing and obedient spirit is essential if God is to
draw near to us in the granting of our requests.

As to the injunction, to *watch* as well as *pray*, the same came from the disappointed heart of Jesus who had taken his disciples with him into Gethsemane that they might have fellowship with him in prayer. During a pause in his prayer-travail he came to his prayer partners but found them *sleeping* instead of praying and said, "Watch and pray, that ye enter not into temptation" (Matt. 26:40, 41). Alas! although those fishermen-disciples were accustomed to keep awake at night to fish, to keep awake to pray, especially after the strain of the previous sorrowful day, was beyond them. How gentle was the reproof of Jesus! *Could ye not watch with me one hour?* Spiritual sleeping and lethargy is one of the church's greatest sins, weaknesses, and dangers today. While she sleeps, the world hurries on, wide awake, to hell.

> Principalities and powers,
> Mustering their unseen array,
> Wait for thy unguarded hours,
> Watch and pray.

HIS EXAMPLES OF PRAYER

The disciples had the inestimable privilege of both seeing and hearing Jesus offer up some of his prayers with strong crying and tears. On one of these occasions, as he ceased praying, one of his disciples asked, "Lord, teach us to pray." This request elicited, not only his doctrine on *prayer*, but also one of the most perfect models of prayer ever composed, and which we call the Lord's Prayer (Matt. 6:8–15; Luke 11:1–13). While the disciples doubtless fashioned their prayers after this pattern-prayer, after almost two thousand years it is still repeated publicly and privately by countless thousands, yet it was not a prayer Jesus could offer.

In his reply to the request, "Teach us to pray," Jesus said, "When ye pray, say," not "When *we* pray." As the sinless Son of God, he could not offer this prayer simply because he had no sins to be forgiven and required no deliverance from evil as the one "holy, harmless, undefiled, and separate from sinners." The only kind of prayer Jesus could pray is the High Priestly Prayer of John 17. In the Lord's Prayer Jesus sets forth what his disciples needed and should desire for themselves. But in the intercessory prayer of John 17, he indicated what he desired for his own. It is also very interesting to study the forms in which the ideas expressed in the Lord's Prayer are reproduced and developed in the High Priestly Prayer.

The Lord's Prayer

Jesus never gave his disciples this sample prayer as the one and only they were to repeat. He meant it to be a pattern after which they were to shape their own approaches to God. What are the constituent elements around which the prayer is built?

Invocation. Give God the first place and magnify him for all he is in himself. Too often we come to him as beggars. Afflicted with so many needs, as soon as we come before him it is "Give me! Give me!" But Jesus taught that we must, first of all,

enter his presence as worshipers, recognizing God
as our Heavenly Father.

The Fatherhood of God is the keynote of all
prayer in the thought of Jesus, who often referred to his own reverence for God as the Father. In the Lord's Prayer and also in the High
Priestly Prayer, Jesus grounds true and effective
prayer upon a distinct relationship brought about
through the new birth by which a sinner becomes
a child of God. He himself came as the Son of
God. God, as God, is the creator who brought the
universe into being and controls it, but his heart
glows with all the affections of a Father toward
those in his universe who are his children through
faith in Christ.

Petition. At the heart of this incomparable
model is petition for our own needs, physical and
spiritual, and also prayer for others. Having the
almighty God as our loving Father, we can rest in
the fact that he knows what we need *before* we ask
him and is well able to undertake accordingly. Ori-
gen, one of the early fathers, said that "to pray for
earthly things was disobedience to God." But this
cannot be so since Jesus taught men to pray, "Give
us this day our daily bread." Thomas Aquinas also
affirmed that "Prayer is concerned only with awak-
ing trust in men and with contemplating of God's
love, and with the elevation of the pray-er." St.
Augustine put it, "You shall pray for nothing else
but God himself." Yet, surely, when Jesus said,
"*Whatsoever* ye shall ask," he included things of a
physical and material nature, as well as spiritual.
Although God knows beforehand all about the
matters that weigh heaviest with us (Luke 12:30),

he yet loves his children to talk these matters over with him.

Doxology. As given in the Authorized Version, the Lord's Prayer ends with praise, adoration, and gratitude to our Father-God, due to him for all his accomplishments—past, present, and future. So the prayer is a *sandwich* one, with God at each end and ourselves in the middle. Prayer covers not only forms of speech, such as personal requests and confession of sin, but the glorifying of God for all he is in himself. Prayer is not a means by which we try to influence deity or win God over to our side, or an effort to get him to change his mind, or merely to gain freedom from earthly ills and dangers, but an expression of our trust in, and acceptance of, the perfect will of God. Spirit-inspired prayer is the outpouring of the soul (Ps. 42:4).

Bishop Gore, who reckoned that the distinctive character of true prayer is shown by this example and that it is "the pattern of all prayer" in Christ's name," also wrote in *Jesus of Nazareth* that "the order of the clauses given in the Lord's Prayer suggests the whole philosophy not only of prayer but of life . . . It may be said that any child can understand this prayer: but to pray it with honest and full purpose of heart requires both the faith of a child and the courage of a hero."

High Priestly Prayer

The writer to the Hebrews reminds us that while on earth Jesus "offered up prayers and supplications" (Heb. 5:7). Alas! however, so very, very few of them were recorded. What a marvelous, spiritual classic it would be if only *all* the prayers he prayed, especially those he offered during those long nights of intercession beneath a Syrian sky, had been treasured up for our edification. Saturated with his tears, perhaps they were too sacred to preserve! As it is, only a few phrases out of the divinely rich prayer life of Jesus are found.

Fortunately, one complete prayer Jesus offered is found in the Gospels, and it is the most remarkable prayer ever prayed. Lifting up his eyes to heaven, he poured out his heart to his father in priestly intercession. It is not our purpose to expound fully the various declarations and desires forming this most wonderful, heart-moving prayer but to point out that in its superb construction is another pattern prayer to emulate. It has been said that "Order is Heaven's first law." Well, there ought to be the observance of order in our prayer lives as there is in the ordering of our homes or business lives. Prayer will never be effective if we rush into the presence of God with no idea of how to address him and to present our petitions. Both of these model prayers have *order* written all over them.

The High Priestly Prayer as recorded in John 17 moves in three circles—personal, particular, and general. What a profitable method Jesus gives us to follow.

Personal (John 17:1–8). In this section, the Son speaks to his Father about himself. As he taught his disciples to commence their prayers with "Our Father in heaven," so here his prayer commences *Father*, the simple filial term he used when only twelve years of age and which he also uttered as he drew his last breath. Reviewing his brief but blessed ministry on earth, Jesus, without assumption, said: "I have glorified thee on the earth: I have finished the work thou gavest me to do" (John 17:4); "I have manifested thy name" (John 17:6); "I have given them the words thou gavest me" (John 17:8, 14).

Particular (John 17:9–19). This central part of the prayer has an exclusion. "I pray for them," that is, for those given him of the Father (John 17:6, 7), but then Jesus went on to say, "I pray not for the world," neither did he in this middle section. His intercession focused upon all those redeemed by his blood, for he viewed his sacrificial work as being already accomplished. "I have finished the work thou gavest me to do." "It is finished." The burden of his intercession for his own is clearly evident. He pleads that they might be kept by God (John 17:11), that they might experience the fullness of joy (John 17:13). He pleads that they should be left in the world to witness (John 17:14, 15, 18), that they might be sanctified (John 17:15–17, 19).

Jesus offered these petitions for his own while here in the world, but when he ascended to heaven, he did not cease to pray for his people. Are we not assured that "He ever liveth to make intercession for them" (Heb. 7:24–28; Rom. 8:34)?

> He ever lives above
>   For me to intercede.
> His all-redeeming love,
>   His precious blood to plead;
> His blood atoned for all our race,
>   And sprinkles now the throne of grace.

Five bleeding wounds He bore,
Received on Calvary,
They pour effectual prayers,
They strongly plead for me:
"Forgive him, oh, forgive," they cry,
"Nor let that ransomed sinner die."

As believers, however, we are doubly blessed in the provision of divine intercessions, for we not only have the Lord Jesus as our prevailing intercessor in heaven, but the Holy Spirit as the continuous intercessor in our hearts. We do not know how to pray as we ought, but the Spirit himself intercedes for us, and sighs for us, too, with longings too deep for words (Rom. 8:26, 27). The Spirit is our intercession within that we might not sin, and the Savior is our Intercessor above to plead his efficacious blood if we do sin.

Christ is our Advocate on high;
Thou art our Advocate within;
Oh, plead the truth, and make reply
To every argument of sin.

C. Rawson's expressive hymn, "Comforter Divine," says:

In us, for us, intercede,
And with voiceless groanings, plead
Our unutterable need,
Comforter Divine.

General (John 17:20–26). In the remaining section of this true Lord's prayer, the one he actually offered to his father (see "About God," Vol. I), we move in a wider circle. At the outset there is a change of emphasis in this perfect example of intercession, "Neither pray I for *these* [his own, given him of the Father] but for them also which shall believe on me through their word" (John 17:20). Here Jesus looks down the vista of the ages and sees a great multitude no man can number being won for him through the life and witness of those redeemed by his blood. Through the testimony of his disciples the teeming godless in the world must be brought to know that they are loved by the Father (John 17:23).

What an all-embracing prayer, then, this is! The most perfect model of intercessory prayer in which Jesus prays about *himself*, about his *church*, and about his *world*. "Them also which shall believe" is a phrase indicating that he was making "intercession for the transgressors," even as he did when he died for their salvation at Calvary (Isa. 53:8, 12).

HIS EXPERIENCES OF PRAYER

Jesus' private prayer is eloquent of his secret life of communion with God his Father. His whole life exhibits the fulfillment of the apostolic prayer, "Pray without ceasing" (1 Thess. 5:17). He not only taught men about *prayer,* but embodied all his enunciations on such a topic. The four Gospels and the Epistle to the Hebrews lay emphasis on his prayer life.

He chose a quiet and solitary place for prayer (Mark 1:35; Matt. 14:23). Eager to begin the day with God, Jesus withdrew, early in the morning, to the silent desert.

He often continued all night in prayer (Luke 6:12). While men slept, he supplicated for his own and for the lost. Wearied by crowds thronging him during the day, he found spiritual invigoration in those all-night prayer sessions.

He was never too busy to pray and made time to pray when he was heavily pressed by service (Mark 6:31).

He prayed before he chose his disciples and before any important phase of his mission or threatened temptation and trial (Matt. 15:36; 26:39; Luke 6:12, 13).

He prayed on the return of the seventy from their successful missionary tour (Luke 10:17–22). The gratitude of God which Jesus expressed was an aspect of prayer.

He prayed at the Mount of Transfiguration and in Gethsemane (Luke 9:29; 22:41), and his prayer habit persisted even in the hour of his death (Luke 23:46).

Although very few of the prayers of Jesus are recorded, those we do have are full of spiritual instruction. John Peter Lange, in his most valuable *Commentary on the Holy Scriptures,* summarizes the pearls of Jesus' single prayers that are preserved for us.

> The prayer given in the Sermon on the Mount for the use of his people—*Our Father,* Matt. 6:9–13.
> The ascription of praise to God at the departure from Galilee, Matt. 11:25.
> The prayers at the grave of Lazarus, and within the precincts of the Temple, John 11.
> The high-priestly prayer, supplication in Gethsemane, and the prayer-words of the Crucified

One—*Father, forgive them—Eli, Eli*—and the closing prayer to which is added his exultant cry,
Father, into thy hands—It is finished.

Add to these the mentions of prayers, the thanks-
givings, the heavenward sighings of Christ, as also his
summonses and encouragements to prayer, and he
appears as the Prince of humanity, even in the realm
of prayer; in the manner, likewise, in which he concealed his prayer-life, exhibiting it only as there was
necessity for its presentment. If we regard his work
as a tree that towers into Heaven and overshadows
the world, his prayer-life is the root of this tree; his
overcoming of the world rests upon the infinite
depth of his self-presentation before God, his self-
devotion to God, his self-immersion in God, his self-
certitude and power from God. In his prayer-life the
perfect truth of his human nature has also approved
itself.

For a study of Jesus' actual prayers, ponder these
references: Matt. 11:25, 26; 26:36, 44; Luke
22:41, 42, 44; John 11:41, 42; 12:27–36; John 17.
With our finite understanding of the ways of
God we come up against the problem of unanswered prayer, and T. R. Glover suggests in *The
Jesus of History* that the Gospels even mention what
we might call the unanswered prayers of Jesus.

The prayer before the calling of the Twelve does not
exclude Judas who betrayed his Master—the Cup
does not pass in spite of the prayer in Gethsemane. It
is as if we had something to learn from the unanswered prayers of our Master. Certainly the content
of the Gospel for us would have been poorer if they
had been answered in our sense of the word; and this
fact, taken with his own teaching on prayer and his
own submission to the Father's will, may help us over
some of our difficulties. But Jesus had no doubt or

fear about prayer being answered, Luke 11:9. It is worth thinking out that the experience of Jesus lies behind his recommendation of prayer.

Prayer is a gift of grace from God, not an independent activity of man, and by the exercise of such a gift we grow like the praying Christ. We have the axiom that "we grow like those we live with" (2 Pet. 3:18). Michelangelo expresses this thought:

> The Prayers I make will then be sweet indeed,
> If Thou the Spirit give by which I pray:
> My unassisted heart in barren clay,
> That of its nature self can nothing feed.

In the quiet hour of prayer, our spirits are hushed as we realize the presence of our divine intercessor who waits to communicate to our needy hearts the fruits and graces of his Spirit.

Every day we need the fresh touch of his hand as we go out to live for him in our feverish age.

Every day we must hear the fresh whisper of his voice to keep us calm and serene amid the rabble of a coarse world.

Every day we require the fresh appropriation of his grace, peace, and wisdom, enabling us to be victorious over all satanic opposition. If, therefore, we strive to live in unbroken fellowship with the ever-praying Master, our lives will reflect his likeness and will be a continual benediction wherever in his providence he has placed us. Shall we allow Tennyson to have the last word?

> Thrice blest, whose *lives* are faithful Prayers,
> Whose lives a higher love endure!
> What souls possess themselves so pure?
> Or is there blessedness like theirs?

BIBLE STUDY QUESTIONS

Take time to turn to each Scripture reference and mark the verse or a portion in your Bible.

1. How and when must we pray?
2. What three qualities should be in our prayers?
3. Compare the two recorded prayers of Jesus.
4. How did Jesus' experience in prayer set an example for us?

— 17 —

The Sabbath

Although the first use of the term *sabbath* is in connection with the gathering of the manna when Moses said to the people of Israel, "Tomorrow is the rest of the holy sabbath unto the Lord.... Today is a sabbath unto the Lord" (Exod. 16:23, 25, 26), all that the day represents goes back to creation. When God finished his creative work, "On the seventh day God ended his work which he had made, and he rested on the seventh day from all his works which he had made. And God blessed the seventh day, and sanctified it, because that in it he had rested from all his work which God created and made" (Gen. 2:1-3).

The word *sabbath* means "cessation" or "rest," so we can read, "He *sabbathed* on the seventh day." God, then, is prominent as the world's first sabbath keeper. Thereafter, he instituted a day of rest for all men, for which the seventh day was set apart. "The seventh day, which is the sabbath ... the Lord has given you the sabbath" (Exod. 16:26, 29). Thus, in keeping with this divine command and provision, "The people rested on the seventh

day" (Exod. 16:30). James Grahame, early eigh-
teenth-century poet, has the line, "Hail, Sabbath!
thee I hail, the poor man's day." But the sabbath
was not only designed for the poor, but for all
men. The great word of Jesus was that "the sabbath was made for man, and not man for the sabbath," and therefore, God meant the day to be
one of relief and rest. The first part of our Lord's
statement looks back to the creation of man and
implies that the necessity for a day of rest is
rooted in human constitution so that it must last
as long as man is what he is.

But the sabbath not only has primeval sanction,
holding the place in the law of creation; it also
carried the authority of the Decalogue, being
found among the Ten Commandments (Exod.
20:8–10). The divine fiat is repeated: "The seventh day is the sabbath of the Lord thy God"
(Exod. 16:23; 20:10). God *sanctified* this day, or
made it holy, or separated it unto himself, and
exhorted his ancient people to keep the day holy.
After six days of *work*, the seventh day was for
worship—a day of physical rest but of spiritual activity through prayer, reflection, and service.
Keats, in "The Eve of Saint Mark," wrote:

> Upon a Sabbath day it fell;
> Twice holy was the Sabbath-bell,
> That call'd the folk to evening prayer.

Dear old George Herbert, quaint poet of the sixteenth century, has this verse on Sunday:

> The Sundays of man's life,
> Threaded together on Time's string,
> Make bracelets to adorn the wife

Of the eternal glorious King.
On Sunday Heaven's gate stands ope;
Blessings are plentiful and rife,
More plentiful than hope.

All the time Israel kept her sabbath unto the Lord, he blessed and prospered her. The story is told of Stephen Girard, the free thinker, millionaire of Philadelphia, Pennsylvania. One Saturday night he bade his clerks come the following day and unload a vessel in the dock. One clerk refused to comply with the demand. "Well, sir," said Girard, "if you cannot do as I wish, we can separate."

"I know that, sir," said the spiritual hero. "I also know that I have a widowed mother to care for, but I cannot work on Sunday."

Girard replied, "Go to the cashier's desk; he will settle the wages due you."

One day a bank president asked Girard if he knew of a suitable person for cashier in his bank, and Girard named the young man he had dismissed. "But," said the president, "I thought you discharged him."

"I did," was the answer, "because he would not work on Sunday, and the man who will lose his situation from principle is the man to whom you can entrust your money."

The prophets of the Old Testament found fault with the people because their worship on the sabbath was not spiritual or prompted by love and gratitude. They connected it with the festival of the new moon and came to worship the moon instead of its creator (2 Kings 4:23; Amos 8:5; Isa. 1:13). The nation became guilty of unfaithfulness in profaning the sabbath, one of Israel's most valuable institutions. Confessions of failure to keep the sabbath holy were frequent (Neh. 13:15–22; Isa. 56:2, 4; 58:13; Ezek. 20:12–24). During the period between the Testaments, with the development of the synagogue, the sabbath became a day of worship and of study of the Law, as well as a day of cessation from all secular employment on the part of the pious in Israel (1 Macc. 2:29–41).

Coming to the New Testament, the first use of· the term *sabbath* is found in connection with the sharp conflict Jesus was to have on the subject of sabbath observance with the religious leaders of the Jews (Matt. 12:1, 2, 5). Almost at the outset of his ministry, Jesus set himself squarely against the current rabbinic restrictions as being contrary to the spirit of the original law of the sabbath when instituted by God. From this time on he maintained the most uncompromising attitude of opposition to the traditional mode of keeping the sabbath day and found himself in the sharpest collision on this subject with the ecclesiastical authorities.

At the outset, it must be affirmed that Jesus was not a sabbath-breaker in the sense in which the Jews of old were. In spite of all the controversies he had with the scribes and Pharisees about the sabbath, he himself was a careful and reverent keeper of the day, as his Father ordained it to be observed. He taught the observance of the sabbath, not only by his efforts on such a day, but by his example. As a growing boy in his Nazareth home, Jesus would be impressed by the observance of the sabbath. Throughout his thirty hidden years, one-half hour before sunset each Friday, he would hear the call from the parapet of the synagogue, announcing that the sabbath, we now recognize as Saturday, was about to begin. From sunset to the next sunset all work ceased. Any boy of thirteen and upwards, when he had made the pilgrimage to the Temple and had become a son of the Law, could be called upon to read.

It is not surprising, therefore, to read that when Jesus entered his public ministry, he taught in the synagogues. Luke tells us that when he came to Nazareth where he had been brought up that "*as his custom was*, he went into the synagogue on the sabbath day, and stood up for to read" (Luke 4:16). The record of his frequent visits to synagogues and that he taught the people on the sabbath days is firm evidence that this was his habit and settled custom, and that he made use of the day and place, not only to worship, but to preach and teach the words his Father had given him (John 17:7). It is against this ardent love of his, both for the sabbath and the sanctuary, that we examine the six times the professed lovers of the past preferred against Jesus the charge of sabbath desecration (Matt. 12:1–18, etc.).

THE RELIGIOUS LEADERS HAD CHANGED THE SABBATH—A DAY OF BLESSING—INTO A BURDEN

The teachings and utterances of Jesus about the sabbath arose out of his controversies with the scribes and Pharisees over his miracles of healing and mercy which he undertook on the sabbath. In every instance he rebuked his critics for their misinterpretation of the law concerning such a day and for their efforts to make it a burden instead of a benefit. Some of the regulation and petty restrictions with which the gracious and beneficent law of the sabbath was weighted down were ludicrous. For instance, on this holy day a man might lead an animal to the watering trough, but he could not carry water to the thirsty beast. A broken leg could not be set until the sabbath was over.

The many petty and vexatious rules hedged around the sabbath and contrary to true religion and humanity raised the righteous indignation of Jesus and became the chief subject of contention between him and the Pharisees (Luke 13:14; 14:1; John 5:10; 7:23; 9:14, etc.). Professor A. M. Fairbairn in his *Studies in the Life of Christ* gives us this concise summary of the clash between Jesus and the Pharisees over the day of rest.

> If there was anything sacred in Judaism, it was the Sabbath; the most awful sanctities and sanctions hedged it round. It seemed essential to the monotheist, necessary alike to their faith and worship. It stood to them indissolubly connected with the origin of the world and of their nation. The Creator had rested on the seventh day, and Jehovah who had delivered their fathers from Egypt, required the Sabbath to be sacred unto him. They were bound to observe it by reasons alike religious and political; it was the symbol and seal of their right to be the people of God, possessed of the Law he instituted that they might obey.
>
> But the day of rest they had made toilsome

through sacerdotal observances and minute legal restrictions. The Sabbath of Jehovah had been lost in a Sabbath of the Scribes. The greatest of the prophets had declared that he could not endure their "new moons and sabbaths," Isa. 1:13, but the Scribes proved mightier than the prophet, and their day of tyrannical prescriptions and observances was identified with God's. Against this idolatry of the Sabbath Christ protested in the most direct and practical way. He walked through the cornfields, and allowed his disciples to pluck ears of corn, Matt. 12:1-9; Mark 2:23. He healed and in one case made the man he healed carry the bed on which before he had lain, Matt. 12:10-13; Luke 13:14; John 5:10. The scandal was great. Such profanity had not been seen in Israel.

JESUS PROTESTED AGAINST IDOLATRY OF THE SABBATH

All of Christ's replies to those who condemned his sabbath-day actions were most significant, each covering the whole question of his truth and his relation to the Law. Even during his silent years in Nazareth, Jesus observed how people had come to associate the thought of God with stupid and irksome laws, perverting thereby the divine purpose of the day of rest. People came to think more of what they were forbidden to do by the religious leaders, instead of thinking of God with joy as their Father who wanted them to be joyful on his day. Thus Jesus revealed himself as careless about the special silly laws and prohibitions and, in placing himself against those who enacted them, manifested his supreme authority.

Because the mind of Jesus was fixed upon the essentials of life and truth, he showed utter disregard for Pharisaical traditions which, because of their age, had gathered the weight of authority. He regarded such traditions as hindrances to faith and service to God and men, and so differed materially from the prevailing attitude of the scribes and Pharisees. Jesus could dare assert the higher law for man than the quietism of an unsympathetic sabbath, and could risk his reputation by helpful fellowship with sinners. He would not be limited save by his own greatness.

What must not be forgotten is that Jesus never meant to discredit the sabbath as a divine institution. He held it in high regard but fought for a more liberal and lenient interpretation of the law of the sabbath since he was not a rigid sabbatarian. One wonders what Jesus would do if in our ·midst today, when men have gone to the other extreme and have swept aside all law and custom concerning the day, now known as his day, *the Lord's day?* Would he rebuke for its widespread desecration, be less severe, or his anger less burning than it was when he rebuked the scribes and Pharisees for their hardness of heart concerning the original intention of his day?

That Jesus himself paid reverent heed to the sabbath as the day of worship above all other days is shown in the record of the man with the withered hand. He appears to have made a habit of worshiping and teaching in the synagogue until this particular sabbath, when his foes sought to kill him (Luke 4:14, 15). After this, and because persistence would only have meant the risk of a

sudden and untimely ending of his mission by violence, he seems to have ceased to frequent the
synagogue except for one more effort to teach in
his own home synagogue at Nazareth, when
again he was rejected, Matt. 13:54–58; Mark 6:1–6.
*The violent opposition of the Sadducees and Herod-
ians at this time marks a decisive turning point in our
Lord's ministry.*

JESUS PROCLAIMED THE TRUE END
OR FUNCTION OF THE SABBATH

With his superb knowledge of Old Testament
Scriptures, Jesus knew that his beneficial use of
the sabbath was not unprecedented. David had
done a profane thing and was blameless—supreme need was his justification for eating the
shewbread (1 Sam. 21:6; Matt. 12:2–4). Then
there were the Temple priests who, on the sabbath day, profaned the day and were yet blameless (Num. 28:9, 10; Matt. 12:5) What was proper
for the priests is not wrong for the people. Jesus,
greater than the Temple, as the great high priest
believed that the sabbath was a day for showing
mercy. Mercy was the best offering man could
render to God—better than sacrifice.

The notion of the scribes and Pharisees as to
the use of the sabbath was fatal to all true worship
on such a day. Failing to see that the sabbath was
made for man, and not man for it, they missed
the true function of the day, and the laws they
enacted turned it into a burden thus destroying its
end. Passers-by were allowed to pluck a few ears

of standing corn or one or two grapes, but reaping and gathering on the sabbath were forbidden. The Pharisees argued that the disciples were virtually reaping and so breaking the law. But Jesus, as with the question about fasting, raises the whole matter above legal enactment. To him, necessary works and acts are compatible with the sabbath (Matt. 12:1-8; Luke 6:1-5; Mark 2:23-28).

The teaching of Jesus, then, is clear. Man should control the sabbath, its observance in worship and benevolences. The Pharisees were the real, religious sabbath breakers in that they allowed themselves to witness the sufferings of fellow-men without alleviation of pain on the sabbath, but their mercenary plans required attention to their beasts. Money meant more to them than needy men. The sabbath rule is for man's good. If it hampers him in the higher duty of God's service, it must go. The constant attitude of Jesus was a deep reverence for the ordinance of the sabbath, in so far as it served religious ends, with a resolute vindication of the principle that the sabbath was made for man (Luke 4:16).

Six times over the professed lovers of the fact preferred against Jesus the charge of sabbath desecration, but he persisted in the so-called desecration. On such a day, he engaged in pleasant social fellowship with men, for it was on a sabbath that he accepted an invitation to dine with one of the chief Pharisees, and on such an occasion he healed a sick man. In fact, it was by the seven miracles he performed on the sabbath that Jesus demonstrated the higher law of the sabbath through such deeds of mercy. Of the thirty-three recorded miracles, seven were performed on the sabbath day. Doubtless there were others. It was the working of these sabbath miracles which stirred such bitter opposition to Jesus on the part of the religious leaders of the Jews. The seven recorded healings include:

1. *The demoniac of Capernaum* (Mark 1:21-27).
2. *Peter's mother-in-law, in Capernaum* (Mark 1:29-31).
3. *The impotent man, in Jerusalem* (John 5:1-18). Jesus not only healed this man, but ordered him to carry his bed home, even though the Pharisees said nothing should be carried on the sabbath. By this miracle, and the previous two, Jesus illustrated that rest does not mean idleness. Sabbath rest did not imply disengagement from acts of mercy.
4. *The man with the withered hand* (Mark 3:1-6). A normal body and a released sufferer were a greater honor to the sabbath than restrictions against gathering sticks. Jesus taught by his action that to refuse the opportunity of a good act is in effect to do evil. To let die by refusing rescue is in effect to kill. A good, beneficial, merciful act cannot be contrary to the spirit and purpose of the sabbath.
5. *The woman bent over* (Luke 13:11-17). Here, again, Jesus taught that it is wrong at any time to acquiesce in human misery if with divine help we can relieve it. The contrast is wonderful between Jesus the Benefactor and the synagogue ruler, the critic, when the poor woman was relieved of her bondage and suffering. The synagogue became a cathedral of praise.

6. *The man with dropsy* (Luke 14:1–6). Once again, by his act, Jesus emphasized that no law of God can be a barrier to work of mercy.

7. *The man born blind* (John 9:1–14). This afflicted man at the Pool of Siloam, when healed, was willing to brave the censure of the religious leaders for having violated the ordinance about the sabbath, for the divine healer had given him what no other person had attempted to bestow. According to the traditions of men, it might be wrong to heal on the sabbath, but the rejoicing, now-seeing man accepted the word of his divine benefactor and recognized Jesus' higher authority. (See my book, *All the Miracles of the Bible,* for additional material on these seven sabbath miracles.)

JESUS DECLARED HIMSELF TO BE LORD OF THE SABBATH

Perhaps more than for any other reason, the scribes and Pharisees opposed and persecuted Jesus and conspired to slay him because of what seemed to them his blasphemous claim to lordship over the sabbath. The intention of Jesus in all his contacts and conversations with his foes about the sabbath was that out of its sacred hours there should be derived the rest and the strength required for living, on the other days of the week, a life of "judgment, mercy, and faith." Such an end gives force to his assertion, "Therefore the Son of man is Lord also of the sabbath." Standing above ordinary men, even the religious men he acted against, Jesus yet likened himself with humanity by the title he used of himself. Jesus, as the Son of man, is so connected with all men as to be fit to be the mouthpiece of all in vindicating their claim to a gift given them at Creation against the encroachments of all who, under whatever pretense, would deprive them of their birthright.

As *Lord* of the sabbath, Jesus had the right to order it for man's good, to institute or modify it so as to serve his true weal. If man needed help on the sabbath, he had the right to it. Acts of healing were worthy of the day. "The better the day, the better the deed." It was God-like to do good on the sabbath, and as God the Son, Jesus went about doing good on *all* days. As the Messiah, he was not subject to the restrictions of men regarding the sabbath—a day he always held in high regard. But because of who he was in himself, he could at any moment assert his lordship over the sabbath, as he did (Mark 2:28). May grace be ours to spend our sabbaths for the worship of the Lord and works of mercy!

A Sabbath well spent,
Brings a week of content,
And strength for the toils of the morrow.
But a Sabbath mis-spent
What'er may be gained,
Is a certain forerunner of sorrow.

JESUS, BY HIS DEATH AND RESURRECTION, CHANGED THE SABBATH INTO THE LORD'S DAY

Not only did the Lord of the sabbath change the nature of such a divinely instituted day by

tearing away irksome restrictions, making it a
bane instead of a blessing; he also, by the finished
work at Calvary, changed its position in the week
of seven days. Up until the time of the crucifixion
both Jesus and his apostles observed the seventh
day sabbath. When he was in the tomb his followers rested on "the sabbath . . . according to the
commandment" (Luke 23:56). Jews and Seventh-
Day Adventists still keep the ancient sabbath and
meet for worship on such a day, which is now our
Saturday. The church in Scotland has retained the
term sabbath but observes the day of rest from
the labors of the past week and church worship
and activities on our Sunday, which is not the seventh day, but the first day of another week.

The name *Sunday* is of heathen origin and
means *Sun*-day, or the day on which the sun was
worshiped. Our consideration, then, of what Jesus
taught concerning the sabbath would not be complete without reference to this change in the Christian world in the observance of the first day of
the week instead of the seventh. While the Gospels record no statement from Jesus authorizing
such change, nevertheless it was made. Christians, from the earliest years in the apostolic era,
marked the first day of the week for special worship and service for God as a memorial of the
Lord's resurrection from the dead. It is worthy of
note that of the ten appearances recorded after
his resurrection, and before his ascension, *six* were
on the first day of the week, the Sunday, and
none on the sabbath, the seventh day. Pentecost
that year fell on the first day of the week, and it
was on this day that the Holy Spirit came down

and the church went out to fulfill her mission in a world of need.

The Christian Sunday offers a contrast to the Jewish sabbath, which it superseded, because it stands, not merely for cessation of work, but for newness of life begun. For awhile in the early church the two days were observed, but the sabbath gradually fell out of observance by Christians, as did worship in the Temple and the synagogue. At the Council at Jerusalem in A.D. 49, there was no mention of sabbath obligation for Christians (Acts 15:28, 29; Col. 2:16, 17). The Christians in the ancient church very soon distinguished the first day of the week, Sunday—however, not as a sabbath but as an assembly day of the Church, to study the word of God together and to celebrate the ordinances one with another. Without a shadow of doubt this took place as early as the first part of the second century. Ignatius, one of the church fathers of the first and second centuries, has phrases in his writings such as, "No longer keeping the Sabbath but living according to the Lord's Day on which also our Light arose"; "The Lord's Day began to dawn"; "Early on the Lord's Day"; "We keep the light day with gladness, on which Jesus arose from the dead."

But the observance of the first day of the week as the day of worship and service for God, which the apostles came to name the Lord's Day, took place before the second century. Christian worship at Troas was on "the first day of the week, when the disciples came together to break bread, Paul preached unto them" (Acts 20:7). For the relief of the impoverished disciples in Jerusalem, Paul exhorted, "Upon the first day of the week let every one of you lay by in store, as God hath prospered him" (1 Cor. 16:2). The inference is that this was the day Christians assembled themselves together and offerings were taken for church needs and for needy saints. John tells us that he was on the Isle of Patmos "in the Spirit on the Lord's Day" (Rev. 1:10), when he received the remarkable revelation of Jesus he recorded. The phrase "first day of the week" is also found in Matthew 28:1, Mark 16:2, Luke 24:1, and John 20:1, 19.

What is clearly evident is the way the early Christians brought over into their mode of observing the Lord's Day the best elements of the old Jewish sabbath, without its petty and nonbeneficial restrictions. Some of the early church fathers like Augustine testified that the change from the seventh day to the first day was made before their time and that such a change could not have been made except by the authority of the apostles and, therefore, by the authority of Jesus himself. That the change of day had his sanction is seen in the appropriateness of the revelation of himself as the exalted Lord on the "Lord's Day" when all saved by his grace could have their minds directed toward his entrance into glory through the resurrection. Comments Fausset in *A Critical Commentary* (by Jammieson, Fausset, and Brown):

> As the O.T. Sabbath was the seal of the first creation in innocence, so the N.T. Lord's Day is the seal of the new creation. The Father's rest after Creation answers to Christ's after redemption's completion.

Today, Christians generally observe Sunday as the day of freedom from their workaday activities, as a day of religious worship in the house of God, as a day for engaging in deeds of kindness and compassion and mercy, and as a day of lofty spiritual conversation. If we reverence the Lord's Day, then what the prophet said concerning the old sabbath will be true of the new day: "If thou turn away thy foot from the sabbath, from doing thy pleasure on my holy day; and call the sabbath a delight, the holy of the Lord, honourable; and shalt honour him, not doing thine own ways, nor finding thine own pleasure, nor speaking thine own words: then shalt thou delight thyself in the Lord; and I will cause thee to ride upon the high places of the earth, and feed thee with the heritage of Jacob thy father: for the mouth of the Lord hath spoken it" (Isa. 58:13, 14).

Neale, the hymnist, gives us the translation from the Latin of an ancient hymn:

> Oh, what the joy and the glory must be,
> Those endless Sabbaths the blessed ones see.

Dryden has the phrase "Or breaks the eternal Sabbath of his rest." Tennyson could write:

> The sabbaths of Eternity,
> One sabbath deep and wide—

But what should occupy our thoughts is the reverent observance of our present sabbaths—dykes, protecting our lives from the invading sea of secularity, bridges from which we walk from time into eternity. Some of the early social reformers, men with Christian ideals, held Moses to be the greatest of labor reformers, seeing his chief labor reform was to give the sabbath to mankind. John Bright, English orator and statesman of the eighteenth century, addressing the toiling masses of Lancashire, speaking on the sabbath, quoted very fittingly the lines of George Herbert:

> Without thy light the week was dark;
> Thy torch doth show the way.

We live in a secular age when Sunday observance for the spiritual culture of the soul is flouted. Travel, sport, centers of worldly amusement capture the time, money, and interest of increasing multitudes, and church attendance is gradually declining. In fact, the majority of churches have a struggle to exist in these days of Sunday desecration. May we ever be found among those who do not forsake the assembling themselves together for worship and service to God on the first day of the week!

O day of rest and gladness, O day of joy and light,
O balm of care and sadness, most beautiful, most
    bright.
On thee at the Creation, the light first had its birth,
On thee for our Salvation, Christ rose from depths of
    earth.
On thee our Lord victorious, the Spirit sent from
    Heaven,
And thus on Thee most glorious, a triple light was
    given.

BIBLE STUDY QUESTION

Take time to turn to each Scripture reference and mark the verse or a portion in your Bible.

1. How did the rabbinical laws profane the sabbath?
2. In what way did Jesus show his higher regard of the sabbath?
3. What made Jesus Lord of the sabbath?
4. How did the Lord's Day become Sunday, the first day?

— 18 —

Sickness and Death

The most casual reader of the four Gospels cannot but be impressed with the fact that Jesus looked upon diseases and death as an intrusion into God's original plan for the human race. He deemed all the ills the flesh is heir to as sin's insurgents—as indeed they are—to be challenged and banished, which he did every time he encountered them. As the Life, he healed all manner of sicknesses and diseases; and as the Resurrection, he restored all the dead of whom he had knowledge. Then, as we are to discover, rich teachings are connected with his miraculous ministry in the realm of the physical. Preeminently, Jesus is portrayed as the Healer-Teacher. Original words from which *sick, sickness* and *disease* come appear in the New Testament some fifty-seven times, principally in the Gospels, where the number of references is significant as proving how much the healing of the sick stands in our Lord's ministry.

Jesus' fame as the perfect healer of diseases, physical and mental, quickly spread, and the needy from far and near sought his aid; such was his sympathy that none were left uncured. He came to bring health of body, as well as health of mind and of spirit, and this characteristic activity fills a large part of the gospel story. Jesus, full of compassion, with a large heart open to the cry of the distressed, ever gentle and tender-hearted yet displaying a power that seemed limitless, lived in two worlds—one *above* and the other *around* him.

Contact with the world above was ever maintained. Although he came *from* heaven, he was ever *in* heaven, paradoxical though it may seem (John 3:13). His was ever the realization that God the Father, as a free agent, was ever ready to hear the call of his creatures and able to meet their needs in rich and overflowing measure.

Contact with the world around was also sustained. Jesus came to live in our world of wonder and was ever doing wonderful and seemingly impossible things while among men. The hidden yet mighty forces of the universe were as instruments ever ready at hand. He had deep insight to see the real needs of those who sought his aid and was able to see and meet, not only the outward ills, but inward diseases too. His was an insight born of love, enabling him to assess each suppliant as a separate person, and act accordingly. Thus, in his miracles he is a revelation of what God is and of what man through him may become.

A rendering of the psalmist's declaration, "He bindeth up their wounds" (Ps. 147:3), is given as, "He giveth medicine to heal their sickness." While here on earth, Jesus himself was the medicine both for broken hearts and for broken bodies, and, as the hymnist reminds us, he is ever the same.

> Christ is my Meat, Christ is my Drink,
> My Medicine and my Health;
> My Peace, my Strength, my Joy, my Crown,
> My Glory and my Wealth.

Recording the healing ministry in our Lord's time, four times over Matthew uses the term *manner* to describe the variety of cures effected. "Jesus went about . . . healing all manner of sickness and all manner of disease among the people" (Matt. 4:23). "He called unto him his twelve disciples and gave them power . . . to heal all manner of sickness and all manner of disease" (Matt. 10:1).

Both the Master and his divinely empowered disciples were able to heal all types and conditions of physical infirmity. No case was beyond them. *All* dealt with were restored to health, not after a time of convalescence, but instantly and perfectly. The miracles of Jesus in this realm had a wide scope, the indefinite mention of all sorts of diseases testifying to his immense power. It is to be understood that the following miracles grouped according to the nature of the ailments treated are limited to the Gospels, since our study only covers what Jesus taught and wrought in the days of his flesh. Further, specified diseases can be found in other parts of Scripture. In this connection the reader should consult the author's work, *All the Miracles of the Bible*.

The terse proverb Jesus quoted, "They that are whole have no need of the physician, but they that are sick" (Mark 2:17), was practiced by him who

came as the Great Physician to heal the sick in
soul, as well as the sick in body.

Physical Disorders
    Blindness, four cases
    Leprosy, two cases
    Fever, two cases
    Lameness, one case
    Deafness and Dumbness, one case
    Dropsy, one case
    Issue of Blood, one case
    Wound, one case
Nervous Disorders
    Demoniacal Possession, six cases
    Paralysis, three cases
    Spirit of Infirmity, one case
Death, three cases.

That there were many others with similar ailments and possibly further forms of sickness is
implicit in the statement that as the fame of Jesus
spread abroad, concerned relatives and friends
"Brought unto him all sick people that were taken
with divers diseases and torments, and those which
were possessed with devils, and those which were
lunatic, and those that had the palsy; and he
healed them" (Matt. 4:24).

In connection with the healing of the woman of
her twelve-year-old hemorrhage, we read that the
poor dear had suffered much at the hands of many
physicians, and that after spending all her money
in the quest of relief, she was "nothing bettered,
but rather grew worse" (Mark 5:26). But with Jesus,
it was so different. He never failed, never lost
a case. "He healed them *all*" without charging

a penny for a complete restoration to health or to sanity.

Some of the *methods* which the Divine Healer employed were as diverse as the diseases he healed. While he gave different processes to his miracles of healing, he could just as easily have dispensed with them. For instance, blind Bartimaeus received his sight immediately without any action on his part, save for his faith in the ability of Jesus to restore sight (Mark 10:46–52). But when it came to the blind man of Siloam, there was a different procedure. Jesus put saliva on his darkened eyes and laid his hands upon him. Partial sight was restored, for he saw people as trees walking. Again Jesus touched his eyes, and sight was fully restored. The ten lepers experienced recovery on their way to the priest. The versatility and adaptability of Jesus can also be traced in his power to heal being present (Matt. 4:23), or being absent (Matt. 8:13), with a touch (Matt. 8:3), or by a word (Matt. 8:8, 13). Anointing with oil is also mentioned (Mark 6:13). The only instance of record where Jesus deals first with a man's spiritual ills and only later with his bodily ones is that of the palsied man (Mark 2:1–12). His first concern was for the sufferer himself in his inner life. Probably his illness was a direct result of past sins, or connected with them, and the word of forgiveness was essential to the man's cure.

Professor Stalker points out in *The Ethic of Jesus* that Christ's miracles of healing were not intended merely to evoke faith in him as a wonderworker but also as a source of higher benefits:

While many reasons may be assigned for the working of miracles, the chief must always be this—that
the healing of the body illustrated the salvation of the
soul. As the bodies of men are afflicted with many
varieties, so are their souls with many kinds of sins;
and, by grappling with all bodily ills, as these were
brought to him, Jesus signified that he was able with
equal success to deal with the maladies of the soul.
How exact the parallel was may be learned from the
fact that to the Woman who was a Sinner, when he
forgave her sins, he said the very same as he used to
say to those cured of bodily infirmities: "Thy faith
hath made thee whole."

Akin to this method of Jesus is the relation of
sin to sickness and disease. Although we may
argue that not *all* suffering comes from sin, the
fact remains that sin is the generic cause of suffering. When God fashioned Adam and Eve, he endowed them with perfect health, but when they
sinned by taking the forbidden fruit, deteriora-
tion of body and soul began. With the entrance of
sin into God's perfect world came pain, suffering,
and death. Thus a race of sinners inherited frailties that brought sickness and disease. Jesus, of
course, knew that suffering and physical disability
could not always be traced to immediate causes of
sin in the life of the sufferer. In the case of the
man born blind, he made it clear that no special
sin in the man himself or in his parents was responsible for the blindness. Yet he also knew that
certain sins have their effects upon the body, and
that the sinner often reaps his harvest of tears and
pain. To the restored lame man of Bethesda, he

said, "Behold, thou art made whole: sin no more, lest a worse thing befall thee." Is there not here the implication that previous sin had caused the disease, as well as a warning to live clean in the future? There are those like Jairus and the Syrophoenician woman who came to Jesus seeking relief, not for themselves, but for their relatives; and healing was granted in answer to their requests. Then, as we have seen, there were cases of bodily illness in which the cure seems to have been given without the cooperation of the faith of the patient. In spiritual healing, personal faith is naturally essential, but it might be awakened by the antecedent faith of friends as in the case of the man brought to Jesus by four anxious friends. "Jesus seeing *their* faith, said to the sick of the palsy, Son, be of good cheer; thy sins are forgiven thee." The four bearers only wanted a bodily cure for their afflicted friend, but Jesus gave him the higher blessing of soul-healing as well.

The woman with the issue of blood came unseen, and apparently Jesus took no active part in her cure. But conscious of the sense of loss of power which he ever possessed, he asked, "Who touched me?" The sensation he experienced was akin to the drawing off of blood from the body. Can it be that in this higher field of transfer of spiritual power there are laws we know nothing of? The only purpose Jesus had in bringing this shy, trembling woman to the front was to assure her that her faith-touch secured her perfect restoration to health.

The method of delay in relieving the critically sick appears somewhat perplexing. In the majority of cases Jesus responded at once to a request, but with Lazarus, whom he loved, it was different. When Martha and Mary saw the distressed condition of their brother, they immediately sent information of his plight to Jesus, "Lord, behold he whom thou lovest is sick." We would have thought that such a heart-moving appeal would have met with immediate, appropriate action on his part; that because his presence was not necessary to healing, he could have spoken the word only where he was, ordaining that the miracle should be performed some two miles distant where Lazarus was on his deathbed. But when Jesus received the sad news, "He abode two days still in the same place where he was." How could he delay in healing the one he loved? To make his action more mysterious, his message on learning that Lazarus was dead seemed heartless, "I am glad for your sake that I was not there" (John 11:15).

Can you not imagine how the nonarrival of Jesus until Lazarus was in his grave disturbed the two sorrowful sisters he likewise loved? Did they have a doubt that perhaps he was not as loving and powerful as they had thought him to be? Did Martha, ever troubled with many things, say to her sister, "Why, oh why, does he not hurry?" What distress of heart must have been theirs! Love's delays are hard to understand, and in the waiting period doubt arises as to their purpose. When the Lord's ear seems heavy that he cannot hear and his heart hard that he does not respond to the urgent plea for help, faith sometimes weakens. Those sisters in Bethany never doubted for

a moment that Jesus would speed with all possible
haste to be at the side of the man he loved and
save him from death, but he left them to see their
brother worsen and die and buried in a grave.

Often divine dealings are dark and mysterious,
and although Jesus loves us, love permits pain
and sickness and death. F. B. Meyer in his *Commentary on John* says that the *therefore* is startling.
"When He heard therefore that he was sick, He
abode two days still in the same place where He
was." Jesus abstained from going to Bethany "not
because he did not love them, but because he did
love them." Although Martha and Mary may have
thought that Jesus appeared neglectful, he is
never so. He was cognizant of all that transpired
in their much-loved home—the gradual waning of
Lazarus, the anguish of his sisters as they watched
him die, the funeral cortége to the rocky tomb.
Jesus knew it all, but he did not go to the sorrow-
stricken home till he saw that he could interpose
with the best possible result. So is it ever. His step
may linger, but his watchful interest never falters.
There is not a sigh, a pang, a tear, that escapes his
notice. There is not a fluttering pulse which he
does not feel, noticing its tremulous anxiety. He
sits as the refiner of silver. He knows our sorrows,
and is acquainted with our grief. He slumbers not,
nor sleeps.

When at length, as the God of love manifest in
flesh, Jesus appeared in Bethany, he accomplished more than the grief-stricken sisters could
have asked or thought, for he not only healed the
sick but raised the dead. The benefit of all gained
by his delay was evident, and the wisdom of divine

patience was vindicated as he made the darkness of the tomb the background against which to set forth the luster of resurrection glory.

The apparent silence of God is ever a perplexing question our finite minds try to fashion. "A silent Heaven is the greatest mystery of our existence," says Sir Robert Anderson in his unique volume, *The Silence of God.* "Martyrs have died, with faces turned to heaven and hearts upraised in prayer to God; but the heaven has seemed as hard as brass, and the God of their prayers as powerless as themselves or as callous as their persecutors." E. Stanley Jones in his heart-moving work, *Christ and Human Suffering,* says:

As the twisted body of Jesus hung on the cross it seemed to turn into a vast question mark against the sky line, and as from his lips comes the cry, "My God, why?" it seems that all anguish and pain of the ages is gathered up in that bitter cry. There is not a single problem that perplexes and wrings our hearts that is not gathered up in that anguished question.

The problems of permitted evil, of unanswered prayers, of unrelieved pain and suffering, and of glaring inequalities are ever present with us. We wonder why infinite Love does not rush instantly to the relief of troubled hearts to stay their grief and dry their tears! In personal experience we have to learn that the Savior does not come until the angel of pain has fulfilled her task. Does not George Matheson remind us of "the joy that seeketh us through pain"? If Jesus himself "learned obedience by the things that he suffered," how can we estimate what we owe to the permitted trials, pain, and suffering overtaking us? Jesus himself as the Man of Sorrows illustrated the truth

> That the mark of rank in nature
> Is capacity for pain,
> That the anguish of the singer
> Makes the sweetness of the strain.

As with our Lord, so with ourselves; there are qualities sorrow and anguish can alone perfect, virtues of the Christian life they alone can develop.

> Where were *Faith*, without trial to test it;
> *Patience*, with nothing to bear;
> *Experience*, without tribulation to enrich it.

Life without trouble, pain, and suffering would be less noble, less compassionate. Character is ennobled by the capacity to bear physical and mental suffering without losing fortitude and faith. There may be times when we find ourselves oppressed by the magnitude of human woe and despondent because of our own personal trials. Yet we triumph still if we have discovered that there is a beauty in suffering which almost explains and justifies its existence. This is the beauty of pain. It blossoms in sorrow. When life's glory is laid in dust, there blossoms red a richer life. When we endure our cross, the heart distills and extracts its rarest gentleness and serenity from its thorns, and our Calvary becomes the gate of pity and understanding. To quote F. B. Meyer again, who was a spiritual guide, with a personal experience of the alchemy of suffering:

Suffering robs us of proud self-reliance, and casts us in an agony at the feet of God. Suffering prunes away the leaves in which we rejoiced, that the sap may find its way into fruit. Suffering isolates the soul, shutting it away from all creative acts, and surrounding it by a wall of fire. The leaves of the aromatic plant must be crushed ere they will emit their fragrance; the ore must be plunged in the furnace ere the gold is set free; the pebble must be polished on the lapidary wheel ere its brilliant colours are apparent.

> Humbly I asked God to give me joy,
> To crown a life with blossoms of delight:
> I begged for happiness without alloy,
> Desiring that my pathway should be bright;
> Prayerful I sought these blessings to attain,
> And now I thank Him that He gave me pain.
> For with my pain and sorrow came to me
> A dower of tenderness in act and thought;
> And with the suffering came a sympathy
> An insight that success has never brought.
> Father, I had been foolish and unblest
> If Thou hadst granted me my blind request.

The strength and greatness of our Lord's personality are manifested in his supreme power to restore health to diseased minds and to heal wounded consciences. Records of his acts of mercy are often prefixed by the phrase, "He was moved with compassion." His heart entered into touch with human suffering, and he is the same today. His power is as great as ever it was and needs only that people open their hearts to receive his help.

There is no place where earth's sorrows are more felt than up in heaven.

While among men Jesus cared for the sick and healed all manner of diseases, and his example became the simple and sufficient motive for the establishment of hospitals with the spread of civilization. In early days, as soon as monasteries were founded, they had their hospitals, and those like St. Thomas's and St. Bartholomew's in London, as well as other ancient hospitals throughout the land, are of an entirely Christian foundation. But in all situations where doctors make conditions favorable for recovery, all agree with the inscription a French surgeon had in his operating theater: *I operate; God heals.*

As to the teaching of Jesus regarding *death,* consideration has already been given to what he taught about death in the miracles associated with his resurrection power. Many more fear the approach of death than they do being attacked by sickness. Death is feared, not only for themselves, but for those they love. But Jesus died, and "by dying, death he slew" and defeated him who had the power of death, namely, the Devil. Now he stands ready to "deliver them who through fear of death were all their lifetime subject to bondage" (Heb. 2:14, 15). Jesus alone

> Can make our dying bed
> Feel soft as downy pillows are:
> While on his breast we lean our head
> And breathe our life out sweetly there.

A few pages back we dealt with three personal contacts Jesus had with Death—the death and resurrection of the widow's son, the death and resurrection of the daughter of Jairus, and the death and resurrection of Lazarus. But Jesus had a fourth contact with death, namely, his own death and resurrection, which was covered in the section concerning what the master taught "About Himself" (Vol. I). The finite mind of man will never be able to explore and explain the depth of mystery found in the apostolic statement that Jesus *tasted* death for every man. We know that on the surface it teaches a general atonement, an efficacious death for Jew and Gentile, elect and nonelect. For *every* man, it means what it says. But although by his death he made possible the abolition of "the fear of death," what were his own feelings as he came to shed his blood for the remission of sins?

From the outset of his teaching ministry, Jesus constantly referred to his coming death. The thought of his vicarious death had been for long his daily companion, from his first reference to it at Caesarea Philippi (Matt. 16:21; Mark 8:31). But as he approached death, the shadow was deepened on his spirit, touching it with a heavier sadness, until in Gethsemane he spoke of being too weak to drink the cup—"the cup of the New Testament in my blood." The contents of such a cup were so terrible as to force from his lips the prayer, "Father, if it be possible, let it pass." Previous mention has been made of the aspect of fear in connection with his imminent death, which throughout he anticipated and foretold.

The great horror expressed in the garden is all the more mysterious when we remember that he came as the Lamb slain *before* the foundation of the world; that coming as the Savior, he was virtually born crucified; that throughout his public ministry he constantly declared his death and resurrection for the world's redemption, the *summum bonum* of his incarnation. Therefore, he could not have feared death in the sense man does who, because of his sin, is afraid to die. The most satisfactory explanation of the apparent shrinking from death represented by "the cup" is that given by Professor A. M. Fairbairn in his *Studies in the Life of Christ.*

> It was not the issues from death Christ feared; it was the way into it, the *drinking* of the cup. He is in a great terror, not at what was personal, but at what was universal in death—what it involved and signified as to man, not what it involved and signified as to himself, his death was to be in a sense, the victory of sin—its victory not over him, but over his life. The spirit that was willing it could not vanquish, but the flesh that was weak it did. Yet in vanquishing the flesh it was vanquished by the spirit. Christ was obedient unto death, and death, in overcoming the life, did not overcome the will, but was rather overcome by it. He surrendered his life, but held fast his obedience ... Christ died on the cross, but not by the cross. He died for sin and by sin, his heart was broken, but his will was strong, inflexible, holy.

A poet has exhorted us to fear the grave as little as our bed, while another would have us sing:

> The fear of death has gone for ever,
> No more to cause my heart to grieve;
> There is a place, I do believe,
> In Heaven for me, beyond the river.

Countless thousands of the people of God on the brink of the river of death have found heart-comfort in some of the most beautiful words, not only in Scripture, but in all literature, and uttered for the consolation of the disciples over the announcement of their Master's approaching death: "Let not your heart be troubled; ye believe in God, believe also in me. In my Father's house are many mansions . . . I go to prepare a place for you."

Since his Ascension after his death and resurrection, Jesus has been active fulfilling this promise, and the believer's assurance is that at death Jesus receives him unto himself to share the prepared place for a prepared people. This is why he can die in peace. Aged Simeon could so die for he had *waited* for the consolation of Israel, and having seen with his own eyes the salvation of the Lord in the babe, death had no terror for him. If we would die well, we must live well. God will give us *dying* grace. What we constantly need is grace to live as he would have us. "Mark the perfect man, and behold the upright: for the end of that man is peace" (Ps. 37:37). Jesus is our exemplar in all things, even in *death*. In life he was the personification of uprightness; consequently his end was one of victory and peace. As we study him in the article of death, we behold him dying, not as a *victim*, but as the glorious Victor. As Fairbairn expresses it so movingly:

> In death and on the cross he fills the eye and prospect of the soul, the shadow of man only helping the better to show him clothed with a light which makes the very place of his feet glorious. In those last hours how dignified his silence, how Divine his speech, how complete his self-sufficiency! Round him there is fretful noise, in him there is majestic calm, about him violence, within peace. In his last extremity, when man's faith in him had perished, he knows himself,

and dies, while he seems to men the vanquished, the conscious Victor of the World. In every moment of the Passion Jesus stands before us as the calm self-conscious Christ. He knows himself, and no event can unsettle his knowledge or disturb his spirit. The hour of greatest prostration is the hour of supreme solitude; where he was most alone there he felt most awed by the magnitude of his mission and the issues it involved. . . . This serene consciousness of His Divine dignity and mission he carries with him to His cross.

Whether we die young or old, naturally or tragically, let our prayer be, "May my end be as his end!" And it will be if only he, the deathless one, is our personal Savior. Only thus can we die in hope that where he is, there shall we be also. Longfellow guides us in what to say to those who may lament our *transition* as he calls Death:

Weep not, my friends! rather rejoice with me!
I shall not feel the pain, but shall be gone,
And you will have another friend in Heaven.
Then start not at the creaking of the door
Through which I pass! I see what lies beyond it!

BIBLE STUDY QUESTIONS

Take time to turn to each Scripture reference and mark the verse or a portion in your Bible.

1. How was Jesus able to become Healer-Teacher?
2. Describe the methods Jesus used in healing.
3. In what way did Jesus taste death for every man?
4. How does Jesus give us hope at death?

Part IV

— 19 —

Love

That the fragrance of *love* permeates the four Gospels is evident from the fact that such an emotion is mentioned over eighty times, principally by Jesus, God's much-loved Son. As H. H. Halley expresses it in his valuable *Bible Handbook:*

> Love is the premier teaching of Christianity, and an undying expression of Jesus' doctrine. It is more potent for the building of the Church than any, or all, of the various manifestations of God's power. Love is the Church's most effective weapon, without which all the various gifts of the Spirit are of no avail. Love is the essence of God's nature, as well as the perfection of human character. Love is the most powerful, ultimate force in the Universe.

Because of the paramount importance of love, then, we need to understand all that Jesus taught of its exercise toward himself, God, and man. In passing, it is fitting to observe that as all the three persons of the godhead are coequal in all of their manifested attributes and virtues, all three share in the affection and in the desire for possession and companionship the term *love* suggests. *God the Father* is love in its highest form and reality

(John 3:16). *God the Son* reflected the essence of
the Father (John 14:21). *God the Holy Spirit*
produces in our hearts the fruit of love (Rom 5:5;
Gal. 5:22). James testifies to a *jealous yearning* in
the Holy Spirit over Christians infected with "love
of the world" (James 4:5; see Eph. 4:13).

Love, in its English form, as found in our
modern Bible represents several different Greek
words, and it is necessary to distinguish the various shades of meaning.

Eros. Running through Greek philosophy and
culture is this term indicating love or desire from
the human side and romantic attachment with sexual overtones. The New Testament, however,
never uses this word for *love.*

Philia is a word standing for love between
friends. *Philcō* means to be a friend and is used in
this. way some fourteen times in the Gospels. The
American city, Philadelphia, means the City of
Brotherly Love. This term indicates a reasoning,
discriminating attachment, founded in the conviction that its object is worthy of esteem, or entitled
to it on account of benefits bestowed. It emphasizes the *intelligent* element of love. The Greek
Philia usually appears, then, in the context of human love.

Agapē. From *Agapaō,* this term is used more often in the Gospels than any other for *love.* It occurs over fifty times, with over thirty of these being found in John's Gospel. This term, as well as
the others above, are all from the same Hebrew
word for love, namely *Aheh,* which has as many
shades of meaning as the English word *love. Agapē*
signifies primarily a voluntary, active affection
and comes from the LXX (the Septuagint, earliest

Greek translation of the Old Testament by seventy translators) into the New Testament in the deeper sense of spiritual affection, the love that links God and man and unites soul and soul in the divine communion. This word represents a warmer, more instinctive sentiment, more closely allied to feeling and implying more passion. It emphasizes the *affectional* element of love. It denotes religious love, the love of God to man and man to God, or man to man under God's covenant (Lev. 19:18). Archbishop Trench speaks of it as "a word born in the bosom of revealed religion." This love, suffused with religion, like *Philia*, implies reciprocity and fellowship—if not existing, then desired and sought.

The epithet *beloved*, found in "Well-Beloved," "Dearly Beloved," and "My Beloved," is a derivative of *Agapē* and is used of Christ by God—of Christians, as dear to God, of Christians, as dear to fellow believers or "the brethren." Let us now endeavor to classify the various features of *love* as taught by the Master.

— 20 —

Divine Love

Under this section we outline what the four Gospels teach about God and love and about Christ and love.

GOD AND LOVE

Love is not one of God's majestic attributes but the essence of his being. "God *is* love" (1 John 4:8, 16); the repetition indicates divine emphasis. "Love is of God" since "God is love." Love comes from him because it is absolutely in him. God is love's prime fountain, and therefore *love* gives the best conception we can form of his nature. With all his wisdom, man will never be able to plumb the depths of phrases like "God so loved" (John 3:16) and "The love of God" (John 5:42; Luke 11:42).

The character of God as "Jehovah" and as the "Holy One of Israel" gives his love its qualities of purity, intensity, selflessness, fidelity, and mercy. Reciprocal love should call forth like qualities in his people. But when his love was affronted, it could break into grief, anger, wrath, and threat-

ening against the wanton and faithless (Ps. 78:40;
Isa. 63:9)— an aspect of love the loving Son of
God also revealed.

God's love for Christ. John, the apostle of love,
records more than any other New Testament
writer the various aspects of divine love. Not only
was God's love exhibited in Christ, it was likewise
showered upon him who came as the Son of his
love, as Jesus himself emphasized. "The Father
loveth the Son" and consequently "sheweth him
all things that he himself doeth" (John 5:20).
Revelation came as the result of a blissful relationship. Further, because of his willing sacrifice,
Jesus was loved of God: "Therefore doth my Father love me, *because* I lay down my life, that I
might take it again" (John 10:17). Then, on his
own confession, Jesus reflected the love God had
toward him: "As the Father hath loved me, so
have I loved you" (John 15:9).

That God wants the world to know about his
love for his well-beloved Son (Matt. 3:17) is evident from the High Priestly Prayer: "That the
world may know that thou . . . hast loved me"
(John 17:23). Loved by God before the foundation of the world, Jesus desired that the same eternal love borne him by the Father might be manifested toward those given him by the Father:
"That the love wherewith thou hast loved me may
be in them, and I in them" (John 17:24, 26). Because of his love for his Son, God made him the
executive of the godhead: "The Father loveth the
Son, and hath given all things into his hand."

This perfect form of love bestowed upon the
Son by the Father was not merely an affectionate
sentiment, but implied an intelligent discernment

of the Son as one worthy of such love and therefore entitled to all the divine benefits bestowed upon him.

God's love for all men. If it is possible for one text in the Bible to be greater than another, surely John 3:16—the gospel in a nutshell—is the greatest verse in the Bible: "God so loved the world"—thankless and evil though it is (Luke 6:35). The perfection of God's character lies in his love heaped upon the worst and seeking out those most alienated from him (Matt. 5:48; Luke 15). By the term *would* we are not to understand the beautiful world in which we live, and which God pronounced *good* after he had created it, but a world of sinners ruined by the Fall. Bring forth the most wretched sinner it is possible to find, who cannot fall any deeper into sin, and I will show you something deeper still—the deep, bottomless abyss of God's love.

Paul says that God *commended* this universal love of his while men were adamantly estranged from him. "God commendeth his love toward us, in that, while we were yet sinners, Christ died for us" —the evidence of such love. The word *commend* carries with it the idea of "recommendation" or establishment. So Phillips translates it, "The proof of God's amazing love is this: that it was *while we were sinners* that Christ died for us" (Rom. 5:8). The love, then, that God "commends" subsisted in him apart from and anterior to the proof of the cross; it actuates all his dealings with mankind—in creation, providence, and moral discipline (Matt. 5:45; 6:23–34; 10:29; see James 1:17; 1 Pet. 4:19). Since the objects of God's love are pitiable, sinners exceedingly, his redeeming love is manifested in *mercy*, in which love predominates (Luke 1:50; see Eph. 2:4; Titus 3:5).

God's love for the disciples. The previous aspect of divine love was universal and general; this feature is particular and personal. All sinners saved by grace are equally loved by the Father and the Son. That the Father has a peculiar love for the saints for two reasons is evident from the teaching of his Son. "The Father himself loveth you, because ye have *loved me*, and *have believed* that I came out from God" (John 16:27). "That the world may know that thou . . . hast loved them" (John 17:23).

While there may be a direct application of these utterances to the first disciples of Jesus, they are not limited to them but apply to saints of all ages —to the church he said he would build. This is the love of God in Christ Jesus from which we can never be separated (Rom. 8:35, 39)—passages in which Paul emphasizes the double love, making the believer forever secure.

> Loved in the past of yesterday,
> And all along our future way,
> And in the present of today,
> Forever loved.

(The reader will refer to the section, "About God," Vol. I, for further material on the different features of his love.)

God commands men to love him. In his answer to his carping critics, the Pharisees, Jesus informed them that the first and great commandment in the Law was, "Thou *shalt* love the Lord thy God with all thy heart, and with all thy soul, and with all thy mind" (Matt. 22:37). Paul also declared that men are bidden to love God (1 Cor. 8:1–6).

To those who obey the divine command and truly love God, "all things work together for good" (Rom. 8:28). Jesus did not invent the two commandments about love in his reply to the question; he was simply quoting from the Law of Moses (Lev. 19:18; Deut. 6:5). He stamped the ancient law of love with fresh honor and authority and "elevated it to shine forever as the sun and the moon of the firmament of duty."

Love to God, holding a prominent place in Scripture and especially in the teaching of Jesus, is not something we can please ourselves about but constitutes obedience to a positive command, "Thou shalt love the Lord thy God." Professor Stalker draws attention to a well-known saying of the English statesman, William Pitt. Chancing to visit a church in which a sermon had been preached by one of the apostles of the Evangelical Revival, the doctrines of which were then only beginning to be heard of, Pitt bounced out at the close of the service, exclaiming in high tones, "Why, that fellow expects us to love God!" But such love is not only expected, but commanded, and anyone refusing to love God is lacking in one of the functions of a complete humanity.

Further, the love demanded is not confined to an emotional feeling but should be a supreme passion according to the sweeping declaration of Jesus when he adopted the Mosaic law of love as his own. God must be loved with:

"All thy heart"—the central part out of which are the issues of life.

"All thy soul"—my soul is my self and includes all self action.

"All thy strength"—this involves the will and means moral and physical strength.

"All thy mind"—this part of our human nature is the intellect with all its power to think and plan.

Such language of psychology claims for God the affection of human nature in all its extent and in all its intensity.

Break through my nature, mighty heavenly Love,
    Clear every avenue of thought and brain,
Flood my affections, purify my will,
    Let nothing but Thine own pure life remain.

CHRIST AND LOVE

The love he taught was not a sentiment but a principle, and likewise the substance of his teaching. It is both comforting and assuring that we are equally loved by the Father and the Son. The appeal of Mary and Martha to Jesus concerning their brother Lazarus brought an immediate response. "Behold, he whom thou lovest is sick" (John 11:3). "Jesus loved Martha, and her sister, and Lazarus" (John 11:5). "Then said the Jews, Behold how he loved him" (John 11:36). The tear-stained face of Jesus as he stood at the graveside testified to his deep love for the friend he raised again from the dead. Thus, he was not the mere channel of his Father's love; Jesus shared in it infinitely so much so that *the love of God* is seen in *the love of Christ* (John 10:11–15; 13:1, 34; 14:21; see Rom. 8:35, 39; Rev. 1:5).

Christ loves God. The eternal love of Jesus for the Father (John 17:4) is seen in his unceasing obedience to the divine will, "I do always the things that please my Father." Love delights in obedience and reveals itself in service and sacrifice (John 14:21). "I love the Father" (John 14:31). "I . . . abide in his love" (John 15:10).

From the dateless past Jesus had been the well-beloved Son of God, and such a close-knit bond was the Master's stay in the dark and lonely hours of his sojourn among men. Those short, swift cries of his, wrung from him in his agony, that seemed to pierce the silent heaven like the sob of a heart grief had broken, were personal, came straight from him, and went straight to his Father, whom he had loved from before the beginning of time.

While we have no biblical record of the first thirty years of the life of Jesus among men, apart from a brief glimpse when he was twelve years of age, all through this long period, as well as during his short span of ministry, he manifested a love to God, equal to any service, making obedience, however seemingly hard, spontaneous. He likewise evidenced a love to man equal to any sacrifice, able with a truly divine freedom to give himself for the life of the world, which he did. As the sons of God through grace, may ours be the undying heart-confession—*I love the Father.*

Christ loved his disciples. Professor Stalker reminds us that the only way of making a commandment of love easier is by exhibiting the object of love in a more attractive light. The great contribution of Jesus to this primary duty of morality was that he made God more lovable than he had ever appeared before, especially in the frequent declarations of his love for his chosen disciples. "He that loveth me shall be loved of my Father, and *I* will love him" (John 14:21). "As the Father hath loved me, so have I loved you; continue ye in my love" (John 15:9, 10).

Because Christ loved the church he brought into being by his death, his express wish is that those whom he loves should be with him where he is (John 14:3; 17:24). Further, in the truth of the fatherhood of God about which Jesus fully instructed his disciples, there is resident the thought of divine love for them. Jesus habitually called God *my Father;* when he denominated God when speaking to his disciples, he called him *your Father* and taught them to pray to him as *our Father.* Such fatherhood was the culminating expression in the revelation for the love of God, a love which, in turn, Jesus manifested toward those given him of the Father.

One of the most impressive affirmations of the love Jesus bore for his disciples is that given by John. "Having loved his own which were in the world, he loved them unto the end [or, *to the uttermost*]" (John 13:1).

As the hymnist expresses it,

> There is no love like the love of Jesus—
> Never to fade or fall.

What is the implication of the phrase, "He loved them unto the end"? Godet translates it, "He perfectly testified unto them all his love" and comments that "unto the end" means *to the utmost, to make an end of it.* John's assuring word does not signify that Jesus *did not cease* to love his own up to the moment when he died for them. Divine love is eternal and cannot, therefore, cease. This phrase signifies therefore the manifestation of his love even to its complete outpouring, in a way to exhaust it, in some sort.

What is true of the Father is likewise true of his Son: "I have loved thee with an everlasting love:

therefore with lovingkindness have I drawn thee" (Jer. 31:3). George Matheson gave us the heart-moving hymn, "O Love, That Wilt Not Let Me Go." Paul, who gave us the paradox of knowing the unknowable love of Christ—a love making us more than conquerors—also confirms that nobody and nothing can ever separate us from the love of the Father and the Son (Rom. 8:35, 39).

> Loved with everlasting love,
> Led by grace that love to know;
> Spirit, breathing from above,
> Thou hast taught me it is so.

Christ loves the individual. The aspect of love just considered is of a particular nature—*his own.* But as we have already indicated, the love of Jesus was also personal, as many proved who crossed his pathway. For instance, there was the rich young ruler: "Jesus beholding him loved him" (Mark 10:21). Behold how he loved Lazarus" (John 11:3, 5, 36). "Now there was leaning on Jesus' bosom, one of his disciples, whom Jesus loved" (John 13:23).

Three times over we have the phrase "the disciple whom Jesus loved" (John 13:23; 20:2; 21:20). That this disciple was John himself is proven by his own statement, "This is the disciple which testifieth of these things" (John 21:24). With all due reticence and reverence, this disciple, who leaned on the bosom of Jesus, did not mention his name. As Godet puts it, if John designates himself by this paraphrase—the Disciple whom Jesus loved—it is precisely from humility that he avoids declaring his name, but with the feeling of the infinite condescension of him who had designed to treat him, during his earthly existence, as *his friend.*

When Jesus focused his love upon an individual, it was because of qualities his deep look discovered in them—qualities and virtues he knew his love was able to enrich and ennoble. The marvel and mystery of grace is that each of us, as the redeemed of the Lord, is the object and recipient of his love. Paul, who reveled in preaching and writing about the love of Jesus, experienced its personal aspect, "The Son of God, who loved *me*, and gave himself for *me*" (Gal. 2:20).

It passeth knowledge, that dear love of Thine,
My Saviour, Jesus; yet this soul of mine
Would of Thy love, in all its breadth and length,
Its height and depths, its everlasting strength,
        Know more and more.

Christ manifested his love by the cross. The Master had much to say about the fact and manner of his death at Calvary (John 3:14). "Greater love hath no man than this, that a man lay down his life for his friends. *Ye are my friends*" (John 15:13, 14). It is undoubtedly a greater proof of love when one is willing to sacrifice his life for his enemies, which Jesus did, seeing "he died for the ungodly." While we were yet sinners, Jesus laid down his life for us, and such sacrificial love founded a new empire of love resulting in a regime and fashion of life hitherto unknown. The wondrous love, willing to bleed and die, binds the redeemed to the service of the Redeemer and transforms them into witnesses of God's covenant of grace in Jesus made with mankind (Matt. 10:4; Mark 16:15; 1 John 2:2).

Inscribed upon the Cross we see,
In shining letters—*God is Love.*

The Christian church of apostolic times cele-
brated the *Agapē*, or Love Feast, which included
the Lord's Supper, and at which there was the
loving remembrance of the broken body and out-
poured blood of Jesus for man's salvation. Saints
still gather for the feast, keeping thereby "the
memory adored."

> His body broken in our stead
> Is seen, in this memorial bread,
> And so our feeble love is fed
> Until He comes.
>
> The drop of His dread agony,
> His life-blood shed for us, we see;
> The wine shall tell the mystery
> Until He come.

Christ expects men to love him and God. Love toward God and Christ is the heart's response to the
Father's love exhibited in Christ (1 John 4:19) and
is a love resulting from faith. "If a man love me,
he will keep my words" (John 14:23). "Continue
ye in my love . . . Abide in his love" (John 15:9–
10). "Lovest thou me more than these" (John
21:15–17)?

In his unique conversation with Peter, Jesus
sought to restore him to his old position as chief
of the apostles, an office he had lost by his denial.
The connection between his threefold denial of
Jesus and his threefold affirmation of love for
Jesus is somewhat striking. There was a sense in
which this threefold profession of his love for the
one he had denied effaced the threefold strain he
had brought upon himself. Jesus asked Peter
whether he loved him "more than these," mean-

ing more than the other disciples over whom he
had felt superiority (Matt. 26:33; Mark 14:29).
The first question of Jesus seems to convey a gentle rebuke for Peter's former extravagant profes-
sions.

Jesus used the more dignified, really the nobler,
word for *love*—to love in the higher and spiritual
sense of the word, love with the love of reverence.
Peter, however, in the ardor of his affection, felt
this to be the colder word for *love* and so substi-
tuted the warmer, more affectionate term of loving in the sense of personal attachment. He thinks
that he can without presumption ascribe to himself this latter feeling; and yet he does not do it
without expressing distrust of himself and without
seeking the guaranty of the testimony of his heart
to which he does not dare to trust any longer in
the infallible knowledge of the hearts of men,
which he now attributes to his Master.

The love Jesus asks of us, and the love he bears
toward us, renovates and purifies the heart, inspires a constant self-devotion to the feeding of
his sheep and lambs, and makes the perfect vision
of God the object of fervent anticipation (John
14:23; 17:24; 1 John 1:1-3; 4:10). May we be
saved from the rebuke Jesus administered to the
church at Ephesus for having left their "first
love" (Rev. 2:4).

> Shall I not yield to that constraining power?
> Shall I not say, O tide of Love, flow in?
> My God, Thy gentleness hath conquered me,
> Life cannot be as it hath hither been.

*Christ taught that love is the sum and substance of the
Law.* It is clear from his teaching on *love* that it is

by such that the Law can be truly kept. It is only as man loves God and his fellow-men that we can fulfill the ancient command. "Love is the fulfilling of the law," Paul affirms. Of old, God showed mercy unto thousands who loved him and kept his commandments (Exod. 20:6), a revelation Jesus emphasizes: "Thou shalt love the Lord thy God" (Matt. 22:37, 38; Luke 10:27). Because God is the source of love, we love him (1 John 4:19). Ancient Israel sinned against divine love, broke the covenant, transgressed the Law; yet love flowed on, ever seeking to bring sinners to share once again in the care of the divine heart.

"How shall I give thee up, Ephraim" (Hos. 11:8)? His banner of love was ever over God's erring children. The many waters of rejection could not quench such pursuing love. In his love and pity, he sought to redeem them, for his love would not let them go.

Coming to the New Testament, we find the self-expressed righteous Pharisees, confident in the security of their own relation to Jehovah, but who deemed publicans and sinners, Samaritans and Gentiles, as being outside of the ancient covenant of love and mercy. But it was against this dark background that Jesus taught the fatherly love of God—a love embracing all without distinction and which could not be dissolved by the ill-doing of its objects. It was because of his own love, so often spurned, that he died for the ungodly. Well might John Milton exclaim:

> O unexampled love!
> Love nowhere to be found less than Divine!

Because, then, of the preeminence of love as proclaimed by Jesus, may we be found resting in, and responding to, and reciprocating such external love, even as Toplady exhorts us:

Loved of my God, for Him again
With love intense I burn!—
Chosen of Thee ere time began,
I choose Thee in return!

— 21 —

Human Love

Jowett of Balliol would have us remember that "The love of Christ is the conducting medium to the love of all mankind." It is like the inspiration of our love to God, as well as to man. From the teaching of Jesus we learn that the spring of human love flows out in four directions, namely, in love for God, in the family circle, among believers, and toward our neighbor.

MAN'S LOVE FOR GOD

Attention has been drawn to this feature of human love. It has been pointed out that the overwhelming preponderance of the New Testament usage is in favor of the essential unity of the love (agapē) which God manifests to his creation and the love (agapē) which Christians are to have for God and for one another. God merits and desires the love of man (1 John 4:19). All pure forms of earthly love point upward to features of the divine love. In the first place, however, the great and incomprehensible in the divine being kindles all the earthly fires of true love. How blessed we are if found among the ardent "lovers of God"!

When Jesus described the end-time period of the Gentile age, he said that one characteristic feature would be that the love of many would wax cold (Matt. 24:12). Coldness certainly sums up the witness of the church today in love for God, for his truth, and for his cause. It is hard in these increasingly sinful times to walk close with God and keep our love for him and all that is dear to him fresh, warm, and active. May grace be ours to emulate the aspiration of Madam Guyon!

> Why have I not a thousand thousand hearts,
>   Lord of my Soul! that they might all be Thine!
> If Thou approve—the zeal Thy smile imparts,
>   How should it ever fail! Can such a fire decline?
> Love, pure and holy, is a deathless fire,—
>   Its object heavenly;—it must ever blaze!
> Eternal Love a God must needs inspire,
>   When once He wins the heart, and fits it for His
>   praise.

LOVE IN THE FAMILY CIRCLE

Jesus was born into and grew up in the loving atmosphere of a godly home and came to experience the close, intimate love between parents and children making a home heaven's twin sister. Yet he made it clear that such human love must be subservient to love for him. "He that loveth father or mother more than me is not worthy of me: and he that loveth son or daughter more than me is not worthy of me" (Matt. 10:37). In all things, even in the realm of family love, he must have the preeminence. These words of Jesus in which he claims our best are remarkable in that he demands for himself a higher affection than any parent or any child can claim. If we would be worthy of being his disciple, we must love him best of all because he loves us more dearly than all. There is beauty all around, not only when there is love at home, but more especially, if Jesus is Lord in the home.

Matthew's "loveth more" softens the harsher expression of Luke's "hateth not" (Luke 14:26). Bible readers are sometimes perplexed over the phrase, "Hateth not his father and mother, and wife and children and brethren, and sisters." What must be borne in mind is that the word *hate* does not mean to hate in the sense in which we use the word today, namely, as expression of intense aversion or to dislike or abhor exceedingly. Such a command to hate in this way would be utterly foreign to the benign character of Jesus and contrary to the tenor of his teaching on *love*.

It will be recalled that Jacob is said to have *hated* Leah (Gen. 29:31), that is, he loved her less than Rachel. "He loved also Rachel more than Leah" (Gen. 29:30), meaning that she had the preeminent place in her husband's affection. This explanation is akin to the reported sayings of Jesus as to true discipleship in which "loving more" takes the place of the yet stronger form of "not hating." What Jesus asked of his own was nothing less than the heart, and that cannot be given by halves. The condition, hard though it may seem, implies that where two affections come into collision, the weaker must give way; and though the man may not and ought not to cease to love, yet he must act as if he hated—disobey, and, it may be, desert—those to whom he is bound by natural ties, that he

may obey the higher supernatural calling. Loving
Jesus more never means loving our dear ones less.
The spiritual affection enriches natural affection.

LOVE AMONG BELIEVERS

Another badge of true and effective discipleship is love among ourselves as fellow believers. If
sinners love fellow sinners, as Jesus indicated
(Luke 6:33, 34), saints should love, not only fellow
saints, but their enemies (Luke 6:35) and "the
evil" (Matt. 5:43–48).

"By this—that ye also love one another—shall
all men know that ye are my disciples" (John
13:34, 35). John, the apostle of love, extends the
teaching of Jesus on *love* and gives us the final
and complete New Testament doctrine of such a
theme. The apostle saw the love of God perfected
in those who "love one another" and thus "keep
God's commands" from whose soul accordingly
"fear" is "cast out." As they "abide" wholly in the
realm of love that is constituted by the one loving
Spirit dwelling in their hearts, they are "perfected
unto one," even as Christ is "one" with the Father
by virtue of the love subsisting eternally between
them, which is love's prime fountain (Matt. 3:17;
John 17:21–26; 1 John 2:5; 3:24; 4:11–21).

We are liars if we profess to love God yet hate
a brother we can see. If we cannot love him, how
can we love God whom we cannot see (1 John
4:20)? In the early days of the church, when the
disciples had a deeper concern for each other, the
surrounding heathen would admiringly say, "See
how these Christians love one another!" Now the

same phrase is uttered with bitter sarcasm by the world that sees the feuds, unhappy divisions, and acrimony among those who profess to be lovers of God. Jesus said that to love one another as he has loved us, was a "new commandment." Would that a loveless church could be found obeying it (see Rom. 12:10, 13–16)!

> Beloved, let us love:
> Love is of God;
> In God alone hath love
> Its true abode.
>
> Beloved, let us love;
> For they who love,
> They only are His sons,
> Born from above.

LOVE TOWARD OUR NEIGHBOR

Jesus lifted "the second great commandment," as he called it—"Thou shalt love thy neighbour as thyself"—right out of the Book of Leviticus and stamped it with his imprimatur (Lev. 19:18; Luke 10:27). The lawyer asked Jesus, "Who is my neighbour?" and he received a new idea as to the identity of his neighbor and of neighborly conduct. *Who is your neighbor?* Is he the one who lives next door to you or across the street? Is he the one of the same nation and race as yourself? Where do we come upon those who are no longer our neighbors?

Among the best-known and best-loved parables of Jesus are the parable of the lost son (Luke 15) and the parable of the good Samaritan (Luke 10:30–37). The first parable deals primarily with the relationship of man to God, while the second emphasizes man's relationship with his fellow-man. Man is "not an island by himself, but a part of the main continent of humanity," as the lawyer learned from Jesus' illustration of who his neighbor was. The Samaritan journeying from Jerusalem to Jericho found another traveler who had been robbed and brutally mugged on the roadside and bestowed upon him every care and attention. As a true neighbor he showed mercy upon the half-dead man.

Does not this superb illustration teach that a man's neighbor is a man in distress and need, no matter of what nation or race or color he may be? This is the loving mercy that God delights to show to man and Jesus taught men to show to one another (see Rom. 12:20, 21). Our neighbor, then, is the one we meet in need and whom it is in our power to help. Chief among the forms of service we can render, says Jesus, are relief to the poor, entertainment of the homeless, tending of the sick, comforting the sorrowful, and the reconciliation of those who are at feud (Matt. 5:9; 25:34-36). Then there are not only the social implications of the gospel so much to the fore today in all our relief programs for those in need at home and abroad, but the spiritual implications as well, namely, the salvation of souls from sin and efforts to help them rise to higher ends of excellence and nobility. Such double help for our neighbor must be disinterested service without any thought of return or reward (Matt. 6:2–4; Luke 6:34). The best service for our neighbor in any sphere loses its grace if we fail to help solely because we love our neighbor.

Discharging our duty toward neighbors, "each according to his ability," then, covers two realms. The seven corporal works of mercy described by Jesus are clothing the naked, giving drink to the thirsty, feeding the hungry, visiting the prisoners and the sick, relieving the poor, sheltering the homeless, and burying the dead. The seven spiritual works our neighbor requires are giving good counsel to those who need it, teaching the ignorant, discreetly correcting those who have offended, comforting those who are cast down, forgiving those who have injured us, patiently bearing reproach, and devoutly praying for those who are our neighbors.

In his teaching on neighborliness, Jesus lays quite an unexpected emphasis on sheer tenderness, on kindness to those in need and to strangers, the instinctive humanity that helps men, if it be only by the swift offer of a cup of cold water (Matt. 10:42). We emulate the example of Jesus, as the good Samaritan did, when we bear another's burden (Gal. 6:2). Illustrating his own tenderness toward those in need, Jesus used the impressive phrase of Isaiah, "A bruised reed shall he not break" (Isa. 42:3). He urged attention going beyond what is natural to man. "Do not even the publicans the same?" Loving our neighbor involves going a little further, even to taking the second mile (Matt. 5:41, 46). T. R. Glover comments that "the man who would use such compulsion would be an alien soldier, the hireling of Herod or of Rome; and who would wish to cart him and his goods even a mile?" "Go two miles," says Jesus, or, if the Syriac translation preserves the right reading, "Go two *extra*." Ordinary kind-

ness and tenderness could hardly be urged
beyond the first mile; yet Jesus goes further still.
With an instinctive love and friendliness he could
even pray for those of his neighbors who despitefully used him (Matt. 5:44; Luke 23:34).

An Anglican prayer for The Twenty-third Sunday after Trinity reads:

> Grant me to love my neighbor as myself, and to do to
> all men as I would they should do unto me,— to hurt
> nobody by word or deed, and to do my Duty in that
> state of life unto which it shall please Thee to call
> me!

Said Marcus Aurelius, Roman emperor of the
second century:

> Every man has three relations to acquite himself in:
>   His body that encompasses him makes one;
>   The Divine Cause that gives to all men all things,
>   another;
>   His neighbour a third.

The poet T. Lyte would have us pray, "Teach
me what I owe to Man below / And to Thyself
in Heaven!"

— 22 —

False Love

That *love,* the ardent emotion of the heart, can be centered on wrong objects of affection, as well as on good and beneficial objects, also emerges from what the Master taught about such a theme. In this particular, the scribes and Pharisees were the worst sinners, and Jesus spared no words in unmasking their false objects of love. He called them hypocrites because "They *love* to pray standing in the synagogues and in the corners of the streets, that they may be seen of men" (Matt. 6:5). These loveless religious leaders knew nothing of the love and joy of praying to God in secret. Truly, these men had their *reward,* by which Jesus meant they got at once *all they will ever get,* namely, the admiration of those who witnessed their show-off.

They *"love* the uppermost rooms at feasts" (Matt. 23:6). By *uppermost,* we understand the "best" rooms that could be had. Because of their hypocritical religious practices they passed over, or neglected, "the judgement and the love of God" (Luke 11:42). They also "Loved greetings in the markets" (Luke 20:46). And because they craved after the honor of men, the love of God

was not in them, said Jesus (John 5:42) Evidently
there were those among the Pharisees who came
to believe that Jesus was the Messiah that Isaiah
had predicted, but they were afraid to confess
him, lest they should be excluded from the synagogue in which they had play-acted because
"They *loved* the praise of men more than the
praise of God" (John 12:43). Godet translates the
phrase, "They loved the glory which comes from
men more than the glory which comes from
God." If only they had loved to live only for God's
glory, what enjoyment of his benediction would
have been theirs!

Paul is not the only apostle to give us a notable
"Hymn of Love," as 1 Corinthians 13 has been
called. John, his fellow apostle, likewise has a vir-
tual hymn to the divine love in his first Epistle.
We find him warning the saints against the wrong
kind of love: "Love not the world, neither the
things in the world. If any man love the world,
the love of the Father is not in him" (1 John 2:15).

It goes without saying that there are so many
wonderful things in God's created world for us to
love. The *world*, however, which John urges the
children of God not to set their heart upon, is the
present world system or the sum total of human
life in an ordered world hostile to God, organized
by Satan, the god of this world of lost sinners, into
"the world of unbelieving mankind upon his cos-
mic principles of force, greed, selfishness, ambition, and pleasure" (Matt. 4:5, 9; John 12:31;
Eph. 2:2; 6:12; 1 John 2:11–17). John, himself,
describes the world he had in mind as being made
up of "The lust of the flesh, the lust of the eyes,
the pride of life" (1 John 2:16).

Such a world is a false object of our heart's love, seeing it is not only detrimental to life now, but is, with its lust, to pass away. It is a world of unsaved humanity inspired by its satanic prince, the atmosphere of which is immoral and which "at every moment of our lives we inhale, again inevitably exhale." The strange thing is that the word John uses for *love* in connection with a lustful, lost world, is *agapaō*, the same word he used of God's love for a lost race of sinners, the love which he is by nature, and the love which is produced in the heart of the yielded saint by the Holy Spirit (John 3:16; 1 John 4:8; Gal. 5:22).

Further, this Greek term *agapaō* is used in the classical meaning of love called out of one's heart by the preciousness of the object loved and thus refers to a fondness, an affection, nonethical in content, for an object because of its value. It is a love of approbation, of esteem. Paul sorrowfully wrote that "Demas loved this present world." This deserter of the apostle found the world of pleasure precious and thus came to love it. The phrase, "love not," carried the idea of "an act of forbidding the continuance of an action already going on." Some to whom John wrote were loving the things of the world, from which they had been saved, and so warned, "Stop loving the world with a love called out of your hearts because of its fancied preciousness."

Emphatically John declares that one who is guilty of the continuous, habitual action of loving the world with its lust is destitute of the love of the Father. Such precious love *is not in him.* Vincent, in his *Word Studies,* comments that "this means more than he does not love God: rather, that the love of God does not dwell in him as the ruling principle of his life." Actually, he is an unsaved person. Westcott, the renowned commentator, cites a parallel from Philo: "It is impossible for love to the world to co-exist with love to God, as it is impossible for light and darkness to coexist."

If "Abba, Father!" is the cry of newborn filial love (Rom. 8:15; Gal. 4:6), then its antithesis is found in false and futile objects of love, such as "the world," "self," "pleasure," and "money" (Luke 16:13; John 15:19–24; 2 Tim 3:2–5; James 4:4).

> Thy name is Love! I hear it from yon Cross;
> Thy name is Love! I read it in yon tomb;
> All meaner love is perishable dross,
>   But this shall light me through time's thickest gloom.

What a fitting end to our topic of *Love* is the exclamation of Thomas à Kempis: "Oh how powerful is the pure love of Jesus, which is mixed with no self-interest, nor self-love!"

BIBLE STUDY QUESTIONS

Take time to turn to each Scripture reference and mark the verse or a portion in your Bible.

1. What is the meaning of love as used in the Bible?
2. Whom did God love and who should love him?
3. How did Christ show his love and what does he expect of us?
4. To whom should human love be directed?
5. What love did Jesus warn against?

— 23 —

Marriage and Divorce

As we are endeavoring in these studies to examine the topics the Master taught, as they are recorded in the Gospels, our findings will reveal how opposed they are to the estimation of our modern, permissive society in the matters of marriage and divorce. Family life would have been on a much higher level today if only it had been fashioned according to the teaching of Jesus regarding marriage and home vows and value. How he denounced the deadly foe ruining homes, and through them, the nation! History proves that the multiplication of broken homes through divorce and the decay of nations and of social systems have gone hand in hand. In his *Decline and Fall of the Roman Empire*, Edward Gibbon wrote of the prevalence of divorce as a prominent cause of Rome's decline:

> When the Roman matrons became the equal and voluntary companions of their lords, a new jurisprudence was established, that marriage, like other partnerships, might be dissolved by the abdication of one of the associates. In three centuries of prosperity and corruption, this principle was enlarged to frequent practice and pernicious abuses. Passion, interest, or caprice suggested daily motives for the dissolution of

marriage: a word, a sign, a message, a letter, the mandate of a freeman, declared the separation: the most tender of human connections was degraded to a transient society of profit and of pleasure.

Laws, the renowned missionary, who had an unsurpassed knowledge of savage peoples, once remarked that the place of any race on the upward or downward scale could be accurately measured by their relation to two of the Ten Commandments—the fifth and the seventh—"Thou shalt not commit adultery" and "Thou shalt not bear false witness against thy neighbour." Dr. Laws could have added, "Thou shalt not covet . . . thy neighbour's wife."

A graver situation has arisen in this twentieth century when marriage is outmoded, and people, principally those in the world of entertainment, live together without any solemn contract, have children, separate, then settle down to live in sin with others. Where marriage is entered into, whether in a religious or civil ceremony, it can be easily dissolved. In fact, a pair can divorce and remarry as often as they like. On the slightest pretext now, a marriage can be broken up, as the soaring rate of divorces proves. Perhaps we should now change the marriage line, "For better or for worse . . . till death doth us part," to "till divorce does us part."

It would seem as if divorce is competing with death as a dissolver of marriages. At the present rate of increase there will soon be more marriages dissolved by the courts than those consummated by pastors and priests and magistrates. The purpose, as well as the perpetuity of marriage, then, make it imperative for us to know what Jesus taught on such a prominent subject and to realize that what he taught has never been abrogated and, therefore, is applicable today. Loose views on marriage and divorce, although they may be hailed as signs of emancipation of society from the fetters of ignorance, superstition, and prejudice, result in a low standard of morality and a weakening of the moral strength of a nation. A true, wholesome family life has a far-reaching influence upon the formation of Christian character of those in the home, and any God-fearing nation owes power and influence to the recognition of Christ in its homes.

Believing that Christ has the answer to any personal or public problem, our task is to state what he taught and commanded. We are not to concern ourselves with the many opinions about marriage and divorce, or even with what the church, Protestant or Roman, may teach and command about such a subject. Our sole criterion is, *What did Jesus teach?* On a few social questions he was noncommittal, but the social matter on which he spoke full and explicitly was the nature and duration of marriage. His high conception is seen in his use of the marriage relationship to illustrate union with himself. Paul could write of being "married to the Lord." The relationship in the home—that of parents with the children—was a picture of the bond between God and his own (Matt. 7:7–11).

THE MARRIAGE OF ONE MAN AND ONE WOMAN IS A DIVINE INSTITUTION

Quoting from the creation record (Gen. 2:23–25), Jesus declared marriage to be of divine origin and as a fundamental social order to be recognized as such. When tempted by the Pharisees to give his opinion as to the divorce of married people, he said, "Have ye not read, that he which made them at the beginning made them male and female, and said, For this cause shall a man leave father and mother, and shall cleave to his wife: and they twain shall be one flesh? Wherefore they are no more twain, but one flesh. What therefore God hath joined together, let not man put asunder" (Matt. 19:4–6).

Such a clear, positive statement was the reply of Jesus to the cunning purpose of the Pharisees to trap Jesus on the legality of divorce. Clarence Macartney says that their subtle purpose was twofold, *first,* to get from Jesus an utterance which might be construed as a condemnation of the ruler of their country, Herod Antipas—who was living with his brother Philip's wife—and so stir up his anger against Jesus; *second,* to draw from Jesus a saying which would seem to be in disagreement with Moses and the Old Testament. But he took his questioners back to Moses and enforcing his teaching declared that *monogamy*—one man living with one woman as prescribed by the Creator —was the divine and original plan for marriage.

The Pharisees went back to the Law, citing the divorce legislation of Moses as the authorization of divorce, but Jesus took them back to the original plan of God and summoned them back to the divine institution of marriage in which man and woman formed a union which was indisoluble once it had been contracted. To break such a union, by violating it and marrying another, was to commit adultery. The human race by the will,

purpose, and power of God began with a monogamous union between man and woman—a mutual
union, natural and inevitable, which only death
could break. Jesus, then, went right back to God's
intent, not to man's treatment of marriage, but to
God's thought and meaning of the institution.
God ordained marriage. He was the one who
planned it, and such a union of man and woman
takes on a solemn significance when it is thought
of in this way. His specific precepts and strong
words in regard to divorce must be connected
with an experience of the home that was happy in
itself and that he regarded as according to the
divine plan (Matt. 5:27–32).

Although Jesus himself did not marry and did
not teach, as the rabbis did, that marriage was
obligatory for all (Matt. 19:12), he considered
such a union to be a divinely established one and
required absolute purity in it, affirming that even
looking at another man's wife "to lust after her"
was adultery. Jesus also taught that marriage belongs to this created world in which we live but
that in the world to come it will have no validity
(Matt. 22:30). Shakespeare's lines on the blessedness and sweetness of the mutual yoke of man
and wife as ordained of God are apt at this point:

> He is the half part of a blessed man,
> Left to be finished by such as she;
> And she a fair divided excellence,
> Whose fulness of perfection lies in him.

The first to pervert the divine order of marriage was Lamech, the descendant of Cain, who
initiated polygamy (Gen. 4:16–24). *Monogamy*
means marriage with but one person at a time, or
the only marriage during life. *Polygamy*, however,

is the state or fact of having a plurality of wives, at the same time. Lamech was the first bigamist and, if alive and in our country today, would be jailed for marrying a second woman while still lawfully married to his first wife. After Lamech, polygamy became more widespread with even leaders of Israel, like Jacob, Saul, David, and Solomon having more than one wife. Like other sins, this one was endured by God but never approved, seeing it was in direct opposition to his original intent of the marriage bond. Mankind began with a monogamous and for life, still stands. A married woman through sin man fell in polygamy, divorce, and kindred corruptions of the divine order.

The apostolic enforcement and extension of the teaching of Jesus as to marriage being monogamous and for life, still stands. "A married woman is bound by law to her husband [and vice versa] as long as he lives; but if her husband dies she is discharged from the law concerning her husband. Accordingly, she will be called an adulteress if she lives with another man while her husband is alive. But if her husband dies she is free from that law and if she marries another man she is not an adulteress" (Rom. 7:2-3, RSV; see 1 Cor. 7:39, 40).

How sweet the mutual yoke of Man and Wife,
When holy fires maintain Love's heavenly life!

THE MARRIAGE OF ONE MAN AND ONE WOMAN IS A DIVINE ACT

Without doubt, the first marriage on earth was made by heaven, but heaven has no part in the six marriages of an actor or actress with all previous wives or husbands still living. What a mockery of such a divine institution this is! Jesus said, "They are no more twain, but one flesh. What therefore God hath joined together, let not man put asunder" (Matt. 19:6; Gen. 2:23-25; 4:1, 2). Both Adam and Jesus emphasize the fact that in creating man, God made one woman for one man, and that monogamy is to be the rule of man; and any rules which covertly or openly permit to man a plurality of wives, stand condemned by the precedent of the Garden of Eden. Adam registered the truth that in marriage man and wife become one flesh; and, being so joined, may not be put asunder.

While our courts rip asunder an ever-increasing number of marriages and allow those parted to remarry others almost immediately, the universal reason of man feels that the grounds of indissoluble union are valid and conclusive and that the proper view of marriage treats it as a union, binding "as long as both shall live." A home happy in itself was regarded by Jesus as being according to the divine plan. While the patriarchs and others in Old Testament times had many wives, and the Mosaic law allowed a man to put away his wife (Deut. 24:1), Jesus taught that his followers must rise above such a level and accept his teaching that the marriage bond must not be severed and that both the man and the woman are equally bound by it (Mark 10:10-12; see 1 Cor. 7:10, 11; Gal. 3:28). For this reason the sacredness and permanence of the marriage relation is likened to the relationship of the Christian to Christ (Eph. 5:28-30).

The happiest marriages are those in which husband and wife believe they were joined together, as such, by the Lord and fully and equally share each other's lives, continually lifting them up to God. Marriages of this sort, in which cares, trials, and responsibilities are met by united prayer and thought and single purpose, are indeed made in heaven and continually blessed by heaven. When two are joined together by the Lord in his sanctuary, then the function of the church is threefold: to bear witness to their lifelong vows when they consent together in holy wedlock; to pronounce God's blessing upon the pair when they enter, of their own accord, into this holy estate; to guard the sanctity of the marriage bond as long as they both shall live.

How appealing are the lines of Lewis Morris on wedded life.

The world hath need of all of you--
Hath need of you, and of thee, too, fair Love.
Oh Lovers, cling together! The old world
Is full of Hate. Sweeten it! draw in one
Two separate chords of Life; and from the loud
Of twin souls lost in Harmony, create
A Fair God dwelling with you—Love, the Lord!

THE MARRIAGE OF ONE MAN AND ONE WOMAN UNIFIES HUSBAND AND WIFE SO THAT THEY CEASE TO BE TWO AND BECOME ONE FLESH

Twice over Jesus used the phrase, "*They* twain shall be *one* flesh" (Matt. 19:5–6). *One flesh.* The term *cleave* he employed denotes a union of the closest and firmest kind. The original word is taken from *gluing* and means so firmly to *adhere* together that nothing can separate or unglue them. Husband and wife were *two* but became united as *one* in law, in feeling, in interest, and in affection. No longer are there separate and personal interests, but both act in all things as if they were one, animated by one soul and one wish.

In his reply to the cunning question of the Pharisees as to marriage and divorce, Jesus declared that since two are so intimately joined as to be one, and since in the beginning God made but one woman for one man, it follows that they cannot be separated but by the authority of God. Man may *not* put away his wife for every cause. What *God* hath joined together, *man* may not put asunder. To divide *one flesh,* or to unmarry two who have been united, is to destroy a living organism. The word *asunder* Jesus used is most suggestive. We read that some early Christians were "sawn asunder" (Heb. 11:37), and this is the kind of murder so prevalent today. The courts of our land, quite easily and quickly, saw asunder those who in God's sight are organically one, and they are thus murdering the home life of our land. "What God doeth, it shall be for ever" (Eccles. 3:14).

Further, the annulment of the marriage bond is foreign to the teaching of Jesus in which he says that marriage binds one man and one woman together in a relationship closer and more binding than that between parent and child. "For this cause shall a man leave father and mother, and shall cleave to his wife" (Matt. 19:5). This quotation which Jesus used with approval from Genesis 2:24 means but one thing, namely, that when a man takes a wife he binds himself more strongly to his partner than he was to his father or mother. In the mind of Jesus the marriage bond is the most tender and endearing of all human relations, more tender even than the bond which unites us to a parent. In his chapter on "The Family" in *The Ethic of Jesus,* Professor James Stalker, dealing with the mysterious attraction drawing opposite sexes into marriage, says:

> No wonder the Saviour alluded to this strong attraction of a pair drawn away from their own home to found a new one with such high appreciation; for, if the aim of Christianity is to purge the heart of selfishness, it can find in the world nothing so akin to itself as pure love between the sexes, which carries the person possessed with it completely out of himself and makes all sacrifices for the sake of the beloved object easy. In some, no doubt, this is transient, the mere blazing up of a flame which is soon extinguished. But in the multitude of cases it is enduring. The choice is a permanent one, and the union only becomes more close and sacred the longer it lasts. If to first love, as it is called, there attached a beauty which has evoked the enthusiasm of poets and romancers, the love of old age is not less beautiful, when it has survived all the changes and chances of life, only becoming mellower with the passage of years.

An anonymous poet of a past century, dealing with the consecration of wedded life lived as God meant, has left us the stanza:

> We in our wedded life shall know no loss,
> We shall new-date our years! What went before
> Will be the time of promise, shadow, dream:
> But this, full revelation of great love;
> For rivers blent take in a broader heaven,
> And we shall bend our souls!

THE MARRIAGE OF ONE MAN AND ONE WOMAN IS A RELATIONSHIP WHICH DEATH, AND NOT DIVORCE, CAN DISSOLVE

In the plan of God, and in the teaching of Jesus, the marriage pact is for life; when man and woman are joined together, they should become heirs together of the grace of life, while life lasts, with death alone being the dissolver of the union. A proverb among the Veddahs of Ceylon reads, "Death alone separates husband and wife." In our human society the enduring length of marriage is a real guide to the strength of love and of its quality. In this remaining section we concern ourselves, primarily, with the question of divorce as dealt with by Jesus. With the alarming increase of broken marriages by this cruel dissolver of the sacred bond, it is most necessary to know what the Master taught in order to combat the growing evil of easy ways out of what is called the Sacrament of Marriage.

When Jesus spoke on any theme, in every case he stated the absolute and uncompromising demand of God. "I have given them thy word" (John 17:14). To the honest reader it is perfectly clear that the New Testament, as a whole, is utterly opposed to divorce and that, in particular, the word of Jesus on the subject is absolute and should be literally obeyed, no matter how such an insistence is contrary to modern practices of dissolving the contract of two who were made one in holy matrimony for better or for worse. It should be the solemn obligation of all who officiate at marriages to state clearly what Jesus taught as the divine intent and permanency of the sacred union

—a union that must not be severed and one by which the man and the woman are equally bound. The only references to divorce in the Gospels are all associated with the one encounter between the Pharisees and Jesus on the subject. Differences can be noted if we set these references alongside each other.

Matthew 5:31

"It hath been said, Whosoever shall put away his wife, let him give her a writing of divorcement:"

Matthew 5:32

"But I say unto you, That whosoever shall put away his wife, saving for the cause of fornication, causeth her to commit adultery: and whosoever shall marry her that is divorced committeth adultery."

Mark 10:5, 6

"Jesus answered and said unto them, For the hardness of your heart he wrote you this precept. But from the beginning of the creation God made them male and female. . . ."

Mark 10:11–12

"Whosoever shall put away his wife, and marry another, committeth adultery against her. And if a woman shall put away her husband, and be married to another, she committeth adultery."

1 Corinthians 7:10–11

"Let not the wife depart from her husband: But and if she depart,

Luke 16:18

"Whosoever putteth away his wife, and marrieth another, commit-

let her remain unmarried, or be reconciled to her husband: and let not the husband put away his wife." teth adultery: and whosoever marrieth her that is put away from her husband committeth adultery."

Matthew 19:9
"Whosoever shall put away his wife, except it be for fornication, and shall marry another, committeth adultery: and whoso marrieth her which is put away doth commit adultery."

Note: Deuteronomy 24:1–4 should be studied along with these passages from the Gospels.

A consideration of these parallel passages leads one to a few observations, important in nature. First, Jesus uses two words, namely, *fornication* and *adultery*, which certainly do not mean the same thing. *Fornication* means uncleanness between those who are unmarried; *adultery* implies uncleanness between persons one of whom, at least, is married.

Moses never gave a writing of divorcement in the case of adultery, for the penalty of adultery was death, and there was no exception. "The adulterer shall surely be put to death" (Lev. 20:10). Jesus at least implied that this was a righteous law when he said, "He that is without sin among you, let him first cast a stone" (John 8:7).

Under the law of Moses the husband was permitted to put away his wife if she found no favor

in his eyes because he had found some uncleanness in her, which evidently referred to sin committed *before* marriage (Deut. 24:1). Discovering
that he had married an unvirtuous woman, he
could put her away, but the words of Jesus give
no permission to remarry, for the phrase, "her
that is divorced," is only one word in the Greek
and means "a divorced woman."

Actually, then, Jesus said that "whosoever shall
put away his wife and marry a divorced woman
committeth adultery." Thus, in the light of the
law of Moses it is clear that Jesus used the word
fornication in its usual sense of uncleanness before
marriage and distinguishes it from adultery (Matt.
15:19; Mark 7:21; see Gal. 5:19). "The writing of
divorcement" was only given to the man who discovered after marriage the unchaste character of
his wife, but even this Jesus declared was due to
the hardness of the hearts of those concerned and
not to any commandment of God. Hence, the emphatic statement, "From the beginning it was not
so" (Matt. 19:8). In such a statement Jesus appeals
from the temporary concession of Moses to the
eternal, original law of God, namely, that he made
male and female, one man and one woman, with
no provision of separation or divorce.

We all know that that first marriage did not
turn out very well, divinely planned though it was,
for the husband was enticed by the wife into sin,
and both husband and wife learned to know what
a broken heart means when they stood over the
corpse of their son, Abel, slain by the hand of his
brother Cain, earth's first murderer (Gen. 4:1–8).
But Adam and Eve remained together and doubtless found family happiness when other sons and
daughters were born to them (Gen. 5:4). It was

Lamech who began the departure from the monogamic bond by introducing polygamy which
opened the gate of promiscuity. When Israel became a nation, a Hebrew could have two or more
wives or concubines, also intercourse with a slave
or bondwoman, even though married, without
being reckoned guilty of the crime of adultery,
because adultery, according to Jewish law, was
possible only when a man dishonored the *free wife*
of a Hebrew (Lev. 19:20 20:10).

In his teaching, however, Jesus was bold
enough to be original in his affirmation that the
Mosaic law of divorce had been an accommoda-
tion to the demand of men's hearts, while the only
true annulment of marriage could be recognized
and declared because of marital unfaithfulness. In
fact, he went further and transferred the sin of
adultery to the lustful desire, the act being fully
condemned. The Pharisees were always on the
alert to trap Jesus with a question, and his answers
revealed the characteristics of his thinking. Instantly, he "recognizes their trickery" (Luke
20:23), and with a certain swiftness, the quick realization of a situation, a character, or the meaning
of a word, had a ready reply. Thus when his persistent enemies, the Pharisees, asked Jesus, "Is it
lawful for a man to put away his wife for *every
cause*," he had but one reply. He deliberately
swept aside all other pretenses for divorce and
named adultery per se destructive of monogamic
family life.

An article by Dr. C. Caverno in the *International
Standard Bible Encyclopedia* states:

> It is the hand of an unerring Master that has made
> fornication a ground of divorce from the bond of
> matrimony and limited divorce to that single cause.

Whichever way we depart we depart from strict practice under the Saviour's direction, we land in polygamy—The society that allows by its statutes divorce for any other cause than the one that breaks the monogamic bond, is simply acting in aid of polygamy, consecutive if not contemporaneous.

Today, there are numerous easy roads out of marriage such as desertion, cruelty, lack of support, drunkenness, incompatibility, and others somewhat ludicrous in character. By affording easy ways out of the trials of married life we invite carelessness about entering marriage. By just as much as a crevice for relief of the miseries of married life is opened by divorce, by so much the flood gates are opened into these miseries. The more solemnly society is impressed that the door of marriage does not swing outward as well as inward the more of happiness and blessing will it find in the institution.

There has developed an idea, particularly in some Protestant churches, that the traditional ban against the remarriage of divorced persons should be considerably softened, and so there is the agreement to remarry *the innocent party* to a divorce. But in the break-up of a home it is to be questioned whether there is any *innocent party*. Usually, the dissolution is caused by mutual, contributing factors. But over against all supposed grounds for divorce is the absolute word of Jesus—"Saving for the cause of adultery." Both Jesus and Paul exalted marriage to heights of significance and sanctity unknown under the old covenant, for in their teaching they sought to restore matrimony to its state and honor as intended by God at creation (Mark 10:9; see Heb. 13:4; 1 Cor. 7:10–16). The phrase "the husband of one wife" (1 Tim. 3:2, 12;

Titus 1:6) is given in the Revised Version as "married only once," the meaning of which is obvious.

Some theologians have suggested that the teaching of Jesus on divorce as given in Matthew 5 is contrary to his words on the subject in Mark 10 and in Luke 16. In Matthew's account divorce is permitted on the grounds of infidelity; in Mark and Luke divorce seems to be forbidden on any ground whatever. The most satisfactory explanation of this seeming contradiction is that what is stated *explicitly* by Jesus in Matthew is *implicit* in Mark and Luke; that the exception stated in Matthew—"Saving for the cause of adultery"—is assumed by Mark and Luke who take for granted Matthew's account of the conversation of Jesus on the divorce question. That Paul is in agreement with Jesus, whose *mind* the apostle said he had, is evident from the command, "The woman which hath a husband is bound by the law to her husband so long as he liveth. . . . So then if, while her husband liveth, she is married to another man, she shall be called an adulteress" (Rom. 7:2–3).

In many parts of the world today divorce is the open sore of mankind, and it is incumbent upon pastors, in particular, to stress that the strictness of the marriage bond as taught by Jesus is the security of morals and of family welfare. All should unite in opposing movements and arguments for permitting divorce for any reason short of the act Jesus mentioned which ruptures the bond between man and wife. Undivided homes are the supreme social necessity for national well-being, religious prosperity, and individual advantage. Whatever those of loose morals may have to say of the increasing sexual permissiveness of today, the fact cannot be disputed that such behavior is totally prohibited by the teaching of Jesus and his apostles. Richard Glover in his most valuable commentary on *Matthew* summarizes the subject:

1. Facilities of divorce, except on the ground of adultery, are proofs of a low state of self-respect in any community, and tend to lower it still more.
2. They work incalculable mischief, for such facilities prevent the healing of quarrels, and unions which might have become sources of honourable comfort, and often promote the sins which are the grounds of separation.
3. Stringency of marriage laws in the interest of the women and the children everywhere. Their rights should be protected.
4. The true secrets for preventing matrimonial misery are:
    Greater care in entering marriage engagements—
    Full mutual knowledge before engagements to marry are made—
    Unselfishness—
    Action in the fear of the Lord—
    The repression of all Lust—
    Above all things—LOVE.
5. The surest way to a happy marriage is:
    To deserve a good husband or wife—
    Only to marry one it is a pleasure to serve—
    To marry only in the Lord, and to bear with all patience and meekness anything not according to expectations—
    If unhappily mated, loving endurance is still both wisdom and duty—
    To keep an unbroken home for children:
        To save them from dishonour and hurt—
        To practice patience—these are things which have great reward.

When Jesus, in reply to the question asked by the Pharisees, "Why did Moses command to give a writing of divorcement?" said, "Because of the hardness of your hearts, suffered you to put away your wives," he implied that Moses acted on the divine principle of suffering evil to exist, but which is divinely disapproved. As Christians, we are not to govern our conduct by the evils which God suffers *but by the law which he gives,* and in his teaching, Jesus gave us the law of God for *all* ages which stated simply is: There may be *divorce* for adultery, and it may be wise to *separate* for other causes, but remarriage *never,* and thus the way is open to repentance and reunion. Pleading with adulterous Israel to turn from her sin, God's plea was, "For I am married unto you" (Jer. 3:14), and he promised to receive her back if only she would repent (Jer. 2, 3). If sin has broken up a home, it is possible for repentance and regeneration to restore it, but such a possibility is forever precluded by remarriage on the heels of divorce.

Both the sacredness and indissolubility of the marriage bond is found in the use of it as a beautiful metaphor of the relationship between Christ and his church. After leaving the home in which he lived for thirty years in an atmosphere conducive to his spiritual development and happiness, his first public appearance was at a wedding. His mother was present, and he contributed to the happiness of the occasion by performing his first miracle of turning water into the best wine. In his parable on the wise and foolish virgins, Jesus used the figure of the marriage to enforce the truth of his Second Advent (Matt. 25:1–13), and John describes for us the marriage of the Lamb (Rev. 19:7–9).

Paul's lofty conception of the bond between Christ and his church is incomparable: "Wives, submit yourselves unto your own husbands, as unto the Lord. For the husband is the head of the wife, even as Christ is the head of the church: and he is the saviour of the body. Therefore as the church is subject unto Christ, so let the wives be to their own husbands in every thing. Husbands, love your wives, even as Christ also loved the church, and gave himself for it" (Eph. 5:22–25). If the relationship between husband and wife can be a figure of the union of the eternal and majestic Christ with his bride, the church, then how high and beautiful ought to be the marriage union between the man and the woman. Paul also uses the divine teaching on the indissolubility of the marriage bond to illustrate his eternal relationship to Jesus Christ his Lord (Rom. 7:1–6).

From Him, Who loves me now so well,
    What power my soul can sever?
Shall life, or death, or earth, or Hell?
    No: I am His for ever.

BIBLE STUDY QUESTIONS

Take time to turn to each Scripture reference and mark the verse or a portion in your Bible.

1. Why is the marriage relationship so important in the New Testament?

2. How did Jesus regard marriage and divorce?

3. What is the explanation of "they twain shall be one flesh"?

4. What actions are Biblical in the matters of fornication and adultery?

5. As Christians what should govern our conduct, and why?

— 24 —

Women

For a rewarding insight into our Lord's attitude toward, and teaching about, *women* while he tabernacled here below, it is essential to understand the Roman and the Jewish estimation of woman during the first century. Born into a world under Roman domination and named a *Jew* by a woman of questionable character, Jesus became familiar with the treatment accorded women by religious and heathen rulers alike. And it is such treatment that lends color to his contact with women and to his conversation with and about them.

Under Roman law, operating at the time when Jesus was born of a woman, women were under the perpetual tutelage of their male relatives. C. Loring Brace, in his erudite work *Gesta Christi* (What Christ Hath Wrought), gives us an insight into the restricted life of women under the old Roman laws. They could not intervene in the government of the family, nor in industrial or commercial affairs, nor in public matters. A court of the relatives of a woman could inflict upon

her the severest penalties in case of certain
offenses. She was not the equal of her husband but treated, more or less, as an adopted
ward. All her property became her husband's; all her earnings were his; her children need not obtain her consent to marry,
for the children were not reckoned to be in
the family of the mother but of the father.
She was not a person in her own right. But
under Justinian laws, absolute power of the
husband over his wife and her property
ceased.

With the coming of Jesus and his gospel,
there developed a new conception of the
worth and position of women, and the tendency toward "the personal and proprietary
independence" of women in modern law and
custom received its first great stimulus in the
religion of Jesus affecting Roman law.
Through Christianity, the elevated position
of women and the character of the relation
between husband and wife, with emphasis on
the absolute sacredness of such a union, became apparent. The new faith threw a halo
about woman she has never lost. As Loring
Brace convincingly proves, such female emancipation came about as the results of the character and teachings of Jesus.

The power of Christianity on the Roman world
was especially the influence of a Person, of a
pure and elevated character who claimed to be a
supernatural Being in His relations with men
and God, and Who was the Founder of a new
religion. His nature alone, from its purity and
elevation, seemed to sweep away unnatural pas-

sions from among men, both in the Roman Empire, and since among all races following Him.

Through the influence of the great Friend of women, their changed position resulted in continual reproach by the early enemies of the Christians because they gave their women high position in the church. And as we know from the Acts and the Epistles, women came to exercise a strong influence in the church. Further, as the result of Christ's teaching, the original conception of marriage as a bond of equal union, and the highest spiritual partnership, was restored. Paul taught that in marriage two became one flesh. Alas! however, in non-Christian lands, the misery of women can be seen whether in marriage among Mohammedans or widowhood in Hinduism.

In Jewish circles, also, the teaching of Jesus concerning women and his treatment of them caused the Pharisees, whose approach to women was so different from his own, to rise up in protest against his respectful and sympathetic understanding of their needs and trials. An old Jewish prayer read, "Blessed art thou, O Lord our God! King of the Universe, Who hast not made me a woman." How wonderfully did Jesus, firstborn of Mary, change the world of women! We never find him warning men against women. As T. R. Glover reminds us in *The Jesus of History:*

> Even the most degraded woman finds in him an amazing sympathy; for he has the secret of being pure and kind at the same time—his purity has not to be protected; it is itself a purifying

force. Jesus draws some of his most delightful
Parables from woman's work. It is recorded
how, when he spoke of the coming disasters of
Jerusalem, he paused to pity poor pregnant
women and mothers with little babies in those
bad times. Matt. 24:19; Luke 21:23.

Bishop Gore, in dealing with various aspects of Jesus' teaching, does not fail to notice his attitude toward women. He comments in *Jesus of Nazareth:*

> There was a good deal in the sacred literature of
> Israel tending to give a high status to women, but on
> the whole it would be true to say that they were still
> treated as the chattels and instruments of men. Con-
> temptuous references to womankind can easily be
> quoted from the Old Testament and the Rabbis:
> Jesus showed no disposition to include women among
> his apostles or official agents: but he constantly
> treated women as of the same spiritual worth as men.
> He is represented as talking freely to them in public
> places contrary to the Jewish custom. When he had to
> do with "fallen women" he totally refused to treat
> them with contempt or under a "taboo." He wel-
> comed their repentance and set them free. In his
> ministry of mercy he showed the same regard to
> women as men. For a part of his ministry at least a
> company of women was attached to the company of
> the disciples and ministered to them of their sub-
> stance. Women, like Martha and Mary, were among
> his friends and he thought them worthy of his high-
> est teaching. He saw in them, that is, the same spiri-
> tual worth and capacity as men.

The attitude of Jesus is of primary importance, for it has been largely influential in the
vast change in women's place in the home
and in society. To him they owe the rights of
persons to be personalities. As we study the

Gospels, we find how all women, good and bad, were attracted to Jesus because, in the true sense of the word, he was a *gentleman*. With all confidence, mothers brought their children to him to be blessed. Sisters, like Mary and Martha, loved to have Jesus in their home, and, as one writer puts it, "It would not be at all surprising if they loved him as a woman loves a true man." Good women, enriched by his teaching, gladly ministered unto him of their substance.

As for his own holy estimation of women, is it not proven, in that before he left heaven, he chose Mary to be his mother, and after his victory over death elected another Mary to be the first herald of his resurrection? Jesus, then, in his attitude to women, referred men's thoughts back to the standard of God's thoughts concerning man's helpmate and supported what he taught by what he *was*. He regarded both man and woman as subject to the same divine laws, which were equally high for both sexes. Always he thought of the woman at least as much as of the man. It is in his human contacts that we discover his chief contribution to the higher view and the better treatment of womanhood. Each contact is a revelation of the mind of Jesus in relation to women who often wept for him.

JESUS AND HIS MOTHER

Although our knowledge of the family life of Jesus for thirty years is somewhat meager, we can safely assume that his attitude toward women generally was an outgrowth of a deep and happy relationship with his mother and sisters, of whom there must have been at least two. Did not his strong words in regard to *divorce* suggest the personal experience of a home that was happy in itself and fashioned according to the divine plan of family life? Can there be any doubt that mother love was a very important factor in the teaching of Jesus, as well as in his life? Do we not have echoes of the home at Nazareth in which he grew to manhood in his keen sense and instruction of the value of the child (Mark 10:13–16; Matt. 18:1–6)? Then what about his strong conviction as to duty to parents when he expressed his deep indignation of the Pharisees who taught negligence of parents as part of their service to God (Matt. 15:1–9)? Does not such explicit teaching imply that from his home life and from his actual relationship to his own parents there emerged his clear ideas of the relation of parents to children and vice versa?

Go back to the joyful song of Mary over the birth of her firstborn and of all the rich promise that such a lowly birth held (Luke 1:46–55). It is not hard to imagine Mary's growing delight and wonder as "the Holy Child Jesus" grew in stature and in favor with God and man; her constant questioning as to what the future held as she pondered in her heart one thing and another; her temporary misunderstanding and desire to drag him back to the sheltered and delightful

home life. Mary knew from angelic and human
announcements at the birth of her illustrious Son
that he was born to die as the Savior of the world
and the deepening appreciation that his great mission could only be fulfilled through pain—a pain
which drove a sword into his mother's heart.

Although it may appear as if he treated his
mother aloofly when he had to rebuke her
gently for giving a personal relationship
precedence over the spiritual bond, he was
ever considerate of her and revered her as
"blessed above women." Had she not his deepest thought in the agony of death? In the
hour of extreme anguish his thought turned
to the future welfare of the mother who had
borne him, and he made provision for her in
the home of John, the disciple whom Jesus
loved. With the weight of the world's sin
upon him, and the endurance of physical
and spiritual agony beyond our imagining,
Jesus addressed two sentences to his beloved
mother and dearest friend, revealing,
thereby, the tender relations which had existed between mother and Son: To Mary his
mother, "Behold thy Son!" To John the disciple, "Behold thy mother" (John 19:26, 27).

A striking evidence of the deep affection
of Mary for her Son, and of her determination to remain near him, encouraging him by
her presence until the last moment of his intense physical suffering, is seen in her attitude at Calvary. Other women who loved
Jesus stood *afar off,* beholding him die. Some
of the disciples had forsaken him and fled.
But what of Mary? We read that *she stood by*

the cross (John 19:25, 26). She was not prostrate on the ground with grief as we might have expected a mother to be as she watched her firstborn die such a terrible death. We further read that her dying Son saw his mother *standing,* along with his beloved disciple, John, and, impressed by her brave watch, provided her with a new home.

The ministry of Jesus, then, grew out of his home life as the bud unfolds on the stem and colored his teaching as to a higher, larger, family life in which God is our heavenly Father and all redeemed by his blood are brothers and sisters. It is to be regretted that unhappy differences and divisions, acrimony and apostasy have greatly impaired the family love-mark that should ever characterize the church Jesus purchased by his precious blood (1 John 3).

JESUS AND WIDOWS

The Gospels record several contacts between Jesus and widows, and how kind, tender, and sympathetic he was in his treatment of them. Here, again, was it experience that made him so considerate of widowhood? After the episode in the Temple involving Jesus, Mary his mother, and Joseph his foster father, we have no further mention of Joseph, who vanishes altogether from the Gospel story. It is generally thought that he died some time after Jesus, at the age of fifteen, left the synagogue school and joined Joseph in the carpentery

business. With his death, Jesus assumed control of
the trade and became known as the "carpenter"
and helped his widowed mother in every possible
way to beat back the beast of poverty from the
home in which its head was missing. With such a
Son, how could Mary the widow be desolate?

It was a very aged widow who welcomed
the birth of Jesus. Anna had long looked for
the Redeemer to come in Jerusalem, and one
day while at her usual prayers in the Temple,
the glad tidings reached her of the Redeemer's appearance in the flesh, and she
gave instant thanks (Luke 2:36–38).

When Jesus entered his public ministry, he
had little sympathy with those religious leaders who took advantage of the helplessness of
widows by devouring their houses (Matt.
23:14). The word for *houses* used here can
denote property or possessions of any kind,
which the scribes and Pharisees got possession of by improper pretenses. Barnes, in his
New Testament commentary, explains:

> They pretended to a very exact knowledge of
> the Law, and to a perfect observance of it. They
> pretended to extraordinary justice to the poor,
> friendship for the distressed, and willingness to
> aid those who were in embarrassed circum-
> stances. They thus induced *widows* and poor peo-
> ple to commit the management of their prop-
> erty to them as guardians and executors, and
> then took advantage of them, and defrauded
> them.

They then added to their heartless treatment of
the poor widows by pretending to make long
prayers for the women they were robbing. Those

hypocrites felt they could the better defraud them by the appearance of sanctity, implying thereby that the widows were devoting their money to religious purposes and not lining the pockets of the callous Pharisees. Truly, the greater damnation is theirs.

With his intimate knowledge of the Old Testament, Jesus drew attention to widows in Israel in the time of Elijah, and particularly to the widow of Zarephath for whom the prophet miraculously provided food in days of famine (Luke 4:25, 26; 1 Kings 17:1–16). How bountifully was this widow's sacrifice rewarded!

The widow of Nain experienced the omnipotence of a greater prophet than Elijah (Luke 7:11 –18). Among the many miracles of Jesus, the utterly unexpected one this sorrowing widow witnessed is one of the few cases where no appeal was made to Jesus to do anything. The action of Jesus was simply the overflow of his loving nature as he watched the only son of this grief-stricken woman being borne to the grave. Neighbors were all moved to pity for her, but there was nothing they could do but mingle their tears with those of the widow who had lost her only stay and support. The first word of Jesus to her was so like him, *Weep not!* The young man in his coffin almost seemed like a secondary consideration. The Divine Comforter's deed of mercy centered around the widow in her loneliness and grief. First, he wiped away her tears; then "he gave him back to his mother." The widow was of supreme importance to Jesus. Should not every bereaved mother find here something of peculiar solace?

Another widow who attracted the attention of Jesus was the one he watched casting all she had into the Temple treasury (Mark 12:38–44). There had been conflict with the Pharisees over their pretext of raising money for religious purposes when, actually, they had been draining away the resources of the very poor. Merciless to the widow and fatherless, these hypocrites, guilty of worthless generosity and empty prayers, gave nothing of their own to God. Jesus, turning from them with righteous indignation, caught sight of a widow quietly stealing up to the treasury and, as if ashamed of her very meager gift, slipping in the only two coins she possessed. Such an act was seen at its true worth by the eyes of him that ever pierces the sham and make-believe. Those *two mites*, representing a day's meat and drink—and *all* that she had—were an illustration of complete self-denial for God's sake. Jesus, who has his own standard of judgment, found in this godly widow a sacrifice winning his approval and commendation. The power to deny herself for God, the love that gives all and instinctively realizes that it will be accepted, is again a woman's.

In his parable of the unjust judge, Jesus describes a widow's importunate demand (Luke 18:1 –8). Doubtless, he had met an actual widow of such persistence and here uses her to illustrate his parable that "men ought always to pray and not to faint." The judge, whose help she sought when pestered by an adversary, is described as *unjust*, "who feared not God, neither regarded man"— not a very commendable character for a judge. To get rid of this persistent widow, he offered judicial help, "lest by her continual coming she weary me." The word used here for *weary* denotes, in the original, the wounds and bruises caused by boxers who beat each other and disable themselves. In his application of the parable, Jesus revealed how different God is from the unjust judge. God values our perseverance and urges us not to faint in our oft coming to him, for suddenly and unexpectedly he will manifest justice on our behalf.

There can be no doubt, whatever, that the contacts of Jesus with widows and his kind and gracious treatment of them influenced the apostles to honor the widows who were widows indeed (1 Tim. 5:3–16; James 1:27). One reason for the election of deacons in the early church was for the caring of the widows who had been "neglected in the daily ministration" (Acts 6:1). Paul became conspicuous in his endeavor to continue and expand the Master's gracious treatment of those bereft of their partners in life. An Order of Widows developed in the church in the second century and lasted into the fourth, being abolished by the Council of Laodicaea in A.D. 364.

JESUS AND THE WOMAN
WHO WAS A SINNER

Simon the Pharisee said "within himself," because he was afraid to say it audibly, "This man, if he were a prophet, would have known *who* and *what* manner of woman this is that toucheth him, for she is a sinner" (Luke 7:36–50). We gather from this that the woman of whom he spoke was an unchaste, disreputable person. No decent man should have any contact with her. Although a defiled creature, she knew Jesus was being entertained by Simon, and believing him to be a friend of sinners, she expressed her love and faith in him by washing his feet with her tears and drying them with the hairs of her head before anointing them with the very precious ointment she had brought. Twice during his life Jesus was anointed by a woman. Here, by one who had trodden dark and evil paths; in the other instance, by a pure saint, Mary of Bethany.

Was not this sinful woman who received the forgiving grace of Jesus—"Thy faith hath saved thee: go in peace"—more akin to the pure and sinless one than to the self-righteous Pharisee. Let it be noted that there is no record of any request from this woman, but hers was the quick instinct assuring her longing heart that here was one who would not spurn her, as men had done after satisfying their lust. She expressed her faith in the willingness of Jesus to deliver her from her sin by an act of pure love, and she was not disappointed. Jesus accepted the gift as an expression of her repentance and forgave her sins, which were many. She loved much and was fully forgiven. By contact with this sinful woman, Jesus was not defiled, as Simon thought he would be, for Simon's concept of a holy man was one who cannot touch evil. But a sunbeam loses nothing of its glory and purity by shining on a dunghill. Jesus, the thrice holy one, ever glories in lifting up the fallen with a tender and redeeming hand.

JESUS AND THE TWO SISTERS

With its mingling of sickness and pain, love and trust, sorrow and death, resurrection and life, the eleventh chapter of John is one of the most heart-moving in the New Testament. All the recorded incidents in it revolve around the close-knit family in Bethany—the spiritual retreat of Jesus. At the age of thirty, he left the Nazareth home in which he grew up, and we have no record of his returning to it during his brief ministry. When by "thronging duties pressed" and in need of relaxation, Jesus found his way to the home of three unmarried friends whom he had come to love. Of the happy association of Jesus with Mary, Martha, and Lazarus in Bethany, F. B. Meyer says in his *Commentary on John:*

> Their home was the one green oasis in the rugged wilderness through which he passed to his Cross; we think of the pure and holy love that broke in upon his loneliness and the true affection that softened the bitterness of his last days, so far at least as human love could.

In this ideal home Jesus found the curse of the sojourner lifted from him, and, in reversal of his own description of his loneliness and penury, found where to lay his head.

The chapter, as a whole, will ever be counted precious since it is saturated with tears, including those Jesus himself shed. In *Commentary on the New Testament* F. Godet says of the chapter that "no scene in the Gospel of John is presented in so detailed and dramatic manner as we find here. There is none from which appears more distinctly the character of Jesus as at once perfectly Divine and perfectly human, and none which more fully justifies the central declaration of the Prologue: *The Word was made flesh.*" As the man Christ Jesus, he wept; as God manifest in flesh, he said to a corpse, "Come forth, and he that was dead came forth" (John 11:35, 43, 44). What a striking combination of tears and triumph, pain and power!

We can also note in passing that Mary, Martha, and Lazarus are the only persons *named* in the

Gospels as being loved by Jesus (John 11:5). John was far too modest to name himself as "the disciple whom Jesus loved" (John 13:23; 21:20, 24). The term used for *loved* is the nobler, more dignified one than that used as an expression of tenderness, appropriate in the mouth of the sisters as they thought of their affection for the Master. The tears of Jesus reveal the loving, tender sympathy he had for the grief of the two sisters and of others mourning the death of Lazarus. One does not raise the dead with a heart of stone. Those tears of his—liquid pain—were not for Lazarus, for one does not weep over a beloved friend whom he will soon see again.

The two sisters, Martha and Mary, were corecipients of divine love, cosufferers in sickness and death, and coparticipants in the miraculous power of the friend who had loved them both (John 11:17-33; Luke 10:38-42). Both of these passages portray the two women as being possessed of the same characteristics, surely an undesigned coincidence affirming a proof of genuineness. The two sisters, so different, as we shall see, were yet each so devoted to Jesus and so confident of his love and power that they stand out among the most interesting characters in John's Gospel. And knowing that they were not on a lower plane than men either spiritually or intellectually, Jesus opened up for Martha and Mary deep wells of truth.

"Men have different gifts, but it is the same Spirit Who gives them. There are different ways of serving God, but it is the same Lord Who is served" (1 Cor. 12:4, 5, Phillips). Paul makes it clear that there is great variety among the Lord's people and that it is evidently not the design of grace to make them all alike as the natural, opposite characteristics of Martha and Mary prove. What marked diversities there were in that Bethany home! The two sisters and their brother were not like peas in a pod, but so different. Yet Jesus loved them each with all their personal, peculiar traits for in the opening of this marvelous chapter is written the affirmation, "Jesus loved Martha, and her sister, and Lazarus."

The fact is evident that the sisters were one in concern for their sick brother and in their faith that the friend who loved them was able to help. While they looked to him for sympathy, they did not ask for it. They felt it was enough to tell him of their trial and then leave the matter with him. "His sisters sent unto him, saying, Lord, behold, he whom thou lovest is sick." These dear women of Bethany had confidence in the continuance of Jesus' love, hence, the present tense *lovest*, not past tense *lovedst*.

To such an affectionate and urgent request, Jesus sent a somewhat puzzling reply. He said that Lazarus would die but that death would not be the end of the sickness laying him low. The tears of Martha and Mary would give luster to the jewels of the crown of Jesus as he proved himself to be the victor over death in the resurrection of Lazarus for the glory of God. What perplexed the sisters still further was the delay of Jesus in coming to the help of the man he loved. They had hastened in sending him tidings of the sickness of Lazarus, but he manifested no haste to come to him. "He abode two days still in the same place where he was." Conscious he was God, and able to cope with the situation, Jesus was in no hurry. He sought to teach Martha and Mary that his delays are not denials, that although he may appear to tarry, he is never too late. In any need that may arise we can with confidence wait for him (Heb. 10:37). To quote F. B. Meyer again:

> To the sisters he must have appeared neglectful but he was not really so . . . The whole situation was constantly present to him, till he saw that he could interpose with the best possible result. So is it ever. His step may linger; but his watchful interest never falters. There is not a sigh, a pang, a tear, that escapes his notice. There is not a fluttering pulse which he does not feel, noticing its tremulous anxiety. He *sits* as a refiner of silver. He knows our sorrows, and is acquainted with our grief. He slumbers not, nor sleeps.

As to the personal characteristics of the two sisters, the record reveals them to be totally different in temperament. Yet theirs was a diversity in unity.

Mary was meditative and reticent, tender and clinging, and gifted with all a woman's delicacy of insight and loving sympathy. She thought little about necessary housework, being unwilling to lose a minute of the precious company of him at whose feet she could sit in silence and rest in his wonderful presence.

Martha, on the other hand, was somewhat impulsive and active, practical, businesslike, abounding in energy, revealing her love by making every preparation, executive and efficient, determined that nothing should lack in the entertainment of the friend she loved. She typifies the strong housewife ever thoughtful of all concerning the comfort and well-being of those for whom she feels responsible. Yet Jesus loved both sisters.

It must not be felt for one moment, however, that Martha was all movement and no meditation, for Luke has the delightful touch, "Martha . . .

had a sister called Mary, which *also* sat at Jesus' feet, and heard his word" (Luke 10:39). So both had tuition in the College of the Feet, but Martha felt that home duties must have some of her time, as well as the spiritual luxury of receiving divine instruction. As for Mary, she had little thought of home service, so long as she could be with her friend. Somehow she felt that he would rather have *her* than the things she could do for him. This is not to say that Jesus did not fail to see that Martha was likewise expressing her devotion in her own way. In his loving rebuke, did he not imply that her fussiness for things mattered little; that what he wanted in the way of hospitality was simplest fare and, above all, *herself*? Jesus loved both of these fine women, not for what they could do for his comfort so much as for the spiritual intercourse he ever sought in the home.

Jesus taught that the one thing most needful in life was fellowship with himself and that this was the good part Mary had chosen and must be nurtured (Luke 10:42). It was Martha not Mary, however, who received from Jesus the most notable and astounding declaration, "I am the resurrection and the life." Hers was the quiet complaint when Jesus ultimately appeared for the burial of Lazarus that had he come sooner he could have prevented her brother's death. Yet she believed that he could secure his resurrection at "the last day" about which Jesus often spoke (John 6:44, 45). But as she was joyfully to experience, the raising of her brother was not to be a far-off event, for the Master said, "I am myself the resurrection." How positive and comprehensive was her reply to the question of Jesus, "Believest thou this?" Without hesitation she replied, "Yea, Lord: I believe that thou art the Christ, the Son of God, which should come into the world" (John 11:26, 27).

When Mary heard from Martha about Jesus' arrival, she "arose quickly" and came to him, expressing, thereby, the eagerness of heart's affection for him. How Mary illustrated that the chariot wheels of love fly swiftly round!

'Tis love that makes our willing feet
In swift obedience move.

Taking up her accustomed place at the feet of Jesus (Luke 10:39; John 11:32), Mary confronted him with the same complaint as Martha, "Lord, if thou hadst been here my brother had not died." Evidently the two sisters had agreed on this matter and up to this point exhibited the same character of faith, but in other respects the faith of Martha was in advance of Mary. Still, the tears of Mary over the death of her brother, as well as the tears of the friends with her, moved, most deeply, the heart of Jesus who, whenever he saw a funeral, upset it and raised the dead. So we have the shortest text in the Bible—*Jesus wept!* The Jews felt that his warm tears were the expression of his love for a much-loved friend whom death had robbed. How touched he ever is with the feeling of our infirmities! Says Hugh Macmillan, "It is the Christian religion alone that reveals to us a God of tears."

Well, as we know, the miracle happened, and Jesus raised the one intimate male friend he possessed outside the circles of the apostles—a miracle that made many Jews turn and believe in Jesus (John 11:45). After this most important and striking, in many respects, of all the miracles of Jesus, he left Bethany for Ephraim (John 11:54) but returned a week later when, in his honor and to celebrate the resurrection of Lazarus, a supper was planned in the home he dearly loved. Martha, practical as ever, served (John 12:1–11). In the previous chapter, Bethany was "the town of Mary and her sister Martha," but now it is the place "where Lazarus was which had been dead, but whom Jesus raised from the dead" (John 12:1). How true it is that in a wonderful way Jesus leaves his mark on all the places and hearts he visits (John 12:9).

That celebration-supper will ever be memorable because of Mary's love-gift to Jesus for his power in calling her beloved brother from the grave. The strong pure love of her heart felt there was no gift too costly for him who was about to die himself and rise from the grave. In fact, Jesus said that Mary had intended the most expensive ointment she had anointed his feet with, to anoint his body on the day of burial (John 12:7). Judas felt that the large amount of money which the gift cost Mary, who was by no means wealthy, had been wasted, or that her money should have been better spent by giving it to the poor. But Jesus saw behind the act of Mary in anointing his feet the intensity of love and that any idea of rebuff to such a gift of gratitude and devotion would be utterly repugnant.

Jesus loved Mary, but the love was not one-sided, and the grateful sister gave to the limit out of an overflowing heart of love. Regardless of cost, love must express itself and approve itself by deeds. Thus the love of Mary justified itself in the eyes of love—his love—which ever kindles love. Wherever the gospel of him who is "the resurrec-

tion and the life" has been preached, Mary's deed
has been proclaimed with it, stirring the hearts of
men and women to yield themselves and their substance to him who broke his box of spikenard very
costly at Calvary. Have you brought him your ala-
baster box, and has the breaking of it filled your
home and the hearts and lives of others with the
perfume of the sacrifice?

> Selfishness seeks a gift,
>   Love loves to give;
> Giving itself away
>   Love loves to live.

> Love's grand munificence
>   Counts not the cost;
> Feeling, though nought is left,
>   Nothing is lost.

JESUS AND THE WOMAN TAKEN IN ADULTERY

The record John gives us of this profligate
woman has been the subject of more eager debate
than any other in the Gospels. In fact, the margin
of the Revised Version notes: "Most of the ancient
authorities omit, John 7:53–8:11." Even Bishop
Westcott says, "The evidence against the genuineness of the woman taken in adultery, John 8:1–11,
as an original piece of the Gospel—both external
and internal—is overwhelming." He goes on to
say what other scholars affirm that the incident is
"beyond doubt an authentic fragment of apostolic
tradition."

But John himself gave the narrative his sanction, as did the early church, and the account of
the woman is in every particular so like other con-

tacts of Jesus that there is nothing in the presentation of this degraded female which would lead us to doubt its authenticity (see Luke 7:36–50). We heartily agree with the conclusion of Dean Farrar that "Were the critical evidence against the genuineness of this passage far more overwhelming than it is, the story would yet bear upon its surface the strongest possible proof of its own truthfulness." Meyer's *Commentary on John* captions this portion "The Penitent's Gospel," and states:

> There is no possibility of accounting for its existence, save on the supposition that the incident really took place. It reveals in our Saviour's character a wisdom so profound, a tenderness to sinners so delicate, a hatred of sin so intense, an insight into human hearts so searching, that it is impossible to suppose the mind of man could have conceived, or the hand of man invented, this most pathetic story.

The characters portrayed by John are the scribes and the Pharisees, the woman guilty of flagrant sin, and Jesus, who by his actions and words teaches us many precious lessons.

The scribes and Pharisees and Jesus. After spending a night on the Mount of Olives, Jesus came to the Temple and, drawing a seat against the treasury wall, sat down and began to teach those who gathered to hear him. But before he had gone too far in his message, a company of his persistent foes, "adorned with their customary badges of sanctity," interrupted his discourse by placing before him a trembling, shrinking woman who had been caught in the act of adultery; they demanded what should be done with her. This was a shameful plot on their part in order to trap Jesus, and some writers suggest that one reason

Jesus stooped down to write on the ground was to conceal the burning shame and holy indignation that leapt to his face over the detestable actions of those scribes and Pharisees.

These "self-appointed inspectors of moral nuisances," who regarded themselves as custodians of public morality, and who regarded publicans and sinners with sanctimonious contempt, were guilty of the very sin for which they desired to have the woman judged. Cowardlike, they brought *a woman*, not the man guilty of abusing her. The Law of Moses, on which the Pharisees prided themselves as being authorities, required that both the adulterer and the adulteress should be judged and put to death (Lev. 20:10). Why, then, was the adulterer not brought to Jesus as well? Why was the woman brought alone as if she were the chief sinner—the one sinning rather than sinned against? Can it be that the adulterer was a Pharisee, one of the company of the accusers, and that policy required that he should not be exposed? Their judgment of the woman was not "without partiality" (James 3:17).

Further, nothing could have been more cruel or harsh than the publicity those Pharisees exposed that weak woman to as they set her "in the midst" of all who were gathered around Jesus. While justice demands the exposure of the guilt of sinners, it is the very nature of love to shield them from public gaze (1 Pet. 4:8). Thus, as Dean Farrar expresses it, "Their conduct showed on their parts a cold, hard cynicism, a graceless, pitiless, barbarous brutality of heart and conscience." These heartless men, clad in the robes of virtuous horror, were incapable of measuring the anguish of the sin-stained heart of the woman they had dragged before Jesus.

Truly, it is a sorry state of things when a sinner falls into the hand of fellow sinners whose sin has blinded them to their own faults and sharpens their detection of the sins of others. Those Pharisees took a prurient pleasure in enumerating all the details—*in the very act*. They held the sinful woman up as a public spectacle—setting *her in the midst*—and left her to her fate which, according to the Law, was death by stoning. Testing Jesus, the Pharisees brought him face to face with the Law of Moses and said, "The law commanded us, that such should be stoned: but what sayest thou" (John 8:5)? They appealed to Moses because he represented a standard Jesus himself regarded and honored (Ps. 40:8). Previously, Jesus had said that Moses was the accuser of the scribes and Pharisees, and it was therefore strange that in accusing the woman they should appeal to Moses (John 5:45).

But the Law could not forgive the woman and transform her life. All it could do was to condemn and demand punishment for sin. The Law of Moses was framed for the purpose of dealing with sin *judicially*. Tenderness and clemency it did not countenance, for in its austerity it implied

> —and in the course of justice none of us
> Should see salvation.

The Law, as an executioner, is commissioned to do its work; and "the offender falls beneath its curse and penalty." Meyer further says:

> The function of the Law is two-fold. *First* it has to reveal our need of salvation; to hold up the looking-glass that we may go for soap; to convince of our disease that we may hasten for the physician; to make

us feel the badness of our best till we are shut in Christ. *Next*, it has to smite, and scourge, and punish us, when we go aside from the narrow thread-like path of perfect goodness. The sinner therefore has no hope as he stands beneath Mount Sinai. He cannot climb those cliffs. Nay, he is smitten down by the pieces of the broken tables as they leap downwards from crag to crag. And Moses, with one blow of his fist, so John Bunyan tells us, completes the work.

Jesus and the woman. In the second part of the story we breathe purer air. There stood the woman before Jesus, not of her free will. She had been forced, ashamed and unresisting, to appear before Jesus as a judge of morals, but she came to know him as the lover of her soul. The exposure of her sin by her accusers led to the remedy for her sin in Jesus. How the delicacy of Jesus shines forth in his treatment of this degraded woman! The Pharisees, after presenting their case against her, asked Jesus, "What sayest thou?" but he said nothing, no reply to the Pharisees, no word of condemnation for the sinner. We have the dramatic, expressive silence of Jesus: "But Jesus stooped down, and with his finger wrote on the ground, *as though he had heard them not.*"

Why did Jesus wait before uttering the words of peace the sinful woman needed to hear? Why he stooped to write in the dust at his feet, and what he wrote, we are not told. If what he wrote was legible, did the adulteress read it and gain life? Many are the reasons conjectured for the action of Jesus in stooping and looking down. One reason is that his pure nature shrunk from gazing at the guilty woman who had been dragged into his presence. Men of corrupt hearts, "having eyes full of adultery" (2 Pet. 2:14), as the Pharisees had, might stare at her, but the holy, loving, compassionate Jesus must look another way.

Another conjectured reason for his downward look is that he wanted to reflect upon the holiness of the divine law. He could not condone the woman's sin. She had broken the Law, and he must honor it. It may be that he paused to say anything that his treatment of her might be delayed. Righteous wrath must have been his over the hard, callous, supercilious attitude of the Pharisees, but Jesus was "slow to anger" even though they kept on asking him for an answer to their question. Little did those loveless, pitiless accusers realize that the averted face of Jesus would make them bow their heads in shame, as conscience-stricken they slunk away, crushed by his simple yet piercing words.

Lifting his head, his first word was not for the sinner trembling before him but for the Pharisees, and how it stung them—"He that is without sin among you, let him first cast a stone" (John 8:7). When Jesus said "without sin," he meant the particular sin of adultery of which the Pharisees condemned the woman, caught in the act, to be guilty. He determined that no stone must be thrown at her save by those who were innocent of the sin with which she was charged. The only one in the group that day who was perfectly holy, and therefore "without sin," was Jesus, but he lifted no stone against the defenseless woman.

The shaft went home and, "convicted by their own conscience, went out one by one, *beginning at the eldest*, even unto the last." The phrase, "beginning at the *eldest*," speaks volumes. In spite of his seniority, he was exposed as an adulterer himself. Says Matthew Henry, "They that are convicted by their own consciences, will be condemned by their Judge if they are not acquitted by their Redeemer. Had those Pharisees stayed there might have been a further revelation of their guilt." But if that mysterious writing on the ground was a record of the iniquity of which they knew they were guilty, then we can understand their humiliating retreat from the presence of the thrice holy one.

The second time Jesus stooped down and wrote on the ground represented another dramatic pause before he dealt with the woman; and seeing no other, he asked, "Woman, where are those thine accusers? Hath no man . . .? She said, No man, Lord" (John 8:10). She might have fled when her convicted accusers did, but she was constrained to remain with the one she had come to see had the only right to judge her. The Pharisees cried, "Stone her." Somewhere she felt Jesus was there to "save her," which he did, for he was not there as a judge and therefore passed no sentence. If the Pharisees could not condemn her, how could he? So the heart of the woman taken in adultery was strangely warmed as she heard her deliverer say, "Neither do I condemn thee: go, and sin no more." Jesus would not have used the words, *sin no more,* if she had not been guilty. In his contacts with women, there were at least three who had been guilty of adultery—the woman of Samaria, the woman who came to him in Simon's house, and the woman we have been considering. Lovingkindness and tender mercy characterized his dealings with each of them. "Go, and sin no more." This last word of Jesus is in perfect agreement with his blessed purpose to save sinners, even the most degraded and the most disgraced.

How full of encouragement this story is for the fallen womanhood of our day! For the crushed and sinning all around us, it offers a ground of hope and an assurance that there is a heart that cares. For women, sinning and sinned against, and generally condemned, what a new world opens when they hear and respond to the Savior's message of forgiveness and warning, "Neither do I condemn thee: go, and sin no more."

> His blood can make the vilest clean,
> His blood avails for me.

JESUS AND THE DAUGHTERS OF JERUSALEM

We cannot think of any other great religious teacher whose contacts with women were so full of meaning and formed so important a part of his life as the one "born of a woman." There was something dynamic in his treatment of women, and the place of women in the world's life and their rights in social and family life have been won largely through those who have caught the spirit of Jesus. We have only to think of the plight of women in those lands where his redeeming Gospel has not penetrated to appreciate what those who are not the mere slaves of the passion of men owe to his ennobling influence.

Among the honorable women Jesus encountered in the days of his flesh were those he named "Daughters of Jerusalem" (Luke 23:27–31) and to whom he had some striking things to say. Among the great company of people following Jesus to Calvary was a group of women who also bewailed and lamented him. It has been suggested that

these devout women formed one of the sister-
hoods in Jerusalem whose gracious task was the
mitigation of the sufferings of condemned crimi-
nals by narcotic drinks. Mary and Martha may
have been among the sorrowful women accompanying Jesus to Calvary.

How characteristic it was of the Master to bury
his own sorrow in the thought of others who wept
and mourned. The tenderness of our Lord's sympathy can be seen in these first words coming
from his lips after he left the presence of Pilate.
The mocking, the scourging, the spitting had all
been borne in silence. Now he speaks and his
thoughts are of the far-off sufferings of others,
rather than those that were then falling upon himself. What tenderness there is in his message to
the female sympathizers. "Weep not for me, but
weep for yourselves, and for your children." He
himself had wept over the sinners in Jerusalem
(Luke 19:41); now he urges the women not to
weep for him, not that it was wrong of them to
show their sympathy, but to weep for a far greater
reason, namely, the destruction of their city and
the overthrow of their nation, which took place
when the Romans ravished Jerusalem and slew its
inhabitants. The beatitude of Jesus, "Blessed are
the barren," implies that women with no children,
during the siege of the city, were spared the hor-
rors of seeing children slain, as so many fond
mothers witnessed.

Jesus predicted that the great calamities and
judgments about to overtake the city and its people would cause them to cry out for shelter and
for the hills to cover them. The same figure is
used of the godless in tribulation judgment (Rev.

6:16, 17). Then the metaphor Jesus used of "the green tree" is a proverbial expression calling for an explanation. "If they [Roman powers] do these things in a green tree, what shall be done in the dry" (Luke 23:31)? Barnes' *Notes on the New Testament* has this satisfying interpretation:

> A green tree is one that is not easily set on fire. A dry one is easily kindled, and burns rapidly. By a green tree is represented, evidently, a man of truth and purity. And the meaning of the passage is: "If they, the Romans, do these things to me, who am innocent and blameless—if they punish me in this manner in the face of justice—what will they not do in relation to this guilty nation? What security have they that heavier judgments will not come upon them? What desolations and woes may not be expected when injustice and oppression have taken the place of justice, and have set up a rule over this wicked people?" Thus applied, the proverb means that the sufferings of the Saviour, compared with the sufferings of the guilty, were like the burning of a green tree compared with the burning of one that is dry. A green tree is not adapted to burn; a dry one is. So the Saviour—innocent, pure, and holy—stood in relation to suffering. . . . The sinner is adapted to sufferings— like a dry tree is to the fire. Guilty, he suffers all the horrors of remorse of conscience.

JESUS AND MARY MAGDALENE

As Luke is preeminently the "Gospel of Womanhood" because of the many figuring in the life of Jesus, so John stands out as the "Gospel of Conversations" since it gives more largely than the other Gospels the individualism of Jesus as expressed in his interviews. John records twenty-four conversations held with seventeen different people. These conversations were often brief monologues of Jesus, and some were directions for his miracles. Conspicuous among his personal talks is the contact with Mary Magdalene in the garden, just after he had risen from the dead (John 20:11–18).

Are you not impressed by the fact that the only friends to stand by Jesus in the closing scenes of his life were *women?* His disciples forsook him and fled, but the women remained near him with tortured hearts, being unable to leave him alone in his terrible plight. They ministered unto him of more than their substance, for as the curtain falls, the small band of loyal and loving women are there, standing by the cross. They were the last to leave the grim spot and the first at his tomb after his burial. And how eloquent are his few words of his relation to them. They had been his friends, bringing him much comfort and strength in his life of strenuous service for others, and they were faithful to the end.

We learn that the encounter with Mary Magdalene was his first appearance after he arose from the dead (Mark 16:9–11). Peter and John and the other women had left the garden tomb where the body of Jesus lay, but Mary Magdalene remained there alone, weeping her heart out for him to whom she owed so much. Even when the angel announced to her that Jesus had risen, the good news did not seem to register. Grief numbed her senses for a few moments. With the rest of the disciples she had heard Jesus say repeatedly that he would rise the third day, but somehow his declaration was not understood. Well, he had gone, and she thought his body had been stolen as she gazed at the empty tomb and begged the angels to tell her where that precious body had gone.

Then it happened. Turning around, she saw Jesus standing, but she knew not that he was the one she loved so much and over whom she had shed so many tears. Then he said to Mary, "Why weepest thou? Whom seekest thou?" It would seem as if Jesus disguised his voice a little to lead her on, for she supposed the speaker to be the gardener who had transferred the body of Jesus to another tomb. How pathetic her plea—"Tell me where thou hast laid him, and I will take him away"! What utter devotion such a plea reveals! But then Jesus uttered only one word in a voice that could not be mistaken—*Mary!* She recognized the tender tone and cried out in ecstatic joy, *Rabboni!* which means "master" (see John 20:16, R.V.). It was not an occasion for many words. "There are spiritual experiences that almost deprive men of the power of utterance, and all they can do is to wonder and adore." It was so with Mary.

Later on, Jesus appeared to the other women (Matt. 28:9–10), but Mary was the first to see him, alive forevermore. The well-loved inflection of the Master's voice opened her eyes, enabling her to see that wonder of all wonders, Jesus alive whom she last saw dead upon the cross. His further words to Mary have received various interpretations, but the simplest explanation of them is that Mary, in her exuberance, tried to detain Jesus. But he meant, "Do not detain me now: for I am not yet ascended to my Father and your Father, and to my God and your God" (20:17). Pause over the phrase, *my Father and your Father,*

for in it Jesus identified himself with Mary and
Mary with himself. Both had an eternal relationship with the Father. Following the command of
her Lord, Mary went and told the disciples the
glorious news, and although a woman, became the
first herald of the resurrection. How privileged
she was!

A concluding word is necessary as to who Mary
Magdalene actually was. She is named more than
any of the other women who followed Jesus, and
usually first; she was the outstanding leader of
them (see Matt. 27:56, 61; 28:1; Mark 15:40, 47;
16:1, 9; Luke 8:2; 24:10; John 19:25; 20:1, 18).
Named among the women who ministered unto
Jesus of their substance, she was evidently a
woman of wealth. The label she wore was, "Out of
whom went seven devils." But this is no indication
that she was unchaste or like the sinful woman
Luke describes (Luke 7:36–50). Nowhere is
Mary Magdalene associated with human immo-
rality. In this respect she has been maligned, for,
in the past, homes and institutes for prostitutes
and fallen women have been given the name of
Magdalene, inferring thereby that she was a
woman of shame whom Jesus rescued. It is un-
thinkable that Jesus would accept such a woman
as the leader among the women who followed
him. When demons invaded human beings, they
caused sickness and disease of various kinds, and
it was in this way Mary had been afflicted (Mark
5:1–20). The sacred record stamps her as a
woman of unblemished character and worthy of
the honor of being the first to proclaim, *He is
risen!* Says Sibbes, "A woman is sent to be the apostle to the Apostles."

BIBLE STUDY QUESTIONS

Take time to turn to each Scripture reference and mark the verse or a portion in your Bible.

1. How did Jesus' regard for women contrast with Roman law?

2. Describe how Jesus regarded widows.

3. What are some of the lessons learned from Jesus, Mary, and Martha?

4. How did Jesus show love to the woman taken in adultery?

5. In what way was Mary Magdalene made a leader of the disciples?

— 25 —

Children

When the Lord of glory became the holy child
Jesus, he entered into a personal experience of a
child's nature and needs; thus his mandate is as
clear as it is challenging, "Suffer the little children
to come unto me, and forbid them not: for of such
is the kingdom of God." "The babe wrapped in
swaddling clothes, lying in a manger" was a sign
that there had been "born in the city of David a
Saviour, which is Christ the Lord" (Luke 2:11).
Gabriel referred to the royal babe as *that holy
thing*, an expression never applied to any other
child in all the world save Mary's child. Alexander
Whyte says in *Walk, Conversation, and Character of
Jesus Christ Our Lord:*

> It is a very startling, and indeed staggering expres-
> sion to be found applied to her Child, to hear him
> called that *thing*, even when it is added, that *holy*
> thing. But the evangelist's so startling expression has
> the seal of the Holy Ghost upon it . . . Human nature
> in all its stages and in all its conditions is a very won-
> derful thing. But as soon as the *thing* we call human
> nature is taken up into himself by a person, that hu-
> man nature is no longer a mere thing. . . . In like

manner, when "that holy thing," which was conceived by the power of the Holy Ghost in the womb of the Virgin Mary, was taken up into himself by the Son of God, that holy thing henceforward and for ever becomes and abides part and parcel of the Son of God.

Many poets wrote feelingly about the nativity. In the sixteenth century, Richard Crashaw wrote:

> Gloomy night embrac'd the place
> Where the noble Infant lay.
> The Babe look't up and shew'd his face;
> In spite of darkness, it was day.
> It was Thy day, sweet! and did rise
> Not from the East, but from thine eyes.

Then in his "Hymn on the Morning of Christ's Nativity," John Milton says:

> It was the winter wild
> While the heaven-born Child
> All meanly wrapt in the rude manger lies;
> Nature in awe to Him
> Had doff't her gaudy trim,
> With her great Master so to sympathize.

C. F. Alexander, who wrote many of our well-known hymns, gave us this Christmas one:

> Once in royal David's city
>   Stood a lowly cattle shed,
> Where a Mother laid her Baby
>   In a manger for His bed:
> Mary was that Mother mild,
> Jesus Christ her little child.

Children love to hear and read about his birth and childhood because

> He's a Friend for little children,
> Above the bright, blue sky.

C. G. Alexander further expresses this thought.

> For, He is our childhood's pattern,
>   Day by day like us He grew,
> He was little, weak, and helpless,
>   Tears and smiles like us He knew;
> And He feeleth for our sadness,
> And He shareth in our gladness.

Then there are the appealing lines of Bishop Heber:

> O Thou, Whose infant feet were found
>   Within Thy Father's shrine,
> Whose years, with changeless virtue crowned,
>   Were all alike Divine;
> Dependent on Thy bounteous breath,
>   We seek Thy grace alone,
> In Childhood, Manhood, Age and Death,
>   To keep us still Thine own!

As God ordained marriage for the creation of children, let us begin by examining the *value* Scripture places upon them. Says the psalmist, "Children are an heritage of the Lord. . . . Happy is the man that hath his quiver full of them" (Ps. 127:1–5). The truly happy home is the one where children are like "olive branches round about the table" (Ps. 128:3). Wordsworth in his "Ode: Intimations of Immortality" reminds us:

> But trailing clouds of glory do we come
>   From God, who is our home:
> Heaven lies about us in our infancy!

As for Tennyson, he would have us know that the ideal home is one in which can be found "Household happiness, gracious children, debtless competence, golden mean." Of old, the firstborn son was claimed as Jehovah's and dedicated to him. Thus Mary brought Jesus, her firstborn, to the Temple. Throughout Scripture, the gift of a son from Jehovah was the height of joy; the loss of a child marked the depth of woe (Gen. 21:16; 33:5; Job 29:5; Matt. 19:13; Luke 2:48, etc.). It was because children were regarded as divine gifts, pledges of God's favor (Gen. 4:1; 33:5), that barrenness was deemed a reproach, a divine punishment involving disgrace in the eyes in the world (Gen. 16:4; 30:1). This is why Elizabeth rejoiced when the Lord took away her "reproach among men" (Luke 1:25), and Jesus referred to the joy of a woman at the birth of a child into the world (John 16:21).

But although children are divine gifts, after they enter the world, their spiritual and moral development depends upon the atmosphere of the home in which they find themselves. Many who heard of the birth of John the Baptist asked, "What manner of child shall this be?" His growth in grace, however, was assured, not only because of his saintly parents, but because "the hand of the Lord was with him" (Luke 1:66). Elizabeth and Zacharias fulfilled the admonition of Sir H. Baker, centuries before he was born.

> O ye who came that Babe to lay
> Within a Saviour's arms to-day,
> Watch well the guard with careful eye,
> The Heir of Immortality.

A prayer used in the Anglican church at the consecration service of children reads,

Grant, we beseech Thee, O Lord, that this child may hereafter not be ashamed to confess the faith of Christ crucified, and manfully to fight under His ban-

ner against sin, the World, and the Devil, and to continue Christ's faithful soldier and servant unto his (or
her) life's end.

PARENTS AND CHILDREN

Whether from the cradle of an infant there
grows a child of God or a child of the Devil depends to a very large degree upon the quality of
the home and the training received. Solomon,
who in *Proverbs* has a great deal to say about children, wrote, "Train up a child in the way he
should go: and when he is old, he will not depart
from it" (Prov. 22:6). The standard of family life
develops or degrades a child. Great, then, is the
responsibility of parents, especially mothers, from
whom naturally children receive their first lessons. Ancient Jews regarded the education of a
child as a religious duty in itself and to be discharged with the religious purpose of bringing
him up in the fear of the Lord.

The home in which Jesus was born was poor
but *pious*, and he found himself in an environment in harmony with his holiness as "the holy
thing" born of Mary, from whom he would be
taught the Old Testament before he was old
enough to go to the village synagogue school.
When, ultimately, Jesus entered his public ministry, he illustrated in his teaching the relation of
father and child in its affection and authority
(Luke 11:11, 12; Matt. 21:28–31). Further he
upheld the paramount duty of the fifth commandment. "Honour thy father and thy mother
[against the tradition of the elders]" (Mark 7:9–13).
Jesus also set all children an example by his own

conduct while at home in which he was subject to his parents (Luke 2:51). He lived out the apostolic injunction, "Children, obey your parents in the Lord: for this is right" (Eph. 6:1). We catch many glimpses in his teaching of experiences and scenes he observed as a growing child.

Alexander Whyte concludes chapter two of his volume with this appeal to parents:

> Pray importunately that your child also may be made of God, both to him, and to you, a twin-brother of the Holy Child Jesus. Pray without ceasing that your child may be sanctified with the self-same sanctification as Mary's Child. And if that may not be perfected all at once, as his sanctification was, pray that at least it may be begun as long as you are here to see it and to have a hand in it. Take your child apart, as long as he is docile and will go with you, and ask on your knees, and in his hearing something like this—
>
> "O God, the God and Father of the Holy Child Jesus, make this, my dear child, a child of God like him. And after I am gone make him and keep him a man of God like him."
>
> Take no rest to yourself, and give God no rest, till you see a seed of God not only sown in your child's heart, but till you see him, as Mary saw her first-born Son, subject to her in everything in her house at home, and growing up every day in wisdom, and in stature, and in favour with God and man.

JESUS AND CHILDREN—MIRACLES

No one can meditate upon Jesus' contacts with children and his teaching concerning them without coming to the conclusion that he had a deep affection for the young. The simple chorus

children of today often sing is true of him who
came as the personification of divine love for old
and young alike.

> Jesus loves the little children,
> All the children of the world,
> Red and yellow, black and white,
> All are precious in his sight.
> Jesus loves the children of the world.

This is why they were, and are, instinctively
drawn to him. The native innocency, simplicity,
and artlessness of children make it easy for them
to believe the stories of Jesus. Their minds are not
lumbered with the doubts and questions affecting
more adult minds and thus decision to love the
Savior comes without effort as they learn to sing:

> Gentle Jesus, meek and mild,
> Look upon a little child;
> Pity my simplicity,
> Suffer me to come to Thee.

First, let us think of his contacts with children,
especially those who figure in his miracles. Jesus
was always deeply moved when he encountered
human suffering, particularly in the young
through no fault of their own. Some of his most
pungent sayings arose out of his miracles. Those
wrought on children were accompanied by exquis-
ite touches of humanity toward the parents.

Nobleman's son (John 4:46–54). John says that
this healing of the nobleman's son was "again
the second miracle that Jesus did" (John 4:54).
This does not mean his miracle in the turning
of water into wine in Cana (John 2:1–12). After
this, Jesus performed many miracles elsewhere,
but he "came again into Cana of Galilee" out of

Judea (John 4:46, 54); thus the healing of the sick boy was his second miracle in Cana. The reputation and influence of his first miracle in Cana lingered on, and as soon as the nobleman heard that Jesus was back in Galilee, he sought the aid of Jesus for his dying son, believing that if he could change water into best wine, he could transform a very sick child into a healthy one.

But when the distressed father and Jesus met, the reply given to the request for Jesus to come to the home and heal the child appears perplexing. "Except ye see signs and wonders, ye will not believe" (John 4:48). This cannot mean that the man would not believe in the power of Jesus to restore his child until the miracle actually happened. The very fact that he came with haste to Jesus for help as soon as he heard that he was back in Galilee was surely an evidence that he believed Jesus was able to stay the hand of death. "Sir, come down ere my child die." What is implied in the reply of Jesus is his reflection on the man's request. "If ye see, ye will believe." The man had not thought that the physical presence in the sick chamber was not necessary to performance of the miracle requested.

Thus, the response of Jesus actually meant that unless he personally went to the sick child, and the father saw with his own eyes the healing sought, he would not believe. But he felt that the remark of Jesus was not an answer, and consequently not a refusal, and so renewed his request, making it more touching but using a term of affection, "Come down ere *my child* die." Godet says that in the granting of the request by Jesus there was also a partial refusal, which was a test.

Jesus yields to the faith which breathes in the prayer, but in such a way as immediately to elevate faith to a higher degree. "Go thy way, thy son liveth." The healing is granted: but without Jesus leaving Cana; he wishes this time to be believed on his word. Until now the father had believed on the testimony of others. Now his faith is to rest on a better support, on the personal contact which he has just had with the Lord himself.

On his way home, the nobleman met his servants and was greeted with the good news, "Thy son liveth." Faith had been rewarded, for the father "believed the word that Jesus had spoken unto him." Inquiring of his servants about the hour his boy began to mend, the father was told "the seventh hour." He remembered that that was "the same hour in which Jesus said unto him, 'Thy son liveth,' " and learned how Jesus could heal by remote control—a divine ability the centurion recognized when, meeting Jesus, he said, "Speak the word only, and my servant shall be healed." Reaching home he found that his servant was healed the very hour Jesus said, "Go thy way; and as thou hast believed, so be it done unto thee" (Matt. 8:5–13).

The Syrophoenician's daughter (Matt. 15:21–28; Mark 7:24–30). This further miracle bringing relief to the daughter of a woman of Canaan affords another instance of an occasion providing Jesus with the opportunity of uttering some startling truths. First, when he sent his disciples forth, it was with the precept, "Go not into the way of the Gentiles," yet here he is heading in the direction of Tyre. Why did he go? Mark tells us that it was partly because of rest (Mark 7:24) and,

as the narrative shows, partly because a soul desired mercy. Because of his omniscience, Jesus
knew that his rest would be invaded by the Gentile woman of Canaan.

Evidently a change had come over this heathen
worshiper of Ashtoreth, or "Queen of Heaven,"
prayers to whom for her demon-vexed child fell
on dead ears. It would seem as if the distressed
mother was a widow, and the fear of losing her
daughter after her husband's death filled her with
despair, seeing intercession to the goddess was un-
availing. Some from Tyre and Sidon had seen
Jesus and been healed by him (Luke 6:17); so she
made her way to him, calling, "Lord, thou son of
David." Afflicted people reason very boldly, and
this Gentile woman with a broken heart cried to
Jesus the Jew, reverently and lovingly, "My daughter is grievously vexed with a devil." Believing him
to be "a very present help in trouble," she pleads
for mercy. But alas! her faith and plea were not at
once successful.

It seemed as if her prayer to the living God had
fallen upon deaf ears, just as her cries had upon
the dead ears of the "Queen of Heaven," for we
read, "Jesus answered her not a word." But, as
she was to learn to her joy, his failure to respond
was not rejection of her plea. The disciples besought Jesus to grant the desperate woman her
wish and send her away, to which came his reply,
crushing though it might have been to a Gentile
mother pleading for her child, "I am not sent but
unto the lost sheep of the house of Israel." The
loving face of Jesus may have seemed to contradict his silence, but he has more reasons for silence than we think. The psalmist cried, "Be not

silent unto me," but divine silence is always golden in its purpose, as the distraught mother was to prove. Jesus had not come seeking her; she sought him and, prostrating herself before him, cried, "Lord, help me!" Can you not read the heart's anguish in such a cry, as she continued knocking at a door that seemed to be closed against her?

Because God's blessings were for God's children, how could a worshiper of a heathen deity expect to share the same? Such appears to be the gist of our Lord's somewhat apparent harsh reply: "It is not meet to take the children's bread, and cast it to dogs." Jews were reckoned to be *children*, and salvation was theirs (John 4:22). Gentiles, however, were classed as *dogs* (Ps. 22:16; Matt. 7:6; Phil. 3:2; Rev. 22:15). But such a reply did not destroy the mother's hope so much as the fact of his replying increased it. Willingly, she owned that those of her nationality were as *dogs*, outsiders altogether, and without any claim upon mercy; but dogs get scraps, and what she desperately needed for her tormented child would not impoverish the *children* privileged to eat the rich food on the table. Like Jacob of old, the persistent mother wrestled with God in the flesh and prevailed. Deeply moved by her determination not to let him go, Jesus uttered one of the most remarkable sayings ever to leave his holy lips: "O woman, great is thy faith; be it unto thee even as thou wilt."

No longer silent, Jesus approves the boldness of the pleader, honors her faith, and grants her heart's desire in his last words to her. "There never has been a true prayer which did not somewhere, sometime, and in some shape, get completely answered." The Lord ever answers true, believing, and fervent prayer, if not in our way, then in his own way, which is ever the best way. For the Syrophoenician woman, the very letter of her request was granted. On reaching home, she found that her daughter was made whole the very moment Jesus uttered a commendable reply to her request.

This further miracle Jesus performed for a very needy child is additional proof that his presence was not necessary for the manifestation of his power. When he said to the anxious mother who would not take no for an answer, "Be it unto thee even as thou wilt," although there was considerable distance between the demon-possessed girl and Jesus, the miracle immediately happened. She was made whole and was resting calmly and comfortably on her bed when her mother returned. While it is true that "his *touch* has still its ancient power," it is likewise true that "his *thought* has still its ancient power"; no matter where we may be, he is able *to will* our relief in the hour of need.

The lunatic son (Matt. 17:14–21; Mark 9:14–29; Luke 9:37–43). The cry of the father in this incident is all the more bitter for this was his *only* child (Luke 9:38). For a full understanding of all that took place on this occasion, it is imperative to compare all the accounts of it found in the Gospels. Perhaps there are no other episodes in the ministry of Jesus so heavy with striking and instructive contrasts as those exhibited between the Mount of Transfiguration and the valley beneath. On the former there was *glory;* in the latter, *grief.* On the mount, *transfiguration;* in the valley, *tragedy.* On the mount, the three disciples wanted to bask in heavenly company forever; below, they miserably failed to assist Jesus and distressed souls. Instead of bringing the shining light of the mount into the darkness and despair of the valley, the disciples only added to the hopelessness of a panic-stricken heart among the multitude, as Matthew, Mark, and Luke narrate, Mark describing the situation with fullness.

But amid all the contrasts, there is the never-changing one, the outflashing of whose inherent glory Peter, James, and John had witnessed. The same compassion which brought Jesus down from heaven likewise constrained him to descend from the mount, with its conversation with glorified saints, to serve and save the sinful, suffering multitude in the valley below. Thus, vision and vocation are united, for what is the use of sublime spiritual experiences when "heaven comes down our souls to greet," unless they thrust us out into a world of suffering and sin to witness to the power of the crucified, glorified Christ to sympathize and save. May we be delivered from taking up the vocation without first having the vision!

1. *The miscellaneous multitude.* When Jesus came down from the mount with his three privileged disciples, he joined the other disciples left below, only to find them surrounded by a mixed multitude, among whom were the scribes and the father distressed about his demon-possessed child. That *great* multitude (Mark 9:14) revealed all the faults and better qualities of a crowd. There were curious scribes asking questions, and the depressed disciples asking theirs. Yet the majority of the multitude that day were "greatly amazed" when they beheld Jesus and, gathering around him, sa-

luted him. They hailed his arrival as if he had mysteriously appeared at the opportune moment to answer all questions and to bring to an anguished heart relief from a most tragic experience. Luke tells us that once Jesus performed the needed miracle, "they were all amazed at the mighty power of God. But ... they wondered every one at all things which Jesus did" (Luke 9:43). But crowds can be fickle, as Jesus experienced when one day they shouted as he rode in triumph, *Hosanna!*—but almost the next day, *Crucify him!*

2. *The questioning queue.* When Jesus joined the large concourse of people, he found the scribes questioning the people, but what about we are not told. Doubtless these critics of his were abashed by his appearance, and meeting them he asked, "What question ye with them?" (Mark 9:16). Could it have been the same question that troubled the disciples, namely, their failure to cast out the dumb spirit causing the child so much pain and anguish? Evidently the disciples who were left behind in the valley when Jesus went up to the mount must have tried to rebuke the foul spirit possessing the boy in the presence of the people and the scribes before Jesus came on the scene. Seeing the helplessness of the disciples in the hour of need, the scribes probably debated with them over their failure and tried to confound them. "Error," says Barnes, "is always subtle, and often puts on the appearance of calm and honest inquiry."

What glorious results there might have been if only those critical, crafty scribes had encouraged the distressed disciples to persist in prayer for the lunatic child and had knelt down with the distraught father, joining the disciples in intercession to God for power to cast out the hellish spirit from his only child. In this way they could have prevented the failure they came to question and denounce, and argue that ill success in one case proves deception in all. As Richard Glover comments in *History of Jesus,* "Pity the woes of men, so often intensified and perpetuated by men disputing as to who is to blame for them, instead of uniting in the effort to cure."

3. *The pleading parent.* It is impossible to describe all the anguish of parental love behind the cry, "Master, I beseech thee, look upon my son: for he is mine only child"(Luke 9:38). The request was more intense because the father was pleading for his *only* child. If he died, the shadowed home would be without hope. Prostrate with grief, the father revealed reverence for the one whose help he sought for he "kneeled down to him." He likewise recognized the power of Jesus to meet the pressing need, for he called him, *Lord!* Thus high regard and earnest entreaty were combined. The prayer of the father was brief yet expressive of intense solicitude for his child he may have felt to be too hopeless a case to expect a cure. But he linked his despair and weakness in himself on to omnipotence and prevailed.

The extreme condition of the child added pathos to the parent's plea, for he was *lunatic,* or smitten with some form of insanity. He was *sore vexed,* meaning, the boy suffered greatly from his affliction. He *fell suddenly,* as persons do when overcome by an epileptic fit. He was *dumb,* except when a fit came upon him, for then *he suddenly cried out.* He *foamed and gnashed with his teeth,* that is, he convulsed, and *wasted away,* or became emaciated. *It tore him,* the demon-spirit bruising him, "hardly departed from him." *It hath cast him* into the fire and into the waters to destroy him. It was an *unclean spirit, foul spirit, dumb and deaf spirit, a devil,* or demon. What a terrible plight for a boy to endure. No wonder his father, whose anxious days and sleepless nights caring for his only child must have aged him, cried to Jesus, "If thou canst do any thing, have compassion on us, and help us."

4. *The sympathizing Savior.* Ever touched with the feeling of human infirmities, Jesus was deeply moved by the father's description of the terrible plight of his only child and also by the intensity of the parent's prayer for help. What immediately distressed the only one who could liberate the lunatic was the failure of his disciples to cast out the demon of hell, seeing he had delegated them power to perform such a miracle. Thus, his grief was mixed with sore displeasure that the disciples had caused both parent and child needless anguish. What a sting there was in the confession of the father, "I brought him to thy disciples, and *they could not cure him*" (Matt. 17:16). Do we realize that it is still a pain and a wound to Christ to see his church stand impotent and depressed amidst woes she might cure, if only she would stir up the power in her?

In his rebuke, Jesus used two words—*faithless* and *perverse.* The former was for the disciples whom the Master condemned with *unbelief* and lacking *faith as a grain of mustard seed.* The latter was for the questioning, critical scribes who, in

their perverseness, prolonged the woes of the afflicted by their strife. How the troubles of the
world today are accentuated by unbelief and per-
versity! But no disappointment could lessen the
love of Jesus, and so there came his answer to the
father's heartfelt cry as he met a human *if* with a
divine *if*. "*If thou canst do* anything," was met with,
"*If thou canst believe*, all things are possible to him
that believeth" (Mark 9:22, 23).

In this reply, Jesus throws the burden of the
situation back on the parent who, smitten with
tears, cried out, "Lord, I believe; help thou mine
unbelief." Here we have an honest and earnest
confession, asserting faith, yet admitting unbelief
and asking for a bigger blessing than his faith can
hope for. There is an authoritative ring about our
Lord's sweet invitation to the grief-stricken, exhausted father, *Bring him hither to me!* "Where the
word of a king is, there is power" (Eccles. 8:4).
Smitten and suffering from early childhood, the
lad's case seemed hopeless, but none are beyond
the king's power to liberate. The demon possessing the father's only child was rebuked in such a
way as to cause the foul spirit to depart, and the
child was cured from that very hour.

It will be noted, however, that there is a change
of the divine healer's method here. In the two
previous child-miracles, the presence of the healer
was not necessary, nor were the sick brought to
him. He healed them at a distance without seeing
or speaking to them. But now Jesus commands
the lunatic lad to be brought to him. Why? Can it
be for the sake of the disciples who, failing to cast
out the demon in the presence of the multitude,
thereby lost the opportunity to reveal publicly

what God was able to do through them? Perhaps Jesus asks for the presence of the afflicted child in order that the carping scribes and the people could witness what "the Son of God with power" was able to accomplish. All could see that he succeeded where others through unbelief had failed. In summarizing the lessons to be learned from this miracle of healing, Richard Glover has these guides:

1. There is no impotence in Christ, every woe of the human heart yields to His control.
2. Where He finds any faith, even as a grain of mustard seed, He can and will impart salvation.
3. When we fail, He will come and turn our failure into humility and victory.
4. There are many ills in life which, though physical, have their origin or their aggravation in the soul, and must find their relief or cure there.
5. There is no morbid condition of the body which the enemy will not take advantage of.
6. When Christ heals He works a permanent cure, saying, *Enter no more into him*, Mark 9:25. What gladness brought and still brings into the world! Let Him cast the evil out of your heart.
7. *Faith, Prayer, Fasting.* What the Church needs today to change her failure into success is, not a new creed, or new methods, or eloquence, or learning, or music but the three requisites of Faith, Intercession, and Fasting which make self-denial easier, and prevent indolence. With these, the *mountains* of drunkenness, of infidelity, of impurity, will remove at the Spirit-empowered Church's command.

Jairus' daughter (Matt. 9:18–26; Mark 5:22–45; Luke 8:41–56). The *little daughter* of this ruler, Mark tells us, was only *twelve years* of age. This account affords another illustration of the loving sympathy of Jesus for afflicted children. The miracle on this girl, the *only* daughter of Jairus, is unique in that it is a miracle wrapped up in another miracle. Following the ruler's request for Jesus to come to the house of gloom and lay his hands on his dying daughter, a woman with a twelve-year hemorrhage—the same length of time as the age of the girl Jesus was on his way to heal —hearing that the Great Physician was passing by, joined the crowd and, pressing close to him, touched his garment and was made whole. *His touch* brought life to a dead girl, but *the woman's touch* of him brought healing for her diseased body. In the narratives given by Matthew, Mark, and Luke, a miracle springs out of a miracle. The healing of the woman was a casual service performed on the road to another act of love and power. Before Jesus entered the house of Jairus, he accomplished a miracle on the way, and when he left the house, another miracle was experienced by the two blind men who cried to Jesus for mercy, and mercifully he restored their sight.

The raising of Jairus' daughter is another instance of home sorrow because of a child and of Jesus' power to banish grief and bring gladness to a shadowed household. How the Great Physician was in constant demand! There was never an hour in which he was not wanted for the work of love in which he was unceasingly active.

Resolve and reverence (Matt. 9:18; Mark 5:22, 23). Examining the miracle before us, we note first the attitude of Jairus himself as he approached Jesus with his intimation and invitation. "My daughter even now is dead: but come and lay

thy hand upon her, and she shall live." The child
was dying when her father left home, and he felt
that by now she must be dead. As a ruler of the
synagogue, Jairus held a responsible position and
had heard the words of Jesus and witnessed his
works. Therefore, he had no doubt as to Jesus'
ability to raise his daughter from the dead. "Lay
thy hand upon her, and she *shall* live." Coupled
with his resolve to contact Jesus, in his desperate
need, was his recognition of Jesus as one worthy
to be reverenced, for coming into his presence,
Jairus worshiped him. Mark and Luke tell us that
"he fell at his feet" and "besought him that he
would come into his house," but Jesus needed no
urging to go to those in dire need of his assistance. With the chance that the girl was still alive,
her father was eager for Jesus to come as quickly
as possible.

Affliction quickens reverence and entreaty. The
possibility of a great sorrow brought the ruler to
his knees; he felt that if death claimed the child
he dearly loved, everything would be changed in
the home. A child is one of God's most precious
and great gifts, one binding parents' hearts to
each other. What would be your reaction *if* your
child was taken from you? From Jairus we learn
the power of sorrow to quicken faith and seek
relief from one able to give it. Nothing is said
about the dying girl's mother, whose anguish
must have been deep. Jairus, who could not nurse
as well as his wife, runs for the Savior. The
mother who could not run so well, stays and
nurses. Thus, they were workers together for the
welfare of their dying child.

The petition Jairus presented to Jesus was the
art of brevity—*only one sentence*—but that was suffi-

cient. We are not heard for our much speaking. How much more effective our approach to the Lord would be if only we would take time to know what we actually need and then tell him in as few words as possible what is on our heart! Some of the greatest prayers in the Bible are the shortest. After all, did not Jesus himself teach that God knows what we have need of *before* we ask him? Then why waste breath and words on long prayers telling him what he already knows?

Response and rebuke (Matt. 9:19, 23, 24; Mark 5:24, 38–40). The response to the appeal of Jairus was immediate, for "Jesus arose, and followed him." How marvelous the compassion, the faith shown, in this promptitude of Jesus! This was the king's business and required haste. He had been discussing theological questions with his disciples, but these were quickly terminated for the cry of need. If you want to find Jesus still, you will more often come on his presence at the bedside of sufferers than in the books of scholars.

After an interruption on the way to the ruler's house, during which a woman who had spent all her money on doctors for relief from her issue of blood, without result, was completely healed, Jesus continued his journey. But he was met by a servant from the ruler's house who said to Jairus, "Thy daughter is dead: why troublest thou the master any further?" How crushed he must have been by such a bold statement! Jesus, when he heard of the needlessness of his help, did not turn round at the face of death but said to Jairus, "Be not afraid, only believe," which must have seemed a word of strange comfort. Yet it was a message preparing Jairus for a wonderful surprise.

Reaching the house, Jesus encountered a great

hullabaloo. Loud lamenting, tumult, and tears were much in evidence, similar in fashion to an old Irish wake. The howling for the dead and the inordinate, mournful sounds were mock grief, jarring the sorrowful occasion. These professional mourners could not comfort the parents in their loss by their *noise,* as Matthew puts it. Calming the tumult by his commanding presence, Jesus uttered the assuring announcement, "The damsel is not dead, but sleepeth." In the house, where the spoils of death were evident, he called death by the beautiful name *sleep.* Jesus did not deny that the girl was dead but denied that death is death in the sense of that hopeless separation the mourners felt. As quickly as they turned on their crocodile tears, the mourners turned them off, for they *"laughed* Jesus to scorn." As these scorners were not fit to witness his miracle-working power, "he put them all out."

Those whose mockery was out of harmony with the occasion scorned Jesus because they thought that he meant natural *sleep* when he used it as a symbol of death. It is contrary to his consistent teaching as to what happens after death, however, to assume that when a saint—or sinner, for that matter—dies, he or she remains unconscious until the resurrection of the dead. *Soul-sleep* is not a Scripture truth. When the figure is used in connection with death, it is always in connection with the body, never the soul (John 11:11, 14). Both Dives and Lazarus were conscious in their respective abodes *after* death (Luke 16:19–31). Paul assures us that the moment we depart from the body at death, we are immediately at home with the Lord.

Contact and command (Matt. 9:25, 26; Mark 5:40 –43). Having expelled the callous weepers from the house, Jesus took the sorrow-stricken parents and Peter, James, and John into the room where the child was laid out, still and cold in death. They were privileged to witness him beard death in its den. They were to witness that the *dead* are living and can hear his voice although at home in the other world, and that he is the Lord of death, and it obeys him who is "the resurrection and the life." Life contacted death as Jesus took the damsel by the hand and said unto her *Talitha cumi,* meaning, "Damsel, I say unto thee, arise" or "Little one, get up!" perhaps words used daily by her mother to wake her.

As death could not keep its prey when it came to Christ's resurrection from the dead, so here, for as soon as he uttered the all-commanding word *arise,* "the maid arose." Jesus arose to journey to the house to meet her need (Matt. 9:19); now she arises to meet him. The child had not been spoiled for earth by her short visit to heaven but woke as if from a sweet dream to see the face of him who was able to deliver from the power of death, and the faces of her dear, astonished but delighted parents.

The impressive story closes on a most practical note. So real and complete was the girl's restoration to life that Jesus had wrought that she needed food. Jairus and his wife were too bewildered to think about food at such a time, but Jesus, intrinsically holy, was always intensely human and knew that health brings hunger; and so he "commanded that something should be given her to eat." How strange are the two precepts in succession—*Arise! Give her meat!* When the Savior himself rose again, he gave evidence of his own resurrection by eating with his disciples (John 21:1–13). Jesus raised Jairus' daughter by *extraordinary* power, but willed that she should be sustained by *ordinary* means. No wonder the fame of Jesus spread abroad in spite of his explicit wish that no man should know of what he had accomplished. How grateful we are that the first three evangelists recorded the miracle so that it has reached us through all the distance of time and space to comfort our hearts in sorrow and to strengthen our faith that one day all the dead in Christ shall rise again.

The widow's son (Luke 7:11–18). Although this is one of the most decisive and instructive of our Lord's miracles and resulted in his being a great prophet raised up by God, it is not actually within the scope of his contact with *children,* even though the one raised from the dead was the only son of his widowed mother. He is referred to as a *dead man,* and Jesus, who because of his omniscience knew all about him, called him a *young man*—probably about Jesus' own age. The resurrection of the children and of this young man and of Lazarus, who was somewhat elderly, prove that age makes no difference to Jesus when it comes to the manifestation of his power whether it be in physical resurrection or spiritual resurrection.

JESUS AND CHILDREN—TEACHINGS

Having considered many precious truths associated with our Lord's miraculous ministry among

the children, let us now look at his direct teachings occasioned by the young as they crossed his
pathway. How apt he was at using them as symbols of spiritual instruction which his disciples and
others needed! That those around Jesus did not
share his love, enthusiasm, and care for children
comes through in a lesson he taught the disciples
on the inclusion of the youngest in the divine
plan. Devout mothers brought their infant children to Jesus that he might put his hands upon
them and pray for them (Matt. 19:13-15; Mark
10:13-16; Luke 18:15-17). Often those who do
not seek the Savior for themselves desire him for
their children, but parents who are truly the
Lord's know the surety he can afford their young
ones when they are safe in his arms. If only more
mothers and fathers had brought their children to
Jesus to be blessed of him, we would not be faced
with profligate youth so common today.

The disciples, with little time for children, and
feeling that Jesus had no time for them, rebuked
the parents for interrupting the Master in his
busy life. Failing to understand his desire to welcome even infants to his heart, the disciples, in-
sufficiently reverent to childhood, and thinking
the mothers intrusive, felt that little children
would not understand him and therefore should
wait until they were older to receive his blessing.
But the disciples' rebuke of the mothers earned
the rebuke of the Master: "Suffer the little children, and forbid them not to come unto me; for
of such is the kingdom of heaven."

The word *suffer* here means "do not hinder
them" or "let them come." Phillips translates "forbid them not"—*you must never stop them.* "Let them

alone," said Jesus. He welcomed the fresh faces and their innocent, artless smiles and rejoiced in the mothers' desire for him to bless their children and also in the attraction the young found in him. Jesus did not believe in letting the children go wrong and afterwards setting them right; he therefore welcomed them, weak though they were. It is better to build a strong barricade round the edge of a high cliff than to have an ambulance below. "Prevention is better than cure." Hence Jesus said, "Let them come unto me: for of such is the kingdom of heaven," or "the kingdom of heaven belongs to little children like these," as Phillips translates it. The kingdom includes a great multitude of children. In fact, only the childlike can enter the kingdom (Matt. 18:3). The children brought and blessed afford a strong contrast to the story that follows of the rich young ruler who, childlike, came to Jesus seeking a blessing but departed without it (Matt. 19:16–22; see Luke 18:17).

Jesus had already taught his disciples about God's interest in little children and that it was his desire that every child should be saved (Matt. 18:14) and that Jesus himself was their Savior (Matt. 18:10, 11). Knowing, therefore, how impressionable the child-mind is, and that childhood is a most convenient season for conversion and that a child enters the kingdom with ease, Jesus said, "Let them come unto me." Further, Jesus loves the little children because they are childlike and he can use them to make an entrance into other hearts for himself (Matt. 18:4–7). "A little child shall lead them" (Isa. 11:6). Once in the kingdom, they have his protection and the highest angels in heaven to guard them. Parents, teachers, and all workers among the young should share with the angels the sacred task of protecting them from the evil of the world (Matt. 18:10).

Mark gives us a beautiful glimpse of the Master's gratitude to the mothers for bringing their children to him: "He took them up in his arms, put his hands upon them, and blessed them" (Mark 10:16). In ancient Hebrew custom, this was a father's act, a blessing Esau sought from Jacob (Gen. 27:38). Bengel, the commentator, has the note on the benediction Jesus pronounced over the children of the mothers of Salem, "He had no children that he might adopt all children." He certainly charmed those young hearts to love him and is ever ready to fill with his love the little hearts that look up at his serene, smiling face. Richard Glover in his *History of Jesus* deals with Jesus' association with children:

> How Jesus likes children!—for their simplicity, Luke 18:17, their intuition, their teachableness, we say. But was it not, perhaps for far simpler and more natural reasons—just because they *were* children, and little, and delightful? We forget his little brothers and sisters, or we eliminate them for theological purposes.

What about your own children or those entrusted to your care? Have you brought them to Jesus to be saved and blessed by him? It should be our preeminent desire and effort to bring the young to him ere their precious lives are damaged by sin.

> Little children are remembered in the Saviour's promise,
> They may early share the blessings of redeeming grace:

He is watching kindly o'er them, and His word assures us,
That in Heaven their angels ever see the Father's
face.

We have a further illustration of the Savior's
interest in children and what can be learned from
them when he had to rebuke his disciples for
squabbling among themselves as to who should be
the greatest among them. This episode gave Jesus
the opportunity to teach his own—and us—a most
precious lesson (Matt. 18:1–6; Mark 9:33–37;
Luke 9:46–48), one that is very hard to take by
those passed by all others for the chief seat at the
feast. Mark's account describes the action of Jesus
in taking a child out of the crowd and using him
as a symbol of lowliness, of his identification with
the child in humility, and of the necessity of caring for the child in his name. The Greek partici-
ple that Mark uses for "when he had taken him in
his arms" (Mark 9:36; 10:16) actually means that
Jesus was sitting with the little child on his knee
and "in the crook of his arm." What a vivid and
delightful glimpse this is of the loving way he nes-
tled the child to his heart! Although we have instances of his happy way in dealing with children,
we have no record of what he spoke to them
about as they looked into each other's faces. Yet
with them near to him, what important truths he
taught others.

Jesus was "moved with indignation" at the way
the disciples failed to realize the importance of
children and of what can be learned from them
(Mark 10:14). A little child is not only teachable,
trustful, and loving, but also simple, unsophisti-
cated, and free from mental pride. This was why

Jesus, as he nursed the child, reminded those around him that heaven is exclusively occupied by childlike people (Matt. 18:3). Those who want to be first strut around as if they owned the universe and court dislike because of their pomposity. They are not fit company for heaven where saints cast their crowns before him who is the first and the last.

Correcting the fleshy ambition of his disciples, Jesus teaches the importance of the child-spirit and that those lacking it needed to be *converted* and become as little children. The Savior speaks as if two conversions are necessary for our salvation; namely, one conversion *backward*, of the man into a child, and then a second conversion *forward*, of the childlike man into a Christian. Christ does not say, "Except children are converted into men" by flow of time, "they cannot enter the kingdom"; but, except men are converted into children, *they* cannot. Children have only to learn not to unlearn; only to do, not to undo. Ambition keeps men from entering; but children easily enter the kingdom.

What are some of the characteristics of this necessary conversion into the child-spirit Jesus emphasized?

Simplicity, acting on simplest grounds and from directest motives;

Freedom from self-consciousness, responsible for adult entanglement;

Deliverance from calculation, as to what others may say, or other days bring—children live in the present and are less overawed by the future;

Humility, or contentedness to be little and obscure if only loved. The secret of Christian greatness is the willingness to stoop, obey, love, forget self in others. *Humility*, like a child's, is the secret of *entrance* into the kingdom and *eminence* in it.

Lowliness within the heart permits the king to enter the heart. "Whoso shall receive one such little child receiveth me." We admit the Lord of glory to our souls when we give welcome to childlike lowliness instead of the pride of life. May ours be the "stainless peace of blest Humility," the poet wrote of! Jesus humbled himself and was among men as one that served; he left us an example that we should follow his steps.

> His life while here, as well as birth,
> Was but a check to pomp and mirth;
> And all man's greatness you may see
> Condemn'd by His humility.

Among the other references to children by Jesus, and teachings attached thereto, we have the *hosanna* of the children greeting him as he entered the Temple on the day of his entry into Jerusalem—hosannas which sorely displeased the chief priests and scribes who had no praise for Jesus. The hosannas of the crowd meant little to him, for he knew how quickly they could change to hate. Infant praises, however, greatly cheered his heart (Matt. 21:1–17). "Out of the mouth of babes and sucklings thou hast perfected praise." Those who loved the clink of money, received from the sale of doves for sacrifice, more than children singing praises to Jesus urged him to forbid their hosannas, but he only approved and invited them. Are you helping to gladden the Master's heart by teaching the children around you to praise him as the king of heaven?

How true it is that in old classical literature and in Christian literature of past ages no parallel can be found to the interest and joy Jesus found in children! His amazing love for the young can be traced in his lament over Jerusalem, in which he prophesied its coming disasters and paused to pity poor pregnant women and mothers with small babies in such perilous times (Matt. 24:19; Mark 13:14–23). Josephus reckons that in the destruction of Jerusalem in A.D. 70, over one million perished. (Consult the author's work, *All the Children of the Bible*.)

Jesus is also found using the term *children* as indicative of a relationship, in a figurative sense. Thus, he called the hypocritical Pharisees "children of hell" (Matt. 23:15; see Acts 13:10; 1 John 3:10). He addressed his own as "children" and "little children" (Mark 10:24; John 13:33; 21:5). Those whose lives are dominated by wisdom, he spoke of as "children of wisdom" (Matt. 11:19). Moral likeness or spiritual kinship is implied when he referred to those who claimed to be Abraham's seed as "children of Abraham" (John 8:39). What are we all if ours is a relationship based on regeneration but children! Tennyson asks in "In Memoriam":

> But what am I?
> An infant crying in the night;
> An infant crying for the light,
> And with no language but a cry.

Our final word is that we cannot meditate upon Christ's associations with children without realizing that all he taught concerning them forms the

Magna Carta for all parents and workers among the young. No efforts are more rewarding than those that are taken up with leading the lambs into his fold. Professor James Stalker says in *The Ethic of Jesus*:

> By the scene in which he blessed the little children he took possession forever of the heart not only of childhood but of motherhood; and it would be difficult to exaggerate the revolution in the condition of children and the estimation in which they are held which has been due to this incident alone. In all the centuries since, the words fall like leaven, and their virtue is not yet by any means exhausted.

Jesus had a keen sense of the value of the child and has taught us how children should be treated in the home and in society. The future of any country is in the hands of its children, a significant fact that must not be lost sight of in homelife, in our systems of education, and in all organizations concentrating upon childcare and welfare. Although there are still some parts of the world where Christ's estimate of the child is neither accepted theoretically nor applied in practice, for us in civilized lands his command still stands, "Bring the child to me" (Matt. 17:17).

BIBLE STUDY QUESTIONS

Take time to turn to each Scripture reference and mark the verse or a portion in your Bible.

1. Of what value and responsibility are children?

2. In healing the nobleman's son and Syro-phoenecian's daughter how did Jesus test and prove faith?

3. How was healing the lunatic son different from the previous two miracles?

4. How did Jesus show his concern and care for Jairus' daughter?

5. How did Jesus use children in his teaching?

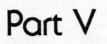

Part V

— 26 —

Ministry

All who received and believed Christ's teachings were signally blessed, spiritually and physically. The same sun, however, that melts the wax, hardens the clay, and the utterances of our Lord only hardened the hearts of the scribes and Pharisees, who rejected them because they exposed their hypocrisy. Let it not be forgotten that Jesus' enemies sought to kill him, not so much for his works, but for his *words*. Jesus was ultimately crucified, not for doing things, but *saying* things. Disputing with Pilate over the epitaph he had placed on the cross, the chief priests said, "Write not, The King of the Jews: but that he said, I am King of the Jews" (John 19:21, 22).

Whenever men drank in those loving, unforgettable words, their emancipating power was experienced because behind them was the spotless life of the divine teacher himself (John 8:31, 32, 36). What he taught his disciples in private and the people in public was enforced by a life in which man could find no fault, hence, the authority and power of his words. The importance of the teachings of Jesus is found in his own assertion that they are to form the basis of judgment at the final assize (John 12:48).

The Hebrew word for *teach* means "to beat," "to chastise," or "to beat with a rod" and most likely had its origin in the striking and goading of beasts by which they were curbed and trained. By a noble evolution the term came to describe the process of disciplining and training men in war, religion, and life (Isa. 2:3; Hos. 10:11; Mic. 4:2). As teaching is both a condition and an accompaniment of discipline, the word often means simply "to teach," "to inform" (2 Chron. 17:7; Ps. 71:17; Prov. 5:13). "The glory of teaching was its harmony with the will of God, its source in God's authority, and its purpose to secure spiritual obedience" (Deut. 4:5, 14; 31:12, 13). It was the outcome of such obedience Jesus looked for in his instructive teaching (John 13:17; James 1:22–23).

As the public ministry of Jesus lasted just over three years, as soon as he appeared as a teacher sent from God, he set about choosing those who would follow him, imbibe and live by his teachings, and help to perpetuate them. A. B. Bruce in his unique work *The Training of the Twelve* gives us an insight into the ways Jesus sought to equip them. Principally, there was the impact of his life and example upon their lives; and then came the mighty influence of his teachings which, because they were always with Jesus, the disciples heard *in toto*. Being their master and teacher, he was ever at the service of the slowest of his disciples to understand his truth. He was never in a hurry. He

gave himself to them in earnest and was ever at
their disposal, becoming theirs in a great intimacy.
He was careful in taking every opportunity of
planting the seed of truth in the minds of his own
since they were to become the pillars of the Christian church he had come to build.

Socrates affirmed that the teacher's real work,
his only work, was to implant the idea, like a seed,
able to look after itself. This was the method Jesus
pursued so patiently. If his teachings perplexed
his disciples, they could cross-question him at lei-
sure (Matt. 15:15). Sometimes they doubted the
wisdom of his open speech (Mark 8:32) and felt it
necessary to criticize what he taught (Matt. 13:10).
They also told Jesus what the Pharisees did not
like about what he said (Matt. 15:12). When his
teachings were hard to understand, the disciples
kept on asking Jesus till he made them plain.
Ultimately, they were captured by the truth he
taught, and one of the greatest miracles in history
is the transformation Jesus wrought in the twelve
by his daily ministry of the Word, Judas excepted.
As the result of the effect of his character and
teachings, those disciples came to establish Christianity in the world, as the Acts and the Epistles
prove. They not only walked in the footsteps of
their Master, but the inculcation of his truth enabled them, by the Holy Spirit's ministry in their
lives, to formulate the Christian faith. The discourse of Jesus in Capernaum seems to mark a
turning point in his ministry in Galilee. Soon after
he retired from public teaching and devoted himself to the instruction of his apostles (Matt. 15:21;
Mark 7:24). Since he was to leave them in the

world after his ascension, such private tuition was necessary.

Our Lord's constant instruction, not only to the twelve but also to the seventy, had as its objective their equipment for a ministry like his own and reveals his conception of a society which should carry on his work of preaching and teaching. Thus, after his resurrection Jesus laid on the consciences of those commissioned to go into all the world and *teach* the nations, "to observe all things whatsoever I have commanded you" (Matt. 28:19, 20). Here the work of Christianity is presented in educational terms. Obediently those disciples went forth and "ceased not to teach and preach Jesus Christ" (Acts 5:42).

Under the inspiration of the Holy Spirit, the apostles remembered the words of the Lord Jesus and set them forth in the four Gospels which were written years after Jesus returned to heaven. The rest of the New Testament likewise proves the certainty of those truths wherein they had been instructed by the peerless teacher himself (Luke 1:1–4). In his preface to Acts, Luke tells us that his purpose in writing the Gospel called after him was to record "all that Jesus began both to do and *to teach*" (Acts 1:1, 2). In the Acts the practice of the apostles is quite uniform; their teaching was the expression and exposition of what they had received from the Master (Acts 2:42); and wherever they went, teaching was correlated to preaching in "the things concerning Jesus Christ" (Acts 5:25; 28:30, 31). Thus, his principles and methods of teaching constitute "the standard by which all true pedagogy is measured, and the ideal toward which all subsequent teachers have toiled with only partial success" (Matt. 7:28, 29; John 1:49; 6:45).

Paul, the greatest teacher of Christian truth next to Jesus, makes clear certain aspects of the teaching function of Christianity.

1. Teaching of Christian truth is necessary for the development of Christian character and for the highest efficiency in Christian service (1 Cor. 12:4–11, 28, 29; Eph. 4:11, 12). In substance, everything Jesus taught in the Gospels comes out in the Epistles: his preexistence (John 1:1; 8:58; 17:5); his share in divine attributes, in divine works, in divine worship, and in divine names and titles receives great emphasis (1 Cor. 8:6; Phil. 2:9–11; Col. 1:16, 17; Heb. 1:2, 8; Rev. 1:8; 3:14; 5:11, 12).

2. The qualifications of the pastor are vitally connected with the teaching function of the church. The pastor must hold the truth, that is, be orthodox; apply the truth, or be practical; teach the truth, ably and tactfully; and study the truth to be informed (1 Tim. 4:13, 15; 2 Tim. 2:2). Above all he must practice what he preaches and live what his lips teach others (1 Tim. 4:16; 2 Tim. 2:2). Paul's dictum, not only for teachers of the Word, but for all believers, is summed up in his challenge to the young church at Philippi: "Whatever happens, make sure that your every day life is worthy of the gospel of Christ" (Phil. 1:27, Phillips trans.). John Bunyan describes how Interpreter led Christian into a private room where he saw the picture of a very grave person hanging on the wall, and this was the fashion of it:

Eyes lifted up to Heaven,
The best of books in its hand,
The law of truth was written upon its lips,
The world was behind its back;
It stood as if it pleaded with men,
And a crown of gold did hang over its head.

Then Christian asked Interpreter the significance of such a picture, and his reply was:

The man whose picture this is, is one of a thousand.
He can beget children [1 Cor. 4:15], travail in birth
with children [Gal. 4:19], and nurse them himself when they are born.
And whereas thou seest him with his eyes lift up to
Heaven, the best of books in his hand, and the
law of truth writ upon his lips: it is to shew thee
that his work is to know and unfold dark things
to sinners, even as also thou seest him stand as if
he pleaded with men:
And whereas thou seest the world cast behind his
back, and that a crown hangs over his head: that
is to shew thee, that, slighting and despising the
things that are present, for the love that he hath
to his Master's service, he is sure, in the World
that comes next, to have glory for his reward.

Then Interpreter explained to Christian why he
had shown him this picture before anything else in
the house:

I have shewed thee this picture first, because
the man whose picture this is, is the only man
whom the Lord of the place whither thou art
going hath authorized to be thy guide, in all difficult places thou mayest meet with in the way.
Wherefore take good heed to what I have shewed
thee, and bear well in thy mind what thou hast

seen; lest in thy journey thou meet with some that pretend to lead thee right; but their way goes down to death.

In all literature there is no finer portrayal of those whom the Master calls to preach and teach his wonderful words of salvation and life. If such is your privilege, may you be found eminently successful as an authorized guide to all you meet on life's pilgrimage. All who worthily bear the joint title of pastor and teacher are ever careful

By day and night strict guard to keep,
To warn the sinner, cheer the saint,
Nourish the lambs and feed the sheep.

— 27 —

Angels

We often question whether the average church-
goer who lustily sings, "Angels of Jesus, Angels of
Light, / Singing to welcome the pilgrims of the
night," actually believes the teaching of the Bible
as a whole that there *is* a vital ministry of angels:
that there is angelic interposition in the affairs of
mankind and, in particular, in the circumstances
of Christ's advent to earth, and that what he
taught concerning the angels of God is so essentially a part of Christianity as to be inseparable
from it. Because there are so many things written
about angels in the Bible, and especially in the
New Testament, it is our solemn obligation to find
out all we can of their ministration. The reader
will find in the author's paperback volume, *The
Unseen Army,* a full coverage of the subject of angel-
ology.

In this topic we confine ourselves to the angels
associated with the Master and to his frequent
teaching that through "the sending of angels" the
Father's purposes were fulfilled. When he tells us
that, if we belong to him, in the world to come we

are to be "like to the angels," then surely these present wonderful ministering spirits claim our prayerful consideration and reverent attention. Repeatedly, Jesus brought the intervention of the holy angels before the minds of his hearers. In some of his parables, angels are described as the reapers of the last harvest, the executors of the last sentence, the devoted servants of their master, and as his retinue when he returns (Matt. 16:27; 24:31; Mark 8:38). References to angels in the four Gospels group around two aspects, namely, associations of angels with Jesus, and announcements about angels by Jesus.

ASSOCIATION OF ANGELS WITH JESUS

It is essential to have in mind what beings *angels* actually are. Cognizant, as we are, that the term itself means "messenger" and is applied in various ways to human messengers (Luke 7:24; 9:52; Mal. 3:1) and to providential circumstances (Ps. 104:4; 148:8), the word is chiefly used in the Bible to represent those superhuman beings whose abode is heaven and who function as the unseen agents in the execution of the will of God. To them also are assigned functions in the administration of nature and of nations as well as in communications to man. They do not exercise independent power. Angels are not inferior deities interposed between God and ourselves, but instruments he uses (Ps. 148:2). They are not permitted to be the objects of our personal regard or to receive the worship due alone to their creator (Col. 2:18; Rev. 22:8–9).

Wherever angels appear in Scripture, it is in the capacity of God's messengers and as personal agents in the fulfillment of his purpose, endowed with faculties fitting them for their higher sphere of existence and ministry. Excelling in strength, they are ready to catch the slightest intimation of God's will and carry it out (Ps. 103:20) and never add to or diminish the message they carry. Theirs is no preference as to service, and no errand is beneath them. It is all one to the unseen army of angels whether they are sent to control the opposing forces of Persia or of Greece or to maintain the cause of Israel or *to spread a meal* for a weary traveler like Elijah (Dan. 10:20; 12:1; 1 Kings 19:5). Would that we, like the angels, considered not the nature of the command but alone its author who demands obedience.

As cocreator of these angelic beings, and having in his preexistent state lived with them in the Father's abode, Jesus knew all about their nature and office which enabled him to speak with all authority about their existence and service as he did. Such intimate knowledge of their created purpose also adds color to their close association with Jesus from his incarnation to his ascension when they carried him back in triumph to heaven.

An angel announced to Zacharias that he would be the father of John the Baptist, forerunner of the Lord Jesus. Although it is stated that the Lord calls *all* the stars by name, among the myriads of angels only two are named in Scripture, namely *Michael* and *Gabriel*. There is, of course, Lucifer, an angel of the highest order who, because of his rebellion in heaven, became Satan and who is prince of the fallen angels deposed with him. Michael is named an *archangel,* and Gabriel must have been in a very near relationship to God, for he is referred to as "standing in the presence of God" (Luke 1:11, 19).

It was an angel, even Gabriel, who was sent from God to announce to the virgin Mary that she was to be the mother of the long-expected Messiah. How the grand words of this prince of angels must have sounded mysterious to the virgin in soul and spirit who was to become, not a dispenser of favor, as the Roman church falsely affirms, but a recipient of such favor with and for the rest of us!

It was an angel who set the troubled mind of Joseph to rest when he found Mary "with child of the Holy Spirit" and told him not to fear to take Mary his espoused wife. As this angel is referred to as the "angel of the Lord," the same title Gabriel is called, the assumption is that it was he who appeared to Joseph (Matt. 1:18–25) and who gave this just man his honorable title "son of David," thereby reminding him of the great promise given to the house of David concerning the coming of the Messiah.

It was the "angel of the Lord" (see Luke 1:11, 19; 2:9) who proclaimed to the shepherds watching over their sheep by night that in "the city of David" Christ was born (Luke 2:8–12). At the same time a vast angelic host appeared with "the angel," magnifying God for his love and grace in sending his Son into the world as its Savior (Luke 2:13–20).

It was the same "angel of the Lord" who appeared to Joseph in a dream, telling him to flee into Egypt with Mary and the infant Jesus, and who, after Herod, who sought to kill the holy child Jesus, was dead, reappeared to Joseph instructing him that he and his precious ones could return safely to their own land, but with the warning to turn aside to Galilee (Matt. 2:19–23).

It was a band of angels who came and ministered unto Jesus after the forty exhausting days in the wilderness and his grueling combat with Satan. What form of assistance they gave, whether physical or spiritual, or both, we are not told (Matt. 4:11). The same applies to the angel who came to Jesus and strengthened him during his agony in the garden (Luke 22:43).

At this point we can consider their constant attendance upon Jesus as indicated in his conversation with Nathanael, "Ye shall see heaven opened, and the angels of God, ascending and descending upon the Son of man" (John 1:51). John is sparing of the use of the word *angel*. He only employs it three times in his Gospel (John 1:51; 12:29; 20:12); never in his Epistles is there a reference to their being or ministry. His Revelation, however, is full of references to angels.

The image Jesus presented to Nathanael was drawn from the history of his ancestor Jacob who, in a dream, beheld "a ladder set up on earth, and the top of it reached to heaven: and behold the angels of God ascending and descending on it" (Gen. 28:12). Such a picture represents the continual protection of divine providence and of its invisible agents assured to the patriarch and extended to Jesus. What the disciples were to witness was a

higher realization of the truth represented by the
ancient symbol. In applying the far-off vision of
Jacob to himself, Jesus pointed to his own divine
humanity as the center of this spiritual intercourse continually carried on between earth and
heaven; and on one occasion, previous to his last
prophecy (Matt. 24:30; 25:31), he spoke openly of
the coming of the Son of man with his angels
(Matt. 16:27; Mark 8:38). What is conspicuous is
the absence of the substance of angelic communications between our Lord and the angels during
the exalted intercourse between them while Jesus
was on earth.

What impresses one in this reference to angels
is that their movements appear to be the wrong
way round—*ascending, descending.* As they dwell in
the immediate presence of God, should it not be
descending from him to fulfill his mission, then
ascending to receive fresh commands? One explanation is that "these servants *ascend* first to seek
power in the presence of God; afterwards they
descend again to accomplish the work." But even
this statement recognizes that their presence is
first on earth, that the angels do not come down,
then go up, but *go up* and *come down.* Milton
speaks of "millions of spiritual creatures that walk
the earth," and while on earth, Jesus was always
surrounded by angels to succour in time of need.
If they *ascended,* it was at the call of God to receive
instruction, but they promptly *descended* to fulfill
their tasks.

Archbishop R. C. Trench, in his work *Studies in
the Gospels,* cites a beautiful passage of Plato in
which he speaks of love as being suggestive of

Christ's words in John 1:51: "He is good spirit, and like all spirits he is intermediate between the divine and the mortal. He interprets between God and men, conveying to the gods the prayers and sacrifices of men, and to men the commands and replies of the gods; he is the mediator who spans the chasm which divides them, and in them all are bound together, and through him the acts of the prophet and the priest, their sacrifices, and mysteries and charms, and all prophecy and incantation find their way. For God mingles not with man, but through *Love* all the intercourse and speech of God with man, whether awake or asleep, is carried on." (Jowett translation.)

It was the presence and announcement of two angels that assured Mary Magdalene that her beloved Jesus she saw crucified was alive forevermore (John 20:11). This woman became the first herald of the resurrection. Mary came seeking the crucified one and found a risen Savior. But those who would find the risen Savior must still seek and receive him as the crucified. Luke speaks of the two angels John mentions as "two men in shining garments," and announcing his ascension and also his second advent were "two men in white apparel" (Acts 1:10). Several writers are persuaded that the latter two who appeared to the disciples who witnessed the return of Jesus to heaven were not angels, but two of the glorified saints who appeared on the Mount of Transfiguration, namely, Moses and Elijah.

These visits of superhuman beings to earth from heaven indicate that they are not subject to the limitations of space and time as we are. In our

movements from one place to another, consideration is given as to how long it will take us to go so
far. But with angels it is different. They are trans-
ported immediately to where their ministry is
needed on earth. As occasion occurs, they are on
the spot at once, and, like their creator, "a very
present help in trouble" (Ps. 46:1).

ANNOUNCEMENTS ABOUT ANGELS
BY JESUS

Gathering all the Master's references to *angels*
in the Gospels we have the following features of
their nature and ministry. These heavenly beings
he depicted were not angels of fancy or of fiction,
but of fact. "Seen of angels," Jesus also saw them
before his birth and after and accurately describes their worth and work. The reader is ad-
vised to follow the rich teaching of Jesus as found
in the Gospels with that to be found in the Book
of Revelation in which angels are so prominent in
connection with the unveiling of Jesus which John
received from an angel (Rev. 1:1).

1. *Their divine charge to keep the obedient* (Matt.
4:6; Luke 4:10). Satan, who has sought in every
possible way to prevent the production of the
Scriptures, which he knows so well, and fears
their authoritative power, often quoted them to
suit his own purpose. In connection with our
Lord's temptation, this hater of truth failed to
quote the Word accurately. Dr. C. I. Scofield comments in his *Reference Bible:*

> After Satan's failure to tempt the Lord away *from* the
> Word, he seeks to tempt Him *by* it. He, however, *mis-*

quotes by the omission of "in all thy ways," Ps. 91:11.
The Lord's *ways* were those marked out for him in
perfect dependence upon His Father's will, Heb.
10:7, 9.

With his intimate knowledge of the psalms,
Jesus knew that Satan had left out part of the
quotation—*Thou shalt tread upon the lion and adder*
(Ps. 91:13)—which Satan symbolically was. In answering the tempter by quoting, correctly, another portion of the Word (Deut. 6:16), Jesus did
indeed tread upon him. Forbidding Satan's experi-
menting with God settles the action of Jesus who
took no liberties with God and knew that he could
expect the angels to protect him as he sought to
be obedient to the divine will.

The beautiful words, simple for all to understand but precious enough for the guardian angels themselves to envy, are meant for any believer who is now "dwelling in the secret place of
the Most High." The gracious, angelic oversight
promised in the psalms, from which Satan quoted,
is individual, as pronouns *he* and *thou* indicate.
The angels are charged "to keep *thee* in all *thy*
ways." Latham in his work, *Service of Angels,* says
that "the word *angels* being in the plural, favours
the idea that their action, unless when on special
service, may be corporate and collective rather
than individual." Still, one finds comfort in the
pronouns of personal possession in which Scripture abounds.

2. *Their solemn task as reapers* (Matt. 13:39, 41,
49). In his parable of the tares, Jesus taught the
existence of a personal spiritual enemy of God
and man, by whom evil is prompted in the world.

"The enemy that sowed them is the devil" (Matt. 13:39). This is the one who is ever active sowing tares—hard to distinguish from wheat in its earliest stages because of its resemblance to wheat—side by side with all God's wheat of truth and goodness. To pluck out tares often means plucking up the wheat with them. God allows both to grow together until they are ripe, and when harvest comes at the end of the age, the angelic reapers will gather out all the offensive tares and garner the wheat into God's storehouse (Matt. 13:41, 43).

"The angels shall come forth, and sever the wicked from among the just" (Matt. 13:49). Mark puts it that the angels will gather together the Lord's elect from "the four winds" (Mark 13:27). Theirs will be the solemn task of severing the wheat from the tares. Our Lord's teaching, then, in the parable of the tares is patience and judgment. The *wheat* represents children of his kingdom, and *tares*, children of the wicked one. Many churches are made up of regenerate and unregenerate members. Tares and wheat grow up together, and as Richard Glover expresses it in *History of Jesus*, many like to try tare-grubbing which requires more grace than man possesses:

> Pluck away hypocrites, and you will pluck up formal Christians who are not hypocrites along with them. Pluck up those "unsound" in doctrine, and you will pluck up some Christians who are travelling by paths of sincerest inquiry to the grandest views of truth.

Ours is the highest wisdom when, following the teaching of Jesus, we exercise patience that leaves the separation of the tares to the angels, and the deserved future of both the tares and the wheat to the Savior (see Jude 15, RV margins).

3. *Their share in the glory of Christ's second coming.* Often in his teaching about angels, Jesus spoke of them accompanying him when he comes in the glory of his Father (Matt. 16:27; 25:31; Luke 9:26). Here, again, we have the truth of final separation in his teaching on the judgment of the unprofitable and the reward of the profitable when all nations are gathered before him. The figure is changed from tares and wheat to sheep and goats. What a pregnant phrase that is, "He shall separate them one from another" (Matt. 25:32)! In the mind of Jesus, there are only two classes, sheep and goats, saved and lost, and he alone is fit to be the judge of who should go to the right hand of honor or to the left hand of shame.

When he comes in all his glory to sit upon the throne of his glory, "the holy angels" will form his retinue and assist him in his judicial function. What prestige is to be the portion of his glory-clad attendants! Jesus further declares their privilege of rank when he says, "Whosoever shall confess me before men, him shall the Son of man also confess before *the angels of God:* But he that denieth me before men shall be denied before the angels of God" (Luke 12:8–9). In his marvelous description of his coming "in the clouds of heaven with power and great glory" (Matt. 24:29–35), Jesus gave utterance to a phrase which has troubled theologians down the ages. As the Son of man with his self-imposed human limitations, he was content to be without knowledge of the day of final judgment, even as the angels were (Matt. 24:36; Mark 13:32). For us to fix dates is to falsify our position and contradict the clear teaching of Jesus. To quote Richard Glover again:

> No day is named, that every day may be hallowed by the sense of the possibility of its being the day of his Advent. It helps to hallow each day of life, to realize that before its close we may be in the presence of Christ's glory.

While the knowledge of angels as to the unseen world is far beyond us to contemplate, it is limited when it comes to the time of the solemn divine completion, when saints are rewarded and sinners punished. Such a final assize is known to the "Father only" (Matt. 24:36), although now back in glory at the right hand of his Father, Jesus doubtless shares his secret and patiently awaits his finest, glorious hour in which the angels are to share.

4. *Their guardianship of the young* (Matt. 18:10). One of the most precious aspects of our Lord's teaching about angels comes as a climax in his lesson to the disciples on the theme of *humility* (Matt. 18:1–14). This section has been called the "Magna Carta of Workers among the Young," seeing the truth enunciated in the blessedness of childhood and of the child-spirit. The object Jesus chose for his discourse was a little child—one old enough to be called, but young enough to be "taken in his arms" (Mark 9:36). Drawing attention to the child, Jesus administered his testimony against ambition by speaking as if two conversions were necessary for salvation.

First, conversion *backward,* of the man into a

child. Children have only to learn, not to unlearn; only to do, not undo. Children easily enter the kingdom; pride keeps men from entering.

The second conversion, *forward,* is the transformation of the childlike man into a Christian—the daily crucifixion of pride of heart, so necessary because the passion to be great destroys the power to be great.

Then, unmasking the worldliness of ambition, declaring that everything heavenly must be free from the taint of pride, Jesus emphasizes that the angels—children's angels, the guardian protectors, glad to stoop and take care of little ones—are free from injurious ambition. Jesus himself was void of pride; mercy moved him to lay aside the insignia of his past majesty and come to save the perishing, and also "the little ones" (Matt. 18:11–14). Further, there is the underlying thought in what the Master taught that parents and teachers should seek the salvation of children and worthily discharge the office they share with the guardian angels (Matt. 18:14).

But what exactly did Jesus mean by his assertion: "In heaven their [the little ones'] angels do always behold the face of my Father which is in heaven" (Matt. 18:10)? Do children have angels of their own? When they cease to be children, have they no further need of angelic guardianship? We do not feel that Jesus meant that each child born into the world is given in charge to some individual angel whose responsibility it is to watch over it and, in some way or other, render the child aid in the critical junctures of its life. The language Jesus used suggests that a certain company of angels *collectively* cares for children in general; the idea is that of *collective* rather than a *personal* and *particular* guardianship. Jesus did not say their *several* angels, but "their angels," the plural *angels* favoring *corporate* rather than *individual* care. Each among "the little ones" is not to have his own angel, but angels. To the multitude of the children are assigned angels many in number. These are the heavenly beings, "beholding the face of my Father," which implies that they catch from the Father's face his love for little children and also their warrant for bringing the saving truth into the mind of the child or those who are about it who should be in harmony with the angelic guardianship of the young.

Paul, however, reminds us that the care of angels is not confined to children. "Are they not all ministering spirits, sent forth to minister for them who shall be heirs of salvation" (Heb. 1:13, 14)? Just how they minister unto us, we are not told, but as they ministered to Jesus in the days of his flesh, so they undertake in unseen and unknown ways for the heirs of salvation, the redeemed of the Lord, whether they be young or old. Charles Kingsley has the phrase, "The angels, ministers to God's elect." E. Young, writing of the way archangels and angels undertake for man, speaks of them as "Sent by the Sovereign; and are these, O man, Thy friends, thy warm allies?"

An unknown poet would have us remember that "God sends great angels in our sore dismay; But little ones go in and out all day."

Do you not love the lines of John Keble as to the untiring care and attention of these warm angelic allies of ours?

Lord, make my heart a place where angels sing!
    For surely thoughts low-breathed by Thee
Are angels gliding near on noiseless wing;
    And where home they see
Swept clean, and garnish'd with adoring joy,
    They enter in and dwell, and teach that heart
        to swell
With Heavenly Melody, their own untired employ.

5. *Their likeness to resurrected saints* (Matt. 22:30; Mark 12:25). Another saying of Jesus about angels is found in his answer to the Sadducee who came to him in the Temple with his carefully prepared difficulty of the woman who had had seven husbands and who wondered which out of the seven would be her husband in heaven. The reply of Jesus was uttered to point the comparison or perfect the illustration: "In the resurrection they neither marry, nor are given in marriage, but are as the angels of God in heaven" (Matt. 22:30).

What the Sadducee—who represented a sect that did not believe in resurrection—did not know was that conditions in the next world are not the same as here. Where there is no death, there is no need for the arrangements necessary here to keep the world peopled. In heaven, there is certainly love, but not marriage. All who are the sons of God are sons of the resurrection and equal unto the angels who neither marry nor are given in marriage (see Luke 20:34–36). Incidentally, angels in Scripture are uniformly depicted as being of a masculine order. No female angel is mentioned.

6. *Their immense number* (Matt. 26:53; Luke 2:13). As spiritual beings, angels seem to be limitless in number. They appear before us as myriads. Thus, when it comes to instruments and intermediaries of his providential care, it would seem as if God has enough and to spare. Rebuking Peter for his unholy act in cutting off the ear of the high priest's servant, Jesus as good as told him that the only proper place for his sword was in its sheath and that what he desired was not someone to draw a sword for him but to bear the cross with him. Then, in his teaching came what Richard Glover aptly calls "The Unused Prerogative." "Thinkest thou that I cannot now pray to my Father, and he shall presently give me *more* than twelve legions of angels" (see Daniel 4:35, "Army of Heaven")?

In the ancient Roman army a *legion* represented about six thousand soldiers, and thus twelve legions would mean a force of some seventy-two thousand men. Had Jesus wanted the assistance of angels, his Father would have sent *more* than seventy-two thousand to deliver him from those about to crucify him, but he refrained from asking for such overwhelming angelic assistance. The reason Jesus did not ask for such heavenly aid is found in the next verse, "How then shall the Scripture be fulfilled, that thus it must be" (Matt. 26:54)? Such a question, put in another form, means, "I wish God's plan of my life to be carried out, not my preference." We, too, must pray not for angels to preserve us, but for the fulfilling of

God's plan. "Thy will be done." Such teaching was hard for the disciples, for we read that they *all* forsook him and fled.

Often in Scripture, the immensity of the angelic host is mentioned. The angels of God were massed together to praise God for creation, "When the morning stars sang together, And all the sons of God shouted for joy" (Job 38:7). Among those who welcomed the birth of Jesus were those who composed "a multitude of the heavenly host" (Luke 2:13). Among those thronging the heavenly Jerusalem are "the innumerable company of angels" or, as the margin puts it, "myriads of angels" (Heb. 12:22). Phillips gives us the translation "the countless angelic army." Then, bearing in mind what we have already said as to the angels being reapers, the "ten thousands of his holy one" which Jude 14 mentions may refer to angels. Further, John, in his description of the whole company of heaven encircling the throne of God, mentions angels as being among the "ten thousand times ten thousand, and thousands of thousands" (Rev. 5:11). It was such myriads John Milton had in mind when he penned the lines:

Nor think—though men were none—
That heaven would want spectators, God want praise!
Millions of spiritual creatures walk the earth
Unseen, both when we wake and when we sleep.
All these with ceaseless praise His works behold
Both day and night.

7. *Their joy over the salvation of sinners* (Luke 15:7–10). The priceless teaching of Jesus about *angels* would not have been complete without his revela-

tion that they share unbounded joy when sinners repent and turn to Jesus as Savior. However lightly the conversion of a soul may be thought of among men, angels receive it with unbounded delight! Nothing so pleases them as the deliverance of a sinner from the power of darkness and his translation into the kingdom of God's dear Son. They do not originate the joy they express; it is *joy in their presence.* They share the joy of the Father, Son, and Holy Spirit.

"There is joy in the presence of the angels of God over one sinner that repenteth." This verse occurs twice—at the end of the parable of the lost sheep and at the conclusion of the parable of the lost coin (Luke 15:7, 10), but not, as we might have expected, at the end of the parable of the lost son. This does conclude with the merriment and gladness of the father who, in his joy over the return of his prodigal boy, reflected the joy of heaven (Luke 15:32).

Then does not the language of Jesus seem to indicate that the angels are ever on the alert, marking what goes on in the sinner's heart, and delighting in every motion of repentance which they can detect? Latham asks, "If man can cause joy to the Angels of Heaven, can he dream of any goal of existence better worth reaching and more sufficing than this?"

No single angel takes the lead in rejoicing; the gladness caused by the repentance and salvation of the sinner is equally diffused; he is an object of interest to all the heavenly host. Angels share the joy of the shepherd after recovering his lost sheep and of the woman finding her lost coin and of the father whose son was lost but found again. Can we say that we share the joy of angels over sinners when we hear of them being gloriously saved by grace?

While angels sang with joy at the coming of the Redeemer and rejoice over those redeemed by his blood, they cannot sing the song of the redeemed which is

> A song unknown to angels' ears,
> A song that tells of banished fears,
> Of pardoned sins and dried-up tears.

BIBLE STUDY QUESTIONS

Take time to turn to each Scripture reference and mark the verse or a portion in your Bible.

1. What can we learn about angels from their association with Jesus?
2. With what two tasks are angels charged?
3. What part do angels have in Christ's Second Coming and with children today?
4. What is the state, number, and attitude of angels in heaven?

— 28 —

Heaven

.

It is impossible to miss the "otherworldliness" of Jesus in his teachings. He had a constant sense of a life beyond, both for saints and sinners. Dealing with the hereafter, he appealed to the hope of heaven and the fear of hell, both of which were real to him, for he spoke often of the joy and blessedness of the redeemed and of the unhappy fate of those who die lost. Occasionally he would set the one over against the other (Matt. 7:21–27, etc.). Jesus refused to believe that this world is the only abode for humans. He often referred to the life to come, with this world simply as a "vale of soul-making," a sphere of kingdom building, with each person reaping in the future what he has sown here.

To Jesus, heaven was no "pie-in-the-sky," but the Father's home with spacious dwelling places and its vault resting upon pillars (Job 26:11), divided by the firmament from the waters and the world beneath (Gen. 1:8; Prov. 8:27). Men argued for years about the possibility of there being a new world out yonder toward the West. One day,

Columbus sailed out and on until he discovered land. Returning to Spain, the explorer was able to report: "There is a land out yonder. I have been there." Jesus is our heavenly Columbus and could speak so authoritatively about heaven for he had been there. At his incarnation, he came as the eternal Son from the bosom of his Father in heaven.

The teachings of Jesus as to immortal hope were not garnered from Old Testament writers. They had a ring of originality about them. When we think of what he taught about heaven, we immediately discern that he spoke as one who had been there and who had come to bring immortality to light through his gospel. Further, it is not true to refer to the other side of death as an undiscovered country, from which no traveler has returned. Coming from heaven to put away our sins, Jesus died and was buried. But he did not remain dead. He arose and appeared to his disciples as the traveler who had returned to declare the reality and glories of heaven. Thus, Jesus would have us believe that when we come to "bow our heads at going out," then we

Enter straight another golden chamber of the King's,
Larger than this we leave, and lovelier.

The term *heaven* occurs well over one hundred times in the four Gospels, and in the majority of references the word came from the lips of Jesus. From the language he used, we gather that he knew that heaven was the eternal dwelling place of the Father from which Jesus, as the eternal Son, descended and from whence the Holy Spirit is received and which is also the everlasting abode of the redeemed. Just as God spoke of the Temple at Jerusalem as his earthly dwelling place (John 2:16), so he could also say, "Heaven is my throne" (Matt. 6:9; Acts 7:49; see 1 Kings 8:30; Ps. 2:4). When the plural *heavens* is used, the reference is to the celestial or stellar heavens (Ps. 8:3; 115:16).

JESUS TAUGHT THAT HEAVEN IS A PLACE

Among the fascinating contrasts Jesus employed in his teachings is the one in which he urged his disciples not to lay up treasures "upon earth" but "in heaven" (Matt. 6:19, 20). Although a very tangible place, "earth" is insecure and fleeting, for Jesus said it is to pass away, but heaven is permanent and eternal. To him, it was the Father's home from the dateless past (John 14:2) to which he was returning to "prepare a place" for his own. Then came his promise to come back to gather the redeemed unto himself. "It is true that I am going away to prepare a place for you, but it is just as true that I am coming again to welcome you into my own home, so that you may be where I am" (John 14:3, Phillips).

Phrases Jesus uttered during his oral ministry likewise prove heaven to be an actual sphere and not a state of being:

"Our Father in heaven" (Matt. 6:9, 14; see Eccles. 5:2).

"Things of heaven" (John 3:12).

"Powers of heaven" (Mark 13:25).

"The angels of heaven" (Mark 13:32).

"Bread from heaven" (John 6:31, 32).

"Sinned against heaven" (Luke 15:18).

Although in the majority of references to heaven, symbols are used, they are figures of the truth. To some of the ancient saints, the Father's home was a heavenly country of which God is the heavenly Father (Heb. 11:16; Luke 11:13). As to its exact location, the Bible is silent. Heaven is usually spoken of as being *up*. Stephen looked up into heaven. Jesus lifted up his eyes to heaven and ascended into heaven. We are content to sing "Where Jesus is, 'Tis heaven there."

A wonderful feature of our ultimate presence in heaven will be the fact that we are there because of the express wish of the Savior himself. In his High Priestly Prayer we have his express request: "Father, I will that they also, whom thou hast given me, be *with me where I am;* that they may behold my glory, which thou hast given me: for thou lovedst me *before* the foundation of the world" (John 17:24). These precious thoughts were uppermost in the mind of Paul when he wrote that the moment he was absent from his body he would be "at home" with the Lord (2 Cor. 5:1–6, 8). Such a hope of heaven was not based upon natural instinct or desire, or even on the completion of an obviously incomplete life here, but upon the authority of Jesus. Paul, who was immersed in the teachings of the Lord he dearly loved and sacrificially served, clung to his explicit affirmation, "In my Father's home are many dwelling places: *if it were not so I would have told you*" (see John 14:2). But he did tell us all we need to know about heaven and how to reach there, and such is sufficient for faith to rest upon. His presence there is its chief blessedness.

JESUS TAUGHT WHAT CONSTITUTES HEAVEN

Apart from heaven being the eternal abode of the Trinity, of the angelic host, and of the redeemed from earth, there are certain discernible features as to what kind of sphere it is, apart from being the place we enter at death.

Its atmosphere is one of purest joy (Luke 12:36, 37; 15:7, 10; see Ps. 16:11). Its joys and glories are beyond human conception. All the inspired could do was to use material figures to convey to our minds something of the joy unspeakable and full of glory awaiting the saints.

Its ever-wider service. While rewards will be ours for faithful service rendered on earth, "Great is your reward in heaven" (Matt. 5:12; 26:21; see 1 Cor. 3:12–15; 2 Cor. 5:8–11). Such faithfulness will bring us larger opportunities of serving the Master in heaven as he taught his own in the parables of the talents and the pounds (Matt. 25:14–30; Luke 19:11–27). The servant making his master's pound into ten here on earth is to be rewarded with authority over *ten cities* (Luke 19:17, 18; 22:30). The teaching of Jesus as to coming rewards, which he frequently introduced, constrained his hearers to embrace his cause, with all its privations and disadvantages, because of the compensations heaven will bring (Luke 18:29, 30).

It is likewise apparent from his instruction that although *all* who are his *are* going to heaven, all will not have the same position and obligations there. There will be those who, because of their lack of loyalty and full surrender while on earth, earned no crown to wear in heaven. May we be found among the number reaching out after a full reward!

Its selective occupants from earth. Jesus left men in no uncertainty as to who are qualified to go to heaven. In unmistakable terms he described those who will reach there, as well as those excluded from the heavenly abode. He prayed that *those whom the Father had given him* might be with him in heaven, as they are the only ones from earth who will be there. "Except a man be born again he *cannot* see the kingdom of heaven" (John 3:3; Matt. 5:3). Declaring himself to be the *Truth* about his Father in heaven, and as the only *Way* to reach him there, Jesus said, *"No* man cometh unto the Father *but by me"* (John 14:6).

Whether it be access to the Father in salvation or worship or ultimately heaven, we cannot approach him acceptably apart from the mediation of the Savior. Note the exclusion *no man* and then that impressive *but* (see Rom. 5:2; Eph. 2:18). Since his ascension, Jesus has been active preparing a place for a prepared people in his Father's home. When he said, "I go to prepare a place for *you,"* he had in mind his church made up of all redeemed by his blood and regenerated by the Holy Spirit. Therefore, if we are to be heaven-bound, we must be heaven-born because all who are not are excluded from the realms of eternal bliss (Matt. 7:21; 25:32–35; Luke 13:27–30).

BIBLE STUDY QUESTIONS

Take time to turn to each Scripture reference and mark the verse or a portion in your Bible.

1. How did Jesus indicate heaven is a place?
2. What six features are said to constitute heaven?

— 29 —

Satan

As the Bible, in its entirety, is a progressive revelation of every aspect of truth it presents, it is essential to gather together all references to any given topic and systematize them accordingly. It is only thus that we can arrive at a complete unfolding of any theme engaging our attention. That this plan is necessary in connection with the history and work of Satan is obvious to any student of the Word. But in these volumes we limit ourselves to what the Master taught on different subjects. Naturally, what he said as to Satan's nature and activities form only a part—withal a most vital part—of the full portrait of the enemy of God and of man. Yet while the Master's unfolding of Satan is limited in scope, it will be found that all he did say about him is everywhere essentially consistent with what the rest of Scripture records as to his character.

In the background of our Lord's experiences of Satan and his enunciations regarding this constant foe of his is the fact that he knew all about Satan *before* he became *Satan*. In the dateless past when, as the preexistent one, Jesus shared the glory of his Father "before the world was" and was his only-begotten Son whom he loved "before the foundation of the world" (John 17:5, 24), Jesus was acquainted with Satan. He was then known as "Son of the Morning" (Isa 14:12) or "Light-Bearer," but when he fell from heaven, he became the prince of demons, or Satan, adversary of God, of Christ, and of man. Thus the first recorded satanic temptation Jesus endured was not his first meeting with the Devil. They had met long before the Son of God became the Son of man. Further, we cannot conceive of Jesus not being tempted of the Devil during the silent years he spent in Galilee—thirty years of which we have little record.

The highest of all created beings or intelligences owed his existence to Jesus, cocreator of the angelic hosts (John 1:3). This archseraph, with great dignity of person and position, was one of the created angels, formed by the same omnipotent hand and glorious power who created the heavens and the earth and all that is therein. He was not created a Devil but became such through his own volition and folly. That he was given position of high order is seen in the way Jesus spoke of Satan as the "prince of this world" or "prince of the powers of the air" or the recognized chief of all spirit beings who shared their ruler's sin and deposition. When he offered the kingdoms of the world to Jesus, Jesus found no fault with his claim, nor did he tell the Devil that the kingdoms of this world with all their glory were not his to give, for the Devil is "the god of this world." His angels, now demons, are under his government of the earth, filling and polluting the atmosphere which is their God-bestowed habitation.

Conversely, Satan was fully acquainted with the preexistence of Jesus and of his partnership in the godhead. He was under no illusion as to the true identity of the babe born of the virgin Mary. When, before his rebellion, he obeyed the Creator's will, Satan constantly witnessed the glory and authority of God's well-beloved Son and observed him as being in the "form of God" and "equal with God" (Phil. 2:6). Thus, when Jesus became the Son of man and lived among men, Satan and his cohorts had no doubts as to who he was and what he was able to accomplish. Although in the temptation Satan said, "*If* thou be the Son of God," he knew only too well that Jesus *was* the Son of God with power he himself did not possess.

The attitude of demons to Jesus reflected that of their hellish master. They repeatedly addressed him as the Son of God. When the Gadarene demoniac encountered Jesus, he asked, "What have I to do with thee, Jesus, *thou Son of the most high God?*" It was the demon inside the wild man of the tombs who made this astounding confession (Mark 5:7). Another demon Jesus met in the Capernaum synagogue cried out, "I know thee who thou art, the Holy one of God" (Mark 1:24). Then we have the unclean spirits represented as falling down before Jesus, saying, "Thou art the Son of God" (Mark 3:11). On the evening of the day he healed Peter's fever-stricken wife's mother, he cast demons out of many who likewise testified, "Thou art Christ, the Son of God." Jesus rebuked them,

suffering them not to speak of him, "for they
knew that he was Christ," the predicted Messiah
of the Old Testament (Luke 4:41; see also Matt.
8:29). Did not the apostle James have this satanic
witness to Christ's deity and authority in mind
when he wrote, "Thou believest there is one God;
thou doest well: the devils *also* believe, and *trem-
ble*" [which is more than many humans do who
profess faith in him]" (James 2:19).

When one of these denizens of hell shrieked
despairingly, "Art thou come to torment us before
our time?" he actually meant, "Hast thou descended from heaven to earth to torment us before
the appointed time?"—a remarkable witness to
the preexistence of Jesus (Matt. 8:29).

Thus, if we should ask about the religious per-
suasion of the Devil we could say positively:

1. *He is a believer in the Lord.* He is no atheist,
but has ever known the true character and commission of the one he tried to seduce.

2. *He fears the one he constantly fought.* Who,
then, is the better believer—the Devil who believes
and trembles or the modern infidel who believes
neither God nor Devil?

HOW JESUS PORTRAYED SATAN

Scripture as a whole lists a great variety of
names for him who, in his first appearance on
earth, was called the *serpent* (Gen. 3:1; Rev. 12:9).
All the names given him seem to be derived from
and adapted to the several shapes in which Satan
has appeared to undertake his diabolical task in

the world. Further, all his names mark him as a personal being. There are many who deny the existence of a personal Devil. Well, if there is no Devil, we would like to know who is responsible for the devilish world in which we live. That Jesus took the personality of the Devil for granted is evident from the names and epithets he used of him. The Gospels present him as an actual, living, and reasonable being, the embodiment of evil, as Jesus was of holiness.

Satan (Luke 10:18; 22:31). Occurring some eighteen times in the Old Testament and thirty-five in the New of which thirteen references are in the Gospels, this ancient name means the "Adversary" or the "Opposing Spirit." Satan is described as the adversary of Israel (1 Sam. 1:6; 1 Chron. 21:1). The same word is used of God who is the adversary of all who act contrary to his mind and will (Num. 22:22). This proper Hebrew name of a malevolent being is often changed in the New Testament to the Greek *Diabolos,* or Devil, but which is more accurately translated the "Accuser" or the "Slanderer." Both in the experience and in the teaching of Jesus, Satan is revealed as the great and bitter adversary of God, of Christ, and of believers, as well as the malignant author of false accusations (Zech. 3:1–2; Rev. 12:10). Satan is the one cruel adversary we dare not agree with in the way (Luke 12:58), seeing he is adverse to all that Christ represents. With his expulsion from heaven, perhaps as the choicest of all the glorious seraphs, he earned the name of *Satan,* as John Milton suggests in his description of the Devil's original glory.

Satan, so call him now; his former name
Is heard no more in Heaven: he of the first,
If not the first archangel; great in power,
In favour and pre-eminence.

Devil (Matt. 13:39). This further descriptive title
of the Evil One is never used of him in the Old
Testament. Not once do we have the singular to
signify Satan as *Devil* as now understood. Four
times we have the plural *devils* (Lev. 17:7; Deut.
32:17; 2 Chron. 11:15; Ps. 106:37). In the New
Testament both the singular *devil* and plural *demons* occur well over one hundred times. At the
outset, it must be made clear that the Bible is entirely free from the extravagances of popular presentation of the Devil with horns, tail, and a fork-
like implement in his hand, and of his tricks and
appearances. The Scots used to call him, "The
muckle horn'd Dee'l." Consistently, the Bible exhibits a dependable accuracy and consistency of
statement regarding the Devil and his work which
is most reassuring. Just how he became a *Devil*,
with moral evil as his controlling attribute, we are
not told.

Devil is the most popular name of this heaven-
born being of the angelic race and is, in general,
his ordinary name in all languages and in all nations; it is the name by which he and his works are
principally distinguished. True, Scripture uses
names of a coarser kind, some of which follow, to
portray the Devil, but all his other names are varied according to the custom of speech, and the
dialects of the several nations where he is spoken
of: but in a word, *Devil* is his common name in all
the known languages of the earth. Professor W. E.

Moorehead, in his *Old Testament Outline Studies*, says:

> It is noteworthy that nearly all the revelation we have of this great evil spirit is found in the New Testament. Rarely is he mentioned in the Old—in Eden, in Job, David, Joshua the High Priest. God delayed the full disclosure of him to later times, and then gave him 28 names which fully describe him.

As to the significance of this particular name which Jesus often used, some commentators say it means "Destroyer"; others, that it signifies "Deceiver." The Greeks derived it from a root meaning "False Witness," and thus *Devil* is a contracted form of the Greek *diabolos*, which properly implies a malicious accuser and is used in the Greek Testament and LXX (the Septuagint, earliest Greek translation of the Old Testament by seventy translators) as an equivalent of the Hebrew word *Satan*, implying "Adversary." *Devil* is a name conjuring up everything evil, frightful in appearance, wicked in action, horrible in manner, and monstrous in effect. In fact, if you take *D* from Devil, you are left with evil, and the bearer of this terrible name is the personification of all that is vile (to take the *E* and place it last) and evil. When originally created a superhuman, but not supernatural, being, he was no more created the *Devil* as such, that is, as he has been since his Fall, than God created *man* as he now is (Eccles 7:29). God is absolute Good, and nothing therefore alien to this virtue could come from him.

Evil One (Matt. 13:19, 38). This epithet which Jesus used of the Devil depicted his fundamental moral attribute. He is the "wicked one" or "evil one" as the Revised Version translates it, the one whose nature and being are given to evil and who is the direct opposite of God who is the "Holy One" (Isa. 1:4). The phrase in the Lord's Prayer, "Deliver us from evil," reads "from the evil one" in the Revised Version of Matthew 6:13. As presented in Scripture, the Devil is the embodiment and source of evil. No explanation of the origin of evil is given; the fact of its existence is clearly and repeatedly stated, as well as its being the work of the Evil One himself (John 13:27; Rev. 12:9).

Evil, in so many forms, is rampant the world over and is poisoning all aspects of society as never before. The tragedy is that the constant exposure to immoral forces makes us immune to their demoralizing effects and of such being the work of the Evil One to destroy mankind. We are living in demonized times and have need to pray without ceasing as Jesus taught us, "Deliver us from the evil one." Daniel DeFoe remarks in his volume on *The History of the Devil:*

> To believe the existence of God is a debt to nature, and to believe the existence of the Devil is a like debt to reason: one is a demonstration from the reality of visible causes, and the other a deduction from the like reality of their effects.

If there were no Devil, and demons, we would have to invent them to account for the multitudinous forms of moral evil becoming more blatant with the passing days and which surely deserve another flood to rid the earth of its corruption and violence.

Enemy (Matt. 13:25, 28, 39). While it is perfectly

true that Jesus taught us to love our enemies, the
Devil is an avowed enemy we dare not and cannot
love. How deceived those are who pretend to be
Satan worshipers! To use a well-known aphorism,
the Devil must "laugh up his sleeve" at their professed devotion to him since it is his diabolical
purpose to have their eternal company in "the
lake of fire." Without hesitation, Jesus named the
Devil an *enemy* to be held in contempt, challenged,
and overcome.

Jesus' incomparable parable of the wheat and
tares is one of the few parables later given a careful explanation and interpretation. Jesus twice
identified the one sowing the tares as an *enemy*.
"His enemy came and sowed tares." "An enemy
hath done this." Then, in his unfolding of the
spiritual application of this earthly story with a
heavenly meaning, Jesus said to his disciples, "He
that soweth the good seed is the Son of man; The
field is the world; the good seed are the children
of the kingdom; but the tares are the children of
the wicked one; the enemy that sowed them is
the devil" (Matt. 13:37–39).

Here, three epithets are used of the evil sower
—*the wicked one, the enemy, the devil.* The emphasis,
however, is on the *enemy* aspect of the satanic antagonist. Without doubt, the Devil is Public Enemy
No. 1. Since his expulsion from heaven, he has
been the persistent, unceasing enemy of the three
persons of the blessed Trinity, and ever since the
creation of our first parents, he has been the callous and cruel enemy of mankind. The Devil is
likewise the enemy of truth and righteousness,
ever seeking to destroy their effectiveness as

wheat by mixing them with his tares of falsehood
and deceit, or by sowing tares of doubt and unbelief with the good seed sown by Christ's gospel
and church. As the enemy, Satan is constantly at
work in the World, tireless in his efforts to combine truth with error, to uproot good and sow
evil. This avowed enemy of God and of man wins
when he persuades humans that his ways are in
their best interests (see 2 Pet. 2:1–3).

While Scripture consistently teaches that he is
the personification of evil, and the type and example of the confirmed, determined, deliberate evil-
doer who delights in it, it also teaches that believers can triumph over all his malicious hatred.
When the seventy returned from their mission
full of joy because even the devils had been subject unto them through the all-prevailing name of
Jesus, he said unto them, "I give unto you power
. . . over all the enemy" (Luke 10:19). A murderous enemy he may be; yet we are assured that if
we resist him in the name of Jesus, he will "flee
from us" (James 4.7).

> Why should I fear the darkest hour,
> Or tremble at the tempter's power?
> Jesus vouchsafes to be my tower.

The Strong Man. In his defense against the Pharisees, who had charged Jesus that he must have
been in league with Satan to have had power to
cast out a demon from a man who was blind and
dumb, Jesus used one of those priceless illustrations to teach his superiority over Satan. "How
can one enter a strong man's house, and spoil his
goods, except he first bind the strong man? and

then he will spoil his house" (Matt. 12:29)? It is obvious from the context that the "strong man" is Satan, and the one able to bind him because he is stronger is Jesus himself. The first great task of him who came to destroy the works of the Devil was to bind him, which he did by the power of the Spirit, "I cast out devils by the Spirit of God." The strong man is out to rob us spiritually, morally, physically, and eternally. As Michael the archangel and the Devil disputed over the body of Moses (Jude 9), so Satan and Jesus are in conflict for the possession of man and all he has.

Because the strong man can be bound, his scope of power is limited. Satan only has a *time-lease* of activity. When a stronger than he encounters him and binds him, his plunder ceases. Is not the design of the Book of Job to show that Satan is like a dog on a leash and cannot go further than divine permission? In spite of his power, which is tremendous, and like his enmity, which is even greater than his power, Satan can only go the length of his chain. He can afflict only so far and when the Lord for inscrutable purposes permits him. A divine *hedge* was formed around Job through which Satan could not break. As a lion (1 Pet. 5:8), he might prowl round and round that hedge, but always on the outside. After his unsuccessful attempt to bind the strong Son of God in the Temptation, the "strong man" was compelled to leave him "for a season."

> Jesus is stronger than Satan and sin,
>   Satan to Jesus must bow;
> Therefore I triumph without and within;
>   Jesus saves me now.

Beelzebub (Matt. 9:34; 10:25; 12:24). One of the terrible penalties of sin is that we tend to repeat it and sink deeper into it. This was the case with the Pharisees who twice over accused Jesus of being in league with Beelzebub, the prince of demons. The second time they more boldly blasphemed Jesus. In his reply, he identified Beelzebub, the current name for the chief of demons, with Satan (Matt. 12:26; Mark 3:23; Luke 11:15, 18, 19) and used the term as a contemptuous designation of the satanic prince. How silenced his foes must have been when he asked, "Since when has Satan become so foolish as to divide his power and dethrone himself?" Why, foolishness that can believe this is only equaled by the waywardness which indulges such an imagination.

Those religious leaders committed the unpardonable sin of ascribing the miracles of Jesus to Beelzebub, thereby ascribing to the worst source the supreme manifestation of goodness. Because demons had been cast out by the power of the Holy Spirit who indwelt Jesus, the Pharisees had been guilty of blasphemy against the Holy Spirit by ascribing good to evil. The term *blasphemy* in its original form meant "evil-speaking" and represents the most acute form of active hatred, implying intense dislike and inflicting keenest calumny —all of which the Pharisees were guilty when they declared heaven to be in harmony with hell. James asked, "Doth a fountain send forth at the same place sweet water and bitter" (James 3:11)?

Murderer (John 8:44). Surely this was one of the most dreadful of designations of Satan to fall from the lips of the Lord Jesus! "He was a murderer from the beginning." The word he used means "man-slayer" and is the same term describing one who hates his brother (1 John 3:15). In a most remarkable passage giving us the most extended revelation of Satan in the Bible, Jesus indicts him as being a slayer of men. This accusation of Jesus refers, first of all, to the Fall of Adam and Eve which was the murder of the human race. "From the beginning" is strictly related to the happening in the Garden of Eden and is not the beginning of creation as in John 1:1. The term *murderer* then describes the foul act of Satan when he caused man to fall under the yoke of sin and thereby of death. "The soul that sinneth shall die."

But out of that satanic murder there came a human murder, for the slaughter of Abel by Cain came out of the temptation of their parents. This first murderous act is cited as the first example of the hatred *of a man* to his brother, a hatred inspired by Satan (1 John 3:12, 15). "Not as Cain, *who was of the evil one* and slew his brother . . . whoso hateth his brother is a murderer."

In this capacity as murderers the Pharisees acted toward Jesus who said, "You seek to kill me, *a man*" (John 8:40; Acts 4:10; 5:30). Ultimately they succeeded in killing the prince of life, but "by dying, death he slew" (Heb. 2:14–15). The word Luke uses for *murderers*—the Revised Version gives *assassins*—is found nowhere else in the New Testament. From the original *sikários*, we have the Latin *sicarious* from *aica*, meaning a small sword or dagger. The word describes the hired assassin, of whom there were bands in the pay of agitators in Rome in the last days of the Republic, who employed them to remove surreptitiously their political opponents. In the latter days of the Jewish commonwealth, Judaea became infested with the same type of ruffian, and it is natural that the Roman commandant at Jerusalem should describe them by the name so well known in the city.

Satan is the archassassin who has no regard for human life whatever. It was thus that he entered Judas and used him to bring about the murder of Jesus, which the Pharisees so long desired (Acts 3:15). Behind all murders, assassinations, wars, and suicides is the sinister figure of "the murderer from the beginning," whose scheme is to terminate the physical life of men before they repent and receive eternal life. This murderous trait is seen in his wolflike, cruel nature (Luke 8:29; John 10:12).

Father (John 8:44). A bad speaker is one who *tries* to say something, but a good speaker is one who *has something* to say. Jesus is in the latter category, for he always had something authoritative to say, meant what he said, and said what he meant. He never equivocated, or beat about the bush, as we express it. Neither was he ever guilty of verbosity. In his oral ministry his teaching was always clear, direct, and explicit. He was a master at expressing the maximum of truth in the minimum of words. A case in point is his reply to the claim of the Pharisees' ancestral parentage in Abraham in which he scorns their proud patriarchal filiation: "Ye are of your father, the Devil" (John 8:44). John distinguishes between "the children of God and the children of the Devil" (1 John

3:10). In the parable of the tares, Jesus referred to the tares as symbolic of "the children of the wicked one" (Matt. 13:38). The literal meaning, then, of his mention of the fatherhood of the Devil is: "You are sons of the *father* who is the *Devil,* and not, as you think, of that other father who is God."

Twice over Jesus spoke of the Devil as *father,* and as such what a vast evil brood he generated! Not only is he the parent of the numberless legions of the bottomless pit, but of the multitude of godless souls on earth. What a marvelous change takes place in a life when the father of hell is forsaken for "Our Father who is in heaven"!

Jesus went on to describe the Devil as "A liar, and the *father* of the liar" (John 8:44). In one breath he is condemned both as a murderer and a liar, thereby uniting two features of his evil character, namely, hatred of man and enmity of the truth. F. Godet says in his *Commentary on the New Testament,* "We may understand how this double hatred must be concentrated in the highest degree upon Jesus, in whom at length was perfectly realized the idea of man and of man as an organ of truth." In his exposure of the Devil, Jesus said there was "no truth in him." Jesus could say, "I am . . . the truth." But the Devil is cut off from *the truth* because as a liar he is destitute *of truth.*

Doubtless our Lord had in mind the way the Devil lied to Adam and Eve in the garden, and since then he has followed this method in dealing with men. His lying tactics are seen in false apostles, in deceitful workers, and in his role as a quick change artist, transforming himself into an angel of light (2 Cor. 11:13–14). Fundamentally, then, he is a liar, and his kingdom is founded upon lies and conceit. An inveterate liar is a child of the Devil and his lying springs from the devil-nature which is in him. Those who make and love lies are excluded from heaven (Rev. 22:15). Man's only deliverance from the father of lies is to experience the emancipating truth of Scripture (John 8:32).

Prince. The word Jesus used in speaking of Satan as a *prince* indicates one who has ruling power allied to dignity and authority. *King* is a title of absolute authority. Peter has the phrase, "The king as supreme" (1 Pet. 2:13). Although Satan has dignity by creation, absolute supremacy has never been his; that is God's prerogative. *Prince* he may be and as such must realize there is one still above him, even the God who created him.

Thus, although Satan is a real prince, or ruler or head of a vast kingdom which includes principalities, powers, rulers of darkness, and wicked spiritual beings in high places (Eph. 6:11–12), Jesus never named him a *king.* As the *air* is the base of all these evil emissaries of Satan, he is called "the prince of the power of the air" (Eph. 2:2). Let us briefly examine the references of Jesus to his archfoe as *prince.*

Prince of Darkness (Luke 22:53). When the Jewish rulers came to take Jesus with their swords and staves, he met their ominous intention with the words, "This is your hour, and the power of darkness." Although he did not actually name Satan as Prince of Darkness, he implied it. *Darkness* that comes by night has no power, for it is not

a tangible beneficial quality as *light*. Natural darkness is simply the absence of light. But in the spiritual realm Jesus revealed when he used the
above phrase, he used a symbol with the idea of
emphasizing the person behind the power. As
Charles H. Ellicott comments in his *Commentary on
the Whole Bible*, "In identifying the power that
worked through human instruments against Him
with darkness, our Lord virtually claims Himself
to be Himself the Light" (John 8:12).

As the powerful prince of darkness Satan blinds
the eyes of "those that believe not lest the light . . .
shine unto them" (2 Cor. 3:14; 4:4).

> The whole world is lost in the darkness of sin,
> The Light of the world is Jesus.

The Savior alone is able to deliver us from the
power of darkness (Col. 1:13). But for those who
persist in loving darkness rather than light, there
is the judgment of being fettered forever with
chains of darkness (Jude 6; 2 Pet. 2:4).

Prince of this World (John 12:31; 14:30; 16:11).
Repetition of a word, phrase, or verse in Scripture
means divine emphasis. Three times over Jesus
named Satan the Prince of this World in three
different ways. By use of such a repeated title
Jesus recognized Satan's dignity of creation.
When the unfallen highest of all created angelic
intelligences, Satan (when he was Lucifer), was
given the jurisdiction over the kingdoms of this
world, he failed to prove himself anything but
princely in character and works. In his letter to
the church at Pergamos, Jesus said, "I know

where thou dwellest, where Satan's throne is" (Rev. 2:13). The original word for *seat* is *thronos,* and this revelation compels us to recognize that Satan still has a throne on the earth from which he exercises his princely rule—a right he holds by *divine right.* He is, however, continuing to govern as a usurper prince, ever seeking to destroy the authority of him who is the prince of Glory.

First of all, Jesus declared that this unprincely prince had no sway over him, for He was outside his domain altogether. "The prince of this world cometh, and hath nothing in me" (John 14:30). All who are born by natural generation are born in sin, or with original sin within them. They enter the world with a bias toward evil, or something of the Devil in them. Not so Jesus whom no man could convict of sin, simply because he came as the perfect, sinless, Son of God. Therefore, there was nothing in him to which the Devil could appeal. Thus, in his affirmation, Jesus was actually saying, "There is nothing in me which appertains to Satan's domain, which gives him a right and power over me, the object of his hatred." It likewise implies in him who uttered the confession the consciousness of the most perfect innocence.

In the second place, Jesus pronounced the overthrow and defeat of the one who had acted, and still does act contrary to all true princely virtues. "Now shall the prince of this world be cast out" (John 12:31). How his rule over men was to be destroyed Jesus goes on to explain: "I, if I be lifted up from the earth, will draw all men unto *me* (John 12:32, 33).

Weiss, the renowned European theologian, has

reminded us that "with the accomplishment of the redemptive work, the expulsion of the Devil begins." Calvary was his Waterloo. We often sing about "marching *on* to victory." The fact is, however, that we "march *from* victory," for the cross is the condemnation of the moral state of natural humanity, and also of its adversary, the Devil, who through the finished work of Jesus became a defeated foe. Now, through faith, we overcome his snares through the blood of the Lamb (Rev. 12:11). By the magnetism of the crucified one we are drawn to a full surrender to his claims.

Third, since Pentecost the Holy Spirit has unceasingly continued to enforce the condemnation of the cross on the world and its prince. In his teaching regarding the ministry of the Spirit, whom Jesus promised to send after his ascension, he taught that one of the functions of the Spirit would be to "convict the world of sin, of righteousness and of judgment . . . Of judgment, because the prince of this world is judged" (John 16:11). The implication is that the satanic prince is *already* judged, that the Spirit convinces men of a past victory over their avowed enemy, and that by his power they can appropriate such a victory. Satan has been judged, deprived of his power, and as the author of sin received his irrevocable sentence through the "five bleeding wounds" the Savior bears. Since he came from heaven, the Spirit has proclaimed the sentence to those on earth and has continuously called upon sin-bound souls to claim the deliverance Jesus secured for them and to render homage to the prince of life as a new master. "Every sinner rescued from Satan and regen-

erated by the Spirit is the monument of the condemnation of him who formally called himself the
prince of this world." In contrast to the threefold
reference to Satan as the prince of this world, it is
interesting to find Jesus named *prince* in a threefold way (see Acts 3:15; 5:31; Rev. 1:5).

Prince of Demons (Matt. 9:34; 12:24). While we
understand that the plural *devils* is a common
name for evil angels, the original means *demons*
and is so given in the Revised Version wherever
devils occurs. There are an unknown number of
demons, but only *one* Devil—and one is far more
than enough! Jesus recognized him as the prince
or head of those called his angels—"the Devil and
his angels." This headship by Satan of an army of
evil angels was likewise an accepted truth among
the Jews of that time, for when Jesus cast the Devil
out of the dumb man, much to the astonishment
of the onlookers, the Pharisees said, "He casteth
out demons through the prince of demons."
These demons are the willing subjects of the Devil
in the kingdom of Evil (Luke 11:18). DeFoe observes in *Guide to Bible Study:*

> Satan, the leader, guide and superior, as he was the
> author of the celestial rebellion, is still the great head
> and master-devil as before; under his authority they
> still act, not obeying, but carrying on the same insur-
> rection against God, which they began in heaven;
> making war still against heaven, in the person of his
> image and creature, man, and though vanquished by
> the thunder of the Son of God, and cast down head-
> long from heaven, they have yet re-assumed, or
> rather not lost, either the will or the power of doing
> evil.

Satan has the sole sovereignty of the whole army of hell, all the numberless legions of the bottomless pit being his subjects who are the principalities and powers owning him as their prince but who, with him, were overcome at Calvary. Today we live in a demonized world. There is no other explanation for the hideous crimes we daily witness apart from demon-possession. Many types of mental affliction are attributable to the same evil source. These demons gain power only where they are feared or worshiped. An atheistic culture such as Communism represents is not subject to demonism, seeing that it is a philosophy respecting both God and the Devil.

Among the characteristic features of demons found in the Gospels, we have the following:

They confess the deity of Jesus (Matt. 8:28, 29; Mark 1:24; 3:11; 5:7; Acts 19:15).

There are innumerable legions (Mark 5:9). Milton wrote of these hellish legions as being

> An host
> Innumerable as the stars of night,
> Or stars of morning, dew-drops, which the sun
> Impearls on ev'ry leaf, and ev'ry flower.

They are foul (Mark 9:25).
They are unclean (Mark 1:27).
They are cruel (Mark 9:20; Luke 9:42; Matt. 8:28).

For an excellent summary of these rebel angels, the reader is directed to the footnote at Matthew 7:22 in the Scofield Reference Bible. There is no redemption whatever for the Devil and his host of demons, for all are doomed to everlasting fire (Matt. 25:41; Rev. 20:10).

Tempter (Matt. 4:1–11; Mark 1:13; Luke 4:2; 1
Tim. 2:14). It was in this guise that Satan appeared to the first man, Adam, and also to the
second man, the last Adam, the Lord of heaven.
He is likewise the tempter of believers (1 Thess.
3:5). In connection with the study of *temptation* as
a whole, it is essential to bear in mind that while
God *permits* temptation, he does not *provide* it, as
Jesus made so clear: "Let no man say when he is
tempted, I am tempted of God: for God cannot
be tempted with evil, neither tempteth he any
men."

When Jesus came in the fashion of man, he
suffered himself, although God the Son, to be
tempted of the Devil and is forever blessed because he endured the temptation and emerged
from it victorious, as we too can by his power
(James 1:12–14). Doubtless there are those who
have been troubled over the phrase in the prayer
Jesus taught his disciples to pray: "Lead us not
into temptation" (Luke 11:4). The implication
surely is that we are not to pray that we may never
be tempted, but that at all times to be delivered
from the evil lurking in the temptations we meet.
Each victory enables us to win another. From
Jesus' experience and encounter with the Devil in
the wilderness, there are so many things of interest to the whole universe. The Holy Spirit was our
Lord's companion in this time of testing, as the
tempter made three attempts to blast his mission
at the outset; then when the conflict was over,
angels ministered unto him. His successful resis-
tance of temptation confirmed his messianic calling, and he was gloriously victorious because of
his prior messianic consciousness. He knew that

he had come into the world to destroy the works of the Devil.

Further, the conflict of Jesus with the Devil, representing real struggles of soul, gave him a sympathetic contact with tempted sinners; and because he emerged victorious from the battle, he gained the right to speak to others who are tempted of the Devil. Temptation, in itself, is not sin, but yielding to it is. Jesus was tempted in all points as we are, yet without sin (Heb. 2:18; 4:15). As the conqueror of sin and Satan, Jesus earned the right to succour us when we are satanically enticed. Bishop Charles Gore suggests in *Jesus of Nazareth:*

> The three temptations of Jesus represented not so much the temptations of the ordinary man as the typical temptations of the exceptional man, whose soul is possessed with a sense of a divine vocation which absorbs his whole interest.

But when the sacred writer said that Jesus was tempted in all points as *we* are, the plural pronoun includes, not only those Bishop Gore suggests, but all believers. Although Satan may not offer the whole world to any one of us, the temptation of Jesus comes close to human experience, for he offers us a little portion of pleasure or money or fame for which so many men soil and sell their souls. The kingdoms of the world were offered Jesus on condition of compromising with the evil resident in the temptation, but he never yielded. This adds weight to what he taught about God being able to deliver us from tasting the sugar on the stick (see Matt. 26:41).

Further, Jesus described those who "in time of

temptation fall away" because they succ   nb to the
evil at the heart of the temptation (Lul ⸱ 8:12). He
also had a good word for his disciples who had
"continued with him in temptations," or trials and
testings as the term can imply (Luke 22:28; see
Luke 10:25; John 8:6; Matt. 16:1; 19:3).

> O Saviour Christ, Thou too art Man;
> Thou hast been troubled, tempted, tried;
> Thy kind but searching glance can scan
> The very wounds that shame would hide.

Deceiver. The first and last portraits the Bible
presents of Satan are those of a cruel *Deceiver.*
"The woman [Eve] being deceived was in the
transgression" (1 Tim. 2:14; Rev. 12:9). "The devil
that deceived them was cast into the lake of fire"
(Rev. 20:8, 10). Since this first manifestation of his
character, Satan has never ceased to deceive the
whole world and is most active in this role today
among those who dwell on the earth (Rev. 12:9;
13:14; 2 Tim. 3:13). Did not Jesus in his teaching
about the signs of time warn his own of the subtlety of Satan in his effort to deceive the very elect
(Matt. 23:4, 5, 24; see Luke 21.8)? The Pharisees
were so deceived of the Devil that they came to
name the spotless Lamb of God as a *deceiver* (Matt.
27:63; John 7:12). In these evil and apostate times
we need to give heed to Paul's advice about the
satanic deceiver's agents who "wax worse and
worse, deceiving and being deceived" (2 Tim.
3:13). We must strive to live as near as possible to
Jesus who unmasked Satan's falsities, ever praying
for that spiritual intuition enabling us instinctively
to detect his crafty wiles.

In his letter to the church at Thyatira, Jesus wrote of those who had plunged into "the depths of Satan," referring to the false teachers in the city. Professing to know the depths of deity, Jesus said it was rather "the depths of Satan" with which they were familiar. Our only source of refuge from Satan and his endeavors to beguile is "the depths of God" (Rom. 11:33; 1 Cor. 2:10). Jesus spoke of Satan as being cast down from heaven with the swiftness of lightning, and Peter describes how those angels who rebelled with Satan were cast down into hell (Luke 10:18; 2 Pet. 2:4; see Jude 6). This adversary of both God and man can only be kept out of our hearts through the constant claiming of the blood of the victorious Lamb which is ever efficacious to make us more than conquerors over the enemy of our souls.

HOW JESUS ENCOUNTERED
AND OVERCAME SATAN

If the victory of Jesus over his persistent foe is to be ours, then we must know how he met him and what weapons or methods he used to defeat him. In all his contacts and contests with the Devil, Jesus had no fear whatever of his evil designs, for he knew that he was stronger than such a strong one. As *the Truth,* Jesus encountered and exposed Satan as the *liar* and *deceiver.* Because we are *in* Christ, we can share his fearlessness of all hellish forces, for through the cross the Devil is a vanquished enemy. According to the teaching of Jesus, the only one we have to fear is God (Luke

12:5). Through the death and resurrection of
Jesus, the empire of the Devil is already destroyed. Reserved for judgment from the beginning of his rebellion against God, Calvary resulted
in the overthrow of his dominion and forecasted
his final everlasting condemnation.

Coming as the Savior and leader of men, Jesus'
defeat of Satan established his rightful claims
(Matt. 4:10; John 14:30). Such a victory was also
for all believers (Luke 22:31; Acts 26:18; Rom.
16:20) and finally for the whole world (Rev. 20:9,
10). Believing that it was his task to destroy the
kingdom of evil and all its rulers, Jesus proclaimed their overthrow (Mark 1:13; 3:11; 1 John
3:8). Not only did Jesus unmask the personality,
the reality, the power, the subtlety, the perseverance, and the malice of Satan, he also declared
Satan's overthrow. As suddenly as the lightning
flashes in the heavens and as visibly, the empire of
darkness will be destroyed (Luke 10:18). Jesus vanquished Satan by resisting him (Matt. 4:11), by
casting out demons (Matt. 4:24; 8:31, etc.), by giving power to exorcise (Matt. 10:1; Mark 16:17),
and by destroying Satan's works in his (Jesus')
death (Col. 2:15; Heb. 2:14; 1 John 3:8).

In a twofold way, Jesus taught his disciples the
truth about Satan: first, by his own personal experience of the enemy's tactics; and second, by his
exposure of and warnings against such a diabolical adversary. By the evidence of his own complete conquest of Satan, Jesus earned the right
and ability to succour souls when tempted of the
Devil. His brave heart, mindful of the force of
suggestive evil and conscious of the power to con-

quer for others as for self, overflowed with love for the tempted soul. As we have already noticed, the weapon Jesus used to defeat Satan in the wilderness temptations was the infallible Word of God, "the Sword of the Spirit." *One little word shall fell him.* This also is our mighty means of defense and victory when assailed by the tempter. To meet his approach with a "Thus saith the Lord" or "It is written" compels him to leave us for a season.

For the saints, another avenue of protection against all the fiery darts of the wicked one is the intercession of the divine prevailer over him. Their reliance in the conflict with this persistent and dangerous foe is the assurance that "Greater is he that is in you, than he that is in the world" (1 John 4:4; John 16:33). In Peter's battle with Satan, there came the assuring message of the Master, "I have prayed for thee, that thy faith fail not." Is it not written that the glorious victor over sin and Satan "ever liveth to make intercession for us"? Therefore, by his mighty pleadings of his own efficacious blood on our behalf, he is able to save us to the uttermost from all the wiles of the Devil (Heb. 7:25).

> Stand then in His great might,
> With all His strength endued;
> And take to arm you for the fight,
> The panoply of God;
> That having all things done,
> And all your conflicts passed,
> Ye may o'ercome through Christ alone,
> And stand complete at last.

BIBLE STUDY QUESTIONS

Take time to turn to each Scripture reference and mark the verse or a portion in your Bible.

1. What is the origin and religion of Satan?
2. What three names did Jesus give the embodiment of evil?
3. In what four ways is the Devil the antagonist of man?
4. Of what is Satan father and prince?
5. In what two ways does Satan appear to man?
6. How did Jesus show us the way to overcome Satan?

— 30 —

Hell

From the records of our Lord's ministry among men we discover that some of the most solemn utterances about the eternal woe of the lost fell from the lips of him who died that men might not perish. No matter how men may try to do away with hell, it is still in existence and was a grim reality to Jesus who constantly warned his hearers of its terrors. While some of his descriptions of the place of final punishment may be figurative, they yet indicate a dreadful reality. The words he used all imply utter and hopeless ruin and reveal how candid he was when speaking of the eternal destiny of those rejecting him and his witness. We cannot explain away the revelation he gave men of eternal punishment. It was the Savior who came as the personification of divine love who spoke of:

"The broad way that leadeth to destruction" (Matt. 7:13).

"Lose his own soul" (Matt. 16:26; see Matt. 19:23).

"Eternal punishment" (Matt. 25:46, RV).

"Outer darkness" (Matt. 8:12; 22:13; 25:30).

"Unquenchable fire" (Mark 9:43, 44).

"Wailing and gnashing of teeth" (Matt. 13:42, 50).

"Thy whole body cast into hell" (Matt. 5:29–30).

"Everlasting fire" (Matt. 25:41, 46).

"Where their worm dieth not, and the fire is not quenched" (Mark 9:46–48).

"Eternal sin" (Mark 3:29, rv).

Yet, speaking so faithfully of the reality, the fearfulness, the eternity of God's just retribution, Jesus always displayed his matchless love and his unlimited grace, for it was the contemplation of the sinner's doom that caused his tears. Can you not hear the sob of unwanted love in his plea, "How often would I have gathered thy children together as a hen doth gather her brood under her wings, *and ye would not*" (Luke 13:34, 35; see Luke 19:41).

It is not generally realized that Jesus spoke more frequently of the place of woe than of the abode of eternal peace. His most graphic and detailed representation of the place, originally prepared for the Devil and his angels, is the illustration he used for the rich man and Lazarus. The rich man is tormented in hell's flame, not because he was rich, but because his soul's deepest interests were neglected. He prays in agony for a drop of water to cool his tongue, but his suffering and despair are increased tenfold by the sight of the felicity of the beggar whom he had despised and neglected, now at a heavenly banquet, and also by the fact that a great gulf is *fixed* between paradise and perdition. There was no purgatory in which

the rich man could cleanse himself of his sins and
errors and then recline on Abraham's bosom.
Hell, as we understand it from the teaching
of Jesus, means eternal separation from God.
R. Southwell gave us these lines:

> The Lazar pined while Dives' feast was kept,
> Yet he to Heaven—to Hell did Dives go;
> We trample grass, and prize the flowers of May,
> Yet grass is green when flowers do fade away.

What must be borne in mind is that God is not
willing that any should perish but that *all* should
come to repentance (2 Pet. 3:9) and, therefore,
never sends sinners to hell. The eternal punishment of the wicked is not arbitrarily imposed by
God but is the inevitable outcome of sin itself—
the confirmation of sinners in their own self-cho-
sen course, being left by God to reap the full, dire
consequences of sin. Having persistently separated themselves from God, sinners, dying in
their sin, banish themselves from his presence and
abandon themselves to reap the full harvest of
their own evil character and of their rejection of
Calvary's provision for their sin. "God willeth that
all men should be saved" (1 Tim. 2:4, RV), but to
the wicked, Jesus was obliged to say, "Ye *will not
come* to me that ye might have life" (John 5:40; see
John 3:19). Although he was the Son of God, with
power, Jesus never compelled submission. "If any
man will." Because he died that men might be
forgiven all their sin, Jesus gives to men not *a*
chance, but *every* chance to accept his gift of eternal life.

Dr. James Orr's article on Christ in the *Interna-*

tional Standard Bible Encyclopedia reminds us that it adds to the terribleness of the sayings of Jesus about hell when we remember that "there is nothing to put against them; no hint or indication of the termination of the doom. Why did Jesus not safeguard his words from misapprehension, if behind them there lay an assurance of restoration and mercy after the grave? No, when Jesus used the term *eternal* whether of eternal life or eternal damnation, he meant a finality of state. When some men fail to reconcile the Saviour's love with his doctrine of Hell, they drop one of them—Hell. But he who taught—'God so loved the World,' also declared that if men fail to believe in his bountiful provision for their sin then they must *perish*, which means, not annihilation, but eternal banishment from his presence, John 3:16."

If ours is the obligation of preaching the *Woes* of Scripture as well as its *Blesseds*, when it comes to warning sinners to flee from the wrath to come, may it be with tears in our voice. This was how Paul preached (Phil. 3:18). May compassion of heart and tone be ours as we warn the sinner of the peril of being forever lost!

> Come, O my soul, thy certain ruin trace,
> If thou neglect thy Saviour's proffered grace;
> Infinite years in torment must I spend,
> Which never, never has an end.
> Yea, I must dwell in torturing despair,
> As many years as atoms in the air;
> When these are past, as many more
> As grains of sand upon the ocean floor.
> When these are gone, as many yet behind
> As forest leaves as shaken in the wind.

When these are o'er, as many to ensue
As blades of grass or drops of morning dew.
When all these doleful years are spent in pain,
And multiplied by myriads again,
Till numbers drown the thought, could I suppose
That then my wretched years were at a close
It would afford a hope, but O, I quiver
To think upon those dreadful words—
Forever and Forever.

BIBLE STUDY QUESTIONS

Take time to turn to each Scripture reference and mark the verse or a portion in your Bible.

1. How did Jesus describe the reality of hell.
2. Who is responsible for banishment from the presence of God?

— 31 —

The Kingdom

At the outset of our study, when dealing with the Master himself, we touched briefly upon the point that Jesus cannot be separated from what he taught, that he was the living embodiment of the topics he enunciated. The person and proclamations of Jesus are inseparable. His words were the expressed essence of his person; the person, the cause or source of the words. But the person is the greater; the cause must ever transcend the effect, the thinker be more and mightier than his thoughts. Without Jesus, the teaching of Jesus had been comparatively impotent. If his sayings had fallen from heaven like the great Ephesian goddess, they had never made for a man a new faith and a diviner religion. The truths his words embodied, his person incarnated, and without the life lived the words preached would have been spoken into the air.

His life and lips were ever in unison. He not only uttered unique truths, he was, in himself, *the Truth*. Jesus incarnated the truth and found the ultimate for his preaching in the personal experience, exalted and vitalized by his own presence. When Jesus declared his offer of freedom, he emphasized appropriated and experimental truths as the foundation of character. Thus, his counsels were never contrary to his conduct. Both, like the robe he daily wore, were seamless. It is with this characteristic feature of the life of Jesus that we approach his teaching about the *kingdom*.

While, as we shall presently see, he proclaimed many aspects of the kingdom of God, the great truth is that he himself personalized such a kingdom. His very being made the kingdom. As Bishop Gore states, "The whole sustenance of the teaching of Jesus was *The Gospel of the Kingdom* as having now come upon men *in* His person." He was the incarnation of all the kingdom represented, as some of his utterances declare. Dr. A. R. Bond says in *The Master Preacher:*

> His preaching radiated from himself. What he would be and do in the history of men constituted His message. This was His prerogative—
> declared by his words,
> confirmed by his deeds, and
> redeemed in his post-resurrection effects upon men.

Professor A. M. Fairbairn stresses, in *Studies in the Life of Christ,* that the preeminence and uniqueness of Jesus as a teacher is proven by the fact that the teacher made the truth he taught.

> His teaching was His articulated person, His person His incorporated teaching. The divinity of the one expressed the other embodied. He came to found a kingdom by manifesting His kinghood, by declaring

Himself a King. The King was the centre round which the kingdom crystallized ... He knew that He was true and His word true.... His word is imperishable—will outlast heaven and earth.

When, for instance, Jesus cast out a demon from the blind and dumb man and the Pharisees charged him with being in league with the prince of demons, he declared the divine source of power over evil spirits: "If I cast out demons by the Spirit of God, then the kingdom of God is come unto you" (Matt. 12:28). Here the personal *I* and the *kingdom of God* are equivalent terms for Jesus; thus in him the rule of God must reside. Then again there is his declaration when dealing with the spiritual aspect of the kingdom: "Behold, the kingdom of God is within you" (Luke 17:21). The words *within you* should read *in the midst of you*, as the Revised Version margin has it. Jesus, who was in the midst of the Pharisees, was the epitome of the kingdom. As the Messiah, he came without great pomp and splendor and was now among the people. Ultimately the kingdom *will* come with outward glory, but already in the persons of the king and his disciples the kingdom was present.

Kingdom implies a king, and we must therefore understand what qualities the terms *kingdom of God, kingdom of heaven* signify. In our Lord's constant use of these phrases, *kingdom* is the cardinal word and can only be interpreted through its cardinal idea, king. The kingdom did not make the King, but the King the kingdom. In any nation where royalty reigns, the nature of the king determines the character of the kingdom. The reign of Jesus was by divine ideals, by his truths, believed and loved. This was why those who entered the kingdom by his invitation came to believe that such ideals and truths were personalized in him— which brings us to the fact of messianic consciousness.

Coming as the king eternal, Jesus was born king (Matt. 2:2), acclaimed king by God (Ps. 2:6), and affirmed his kingship (Luke 23:1–4). More than once the popular enthusiasm would have crowned him king, but his masterful mind avoided the crisis even although deep in his own consciousness he knew himself to be the Messiah of his people under whose kingship the highest good of man was to be enjoyed. Although it seemed as if he also died as king, seeing they wrote the title over his cross, Jesus missed being the King of the Jews in order that he might be the King of kings and the Lord of lords. One wonders, however, what would have happened if he had ascended the throne of the country and thence ruled the world. What we do know is that the world missed an incomparable splendor when, instead of hailing Jesus of Nazareth as King of the Jews, the inhabitants of Jerusalem cried out, *Crucify him.* When they crucified him as king, the kingdom in all its fullness as envisaged in the prayer, "thy kingdom come," was held in abeyance. Since then he has been gathering out of the world a redeemed people for his name.

Before we come to examine the nature of the various aspects of the kingdom as suggested by the description given it, it may prove interesting to tabulate the frequency of references to the kingdom in the Gospels. George Jackson in *The Teaching of Jesus* says:

> The idea as set forth in the Gospels is so complex, the phrase, 'The Kingdom' is used to cover so many and difficult conceptions, that it is practically impossible to frame a definition within which all the sayings of Jesus concerning the Kingdom can be included.

Next to the sacred name *Father*, no word was more often on the lips of Jesus than *kingdom*. This simple word, or with *his*, *my*, or *thy* attached, occurs in the Gospels between thirty and forty times. The expression *kingdom* occurs some one hundred twenty times and represents about thirty occasions distributed through all periods of the ministry of Jesus and proves that what it stands for is of major importance. There is no record of his use of the term after his resurrection. It was, however, the most frequent topic during his period of preaching and teaching. The phrase "the kingdom of God" occurs some fifty to sixty times. "The kingdom of heaven" is Matthew's favorite term and is found only in his Gospel some thirty-three times. The only term Mark uses is "the kingdom of God," which he employs fifteen times. Luke only uses "the Kingdom of God," mentioning it thirty-one times. John has only two references to the same phrase (John 3:3, 5) but has, as its equivalent as a state of spiritual blessing, "eternal life," which describes the final condition of redeemed man in the kingdom of God (Matt. 24:46; Mark 10:17, 30; Luke 10:25).

Then attention can be drawn to the teaching of Jesus in the kingdom parables, found principally in Matthew 13. (See *All the Parables of the Bible* by this writer.) As to the thirty-four parables of Jesus, they are classified according to a central thought, as Dr. A. R. Bond explains:

These parables divide equally into those whose central thought is that of the kingdom of God and that of personal experience. For Jesus this kingdom filled a large place in preaching and thought. The parables of the kingdom are placed by records first and last in Jesus' ministry.

Five parables describe the beginnings of the kingdom, whose value should justify any sacrifice, but may be disregarded and its benefits may pass to aliens to Israel.

The growth and principles of the kingdom are outlined in five parables, two of which are repeated.

The remaining seven forecast the consummation of the kingdom. As for the Parables of personal experience, these show that the Preacher must not forget the needs of the single heart, even although a Kingdom filled His vision and He should be its King. These occupy the middle part of His ministry.

Bible teachers differ as to whether terms like *the kingdom, the kingdom of God,* and *the kingdom of heaven* are used interchangeably or are synonymous. Some affirm that they stand as different spiritual ideas, while others affirm that they mean the same thing since in thirteen passages in which Matthew employs the term *the kingdom of heaven,* parallel passages in Mark and Luke use the expression *the kingdom of God.* Dr. W. Graham Scroggie points out in *A Guide to the Gospels:*

The word *Church* occurs only 3 times in the Gospels, Matt. 16:18; 18:17, and 68 times in the Epistles; and the terms Kingdom and Kingdom of God occur 18 times in the Epistles, and over 120 times in the Gospels. Clearly, then, the terms are not to be regarded as synonymous. The Church is in the Kingdom of God, but is not that Kingdom. 'The Kingdom of the Son of his love,' is part of the Kingdom of God, Col. 1:13.

Says Bishop Gore: "If the Church was not to be in the full sense the Kingdom, it was at least to be its vestibule, and its representative on earth."

The reader is referred to the extensive coverage Fairbairn gives to the radically dissimilar concepts of the *kingdom* and the *church* in his most valuable work, *Studies in the Life of Christ*. This evangelical theologian conclusively proves that there may be many churches, but only one kingdom; that the kingdom created the church, not the church the kingdom; that of the kingdom, Jesus never ceased to speak, but of the church, he only spoke twice; that the church denotes a structure, a body, a building, but the kingdom does not; that the church exists for the sake of the kingdom, the purpose of the church being to magnify its creator, enlarge the kingdom, promote its extensive and intensive growth; that Christ lives in the church, in and by it reigns that he may put all his enemies under his feet and usher in the time when the kingdom shall be delivered up to God, even the Father, that he may be all in all.

We now come to formulate the distinctive qualities, aspects, and relations of the kingdom as suggested by the various ways it is described in the Gospels.

THE KINGDOM WAS ORIGINAL
AND DISTINCTIVE

Reporting on the first Galilean ministry of Jesus, Mark says that "he came into Galilee, preaching the gospel of the kingdom" (Mark 1:14, 15). As *gospel* means "Good News," the divine herald appeared with a distinctive message of great joy for those who had been bound under satanic dominion. Out of sin had come ruin to the single soul and the collective society, and Jesus was to reveal how his kingdom would destroy the empire of sin both in the individual and in the race. Thus he appeared as the king, and throughout his great yet brief career was conspicuous as the preacher of "the kingdom of God." The kindred term "the kingdom of heaven," most frequent on his lips, reveals that he had penetrated its meaning and knew what he had come to do. When he went forth in his fresh and glorious manhood, his first words, "the gospel of the kingdom," unfolded his mission, expressed his aim, embodied his grand objective.

Old Testament prophets forecast a divine kingdom when ultimately God would establish in undisputed sovereignty his justice and mercy and truth on earth. Their dominant aim was to proclaim the certainty that, although God was content age after age to allow the rebellious wills of men to usurp dominion in the world, and to seem to have unchecked progress, he must come into his own at last. Israel was at first a *theocracy*, being governed directly by God but desiring to be a kingdom like surrounding heathen kingdoms became a *monarchy*, with Saul as her first king. The Spirit-inspired Daniel, and therefore, the far-seeing prophet could look down the vista of the ages and predict the time when "the God of heaven would set up an everlasting kingdom, in which all dominions would serve and obey him" (Dan. 2:34-36, 44; 7:23-27).

But when John the Baptist came as the voice crying in the wilderness, the substance of his preaching was, "Repent ye, for the kingdom of heaven is *at hand*"—not far away, but *near*, or about to be revealed, as it was in the Messiah for whom John prepared the way (Matt. 3:1-3). What, therefore, is original and distinctive about kingdom-truth in the Gospels is the advent of the long-expected new theocracy in which a divine ruler himself would fulfill dreams of a blessed empire of God on earth. The coming of such a kingdom involved, of course, the presence of the king, and Jesus was born as such. The tragedy is that John had to say of the one whose forerunner he was, "There standeth one among you, whom ye know not" (John 1:26, 27) Jesus was the king in disguise.

In order to understand the Master's own revelation of what he meant by the kingdom, it is necessary to consider his individual varied and many-featured presentation of it. His formula for his glorious conception of the rule of God was made up of two phrases of which Fairbairn says, "The phrases were Hebrew, the ideas were Christian. The old terms, transfigured and made radiant with a meaning high as heaven, vast as the universe, inexhaustible as eternity" were *the kingdom of heaven* and *the kingdom of God*.

While we are apt to think of these definitions as

being equivalent, seeing that God's throne is depicted in heaven, there is a difference between the two. It was Jesus who changed the phraseology of *kingdom of God* into *kingdom of heaven,* emphasizing thereby that the kingdom he declared was not of this world at all, an aspect John the Baptist had failed to grasp (Matt. 11:11–13; John 18:36).

The kingdom of God implies that its divine origin and aim proceeds from God that it may fulfill God's ends. The authority of the kingdom is God's, not man's, and its laws are divine, administered from divine presence though obeyed on earth. This aspect of the kingdom contrasts to the kingdom of evil, or Satan, the great empire of anarchy and darkness, creative of misery and death to man. God, through his rule, silently changed man from ill to good, from chaos to order, as well as the world in which he lives.

The gospel of the kingdom Jesus preached emphasized the truth that God has no respect for persons and was a gospel preeminently for the poor and the oppressed. It was "offensive" first of all to the rich and to the highest respected leaders of religion and generally to the privileged classes and their adherents. As for the kingship of Jesus, it was evidenced by his power over diseases and over the spirits of evil. Israel looked for "the kingdom," but the type the people thought of was emancipation from the Romans, a palace and court of their own, of influence and predominance among the nations. Jesus, however, laid the emphasis on *of* God, indicating a kingdom in which the will of God was being done on earth as it is done in heaven. As James Stalker states it in

The Ethic of Jesus, "God is the King of the Kingdom of God, and the Son of God is His viceregent; and without the love of God the Father and
the grace of the Lord Jesus Christ no progress can
be made with the Christianization of the world."

Further, the kingdom of God is distinguish-
able by the fact that it is universal, embracing all
moral intelligences willingly subject to the will of
God, whether angels, the church, or the saints of
past or future dispensations (Luke 13:28, 29;
Heb. 12:22, 23). In his teaching Jesus had much
to say about those who could enter or be excluded
from the kingdom he broadened out into "the
kingdom of God and his righteousness" (see Matt.
21:31, 43). *Righteousness* is a qualifying term describing the nature of the *kingdom.* It creates and
requires righteousness in all its subjects. To seek it
is to seek divine righteousness. Where this righteousness is real, the kingdom is realized (Matt.
5:19, 20; 6:33).

The kingdom of heaven, literally "of the heavens,"
is a phrase peculiar to Matthew and signifies the
messianic earth rule of Jesus Christ, the Son of
David. It is called the kingdom of the heavens
because it is the rule of the heavens over the earth
(Matt. 6:10). The gospel of the kingdom of
heaven was not that of Judaism—so much merit,
so much reward. The heavenly rule of God rules
out all murmuring and cavilling about rate of pay,
as is vividly contrasted for us by Jesus in the parable of the laborers (Matt. 19:30–20:16). The frequency with which Matthew uses the expression
the kingdom of heaven implies that it was the more
familiar term used among Jews. And as the fa-

vorite phrase of Jesus it conserved the best in the messianic hope of his nation and implies that the kingdom came from heaven, was heavenly in character and influence, and is to be consummated in heaven. This is why many of the parables of Jesus begin with the phrase, "The kingdom of heaven is like."

As the kingdom is *of heaven*, it stands opposed to the kingdoms of earth Satan offered Jesus when he tempted him. Great world empires live and rule by the strength of their armies, but the empire of heaven conquers by sacrificial love and seeks to restore on earth an obedience making men as happy and harmonious as heaven. Empires of earth in means and ends, in principles and practice, are far from being heavenly in character. The Lord from heaven, preaching "the gospel of the kingdom of heaven," determined the character of the kingdom, namely, a holy and joyful province of the heavenly Father's empire on earth. Jesus knew that where the will of God is fulfilled among the children of men, there is heaven upon earth. Distinguished according to their meaning then, "The kingdom of heaven indicates the nature and character of the new kingdom Jesus came to establish: and the kingdom of God is its origin and end."

THE KINGDOM WAS MORAL AND SPIRITUAL, NOT POLITICAL

"Comprehensively," says Dr. Graham Scroggie, "the Kingdom is a spiritual commonwealth embracing all who do God's will." The spiritual characteristics of the kingdom are set forth in the nine Beatitudes Jesus expounded at the outset of his Sermon on the Mount (Matt. 5:1–12) and also explicitly by Paul when he informs us that "the kingdom of God is not meat and drink but righteousness and peace and joy in the Holy Spirit" (Rom. 14:17). As the Messiah, the kingdom of God was the realm in which he was to exercise sovereignty, and he habitually made use of the phrase to describe succinctly all the moral blessings which he came to bestow. In his teaching Jesus is to be seen substituting for the political conception the idea of the kingdom which was spiritual in its nature and by consequence universal with its essentially spiritual character revealed in the nature of the blessings it brings. The best half of the parables of Jesus indicate the spiritual nature, principles, growth, and consummation of the kingdom. Stalker, in *The Ethic of Jesus*, reminds us that "Wherever, in a nation or a home, or a heart, the will of God is done, there the kingdom of God exists, and this is something which never grows old." This is why it is referred to as his *kingdom of grace* and his *kingdom of power* and his *kingdom of glory*—phrases stressing the essential spirituality of the kingdom which is its power and glory. "The spiritual far surpasses the material in value, just as the glory of the spiritual far transcends the glory of material kingdoms." Yet the kingdom has its social aspects (Matt. 20:25–28).

How slow we are to learn that every time we obey the divine will by showing kindness, generosity, purity, truth, honesty, or forgiveness, we bring God's kingdom a little nearer. When those around see the individual and general spiritual benefits God's rule brings, they will desire to be subject to that rule themselves (1 Pet. 2:9). As we shall presently indicate, as a spiritual state, his kingdom, which is not of this world, can only be entered into by repentance and faith. To Jesus, then, the kingdom meant his messianic reign in the heart and life of the believer. While not political in structure, the kingdom of heaven can yet influence, purify, and ennoble the politics of any nation. Wherever Jesus is known and obeyed, he reigns, and the kingdom he had much to speak about is realized. The sovereignty of God, exercised through his Son who came as his king, is limited to spiritual force. Political kingdoms represent social prestige, preferment through favoritism, and territorial boundaries, but his kingdom is totally different. As A. R. Bond says, "Whatever externals of land, property, or power might come into relationship with this Kingdom would be considered as correlative benefits and not as constituent elements."

THE KINGDOM IS INVISIBLE AND ETERNAL

Jesus taught that "the kingdom of heaven cometh not with observation" or with the outward show characterizing the growth of earthly kingdoms (Luke 17:20, 21; Matt. 13:31–33). This constitutes the teaching of some of the parables. The *leaven* works till the whole is leavened; the uneasy process is over and the result achieved. In the *seed*, which grows while the farmer sleeps and rises, day and night, the development is more quietly still. The blade silently grows just as the ear forms on the blade, and the seed grows in the ear; and the end is reached. The growth is unconscious, silent, mysterious, and progressive. Its intensive is as silent as its expansive action (Mark 4:26–29). Yet there may be occasions when the reality of God's kingdom in a life comes like a lightning flash—sudden, illuminative, and decisive (Matt. 11:27).

At all times, however, it comes without observation or ostentation. "So quietly it comes," says T. R. Glover in *The Jesus of History*, "that we may not guess how in any particular instance the realization of God came to a soul; but, if we are candid and truth-loving we can know it when it has come to ourselves, and we can recognize it when it comes to another." Although the kingdom is unrecognized, it is yet present, "with you," an already existing reality, but none the less real because unseen or undiscovered by the very men who professed to be looking for it. Yet invisible as it is, it is not ethereal, but very real and an everlasting kingdom enduring throughout all generations. Heaven and earth may perish, but because it is "of God" and "of heaven," it must forevermore endure.

THE KINGDOM IS UNIVERSAL IN SCOPE AND DESIGN

If the divine kingdom had had a parochial or national boundary, the servants of Jesus would have fought for its limited sovereignty (John

18:36). But his kingdom was not of this world, or like it, with its separate kingdoms. "It is expansive, has an extensive and intensive growth, can have its dominion extended and its authority more perfectly recognized and obeyed." Unseen, it is yet actual, and having come in the person of the king, it is always coming and because of its continuous process will expand until the kingdoms of the world become the world-kingdom of the Christ-King (Matt. 6:10; 21:42–44).

In the mind of the ancient Jew, the conception of Messiah's reign was a narrow national one, with the supremacy of Judaism over the haughty Roman, the cultured Greek, and the rude barbarians. Although the Messiah would be a greater king than David or Solomon, his sway would yet be limited. The true prophetical ideal, however, was that of a universal kingdom, and it is this universality that is endorsed and emphasized in Jesus' teaching (Isa. 11:10; Dan. 7:13, 14; Matt. 8:11). In his Great Commission, Jesus stressed the universal sovereignty he claims over all men (Matt. 28:19; Acts 1:8). The Savior's kingdom, therefore, cannot be bounded by earthly limits, and all attempts to map it out according to human rules imply a failure to recognize the true scriptural idea of its universality. Paul affirms that Jesus is king of the universe—"Head over *all* things" (Eph. 1:22; Col. 1:18). Unworldly in origin, and universal in scope, and headed up in the king eternal, the kingdom cannot be propagated by worldly means, and the nonuse of worldly means declares it to be of an unworldly universal and eternal character.

THE KINGDOM CAN ONLY BE ENTERED
BY RELATIONSHIP

If we do not belong to the king, we cannot have any share in his kingdom, which can only transform those who are willing to enter it. Jesus made it very clear in his teaching that it is only by the kingdom's entrance into man and his entrance into it by regeneration and humility that he can become a new citizen of a new, heavenly state (Matt. 18:1–4; Luke 18:17; John 3:3–7). Both John and Jesus insisted on repentance as a preparation for admission into the kingdom. This was the very first word of the preaching of Jesus, and it is a word which has never disappeared. According to his mind, entrance can only be found through a strait gate, but which, although narrow, admitting only one at a time, never excludes any child of Adam who is willing to repent.

A person can live in any kingdom at all on earth and yet be a citizen of the kingdom of heaven if the king reigns in the heart -the heart he alone can create and maintain. His rule in the heart implies, in the first place, a personal experience, a secret blessedness, a spiritual discovery, filling the soul with a joy which suffuses life with color and warmth; and, then, in the second place, is a glorious brotherhood and league of endeavor and victory. Participation in the kingdom of God is impossible with an unequivocal decision, namely surrender to the claims of the king himself and complete obedience to his will (Matt. 7:21). Nicodemus was amazed by the announcement of Jesus that apart from regeneration no one can enter the kingdom. Such condition at once explains the nature of the kingdom and is explained by it. The kingdom is a kingdom of the Holy Spirit, and the birth into it is a spiritual birth, an effect whose cause is the ubiquitous, silently ever-operating Divine Spirit, whose historical symbol or expression is *The Water* that purifies and renews.

Regeneration, then, and faith in Christ himself form the entrance requirements (John 3:1–16). The two things he impressed upon the mind of Nicodemus in relation to the kingdom of God that are impossible to the unregenerate were that they cannot *see* the kingdom and that they *cannot* enter it (John 3:3–5). Having taught men to seek the kingdom, Jesus here teaches how it can be entered. The new birth is the gateway of his kingdom, and therefore all who seek it must seek to know what it is to be born again, or born from above. A man may be a member of a church or preach in its pulpit without being born again, but he cannot be a citizen of the heavenly realm without being born again. The divine command has never been abrogated, "Except a man be born again, he *cannot* see the kingdom of God."

There was the occasion when the disciples disputed among themselves as to which of them should be the greatest in the kingdom of heaven, and, calling a child to him, Jesus sat him in their midst and said, "Verily I say unto you, Except ye be converted and become as little children, *ye shall not* enter into the kingdom of heaven" (Matt. 18:1–3). Here, again, the necessity of a change of man's heart, by repentance and conversion, is emphasized by Jesus. By humility, repentance, regeneration, and faith man enters the kingdom of grace. The religious leaders of the people received the stark authoritative announcement from the lips of Jesus that publicans and harlots would, because of their repentance and faith, enter the kingdom of God, but they themselves, because of their unrepentant hearts, would be excluded (Matt. 21:31, 43; see Gal. 5:19–21).

The term *conversion*, as used by Jesus, means "turning," and he speaks as if two turnings are necessary for our place in the kingdom, namely, the first conversion, *backward*, of the man into a child, and then a second conversion, *forward*, of the childlike man into a Christian.

Further, because the kingdom of heaven is without local or national character, it can have subjects anywhere. None are included because they are Jews, or excluded simply because they are Gentiles. Wherever and however men are made conscious of their lost estate, repent of their sins, manifest the spiritual quality of childlikeness, and are translated by faith into "the kingdom of his dear Son," immediately they are made possessors and heirs, or as Paul reminds us joint-heirs, with Christ (Rom. 8:17), with all the glorious inheritance at their disposal (1 Pet. 1:4).

THE KINGDOM IS PRESENT YET FUTURE

Universal and individual, seen yet unseen, heavenly yet earthly, the kingdom of God is also present yet future, as the two phrases in the Lord's

Prayer indicate—"Thine is the kingdom," "Thy kingdom come" (Matt. 6:10, 13).

Commencing with the coming of the king, continuing to expand through the centuries since his advent, the kingdom will reach its consummation "when the people are gathered together, and the kingdoms to serve the Lord" (Ps. 102:22). When he returns to earth, he will take unto himself his great power and reign and, as the King of kings, transform the kingdoms of this world into his own world-kingdom and finally deliver up the kingdom to God (1 Cor. 15:24, 25; Rev. 11:15, 17; 19:11–16; Dan. 7:14). Johannes Schneider says that Jesus spoke of the kingdom of God in three ways:

1. As the future kingdom that God would bring about at a time concealed from men;
2. As the kingdom that was already a present reality in the ministry of Jesus;
3. As the power of almighty God, increasingly apparent, that lays hold of men and moulds their whole existence.

With the inception of the kingdom, Jesus made it clear by sayings and symbols that all who would share in it must face the stern requirements that come with total commitment. Demand was made —and still is—for unconditional surrender of heart and the willingness to count the cost (Matt. 18:9; Luke 13:24; 14:28). But open attachment to the king and unfailing obedience to his commands only attract a minority—"the little flock"—and for such it is the Father's good pleasure to give them the kingdom (Luke 12:32). Jesus came preaching the good tidings of the kingdom, which actually among men, in his own person, was evidenced by his power over diseases and demons. Yet Professor W. P. Patterson points out in *Christ and the Gospels:*

One of the difficulties of the subject is that in some passages Jesus speaks of the Kingdom as present, while in many others He speaks of it as future: and there has been a wide difference of opinion as to the relation of the two sets of utterances, and the importance to be attributed to the eschatological series.

That the kingdom was a present reality on earth was definitely taught by Jesus, who referred to his mighty works as proof (Matt. 12:28; Luke 10:9; 17:21). Parables, like that of the seed, growing secretly, clearly teach that the kingdom was then present in the world in small and lowly beginnings, which were to be succeeded by a process of wonderful growth and expansion. Once established and present, the great enemy of the kingdom, said Jesus, was the Devil who constantly seeks to destroy the principles of it sown in the hearts of men (Matt. 13:19). At all times, spiritual blessings are the chiefest (Matt. 5:8), and the transfiguration of the natural is suggested by Jesus in a significant particular (Mark 12:25).

As to the future of the kingdom, Jesus describes its consummation in a number of passages. All prophetic students are interested in those passages describing the establishment of the kingdom in the last days and in the sublime events by which it is to be ushered in and finalized (Matt. 5:20; 24; 25:34; Mark 14:62). With the setting up of the future kingdom of God, there will take place, as

Jesus taught, the judgment and final separation of the *good* from the *bad*, the *wheat* from the *tares* (Matt. 13:24, 30, 47). The prayer, "thy kingdom come," will be fully answered when the rule of God is established everywhere on earth (Rev. 11:15; 20:1–22:21). Today, God's will is not done on earth as it is in heaven, but when the king comes and ushers in his millennial reign, then it will be. Jesus proclaimed an end or climax to the world-order he introduced "in which God shall be all in all," says Bishop Gore, "but this final manifestation of judgment and justice He refused altogether to date." This we do know that all who are God's children through regeneration are to inherit the kingdom (Matt. 25:34).

> O King of Glory, King of Peace,
> Bid all these storms and tumults cease,
> Bring in Thy reign of righteousness:
> Thy Kingdom come.

The last and most moving mention of the kingdom of God in the four Gospels came, not from the life of Jesus, but from one of his cosufferers at Calvary. It was the dying thief who, repenting and confessing his sin, gave a marvelous expression to his childlike faith and trust in Jesus as he died. He prayed, "Jesus, Lord, remember me when thou comest into thy kingdom," and Jesus replied, "Today thou shalt be with me in paradise." Here we have the kingdom both as a present experience and a state of the future (Matt. 13:38–43; Dan 2:44; 2 Tim. 4:1). Throughout the New Testament the reality of Christ's coming kingship is stressed beyond all doubt. Every knee is to bow to

him in his eternal kingdom (Phil. 2:9–11; 2 Tim.
2:12; 4:18; 2 Pet. 1:11). What a time that will be
when we see him as "the ruler of the kings of the
earth," as "king of ages" (Rev. 1:5; 5:13), and
exercising universal dominion as "king of kings"
(Rev. 11:15; 17:14; 19:6).

As our conclusion to the absorbing study of him
whose very being made the kingdom and pervades it, we gratefully employ that which Professor Fairbairn has in his most comprehensive coverage of the kingdom of heaven in his *Studies in the
Life of Christ.* What a sublime, masterly tribute it
is!

The Kingdom, then, Christ instituted was sublime
and glorious enough. While it has only an ideal being, or being in the realm of the spirit, it is creative
of the best and noblest realities on earth. It has made
our churches, and inspired these to do every good
work they have accomplished. It is the spring, too, of
our philanthropies, our ambitions to be and to do
good. While it can be embodied in no institution, it
forms and animates every institution that promotes
the common weal. The state feels it in all its highest
legislation, aims, and endeavours. Art in all its
branches pulses with an enthusiasm it creates, is
charmed by the visions it sends, and fascinated by
ideals it raises, making our perfect seem imperfect
still. It is, too, the one power creative of righteousness. It seeks the good of the race by seeking the
good of all its individuals; blesses the masses through
the units that compose it. The rewards of the Kingdom are the virtues of the Kingdom, the holiness that
is happiness, the graces that adorn the saints of God.
While it lives He reigns, and while He reigns men
need fear no victory of evil, either over himself or his

kind, may rest assured that the Divine Father Who guides the world, will guide it, through its shadow as through its sunshine, to the calm and glory of an eternal day.

That Charles Wesley loved to rejoice in the triumph of his Lord as king is found in his stirring hymn, "Rejoice, the Lord Is King."

> His Kingdom cannot fail,
>   He rules o'er earth and heav'n;
> The keys of death and hell
> Are to our Jesus given:
> Lift up your heart, lift up your voice;
> Rejoice, again I say, Rejoice.

BIBLE STUDY QUESTIONS

Take time to turn to each Scripture reference and mark the verse or a portion in your Bible.

1. What place does the kingdom have in Jesus' teachings and in the Epistles?
2. What is the difference in kingdom of God and kingdom of heaven?
3. What are the bounds of the kingdom and how is it entered?
4. How is the kingdom present yet future?

— 32 —

The Second Coming

Closely allied to the theme of the kingdom is what the Master taught regarding his second coming, for when, according to his promise, he returns to translate his church to glory, events will accelerate until they culminate in the millennium when he will personally reign "where'er the sun, doth his successive journeys run." Then "every creature will rise and bring peculiar honors to our king." The future, near and far-off, loomed large in the teaching of Jesus. His eyes ever beheld the land of far distances. Priority, however, is given to what Jesus accomplished during his first coming since that forms the basis of all he will make us the recipients of at his second coming. "First of all . . . Christ died for our sins according to the Scriptures" (1 Cor. 15:1–3). Jesus himself declared that he came among men to give his life as a ransom for their sin.

Nothing that has happened in the long history of the world can compare to all that was involved in the incarnation, the great historic fact of tremendous significance upon which our Christian faith and hope rest. Next in importance is the teaching of Jesus in his predicted and promised return for his redeemed church and for his universal reign on earth as the king of nations. This is why his appearing is referred to as the *second coming,* the word *second* being used to differentiate between his coming in humility and glory as the King of kings. There are those, however, who quibble about the phrase, affirming that the Bible nowhere speaks of a *second* coming, but only of the *coming* or *presence,* because the event, being of great significance, stands by itself. But this contention is entirely wrong, for the Bible *does* use the word *second* in connection with Christ's return. "Christ was *once* offered to bear the sins of many; and unto them that look for him shall he appear the *second* time without sin unto salvation" (Heb. 9:28). The word *again* (John 14:3) surely means a second time!

Whenever Jesus dealt with the topic of eschatology, he knew what he was talking about and made the truth clear and plain, which is more than some theologians are able to do when they seek to expound what he taught. The hymn rebukes us by saying that "if our love were but more simple, we would take him at his word." In the four Gospels, Jesus approaches his return almost twenty times, the earliest reference being when he sent out the twelve to preach the gospel, saying, "Ye shall have not gone over the cities of Israel, till the Son of man be come" (Matt. 10:23). From then on, he gave promises concerning his return and made frequent predictions of events leading up to

and associated with such an event. In his last reference to his second coming before he died, he gave
his own the warning, "Watch therefore, for ye
know neither the day nor the hour wherein the
Son of man cometh" (Matt. 25:13). Jesus laid
great stress upon the duty of watchfulness in view
of his promised coming.

The Greek word for *coming* is *Parousia,* and
usually implies "arrival and presence." Some
verses give prominence to the period of time concept, and others, to the arrival aspect. This term
Parousia is also used to denote the coming or appearance of the Anti-Christ (2 Thess. 2:9). Another expression Paul uses is *Apokálupsis,* which
depicts Christ's appearance in majesty and glory,
his *uncovering of glory. Parousia* implying "presence"
as opposed to "absence" not only denotes the return of Jesus at the end of the Gentile age, but also
his promised return to take his own to be with him
where he presently is (John 14:1–4). And this
brings us to a consideration of what is actually
meant by the phrase *second coming.*

Within the general term *second coming* there are
many events which must be distinguished, otherwise confusion will reign—as alas! it does in the
minds of many who fail to separate aspects that
differ. It is, of course, best not to cloud the hope
of his coming with too detailed a theory as to what
will transpire when he returns. Probably there will
be those dear hearts who will be disappointed if
Jesus does not follow the schedule they have
clearly mapped out for him. On the other hand, it
is just as unwise not to study the various events
and say, "Well, he's coming again, and that's

enough for me." We are urged, are we not, to "rightly divide the word of truth" related to any Bible theme? Unprofitable speculation we shun, but a sane interpretation we welcome.

The reader will understand that for a complete exposition of *all* that is implied in the appearance of Jesus the second time it is necessary to trace such a glorious theme as a whole through the entire New Testament. But as we are confining ourselves in this book to what the Master taught, we are content to follow such. After all, he is the one who is coming, and his teaching on the subject is therefore supreme and authoritative. After his ascension, angels and apostles, under the inspiration of the Holy Spirit, expanded his unfolding of such a truth, even as he said the Spirit would do (John 16:12–15).

That the world owes much to the latest utterances of its eminent saints can be gathered from my work on *Last Words of Saints and Sinners*. While all the sayings of Jesus are of deepest importance and gather and grow in intensity as he nears his end, his later promises and predictions are most precious and of deepest importance. His person came into the foreground; he became the great theme of his farewell sayings. Somehow his consciousness grew more exalted as his way grew more troubled. The shadow that fell upon his spirit was marked by a correspondent change in his teaching. He became sadder, was in speech as in soul more the Man of Sorrows, despised and rejected of men. The gathering clouds, however, left his soul clear. The larger part of his great discourse of future events in connection with his coming again was given within a few days of his death (Matt. 25; 26:2). Taking John's Gospel, the public ministry of Jesus seems to end with the twelfth chapter. Thereafter, his last words were to his own (John 13:1). Knowing that his trial and crucifixion would stun his disciples almost out of their faith, he purposely dwelt on those truths that would realize their hopes of him in a far grander way than they had ever yet dreamed.

In his chapter "The Later Teaching" Fairbairn gives us a most heart-moving description of the peculiarities that distinguish the later teaching of Jesus. In fact, the paragraphs are without parallel in spiritual literature.

We can hardly approach the final words of Christ without reverence. As we study them we almost feel as if we were overhearing His speech, or looking into His spirit, or watching the ebb and flow of emotion on His wondrous face. . . His words have been a source of infinite wonder to the world, a kind of Divine heart and conscience in it. They are but few; we can read in an hour all of His thought that survives, which the forms of human art have created to clothe and immortalize the human spirit.

Nor was He careful to preserve them, wrote no word, commanded no word to be written; spoke, as it were, into the listening air the words it was to hear and preserve for all time. And speech thus spoken into the air has been like a sweet and subtle Divine essence in the heart of humanity. . . . Had the words of Christ vanished into silence, passed into the great halls of oblivion, or had they never been spoken, our world had been quite other than it is, and been far from as wise and good as it is now. So great and infinite in value have been those teachings, in quantity smallest of fragments, in quality greatest and most priceless of the treasures that have enriched the World.

By cataloguing a few of these final advent utterances we can discover the related events.

"I go to prepare a place for you, I will come again, and receive you unto myself" (John 14:3).

"I will not leave you comfortless: I will come to you" (John 14:18).

"When he comes in the glory of his Father with the holy angels" (Mark 8:38).

"They shall see the Son of man coming in a cloud with power and great glory" (Luke 21:27).

"As in the days of Lot . . . so shall it be in the day that the Son of man is revealed" (Luke 17:28–30).

"The Son of man shall come in the glory of his Father with his angels" (Matt. 16:27).

"As it was in the days of Noah, so shall the coming of the Son of man be" (Matt. 24:37).

"When the Son of man shall come in his glory, and all the holy angels with him" (Matt. 25:31).

When the hour dawns for Jesus to leave the Father's home on his triumphant journey back to earth, he will not descend all the way without a break. Two features or events are related to his coming, namely, the *reception of church* and the *reign of Christ,* with several events leading up to the latter aspect. We are cognizant of the fact that prophecy suffers many wounds in the house of its friends and that conflicting interpretations result in many leaving such an entrancing theme severely alone. Some there are, who clump all events together, making no distinction as to their nature or time. All recorded concerning the second coming will be fulfilled when Jesus appears as the august judge at the last judgment.

What Jesus promised his disciples about returning for and receiving them, however, is in a category of its own. If the language has any meaning then the phrase, "I will come again, and receive you unto myself," must imply a *personal* return for not only the disciples who listened to the tender words of Jesus, but for all believers. Those original believers formed the church in representation. There is to be an entrance for his church which he said he would build into an eternal communion with himself. There are those who make the promise of Jesus to mean either his coming in judgment upon Jerusalem in A.D. 70, or the coming of the Holy Spirit on the Day of Pentecost, or his coming at death to take the believer to be with himself. But I am simple enough to believe that when he said *I*, he meant himself.

RECEPTION OF CHURCH

To all who have received him as a personal Savior (John 1:12), he will receive unto himself when he appears the second time. This royal reception will take place on his way to take unto himself his power and reign. The testimony of the two heavenly visitants was that "This same Jesus, who is taken up from *you* into heaven, shall so come *in like manner* as *ye* have seen him go into heaven" (Acts 1:11). How did he go? In the presence of his own (Acts 1:9, 10). How will he return? In the same manner, or in the presence of his own. We differentiate between his coming *for* his church, and his coming *with* her.

Presently, we have the church triumphant in heaven and the church militant on earth. The former, Jesus will bring *with* him, while the latter —"we which are alive and remain"—will be immediately transformed and translated to meet the Lord with the glorified host in the air, to which Paul says we are to be "caught up" (1 Cor. 15:51, 52; 1 Thess. 4:13–18). Jesus said that his coming is to be heralded with "a great sound of a trumpet" (Matt. 24:31), and Paul repeats this expression, "the trumpet shall sound" (1 Cor. 15:52), and similarly as "the trump of God," for the assembly to himself of all the saints in glory, and the saints on earth, on a vast and mighty scale.

> Some from earth, from glory some,
> Severed only till He come.

As to the time of the rapture, Scripture is silent. Jesus may appear at any moment. He himself hinted that his return might be after a long time and seemed to suggest that it would be wise to prepare for a delay (Matt. 25:4, 19). Lest saints should lose hope through apparent tarrying, Peter reminds them that in the Lord's reckoning a thousand years are but a day (Ps. 90:4; 2 Pet. 3:8). What Paul calls "the blessed hope" he links to the commemoration of the Lord's Supper. "For as often as ye eat this bread, and drink this cup, ye do show the Lord's death *till he come*" (1 Cor. 11:26). John would have believers remember that when they ultimately see Jesus, they will be like him (1 John 3:1-3). The question is, Are we like him in character now? Does the prospect of seeing him at any moment exercise a sanctifying influence over the phase of our present life? Is ours

> . . . A life all lily-fair,
> And fragrant as the place
>   Where seraphs are?

Horatius Bonar, the Scottish saintly minister and poet who gave us many of our best hymns, firmly believed in the return of the Lord he dearly loved and preached and wrote about such a glorious event. He taught himself, however, to live constantly as one ready to hail his Lord's arrival. Retiring at night and drawing the curtains, he would repeat the words, "Perhaps tonight, Lord!" In the morning when he awoke and drew aside the curtains and looked out on another dawn, he would pray, "Perhaps today, Lord!" Can we say that this is our attitude?

> Some time, some ordinary day will come—
> A busy day like this—filled to the brim
> With ordinary tasks—perhaps so full
> That we have little thought or care for Him,
> And there will be no hint from the silent skies,
> No sign, no clash of cymbals, roll of drums;
> And yet that ordinary day will be
> The very day in which our Lord will come.

In a few of his parables, Jesus stressed the necessity of having his return uppermost in our thoughts. The parable of the faithful and wise servants is a discourse on watchfulness in view of his coming (Matt. 24:45-51). The parable of the ten virgins teaches the lesson of preparedness in preparation for his coming as the bridegroom (Matt. 25:1–13). The parable of the ten talents implies that service here below is a training for a more glorified form of service above (Matt. 25:14–30).

REIGN OF CHRIST

After our gathering together unto him, which is referred to as "the day of Christ," events move swiftly in connection with the coming of "the day of the Lord." The majority of our Lord's sayings about his second coming, spoken during his last days before his death, are associated with the great tribulation to follow the disappearance of the saints from earth at the rapture, with his judgment of the living nations, the inauguration of his millennial reign when for a thousand years he will rule without a rival, and with the final assize and the assignment of the Devil, of all satanic forces, and the wicked dead to eternal perdition.

In this terminus of a future and final catastrophe, Jesus himself is the judge, and no thought in his teaching is more frequent than this. Thus a marked feature in his solemn words about this concluding judgment is his phrase, "That day!" As this judgment is to be in "the presence of his angels," they will attend him as a king is surrounded by his courtiers and will assist him in his character as the viceregent of God. The angelic host gladly welcomed Jesus as he came to destroy the works of the Devil and now magnify him for his final triumph over him and his diabolical works. There is no more dreadful scene depicted in Scripture than that of the great white throne (Rev. 20:7–15).

If we are at the first judgment, the judgment seat of Christ for believers, and believers only, with its assessment of rewards and positions in future service (Rom. 14:10; 1 Cor. 3:12–15; 2 Cor. 5:10), then, bless God, we shall not be present at the final judgment with its ratification of condemnation already announced (John 3:18, 36). After the description of the new heaven and new earth, forming one of the most precious chapters in the Bible (Rev. 21), we have the concluding chapter of the Bible with its final invitations, warnings, and promises. In Revelation 22, Jesus returns to "the blessed hope" he promised his own when he said, "I will come again." Three times over we have Jesus saying, "Behold, I come quickly" (Rev. 22:7, 12, 20). In fact, we have the last fourfold testimony to his return in the chapter.

The Last Word of the Holy Spirit and the Glorified Church—"The Spirit and the Bride say, Come" (Rev. 22:17).

The Last Word of Jesus in Scripture—"Surely, I come quickly" (Rev. 22:20).

The Last Word of a Saint—"Even so, Come, Lord Jesus" (Rev. 22:20).

Hark! what a sound, and too divine for hearing,
    Stirs on the earth and trembles in the air!
Is it the thunder of the Lord's appearing?
    Is it the music of His people's prayer?
Surely He cometh and a thousand voices

Shout to the saints and to the deaf and dumb!
Surely He cometh, and the earth rejoices,
    Glad in His coming, Who hath sworn, *I Come!*

BIBLE STUDY QUESTIONS

*Take time to turn to each Scripture reference and
mark the verse or a portion in your Bible.*

1. How did Jesus emphasize his second coming?
2. What events are related to his second coming?
3. In what way did Jesus tell us to prepare for the
reception of the church?
4. What happens after the disappearance of the
church?

APPENDIX

EVERYTHING JESUS TAUGHT

THE DISCOURSE MATERIAL

1. Discourses

I. From Passover 27 A.D.

No.	Subject	Audience
1.	Regeneration	Nicodemus
2.	Worship and Salvation	Samaritan Woman
3.	Sowing and Harvest	Disciples

II. From December 27 A.D.

4.	Rejection	Public
5.	Fasting	Disciples and Others
6.	Relation to His Father	Public
7.	Sabbath Observance	Disciples and Others

III. From Early Summer 28 A.D.

8.	Sermon on the Mount	Public
9.	John and Suggested Topics	Public
10.	Forgiveness	Nondisciples
11.	Blasphemy	Public
12.	Signs	Public
13.	First Great Parable Group	Public
14.	Parables Explained and Given	Disciples
15.	Mission and Instruction of Twelve	Disciples
16.	Bread of Life	Public
17.	Traditions	Public

IV. From Passover 29 A.D.

18.	Church Rock	Disciples
19.	His Death and Resurrection	Disciples
20.	Humility and Forgiveness	Disciples
21.	Discussion at Feast	Public
22.	Light and Freedom	Public

to December 27 A.D.

Place	Matthew	Mark	Luke	John
Jerusalem				3:1–21
Near Sychar				4:5–26
Near Sychar				4:27–38

to Early Summer 28 A.D.

Nazareth			4:16–30	
Capernaum	9:14–17	2:18–22	5:33–39	
Jerusalem				5:19–47
To Galilee	12:1–8	2:23–28	6:1–5	

to Passover 29 A.D.

Near Capernaum	5–7		6:17–49	
Galilee	11:4–30		7:22–35	
Galilee			7:40–50	
Capernaum	12:25–37	3:23–30		
Capernaum	12:38–45			
Shore Galilee	13:1–33	4:1–32	8:4–18	
Capernaum	13:36–52			
Galilee	10:5–42	6:7–11	9:3–5	
Capernaum				6:26–65
Capernaum(?)	15:3–20	7 6–23		

to Autumn 29 A.D.

Caesarea Philippi	16:13–20	8:27–30	9:18–21	
Caesarea Philippi	16:21–28	8:31–9:1	9:22–27	
Capernaum	18:1–35	9:33–50	9:48–50	
Jerusalem				7:14–36
Jerusalem				8:12–58

V. From Autumn 29 A.D.

23.	Good Shepherd	Public
24.	Mission of Seventy	Disciples
25.	Eternal Life	Disciples and Others
26.	Prayer	Disciples
27.	League with Evil	Public
28.	Woes for Pharisees	Nondisciples
29.	Against Pharisaism	Public
30.	Repentance	Public
31.	Sabbath Observance	Public
32.	Messiahship	Public
33.	Salvation of Elect	Public
34.	Modesty in Feasts	Nondisciples
35.	Cost of Discipleship	Public
36.	Parables of Grace	Public
37.	Parables of Warning	Public
38.	Forgiveness and Faith	Public
39.	Coming Kingdom	Public
40.	Prayer of Pharisee and Publican	Public
41.	Divorce	Disciples and Others
42.	Rewards of Discipleship	Disciples and Others
43.	Parable of the Pounds	Disciples and Others

VI. During Passover 30 A.D.

44.	His Death and Glory	Public
45.	Belief and Unbelief	Public
46.	Authority Challenged	Public
47.	Three Jewish Questions	Public
48.	The Unanswerable Question	Public
49.	Denunciation of Pharisees	Public
50.	End of Jerusalem and World	Disciples
51.	Precedence in Kingdom	Disciples
52.	Humility	Disciples
53.	Memorial Supper	Disciples
54.	Farewell Discourse and Prayer	Disciples

to Spring 30 A.D.

Jerusalem			10:1–18
Probably Judea		10:1–24	
Probably Judea		10:25–37	
Probably Judea		11:1–13	
Probably Judea		11:14–36	
Probably Judea		11:37–54	
Probably Judea		12	
Probably Judea		13:1–9	
Probably Judea		13:10–21	
Jerusalem			10:22–38
Perea		13:22–30	
Perea		14:1–24	
Perea		14:25–35	
Perea		15	
Perea		16	
Perea		17:1–10	
Samaria or Galilee		17:20–18:8	
Samaria or Galilee		18:9–14	
Perea	19:3–12	10:2–12	
Perea	19:16–20:16	10:17–31	18:18–30
Jericho			19:11–27

Jerusalem			12:30–36
Jerusalem			12:44–50
Jerusalem	21:23–22:14	11:27–12:12	20:1–19
Jerusalem	22:15–33	12:13–27	20:20–40
Jerusalem	22:34–46	12:28–34	20:41–44
Jerusalem	23:1–39	12:38–40	20:45–47
Mt. Olivet	24:1–25:46	13:1–37	21:5–36
Jerusalem			22:24–30
Jerusalem			13:4–20
Jerusalem	26:26–29	14:22–25	22:19–20
Jerusalem			14–17

2. Fragmentary Sayings

I. From Passover 27 A.D. to December 27 A.D.

No.	Matthew	Mark	Luke	John
1.	3:15			
2.	4:4, 7, 10		4:4, 8, 12	
3.				1:38, 39, 42
4.				1:47, 48, 50, 51
5.				2:4, 7, 8
6.				2:16, 19
7.		1:15		

II. From December 27 A.D. to Early Summer 28 A.D.

No.	Matthew	Mark	Luke	John
8.				4:48, 50
9.	4:19	1:17	5:4, 10	
10.		1:25	4:35	
11.		1:38	4:43	
12.	9:2, 4–6	2:5, 8–11	5:20, 22–24	
13.	9:12, 13	2:14, 17	5:31, 32	
14.	12:11–13	3:3–5	6:8–10	

III. From Early Summer 28 A.D. to Passover 29 A.D.

No.	Matthew	Mark	Luke	John
15.	8:7, 10–13		7:9	
16.			7:13, 14	
17.	12:48–50	3:33–35	8:21	
18.	8:26	4:35, 39, 40	8:22, 25	
19.	8:32	5:8, 9	8:30, 39	
20.	9:22, 24	5:30, 34, 36, 39, 41	8:45, 46, 48, 50, 52, 54	
21.	9:28, 29, 30			
22.	13:57			
23.	14:16, 18	6:31, 37, 38	9:13, 14	6:5, 10, 12
24.	14:27, 31	6:50		6:20

IV. From Passover 29 A.D. to Autumn 29 A.D.

No.	Matthew	Mark	Luke	John
25.	15:24, 26, 28	7:27, 29		
26.		7:34		

27.	15:32, 34	8:2, 3, 5	
28.		8:26	
29.	17:17, 20	9:16, 19, 21, 23, 25, 29	9:41
30.	17:25–27		

V. From Autumn 29 A.D. to Spring 30 A.D.

31.			10:41, 42	
32.				9:3–7, 35, 37, 39, 41
33.				11:4, 7, 9–11, 14, 15
34.				11:23, 25, 26, 34, 39, 41–44
35.	19:14	10:14, 15	18:16, 17	
36.	20:18, 19	10:33, 34	18:29–33	
37.	20:21–23, 25–28	10:36, 38–40, 42–45		
38.	20:32	10:49, 51, 52	18:41, 42	
39.			19:5, 9, 10	

VI. During Passover 30 A.D.

40.	21:2, 3	11:2, 3	19:30, 31, 40, 42–44	
41.	21:19	11:14		
42.	21:13, 16	11:17	19:46	
43.	21:21, 22	11:22–25		
44.		12:43, 44	21:3, 4	
45.	24:2		21:6, 8, 9	
46.	26:2			
47.	26:10–13	14:6–9		12:7, 8
48.	26:36, 38–42, 45, 46	14:32, 35, 36–38, 41, 42	22:40, 42, 46	
49.	26:50, 52–55	14:48, 49	22:48, 51–53	11:5, 7, 8
50.				18:20, 21, 23
51.			23:3	18:34, 36, 37
52.	27:46	15:34	23:28–31, 34, 43, 46	19:26, 27, 28, 30

II. THE OLD TESTAMENT QUOTATIONS

1. Direct Quotations

I. From Passover 27 A.D. to December 27 A.D.

No.	Matthew	Mark	Luke	John	Passage Quoted
1.	4:4		4:4		Deut. 8:3
2.	4:7		4:12		Deut. 6:16
3.	4:10		4:8		Deut. 6:13

II. From December 27 A.D. to Early Summer 28 A.D.

No.	Matthew	Mark	Luke	John	Passage Quoted
4.			4:18, 19		Isa. 61:1, 2
5.	9:13				Hos. 6:6
6.	12:7				Hos. 6:6

III. From Early Summer 28 A.D. to Passover 29 A.D.

No.	Matthew	Mark	Luke	John	Passage Quoted
7.	5:21				Exod. 20:13; Deut. 5:17
8.	5:27				Exod. 20:14; Deut. 5:18
9.	5:31				Deut. 24:1
10.	5:33				Lev. 19:12; Num. 30:2; Deut. 23:21
11.	5:38				Exod. 21:24; Lev. 24:20; Deut. 19:21
12.	5:43				Deut. 23:6; 25:19
13.	5:43				Lev. 19:18
14.	11:10		7:27		Mal. 3:1
15.	13:14, 15				Isa. 6:9, 0
16.				6:45	Isa. 54:13
17.	15:4	7:10			Exod. 20:12; Deut. 5:16
18.	15:4	7:10			Exod. 21:17; Deut. 20:9
19.	15:8, 9	7:6, 7			Isa. 29:13

IV. From Passover 29 A.D. to Autumn 29 A.D.

V. From Autumn 29 A.D. to Spring 30 A.D.

No.	Matthew	Mark	Luke	John	Passage Quoted
20.				10:34	Ps. 82:6
21.	19:4	10:6			Gen. 1:27

540 EVERYTHING JESUS TAUGHT

2. Fragmentary Sayings

I. From Passover 27 A.D. to December 27 A.D.

No.	Matthew	Mark	Luke	John
1.	3:15			
2.	4:4, 7, 10		4:4, 8, 12	
3.				1:38, 39, 42
4.				1:47, 48, 50, 51
5.				2:4, 7, 8
6.				2:16, 19
7.		1:15		

II. From December 27 A.D. to Early Summer 28 A.D.

No.	Matthew	Mark	Luke	John
8.				4:48, 50
9.	4:19	1:17	5:4, 10	
10.		1:25	4:35	
11.		1:38	4:43	
12.	9:2, 4–6	2:5, 8–11	5:20, 22–24	
13.	9:12, 13	2:14, 17	5:31, 32	
14.	12:11–13	3:3–5	6:8–10	

III. From Early Summer 28 A.D. to Passover 29 A.D.

No.	Matthew	Mark	Luke	John
15.	8:7, 10–13		7:9	
16.			7:13, 14	
17.	12:48–50	3:33–35	8:21	
18.	8:26	4:35, 39, 40	8:22, 25	
19.	8:32	5:8, 9	8:30, 39	
20.	9:22, 24	5:29, 34, 36, 39, 41	8:45, 46, 48, 50, 52, 54	
21.	9:28, 29, 30			
22.	13:57			
23.	14:16, 18	6:31, 37, 38	9:13, 14	6:5, 10, 12
24.	14:27, 31	6:50		6:20

IV. From Passover 29 A.D. to Autumn 29 A.D.

No.	Matthew	Mark	Luke	John
25.	15:24, 26, 28	7:27, 29		
26.		7:34		

14.	Luke 11:31	1 Kings 10:1–3	Visit of Queen of Sheba to Solomon
		2 Chron. 9:1–8	
15.	Luke 11:32	Jon. 3:5–10	Repentance of Nineveh
16.	Luke 11:51	Gen. 4:8	The Blood of Abel
17.	Luke 11:51	2 Chron. 24:20	The Blood of Zechariah
18.	Luke 17:14	Lev. 13:49	Law for Cleansed Lepers
19.	Luke 17:26, 27	Gen. 7:7	Noah's Generation
20.	Luke 17:28, 29	Gen. 19:24	Sodom Destroyed
21.	Luke 17:32	Gen. 19:26	Lot's Wife
22.	Matt. 22:31, 32 Mark 12:26 Luke 20:37	Exod. 3:6	Moses and the Burning Bush
23.	Matt. 24:38, 39	Gen. 7:7	The Deluge and Noah's Generation

III. THE PARABLES

I. From Early Summer 28 A.D. to Passover 29 A.D.

No.	Matthew	Mark	Luke	Name	Place
1.	13:3–9, 18–23	4:1–9, 13–20	8:5–8, 11–15	The Sower	Galilee
2.	13:24–30, 36–43			The Tares	Galilee
3.		4:26–29		The Seed Growing	Galilee
4.	13:31, 32	4:30–32		The Mustard Seed	Galilee
5.	13:33			The Leaven	Galilee
6.	13:44			The Hidden Treasure	Capernaum
7.	13:45, 46			The Goodly Pearl	Capernaum
8.	13:47–50			The Net	Capernaum

II. From Passover 29 A.D. to Autumn 29 A.D.

No.	Matthew	Mark	Luke	Name	Place
9.	18:23–35			The Unmerciful Servant	Capernaum

III. From Autumn 29 A.D. to Spring 30 A.D.

No.	Matthew	Mark	Luke	Name	Place
10.			10:25–37	The Good Samaritan	Judea
11.			11:5–13	The Midnight Friend	Judea
12.			12:16–21	The Rich Fool	Judea
13.			12:35–40	The Watchful Servants	Judea
14.			13:6–9	The Barren Fig Tree	Judea
(4)			13:18, 19	The Mustard Seed	Judea
(5)			13:20, 21	The Leaven	Judea
15.			14:7–11	The Chief Seats	Perea
16.			14:16–24	The Great Supper	Perea

17.			14:25–30	The Rash Builder	Perea
18.			14:31–35	The Rash King	Perea
19.			15:3–7	The Lost Sheep	Perea
20.			15:8–10	The Lost Coin	Perea
21.			15:11–32	The Lost Son	Perea
22.			16:1–13	The Unrighteous Steward	Perea
23.			16:19–31	The Rich Man and Lazarus	Perea
24.			17:7–10	The Unprofitable Servants	Perea
25.			18:1–8	The Unrighteous Judge	Samaria or Galilee
26.			18:9–14	The Pharisee and the Publican	Samaria or Galilee
27.	20:1–16			The Laborers in the Vineyard	Perea
28.			19:11–27	The Pounds	Jericho

IV. During Passover 30 A.D.

29.	21:28–32			The Two Sons	Jerusalem
30.	21:33–44	12:1–11	20:9–18	The Wicked Husbandman	Jerusalem
31.	22:1–13			The Royal Marriage	Jerusalem
32.	24:32, 33	13:28, 29	21:29–31	The Fig Tree Leaving	Mt. Olivet
33.	25:1–13			The Ten Virgins	Mt. Olivet
34.	25:14–30			The Ten Talents	Mt. Olivet

EVERYTHING JESUS TAUGHT

IV. THE MIRACLES

I. From Passover 27 A.D.

No.	Matthew	Mark	Luke	John	Name
1.				2:1–11	Water Turned into Wine

II. From December 27 A.D.

No.	Matthew	Mark	Luke	John	Name
2.				4:46–54	Nobleman's Son
3.			5:1–11		Draught of fish
4.		1:21–28	4:31–37		Demoniac
5.	8:14, 15	1:29–31	4:38, 39		Peter's Mother-in-law
6.	8:2–4	1:40–45	5:12–16		Leper
7.	9:2–8	2:1–12	5:17–26		Paralytic
8.				5:2–18	Impotent Man
9.	12:9–14	3:1–6	6:6–11		Man with Withered Hand

III. From Early Summer 28 A.D.

No.	Matthew	Mark	Luke	John	Name
10.	8:5–13		7:2–10		Centurion's Servant
11.			7:11–17		Son of Widow of Nain
12.	12:22, 23				Blind-dumb Demoniac
13.	8:23–37	4:35–41	8:22–25		Stilling the Storm
14.	8:28–34	5:1–20	8:26–39		Two Demoniacs
15.	9:20–22	5:25–34	8:43–48		Woman with Issue of Blood
16.	9:18, 19, 23–26	5:22–24, 35–43	8:41, 42, 49–56		Daughter of Jairus
17.	9:27–31				Two Blind Men
18.	9:32–34				Dumb Demoniac
19.	14:13–23	6:30–46	9:10–17	6:1–15	Feeding the Five Thousand
20.	14:24–36	6:47–56		6:16–21	Walking on Water

to December 27 A.D.

Person	Disease	Method	Place	Location
			House	Cana

to Early Summer 28 A.D.

Person	Disease	Method	Place	Location
Boy	Fever	Word	Open-air	Cana
			Open-air	Sea of Galilee
Man	Demon	Word	Synagogue	Capernaum
Woman	Fever	Touch	House	Capernaum
Man	Leprosy	Touch	Open-air	Capernaum
Man	Paralysis	Word	House	Capernaum
Man	Impotency	Word	Open-air	Jerusalem
Man	Paralysis	Word	Synagogue	Capernaum

to Passover 29 A.D.

Person	Disease	Method	Place	Location
Man	Palsy	Word	Open-air	Capernaum
Man	Death	Touch	Open-air	Near Nain
Man	Demon	Word	House	Capernaum
Men	Demon	Word	Open-air	Gadara
Woman	Blood Issue	Touch	Open-air	Capernaum
Girl	Death	Touch	House	Capernaum
Men	Blindness	Word	Open-air	Capernaum
Man	Demon	Word	Open-air	Capernaum
			Open-air	Decapolis
			Open-air	Sea of Galilee

IV. From Passover 29 A.D.

21.	15:21–28	7:24–30		Syrophoenician Daughter
22.		7:32–37		Deaf-dumb Man
23.	15:32–38	8:1–9		Feeding the Four Thousand
24.		8:22–26		Blind Man
25.	17:14–20	9:14–29	9:37–43	Demoniac Boy
26.	17:24–27			Shekel in Fish's Mouth

V. From Autumn 29 A.D.

27.			9:1–7	Blind Man
28.		13:10–17		Woman with Infirmity
29.		14:1–6		Dropsical Man
30.			11:1–46	Lazarus
31.		17:11–19		Ten Lepers
32.	20:29–34	10:46–52	18:35–43	Bartimaeus and Blind Man

VI. During Passover 30 A.D.

33.	21:18, 19	11:12–14		Fig Tree Cursed
34.			22:50, 51	Malcus' Ear

to Autumn 29 A.D.

Girl	Demon	Word	House	Near Tyre
Man	Deafness	Anointed	Open-air	Decapolis
			Open-air	Decapolis
Man	Blindness	Anointed	Open-air	Bethsaida
Boy	Demon	Word	Open-air	Galilee
			Open-air	Capernaum—
				Sea of
				Galilee

to Spring 30 A.D.

Man	Blindness	Anointed	Open-air	Jerusalem
Woman	Infirmity	Touch	Synagogue	Judea
Man	Dropsy	Touch	House	Perea
Man	Death	Word	Open-air	Bethany
Men	Leprosy	Word	Open-air	Samaria or
				Galilee
Men	Blindness	Touch	Open-air	Jericho
			Open-air	Mt. Olivet
Man	Wound	Touch	Open-air	Gethsemane

Bibliography

Barnes, Albert. *Barnes' Notes on the New Testament.* Grand Rapids: Kregel Publications, n.d.

Bernard, T. D. *The Central Teaching of Jesus Christ.* London: Oxford Press, 1920.

Bond, A. R. *The Master Preacher.* New York: American Tract Society, 1910.

Dale, R. W. *Christian Doctrine.* London: Hodder & Stoughton, n.d.

DeFoe, James. *Guide to Bible Study.* London: Society of Christian Knowledge, 1908.

————. *History of the Bible.* London: Gety, 1853.

Ellicott, Charles H. *Commentary on the Whole Bible.* Grand Rapids: Zondervan, 1951.

Fairbairn, A. M. *Studies in the Life of Christ.* London: Hodder & Stoughton, 1900. A spiritual treasure all Bible students should have.

Glover, Richard. *The Gospel of Matthew.* Grand Rapids: Zondervan, 1956.

————. *History of Jesus.* Grand Rapids: Zondervan, 1956.

Glover, T. R. *The Jesus of History.* London: Student Christian Movement, 1917.

Godet, F. *Godet's Commentary on the New Testament.* New York: Funk & Wagnalls, 1886.

Gore, Charles. *Jesus of Nazareth.* London: Thornton Butterworth Ltd., 1917.

Green, Peter. *Our Lord and Saviour.* London: Longmans, Green & Co., 1928.

Halley, Henry H. *Halley's Bible Handbook.* Grand Rapids: Zondervan, 1927.

Handbook of Christian Teaching. London: Sheldon Press, 1939.

Hastings, James. *Dictionary of the Bible.* Edinburgh: T. & T. Clark, 1909.

Hodgkin, Henry T. *Jesus among Men.* London: Student Christian Movement, 1930.

The International Standard Bible Encyclopedia. Grand Rapids: Wm. Erdmans, 1929. See articles on topics with which we have dealt.

Lange, John Peter. *Commentary on the Holy Scriptures.* New York: Scribner's, 1884.

Lee, Umphrey. *The Life of Christ.* Nashville: Cokesbury Press, 1926.

Liddon, H. B. *The Divinity of Our Lord.* London: Pickering & Inglis, 1864.

Lockyer, Herbert. *All the Children of the Bible.* Grand Rapids: Zondervan, 1970.

————. *All the Miracles of the Bible.* Grand Rapids: Zondervan, 1961

————. *All the Parables of the Bible.* Grand Rapids: Zondervan, 1963.

Macartney, Clarence E. *What Jesus Really Taught.* Nashville: Abingdon Press, 1958.

Mackintosh, H. R. *The Doctrine of the Person of Christ.* International Theological Library. New York: Scribner's, 1912.

Moorehead, W. E. *Old and New Testament Outline Studies.* New York: Revell, 1893.

Morgan, G. Campbell. *The Teaching of Christ.* London: Marshall, Morgan, & Scott, 1930.

Patterson, W. P. *Christ and the Gospels.* Edinburgh: T. & T. Clark, 1911.

Pierson, A. T. *Knowing the Scriptures.* London: James Nisbet Co., 1910.

Scroggie, W. Graham. *A Guide to the Gospels*. London: Pickering & Inglis, 1948.

Stalker, James. *The Christology of Jesus*. London: Hodder & Stoughton, 1899.

————. *The Ethic of Jesus*. London: Hodder & Stoughton, 1919.

Vincent, Marvin R. *Word Studies in the New Testament*. New York: Scribner's, 1882.

Warfield, Benjamin B. *The Lord of Glory*. London: Hodder & Stoughton, 1909.

Wescott, B. F. *The Gospels*. Edinburgh: T. & T. Clark, 1884.

Whyte, Alexander. *The Walk, Conversation, and Character of Jesus Christ Our Lord*. London: Oliphant, n.d.

CHRISTIAN HERALD ASSOCIATION AND ITS MINISTRIES

CHRISTIAN HERALD ASSOCIATION, founded in 1878, publishes The Christian Herald Magazine, one of the leading interdenominational religious monthlies in America. Through its wide circulation, it brings inspiring articles and the latest news of religious developments to many families. From the magazine's pages came the initiative for CHRISTIAN HERALD CHILDREN and THE BOWERY MISSION, two individually supported not-for-profit corporations.

CHRISTIAN HERALD CHILDREN, established in 1894, is the name for a unique and dynamic ministry to disadvantaged children, offering hope and opportunities which would not otherwise be available for reasons of poverty and neglect. The goal is to develop each child's potential and to demonstrate Christian compassion and understanding to children in need.

Mont Lawn is a permanent camp located in Bushkill, Pennsylvania. It is the focal point of a ministry which provides a healthful "vacation with a purpose" to children who without it would be confined to the streets of the city. Up to 1000 children between the age of 7 and 11 come to Mont Lawn each year.

Christian Herald Children maintains year-round contact with children by means of a *City Youth Ministry.* Central to its philosophy is the belief that only through sustained relationships and demonstrated concern can individual lives be truly enriched. Special emphasis is on individual guidance, spiritual and family counseling and tutoring. This follow-up ministry to inner-city children culminates for many in financial assistance toward higher education and career counseling.

THE BOWERY MISSION, located at 227 Bowery, New York City, has since 1879 been reaching out to the lost men on the Bowery, offering them what could be their last chance to rebuild their lives. Every man is fed, clothed and ministered to. Countless numbers have entered the 90-day residential rehabilitation program at the Bowery Mission. A concentrated ministry of counseling, medical care, nutrition therapy, Bible study and Gospel services awakens a man to spiritual renewal within himself.

These ministries are supported solely by the voluntary contributions of individuals and by legacies and bequests. Contributions are tax deductible. Checks should be made out either to CHRISTIAN HERALD CHILDREN or to THE BOWERY MISSION.

Administrative Office: 40 Overlook Drive, Chappaqua, New York 10514
Telephone: (914) 769-9000